WHEN CORRUPTION WAS KING

HOW I HELPED THE MOB RULE CHICAGO, THEN BROUGHT THE OUTFIT DOWN

ROBERT COOLEY

WITH HILLEL LEVIN

CARROLL & GRAF PUBLISHERS
NEW YORK

To my father and all that he stood for.
—RC
My gang: MJ, A, A & G. Done. Finally.
—HL

WHEN CORRUPTION WAS KING
How I Helped the Mob Rule Chicago, Then Brought the Outfit Down

Carroll & Graf Publishers
An Imprint of Avalon Publishing Group Inc.
245 West 17th Street
11th Floor
New York, NY 10011

AVALON
publishing group incorporated

First Carroll & Graf edition 2004
Third printing, October 2004

Library of Congress Cataloging-in-Publication Data is available.

ISBN: 0-7867-1330-5

Interior design by Paul Paddock

Printed in the United States of America
Distributed by Publishers Group West

CONTENTS

INTRODUCTION

Most cities have one overriding claim to fame. Say Los Angeles and you think about the movies; say Paris, you think art; Detroit, cars. But when people, the world over, say Chicago, they think of something less marketable: Organized Crime. It is a stain that no amount of accomplishment or image-boosting will ever wipe clean.

The city's grim reputation is rooted back in the Roaring Twenties when Al Capone emerged victorious from gang warfare and went on to become a household name. Oddly enough, far less is known about his successors and their grip on the city during the last half of the twentieth century. But that is when Chicago's Mafia became the single most powerful organized crime family in American history. While Mob bosses knocked each other off on the East Coast, in Chicago they united into a monolithic force called the Outfit. They would literally control the cops, the courts, and the politicians—a corrupt trifecta that Capone dreamed about but never came close to achieving. The Outfit demanded a cut of every criminal enterprise in the region, from a lowly car theft or private poker game to a jewelry heist. To enforce this "street tax," their hit men killed with impunity, knowing that crooked judges would throw out any case against them. Their bookies brazenly took bets in nightclubs, at racetracks, and even in government office buildings, confident that contacts in the police department (at one point as high up as the chief of detectives) would warn them before the vice squad could make a raid. Mobsters ran Chicago union locals, and even national organizations for the Laborers and the Teamsters. This unprecedented combination of brute force and political clout let the bosses feed at the public trough with no-show jobs for their goons, and with municipal contracts for themselves and their associates. Government became one of their most lucrative rackets.

In his 1969 book *Captive City,* investigative journalist Ovid Demaris called the Outfit "the most politically insulated and police-pampered 'family' this side of Sicily" and estimated, even then, that their take was in the billions. With such total domination of their home turf, they could wander far and wide. By the seventies, the FBI reported that Chicago's Mob controlled all organized criminal activity west of the Mississippi—including and especially Las Vegas. Millions were skimmed from casinos like the Tropicana and the Stardust, and bundles of cash, stuffed in green army duffel bags, found their way back to the Outfit's bosses. Meanwhile, New York's mobsters had to content themselves with the slim pickings of Atlantic City.

Although other urban areas had their share of corruption, Chicago remained unique for its mixture of Organized Crime and political organization. The extent of Mafia influence on the city is still not fully appreciated, even by long-time residents. We think of Mobs hijacking trucks or businesses—not ballot boxes. But the ability to deliver votes and manipulate elected officials provided even more muscle to the Outfit than their army of enforcers.

In the shadows, at the controls of the Mob's political machine, was an ex-felon with a vaguely ethnic name and an obscure position in the Democratic Party. Born Pasqualino Marchone, he had been a protégé of Capone and supposedly served prison time for robbery in the thirties. Over the next three decades, he shed his thug exterior and took on a mantle of respectability, along with the new name of Pat Marcy. Most weekdays, he sat in a restaurant across the street from City Hall, ensconced at a corner table with a private phone. Dressed in three-piece suits, smoking fine cigars, he looked like his fellow diners from the local banks, government offices, and law firms.

His official title was Secretary for the Democratic Committee of Chicago's First Ward. To an outsider, his domain may have sounded like some quaint throwback. But for Chicagoans, the First Ward was a city unto itself—a political precinct carved out at the turn of the century like the richest vein in a gold mine. It extended from the slums and factories south of the city, through the central business district, up to the very wealthiest neighborhoods of the Gold Coast. And to see the company Pat Marcy kept at lunch, you'd think he was the mayor. Aldermen, state legislators, judges, congressmen, city officials, police chiefs, and union leaders—all regularly shared meals or dropped by to show the deference reserved for a man of great influence.

In that same restaurant, Marcy had other, less public, meetings away from the spotlight of the "First Ward table." Thursdays he would spend a few minutes in a booth with one or the other of the Outfit's most notorious team of hit men. Out in the adjoining lobby, as office workers rushed past and where no FBI bug could eavesdrop, he barked at lawyers and politicians, demanding that cases get fixed or kickbacks get paid. In bathrooms and unmarked offices elsewhere in the building, he conferred with the elderly bosses at the top of the Outfit. During the seventies and eighties, some of them would shuffle off to prison with the advent of new racketeering laws and federal investigations, but Marcy remained untouchable—along with his coterie of politicians, judges, and lawyers who became known as the Inner Circle of the First Ward.

Although the FBI tried to penetrate the First Ward with Mob informants and wiretaps, Marcy was too careful to be caught and too valuable for the bosses to give up. Besides, his political connections extended through both parties and ran from Chicago to Washington, DC. This clout made him radioactive to the ever-changing cast of U.S. Attorneys who rotated through the Northern Illinois office. It was one thing to target a small-time magistrate or alderman for taking a bribe. It was quite another thing to go after Marcy and charge that a Mafia figure was calling the shots at City Hall and the county courthouses. It sounded too outrageous to be true—a slap not only at the politicians and judges, but an insult to Chicago's business and media leaders, who even before Capone labored to put the best face above the city's "Big Shoulders."

To crack Marcy and Mob rule in Chicago, the Feds needed a lucky break. It arrived on a Saturday afternoon in 1986, when criminal lawyer Bob Cooley popped into the local office of the Organized Crime Strike

Force. By chance, the chief attorney happened to be in, catching up on paperwork. When he asked what Cooley wanted, he replied: "I'd like to help you destroy the First Ward. I'd like to help you destroy Pat Marcy."

Cooley was the last person that Pat Marcy or the Mob bosses would have expected to turn on them. Outside of the Mafia, few others had profited so flamboyantly from the corruption. For four years, Cooley personally handled most First Ward criminal cases involving Outfit soldiers and associates, and it helped make him rich. He took payment from his clients only in cash and at times didn't know what to do with it all. He might bet hundreds of thousands with bookmakers, buy a health club, or put up the money to start an Italian restaurant. Although he had a natural flair for the courtroom and won many cases legitimately, he let his clients know he would do whatever it took to get a favorable verdict. He solidified his reputation as the ultimate fixer when he paid off a "law and order" judge to get an acquittal on a murder charge for Harry Aleman, a hit man dubbed the Outfit's "killing machine."

Unlike the other Mob lawyers, Cooley's relationship with his clients went well beyond the courtroom. He was the life of their parties, hanging out with the young bucks at the hottest bars and nightclubs, dining at swankier spots with the older bosses. He bet with the Mob's bookies, traded girlfriends with the crew leaders, and, on some occasions, got in fistfights with them. A big part of his outlaw charm was that Cooley never appeared to take anyone or anything too seriously. He parked his luxury sedan in the bus stop outside court or, on occasion, in the mayor's spot outside City Hall. He wore a gold chain and open-neck shirt in court when everyone else wore ties. He brought his dog into fine restaurants and office buildings.

But however affable Cooley looked to the Outfit from the outside, he was boiling inside, deeply conflicted about his wealth and the scummy patrons who helped make it. For three and a half years after he walked into the Strike Force office, Cooley would wear a hidden recording device on some of the most dangerous men in America, and he helped the government develop damning cases against them. Always Cooley kept pushing his investigation higher and higher to the top Mob bosses and Chicago's most powerful politicians, even as some of his federal handlers tried to limit his targets to small-fry bookies and judges.

In 1989 the Feds finally brought a halt to his investigation, which they now called "Operation Gambat," for Gambling Attorney. When Cooley suddenly disappeared, and news about his double life leaked out, panic shot through the upper echelons of the Outfit and Chicago's Democratic Party. The FBI reported that the Mob had put a million-dollar bounty on Cooley's head. All the alarm was warranted. Before the end of 1990, the U.S. Attorney General flew to Chicago to announce the first wave of several sweeping Gambat indictments.

Over the course of the nineties, Cooley repeatedly returned to the city to testify as the central witness in Grand Jury proceedings, hearings, and eventually, eight trials. Time and again, he faced renowned criminal defense lawyers. Time and again, their clients were found guilty. When Cooley and the prosecutors were done, twenty-four individuals were convicted or had taken a guilty plea.

But the significance of Operation Gambat went far beyond the head count of all those sent to prison. What had once been a matter of speculation for a few gadfly newspaper columnists and reporters was now fact. No one could any longer deny that the Mob had influence on Chicago's leading politicians. Among those Cooley helped convict were the First Ward Alderman, a Corporation Counsel, and the Assistant Majority Leader in the Illinois Senate. Before a U.S. District Court judge imposed a sentence on one of them, he lamented that democracy in Chicago was "the same as any other banana republic or corrupt regime."

No one could deny that the Mob had influence on Chicago's judicial system, either. Among those sent to prison were the presiding judge for the prestigious Chancery Court and the only judge in America *ever* convicted of fixing murder cases. In yet another legal landmark stemming from the investigation, state prosecutors overturned the Double Jeopardy provision of the Fifth Amendment and retried the hit man who had been previously acquitted (with Cooley's help) in a rigged trial.

In the wake of Operation Gambat, the establishment was finally forced to take action. The Illinois Supreme Court's "Special Commission on the Administration of Justice" reviewed the evidence in Cooley's cases and called for wide-ranging reforms in the way judges are appointed and assigned trials in the state. The First Ward was whittled down to a fishhook fraction of its former size and, with the help of Cooley's testimony, federal trustees wrested control of some unions back from the mobsters. Significant remnants of the Outfit remain, but they have lost much of their power to influence or intimidate. Gangster hits in Chicago, which were once commonplace, are now rare.

With so much impact in so many areas—the judiciary, politics, and crime—and with so many high-profile convictions, Operation Gambat ranks as the crowning achievement of the Organized Crime Strike Force. But until now, the full story behind the investigation has remained largely untold because Bob Cooley has chosen not to tell it. This has not stopped others from speaking for him, starting with the reporters who covered the many trials and his hours of testimony. Several true-crime books have also touched on individual Gambat cases or aspects of the investigation. A character clearly based on Cooley appears in the novel *Personal Injuries* by Chicago lawyer Scott Turow, as well as a quickie TV movie called *The Fixer*, starring Jon Voight.

But none of these accounts—fiction and nonfiction—begin to explain why Cooley decided to cooperate with federal authorities. There have been plenty of theories—most of them propagated by attorneys for the Gambat defendants. Some have him drowning in gambling debts to bookmakers and in fear of their enforcers. Others claim he was on the verge of indictment himself for bribery or tax fraud. Such speculation, intended to discredit Cooley's testimony, became the centerpiece of defense efforts in almost all the Gambat trials. Obviously, it never carried much weight with a jury. In the words of Tom Durkin, the assistant U.S. Attorney who worked most closely with Cooley, "Bob is every bit the hero because he didn't have to do what he did."

As Cooley tells it, several different forces drove his decision to inform. For the most part, it was an act of conscience. This may sound laughable to anyone acquainted with the wild lifestyle Cooley once led. As he is the first to admit, morality was never his strong suit. However, the seeds for his later transformation were sown back in his childhood.

He grew up in a large, loving, and devout Catholic family. His father was a truly incorruptible cop—too honest to advance far in the Chicago Police Department—and both of his grandfathers, also policemen, died in the line of duty. From the start, Cooley was encouraged to follow the straight and narrow path laid down by his parents, although he always felt the tug to stray from it as well.

If anything, Pat Marcy became the mentor for his dark side, and Cooley's struggle with the two conflicting father figures was well under way years before Operation Gambat started. At one point, he refused to betray one of his clients as an informant, and an Outfit crew leader ordered Cooley killed. Although he managed, with his typical moxie, to lift the contract from his head, Cooley lost any sympathy he had had for his Mob benefactors. Gradually, he became filled with self-loathing about what he had done for Marcy and the Outfit. Those feelings only intensified when he learned that a crooked lawyer might have rigged the trial that acquitted his grandfather's killer. When Marcy forced him into fixing one more trial—this one involving the assault on a police-woman—Cooley could take no more. With an impulsiveness that he immediately regretted, he found himself at the Strike Force door.

It's unlikely that any other mole could have taken Operation Gambat as far as Cooley did. His zeal was nearly suicidal and partly fueled by his belief that destroying the First Ward and the Outfit had become his life's mission. But there would be few earthly rewards in the investiga-tion for this lapsed Catholic. Instead, he would star in his own version of the Passion Play. The more good he did, the more he was made to suffer—with each station of the cross that much more degrading and painful. After he "came in" to the government, he became convinced that some of the Feds—the U.S. Attorney in particular—were out to stifle and demoralize him at every pass. First he was stopped from gam-bling, which provided most of his entertainment and social life; and then from practicing criminal law, which provided much of his income. Cash that once gushed into his firm now barely trickled.

When the authorities finally unveiled the full scope of Operation Gambat, Cooley's central role should have earned him some redemption for his years of wrongdoing. Instead, like John Dean and Frank Serpico before him, Cooley discovered that the public and the media reserve a special scorn for informants—no matter how beneficial their information. During the trials, Cooley lost the gold chain and transformed himself from the cocky counselor to a humble witness. Defense attorneys he once considered pathetic pretenders to his throne heaped abuse on him in court and used their media friends to vilify him in the local papers and on TV. The Illinois Attorney Registration and Disciplinary Commission moved to disbar Cooley, based on his admissions in court, before they took similar action against any of those lawyers and judges ultimately convicted in his trials. Finally, as the last nail in the cross—for the sake of his own safety—he was exiled forever from the city he loved so much.

Outside the courtroom, Cooley also broke the mold. He refused the federal Witness Protection Program, and although the government has helped him assume another name, he has not been provided with security or further resources. He trusts his own instincts better than those of the bureaucracy. He has lived in dozens of places around the country and is always ready to move again at short notice.

Despite the extreme changes he has weathered in his life, Cooley remains much the same as he was in Chicago. Garrulous as ever, he keeps in touch with a large circle of family and friends that now includes many of the agents and prosecutors involved with Gambat. In each of his new locations, he finds new hangouts and buddies.

He remains obsessed with his investigation and the legacy it has left behind in Chicago. He wonders if the city has ever come to grips with the enormity of Operation Gambat's revelations. This obsession, as much as anything, has driven him to write this book with me and to finally get his side of the story on the record.

Cooley does not try to buff up his own image. He's open about his flaws and his own illegal activities. His brutal honesty is exactly what makes his story so credible, buttressed by testimony—over hundreds of hours—that was never significantly impeached by any of the defense counsel he faced.

Unlike other witnesses against the Mafia, he offers a perspective on Organized Crime that literally extends from the thug on the street to the equally brutal, if more sophisticated, bosses at the top. Along the way, he details the centrality of gambling to Mob culture, the mindlessly violent nightlife, and the Outfit's bizarre, longstanding relationship with elements of the Chicago Police Department.

Most important, Cooley reveals how easily the criminal world intersected with the supposedly legitimate world of law and politics. Old arrest records were dismissed as ancient history. Sweetheart contracts and rigged trials were laughed off in the press as "business as usual." Cynicism took the place of outrage, and the voting public collectively turned away.

As we complete this book, some individuals from Cooley's old Mob circles are back in the news. The *Chicago Sun-Times* exposed a municipal "Hired Truck Program" that funneled millions in public funds to "organized crime figures." Meanwhile, Richard Daley, in his fifteenth year as mayor, with no challenger in sight, now calls for Chicago to have its very own casino. He assures one and all that he needs no help keeping legalized gambling free of Mob influences. In sum, conditions are ripe for remnants of the Outfit to mount a comeback, and there's plenty at stake to attract them. It is just the time for Bob Cooley to speak up again.

SAINTS
&
SINNERS

CHAPTER 1

A DEAL WITH THE DEVIL

First of all, you should know that Bob Cooley is dead. Actually, I committed suicide several years ago.

It's not like I wanted to be put out of my misery. I gave up a life in Chicago that anyone else would have died for. I had a fantastic career, beautiful sweethearts, wonderful friends and family. There were nonstop parties at the finest restaurants and hottest clubs. It was not just any life. It was a fabulous life.

Now it's over.

I have a different name and will never put my roots down in another city. Like a nomad, I'm here today, gone tomorrow.

The exact date of my suicide is open to debate. Some people would say I pulled the trigger in 1986, when I walked into the Chicago offices of the Organized Crime Strike Force and agreed to wear a wire on some very dangerous people. Others would argue that I was as good as dead three years later, when a dozen FBI agents fanned out across the city with indictments based on the tapes I had made, and the Mob fully realized what I had done to them. I could have easily ended up with a .22 in the head—if I was lucky. If I wasn't lucky, I could have ended up hanging from a meat hook, getting slowly charbroiled by some animal with a blowtorch.

If you ask me, my undoing really started many years before, when I made a deal with the Devil. His name was Pat Marcy, and he wanted me to fix a murder case.

● ● ●

It all began innocently enough: someone asking me to help his son. The year was 1977. I was thirty-five years old and pretty hot shit—if I do say so myself. After working as a cop to put myself through law school, I built one of the best criminal defense practices in Chicago. If you got in trouble—from a traffic ticket to a gambling bust to a murder—you wanted me as your lawyer. I had my own office, in a prime location, right across the street from City Hall. Mornings, after I spent a few hours in court, I would grab a massage and a steam before I got back to the office, usually in time for lunch.

I never entered my building through the lobby. Instead, I would take a walk first through Counsellors Row, the restaurant on the ground floor. It was a big, busy place with lots of tables and leather booths. Everybody hung out there: lawyers, city workers, and all the big shot politicians. Sometimes my clients would grab a bite and wait for me at a table. It was like my second office. People would even leave messages for me there.

One day, as I was doing my walk through Counsellors, I felt a hand at my elbow. "Can I talk to you for a minute?"

I turned to see John D'Arco Senior. He looked for all the world like a kindly old Italian grandfather. Round, smiling face and thick tinted glasses. You might think he was the guy who owned the grocery down the street—but one who made out very well for himself. He wore fancy suits and silk ties, usually smoked big cigars and had a diamond pinkie ring. Once he had been a pretty tough guy—as legend had it, a stickup man for Al Capone. Somewhere along the way he got involved with the Democratic Party and cleaned up his act. For a while he had been a city council alderman, and he was still head of the Democratic Regular Committee for Chicago's First Ward. But whatever D'Arco looked like from the outside, his organization in the First Ward was still part and parcel of the Mob. That much I knew.

I used to see D'Arco in Counsellors all the time. He sat in a corner, in front of the restaurant, at what they called the First Ward table. They had bricked up the window and, on the wall, hung pictures of all their favorite politicians—in those days, Mayor Richard M. Daley and Jimmy Carter. The table even had a little pedestal with their private phone.

But when he wanted to talk to me, John D'Arco didn't take me to the First Ward table. Instead, we walked to the back of the restaurant, where it was pretty empty. We sat down, and he asked, "You know my son?"

"Yeah," I replied. "I know Johnny. I know him quite well." Seven years before, when we were both going to the same college, Johnny picked a fight with me and I beat the crap out of him.

Then Senior said, "I hear you're a fantastic lawyer, and my son's a lawyer too. He's never tried a case, and I'd like to have him learn to be a real lawyer. Would you be interested in teaching him how to defend a case?"

I was caught totally off guard. "Let me think about it," I said, "and I'll get back to you."

Then I walked up to my office in kind of a daze. Whatever I thought of Johnny really didn't matter. Thanks to his father, he had become a state senator—at the age of twenty-six—so I figured he wasn't a punk any more. Besides, I had a soft spot for fathers who looked out for their sons. My own dad was like that.

But a deal with D'Arco could mean more than taking Johnny around by the nose. This was a chance to hook up with the First Ward machine and all its connections.

It's not like I needed their help to be successful. You could have looked at me in 1977 and wondered what more I wanted as a lawyer. I didn't have some big firm, but I liked it that way. I was my own boss, and I had a hand on every dollar coming in or going out. I made all my clients pay in cash; at times I had so much, I didn't know what to do with it. I could spend hundreds of thousands each day on sports bets or blow fifty thousand on a trip to Vegas. I bought the old health club where I got my rubdowns and even owned one of the city's more popular Italian restaurants with one of my bookies.

But working with D'Arco and the First Ward wasn't about money. It was about power, and that was the one thing I couldn't buy. I knew how to *work* the system; these guys *controlled* the system. They could hire and fire cops. They could even make or break judges. When it came to the clients, they were on a higher level as well. I worked with the Mob's crew leaders; they did business with the bosses.

Before long, I was back in Counsellors Row to give Senior a response. Now it was my turn to knock him on his ass—with a much bigger proposition than he was expecting. I told him I would take Johnny around with me, but in return I wanted *all* of the First Ward's criminal business. I knew they were farming it out to ten or fifteen other lawyers. In return, I would split the fees fifty-fifty. I offered to check it out first with D'Arco's son-in-law, who ran their firm, but from the way Senior nodded, I knew it was a done deal. Like all the other Mob guys, he respected my brass balls. More than I knew.

A couple of weeks later, in the middle of the day, Senior called my office and asked that I come down to meet him at the First Ward table. When I got there, he picked up the phone, and a few minutes later, Pat Marcy was staring at us through the door to the lobby.

Pat was in his early sixties, and he dressed like some corporate executive in three-piece suits. He wore tinted dark-rimmed glasses that gave him the expression of a pissed-off owl. We got up and joined him in the lobby. Senior said, "You know Pat Marcy, don't you?"

I said, "Sure, I know Pat." In fact, I knew he was secretary for the First Ward Committee of the Democratic Party. Whatever the hell that meant. I assumed he was somebody ultra-heavy, but I thought Senior was the real powerhouse in the First Ward—even though Pat was at the First Ward table more than anyone else.

The three of us were just standing there, up against the wall in the lobby, as people rushed by to jump in the elevators. Senior looked around to check that nobody was near us. "Pat wants to talk to you about something. It's important."

Pat said, "Listen, do you know a judge at 26th who can handle a case?"

When he said that, I knew exactly what he meant. The criminal court was at 26th Street and California. He wanted a judge to help him fix a case.

Then he added, "It's a very serious case. It's a murder case."

I had fixed cases before, but never a murder case. Still, partly out of curiosity, I said, "I don't know. What case is it?"

"Harry Aleman."

In those days, the name Harry Aleman invoked the same chills as the Luca Brasi character in *The Godfather* movie. The press dubbed him the Mob's "killing machine," and the Chicago Crime Commission considered Aleman responsible for at least eighteen contract murders. I remembered reading in the papers that he had been arrested and charged with killing some union guy.

Maybe I should have backed away right then and done us all a favor. But I was flattered they had approached me. "Pat," I said, "before I say I can help, I'd like to see the police reports, so I know what kind of case they have."

Senior got a little annoyed with that. "If you have somebody, fine. If you don't have somebody, don't say that you do. Because this is a serious matter. Some very powerful people are concerned about this individual, and if you say you can do it, you can't back away."

But Pat respected my response. He saw I wasn't bullshitting, and he promised to get me the police reports.

The next day, I picked up Johnny D'Arco in my Lincoln to go on our rounds of the courthouses. Johnny had started to treat me like a big brother. Whenever we hung at a bar or club, he would order exactly what I did. After spending so much time with me, he knew I loved pranks, like parking in the mayor's spot at City Hall or dropping eggs on people from the balcony of my condo. When he found out I was involved with the Aleman case, he got worried. "This is not something you can fuck around with," he told me. "If you make a mistake on this, it could be a real problem for you. You'll probably get killed."

Later, when we got back from court, I walked by the First Ward table, and Pat Marcy handed me an envelope. Then he reminded me, "I have to know as soon as possible if you've got somebody. And if they say they are going to do it, they have to do it."

Back in my office, I pulled out the police reports. They were the originals. Obviously, Pat had some deep contacts—either inside the police department or the state attorney's office. I don't think I spent more than twenty minutes on the material before I could see that it was an absolute throw-out case—the sort of stuff that would *never* convince a judge or jury that Harry Aleman was guilty of this crime.

The victim was William P. Logan, a Teamster shop steward and part-time cab driver. He was thirty-five and living with his sister after a recent divorce. Shortly before midnight, September 27, 1972, as he was getting into his car to drive to work, another car pulled up and someone called out, "Billy." He turned to run, but got nailed with three quick blasts. His nephew, who was sleeping on the porch, woke up to see him stagger between two parked cars and crumple, face first, onto the parkway. His lunch bag was still on the hood of the car.

Besides what they pulled out of his body, the state had no physical evidence. No gun and no car. All they had was a flaky statement from a neighbor. He said he saw what happened when he let his dog out. He couldn't describe the two white males in the car, but he said one of them got out and nailed Logan with a .45-caliber pistol. In fact, though, the wounds and pellet fragments showed Logan was killed with a shotgun.

The state's first real break in the case came four years later, when some Pennsylvania state troopers arrested a speeder named Louie Almeida. He told them that he was on his way "to kill somebody." Louie was a real piece of work. He had been part of Harry Aleman's crew—the kind of knucklehead who would do whatever he was asked. But somewhere inside that thick skull, a camcorder was always running. Once the coppers got him back in Chicago, they didn't have to push too many buttons before Louie's adventures with Harry started spilling out. One of them was the Logan hit. But what Louie remembered conflicted directly with the other witness. Louie said he was driving a car completely different from the neighbor's description. Also, Louie said Harry never got out of the car, but fired a sawed-off shotgun from the back seat. Of course, Louie had some credibility issues of his own—starting with a rap sheet a mile long, and ending with a prison shrink's diagnosis that he was a Looney Tune psycho. Still, the coppers must have figured Louie was more believable than the neighbor, so they had him change his statement to match Louie's. It wasn't going to take much to tear either one of these losers into shreds once they took the stand.

As for the motive, the state had some trumped-up story about the Mob and union politics. But Logan was only a shop steward, and the Mob already controlled the Teamsters, any idiot knew that.

I went back down to get Marcy and we had another little conference against the lobby wall. "Pat," I said, "they got no case here. I could take this to a jury and walk him."

But Pat didn't want to hear that. "No. No," he said. "We want a judge to handle it." He didn't want Aleman to risk a jury trial. He wanted a bench trial, where the judge would arrive at the verdict. And he wanted to be absolutely sure that the verdict would be Not Guilty. So he asked again, "Have you got somebody?"

"Let me think about it," I said. "I've got a couple of people in mind."

Actually, I had exactly the perfect judge in mind. The last person Marcy would have expected, but I wasn't going to blurt out his name until I had checked with him first.

Frank Wilson was what we called a "state-minded" judge—a hard-nosed law-and-order guy who always leaned toward the prosecution. He could be very mean on the bench, and most lawyers were scared to death of him. But he was also considered totally legit. As far as I knew, he had never taken a dime on any case, let alone a murder rap.

That night, just as I expected, I saw the judge in Greco's, the Italian restaurant I owned. I usually headed down there in the early evening, just after I finished up with my bookies. It was about six o'clock, and Judge Wilson was at the bar, getting a head start on his Canadian Clubs before his friends arrived. The judge had what they call the Irish Disease. He drank the hard stuff every day. He was a big beefy guy with white hair, and he had that stern look of a judge. I walked up to him, shook his hand, and led him a little distance from the bar, where nobody could hear us. My plan was to pop the question and then, if he got offended, to pretend he was too drunk to understand what I was talking about.

"Judge," I said, "I was just approached on a murder case. They want me to find a judge who would handle it."

"You mean the Harry Aleman case?" he asked.

"Yeah." To my surprise he didn't show any anxiety when I brought it up. But then he explained that Aleman's lawyer had already requested that Judge Wilson *not* be given their case. Defense lawyers were allowed to name two judges that they would want substituted, and given Frank's reputation, Aleman's lawyer wanted no part of him. The judge told me, "I don't think you can get the case back to me,"

"I'll check and see," I said. "But if I can get it back, would you be interested in handling the case?"

"What kind of case do they have?" he asked.

I had tried several cases in his court, and he trusted me to know what was a good case for the defense. "I've already read the reports," I told him, "and it's a weak case. It's a throw-out case."

He shrugged his shoulders. "I doubt if you can get the case back to me."

It wasn't a yes, but it wasn't a no either. When his friends came, they had dinner as usual. I just picked up the check and went about my business. I didn't talk to him for the rest of the night.

Anybody else would have been nuts to approach Judge Wilson. But I knew him better than most other lawyers did. We hung out quite a bit, usually at a bar near the courthouse or at Greco's. As a part owner, I may have been biased, but it was probably the nicest restaurant in the area. It looked like an old-fashioned wine cellar with its trellises and vines. Our cooks were the Italian ladies in the neighborhood, so it was real home cooking. The judge lived nearby, and if I saw him there, I would pick up his check. But he was no moocher. To reciprocate, he'd invite me to his country club and take care of those tabs. When he was totally wasted, I was one of the few people he'd let drive him home. Otherwise, he got in a lot of trouble with his drunk driving. Once he drove smack into the side of a house near his country club.

What really bonded us was one experience we had in Las Vegas. Since I was considered a big spender—big loser was more like it—the casinos would fly me back and forth on junkets. They didn't care how many people I brought along, so I used to take the judge. He didn't go to gamble. He went to drink, because the booze was free. Sometimes you'd see him at the craps table with a pile of chips on the pass line. He had fallen asleep on his feet and his bet would keep riding until he lost or woke up.

Once we were at the MGM Grand at three in the morning, and I found him slumped over the bar. I was going to drag him up to his room when I saw some real cute girl giving me the eye from the other end of the bar.

I went over to her and said, "You're not a working girl, are you?"

"Oh, no," she said. "I'm just here for the weekend."

I thought, "What a gorgeous little broad." And I started rapping with her. We had a couple of drinks, but then I remembered sleeping beauty. I said, "Look. My friend here is a judge, and I got to get him upstairs. He's really wasted. Then we'll go back to my place."

We walked over to the judge and woke him up. He started drooling all over her, "Oh, hi, honey." He was fumbling with her dress and everything. I thought he was going to blow this date for me.

But she wasn't fazed at all. She pulled him to his feet and said, "I'll help you put him to bed. My father was like this all the time."

The judge had always had a horrible limp, from some childhood injury, so it took forever to reach his room. When we finally got there, I opened the door and she pushed right past me. "I'll take it from here," she said and shut the door behind her. I must have been waiting twenty minutes in the hall. I figured maybe he's attacking her or something. But finally she appeared, and we went to my room. She had this whole story about just getting divorced, and what she used to do with her ex-husband. They would each take a shower, and then they'd have sex. So I figured, "What the hell." She got the shower running and I climbed inside. But the water hardly hit my face before I started thinking, "Wait! I have a good fifteen thousand in my pants pocket, a big ring and a fancy watch on the nightstand, and I don't even know this fucking broad."

I jumped out of the shower and she was already gone. I tore open the door and ran into the hall buck naked, and there she was, just getting on the elevator. I grabbed the next elevator going down. Inside, wouldn't you know, some nice older couple was headed for an early breakfast, and there was yours truly trying to cover his nuts with his hands. I went straight to the pool, so I could grab a towel and the phone, and I called for security. As it turned out, this broad was a hustler. She flew in from LA and did this all the time. They had her picture and everything. Of course, I was one pissed-off individual. I filled out all the paperwork to file a complaint in case they caught her, and then I practically crawled back to my room. I wasn't asleep for more than a few minutes before the phone rang. It was the judge. "What the fuck?" he yelled. "That girl you fixed me up with stole all my money." He probably had four hundred dollars that she took, but it was a lot for him. You could say we had both been caught with our pants down.

When I told Pat Marcy the judge I had in mind for the fix, he couldn't believe it. Frank Wilson was exactly the kind of judge he was looking for. "But we have to get the case back to his court," I said. Like Judge Wilson, I didn't think that would be an easy matter. First, the current judge had to withdraw from the Aleman case, and then there would be a computer lottery to select his replacement.

But Pat just waved his hand and said that wouldn't be a problem. He could assign that case any which way he wanted. All this bullshit about procedures and lotteries was just a game for the rest of us. Pat told me to offer him $10,000. It sounded like a lot to me, but what did I know? Up to that time, the most I had paid on any case was a thousand bucks, but I never had paid on a murder case before. I took all of those to trial, and I always got an acquittal. And in most of those cases, the state had a lot more evidence against my client than they had against Harry Aleman.

I waited a day before I called the judge at the courthouse and suggested he invite the wife for dinner at Greco's. We had been out together before. She was a real nice Irish lady and would help break the tension.

I brought along Cathy Fleming, a very attractive young woman who was working for me at the time. She was also about to become one of my girlfriends. I thought she could mix with an older couple and make the evening look like a social occasion. At the restaurant, just as we were about to get seated, I said, "Judge, can I talk to you for a minute?"

I took him into the men's room. It was a big place, with plenty of marble for an echo, so I first checked under all the stalls to make sure no one else was using a toilet. Then I said, "Judge, are you still interested in taking the case?"

"If you tell me it's a real weak case," he said, "then yes, I'd be interested."

I said, "Judge, I think we can get the case back to you if you want to handle it."

I told him he would get $10,000 in return, but then I added, "I don't want you to say yes or no now. I want you to think about it first. If you say, 'Yes' and then back away, I will have a serious problem."

He just nodded. Then we sat down and had our dinner.

A couple of days later, we met again at Greco's. We went into the bathroom, and he said, "Okay. Okay. I'll handle it." As a down payment, I pulled $2,500 out of my jacket pocket. Pat Marcy hadn't even paid *me* yet, but I wanted to lock the judge in, right then and there. Maybe, before I gave him the money, I should have thought a little more about the consequences—for our careers and our lives. But I really thought I was doing him a favor. His annual salary was $50,000 at most. He had his membership at the country club. His daughter was ready for college. Things were probably a little tight. He took the cash and almost didn't know where to put it. I'm sure it was the first time he ever took a bribe.

A few days after my first payoff to the judge, I got a call from Marco D'Amico. He was one of the Mob's Young Turks and ran a crew on the city's West Side. We had been hanging out and gambling with each other since I had been a cop. He wanted to meet me at a motel near the airport called The King's Inn. Marco owned it behind the scenes, and we had been there before, so nothing seemed suspicious.

For a motel, The King's Inn was a pretty swanky place. On the lower level, it had a bar and a nightclub. You drove down from the street into the parking area. People couldn't see you coming or going. I brought along one of my girlfriends, and Marco was waiting for us at the bar. Disco was big in those days. There were a lot of flashing lights all around, and pounding music. Marco motioned for the girl to have a seat and told me that someone wanted to meet me. We went upstairs into an empty motel room—just a bed and a little round table in the corner. I could still hear the thump-thump of the disco music coming up through the floor. Obviously, Marco had not called me to The King's Inn just to hang out and get drunk. When Mob guys pulled this cloak and dagger stuff, it was always pretty funny, but you had to play along and act surprised or they'd get mad at you. We were just about to sit down when there was a knock at the door. I had already figured out who I was about to meet before he walked in the room: the killing machine himself, Harry Aleman.

At first sight, Harry did not look all that threatening. At thirty-eight, he had a build, from working out, but he was fairly short and a very fancy dresser. Silk shirts. Leather jackets. He had brown, blow-dried hair with prematurely gray sideburns and a hawk-like nose. You wouldn't know that Harry was a killer until you looked into his eyes and saw his stone-cold evil stare. Once I watched him in my restaurant when he stared daggers at Tony Reitinger, a young Jewish bookmaker, who wasn't paying the Mob's "street tax." Two weeks later, Tony was dead— from a shotgun blast while he sat waiting for someone in a pizza parlor. And wouldn't you know, they had to kill Tony right *after* I had paid him $5,000 on a bet I lost. Poor guy, he probably thought the street tax was a game. But Harry Aleman never played games.

"Hey, how ya doing? How ya doing?" Harry pumped my hand in the motel room like we were long-lost pals. We had met before, but we'd never had much to say to each other.

He asked, "You gonna handle my case?"

"Yeah."

"Are you sure you can handle it? Are you sure this judge is going to throw the case out?"

"Sure. He's going to throw it out."

Then he took a long look at me and gave me his Evil Eye routine. "You realize," he said, "if there's a problem, you're gonna have a problem."

"I understand what's going on," I said. "I wouldn't say it unless it was so."

Harry nodded, like everything was okay, and we sat around the table. As it turns out, he had another mission for this meeting, and it related to his asshole lawyer. "I want to keep Tom Maloney on the case," he said, "and Tom wants to stay on the case."

As far as I was concerned, this was not a matter for discussion. I told him, "Maloney can't stay on the case."

There were several reasons to dump Maloney. First of all, I didn't like the prick—as a lawyer or a human being. He was a big overbearing blowhard who acted like he was God's gift to the legal profession. I hated the way he talked down to the clerks and the bailiffs. And I knew

Judge Wilson hated him, too. But I wasn't going to say any of that to Harry.

Instead, I said, "Maloney already asked for a substitute for Judge Wilson. How would it look if he suddenly turned around and accepted Wilson as the judge? It would look suspicious. You're much better off with another lawyer."

But Harry kept on pushing Maloney. I had already told Pat Marcy that we would have to change lawyers, and now I realized that fucking Maloney had talked Harry into letting him stay on the case. "Look," Harry said, "they're gonna name him a judge real soon. This may be the last case he does as a lawyer. He would be a real good friend to have."

Harry was right. Through Marcy's connections, Maloney was soon to be appointed as a Circuit Court judge to fill a vacancy. Still, if Maloney had been appointed king, there was no way I'd ever work with him. But I wasn't going to sit there and argue about it with Harry. When these guys got insistent, it was no use arguing with them. "Okay," I said. "Let me talk to Judge Wilson and see if I can get him to change his mind." In fact, I had no intention of talking to the judge about Maloney.

Harry was still not finished with me. He had hired a private investigator to check up on the witness who was Logan's neighbor. This guy was an absolute lowlife with three warrants out for his arrest. Obviously, the investigator didn't have to dig too deep to find some dirt on him. "Maybe," Harry said, "you want to meet this investigator."

"No," I said. "I don't want to meet the investigator. I don't want anyone else to know I'm involved in this. Just get me his reports."

This was not Harry's first trial, and we all knew it wouldn't be his last, but I could tell that there was something about this case that really bothered him, and he kept me in that little motel room for another half hour. When he finally got up to leave, he gave me a number and said I should call his wife if I needed to reach him in an emergency. "I don't go home much any more, but she still knows how to get ahold of me."

I told him he was never to call me on my regular phone, and he should use a code name if someone else picked up my private line. We had to be super-cautious to make sure no one could connect me to his case.

That next day, Pat Marcy gave me more bullshit about keeping Maloney as Harry's lawyer, but I held my ground. I told him, "If you want to keep Maloney you have to find another judge." But they didn't want another judge. My judge was perfect and they knew it. Maloney could fuck himself.

To replace Maloney, Marcy got Frank Whalen, an older lawyer who used to handle Chicago Mob cases, but then moved his practice to Florida. The choice was fine with Judge Wilson. He said, "Whalen's been before me, and he's a good lawyer." But the judge didn't want to meet with him. "If there's any problems, I will deal with you." He asked that I help Whalen prepare the case, and before the trial I flew down to see him twice—at my own expense. I still hadn't even asked Marcy about my fee for this deal, but the money really didn't matter to me. If I could get Harry off, I would be locked into the First Ward legal business for some time to come.

Everything looked fine to Whalen down in Florida, but once the trial date got close, and he met with Harry in Chicago, he wasn't so sure any more. He was staying at one of the old hotels in the business district. I'd sneak through the rear entrance and go directly to his room. Whalen remembered Judge Wilson and he knew his reputation, so he kept asking me, "Are you sure this judge will throw the case out? Are you sure you can trust him?"

"That's my responsibility," I told him. "You put the case on, and I'll take the heat if the judge doesn't do what we want."

But Harry Aleman wasn't going to leave anything to chance. Just days before the trial started, I got a call at four in the morning. It woke me up from a sound sleep with a very beautiful girl next to me. It was Harry. "It's important," he said. "I got to see you right away." He told me to meet him by the *Chicago Tribune* tower at a 24-hour diner—a big, cheap Greek place.

When I got there, I ordered some coffee and took a booth by the window. I was facing the loading docks for the newspaper building, and it wasn't long before I saw Harry and his partner, Butch, slinking out of the shadows. Butch Petrocelli had a face like a fist and a skunk's tail for a head of hair—a bizarre splotch of white in the middle of the black.

You could spot him a mile away. They walked into the diner, acting as though they didn't see me. They went to a booth in the back and, after a few minutes, I got up to join them.

Harry was all excited. His brother knew some girl who lived down the street from where Logan was shot. "We can get her to come in and say she saw the shooting and that I wasn't the guy who did the shooting."

"Good." I said. "We don't really need it, but every little bit helps."

"Let the judge know that. I'm sure it will make him happy."

I said, "Okay, Harry. Okay. Whatever you say." But I was thinking, "What the fuck, you asshole? You wake me up at four in the morning to tell me this? You could have waited until tomorrow."

Then Harry said, "We're gonna give her ten thousand."

"Be careful," I told him. "I don't want you talking to this girl. That could get you into a lot of trouble. Don't you *ever* be seen meeting with her."

It was like I popped his balloon. "Oh. Okay," he said. "I won't meet with her."

This girl wasn't such a prize after all. She got second thoughts and went to the police. She tried to lure Harry into a meeting, so the coppers could catch him bribing her, but because of what I told him, he steered clear of her.

Meanwhile, the case got underway. Unfortunately, things didn't go as we had planned. After the first day of testimony, I was sitting in my office when the phone rang. It was the judge. He was calling from a pay phone, somewhere outside the courthouse. "Hi," he said.

"Hello," I said. "See you later," and we both hung up. That was our code to meet at a restaurant near his home. He was there before I arrived, waiting for me at a table by the bar. He was so upset, he hadn't even had that much to drink.

"Is Whalen sick?" he asked. "He's not doing a good job cross-examining the witnesses."

"What do you mean?" I asked.

He said, "You told me it was a weak case, but it's a good case. The state is putting on a good case. You didn't tell me how difficult it was going to be for me." Then he asked me again, "Is this man sick?"

"I don't know," I said. I explained I had never seen him in court before.

"Well, he's not the lawyer he used to be," the judge said.

I told him I'd check up on Whalen and went right over to his hotel.

"The judge is pissed," I told Whalen. "He says you're doing a shitty job. What the fuck is going on in there? I gave you all the information you needed to tear apart these witnesses."

"I'm doing a great job," he bellowed back at me. "What's he talking about?"

Now I had Whalen mad at me, too.

The judge's concerns about Whalen were not a good sign, especially since I had pushed Maloney off the case. The next morning, I went over to see Pat Marcy at Counsellors Row, and we walked out into the lobby. "Pat," I said, "the judge wants to know if Whalen's sick. He thinks he's doing a terrible job in court."

This got Pat all upset. He started glaring at me. "You tell that judge he better throw this case out."

After I left Counsellors Row, I wanted to be close to the Criminal Courthouse, and I drove down to 26th Street. I even entered the building, so I could sneak into the gallery. I went up the courthouse stairs as far as the judges' floor, but from there I could see that they had set up metal detectors outside the courtroom. Since I knew the coppers who were manning them, there was no way for me to pass by unnoticed.

I walked back downstairs, thinking, "What the fuck am I going to do now?" I had the judge upset with me for putting Whalen on the case. I had Whalen upset at me for calling him a terrible lawyer. I had Pat Marcy upset with me for being upset. My life was literally on the line with this trial, and I couldn't do a damned thing about it.

So each night I arranged to be in my office in case the judge wanted to talk again. I could sense he was getting increasingly nervous. It didn't help that the papers were printing their version of the evidence, saying the state had Harry dead to rights. In truth, no matter how weak the evidence, Harry Aleman was their perfect villain. According to the press, in the whole crazy history of Chicago, this was the first time a Mob hit man was ever standing trial for a contract killing.

Finally, the judge called me again from the pay phone, and I raced out to the restaurant. Earlier that day, away from the jury, there was a hearing about Harry's brother trying to bribe the neighbor girl. The prosecutors tried to call her as a witness, but she had only met with the brother. Anything she knew about Harry was hearsay and not admissible. The judge had no problem ruling that the state couldn't call her to the stand. But he was bothered by something else: that they were going to pay her $10,000.

"Did you know about that?" he asked.

"I knew they were trying to get a witness," I said, "but I didn't know what amount they would pay her."

"I am a judge. I am a full judge," he told me. "I am going to lose my job on this thing and all *I'm* getting is ten thousand dollars. It's not fair."

"Let me see if I can get you some more," I said.

But that wasn't all he wanted to talk about. He was reading the newspapers. "I'm going to be in trouble if I find him not guilty."

I didn't like where this was going. "Wait, Judge," I said. "Before you got involved, I told you about this case. You knew what was going on. The state really doesn't have a case. If you find this guy guilty, I'm a dead man."

The next day I went to see Marcy at Counsellors Row. I told him that the judge was getting unbelievable heat in the press. I said he was frightened and realized he probably wouldn't get reelected. Meanwhile, he found out what Harry's brother was going to pay the witness. "The judge thinks he should get some more. Maybe we should give him some more."

Pat glared at me again. "That's all he is going to get. Not a nickel more. He agreed to do it for ten thousand, and he better do what he said or there will be consequences."

As if I wasn't worried enough, behind the scenes I picked up information that was total dynamite. The hit, I learned, had had nothing to do with unions and all the other crap in the indictment. It was strictly personal. Billy Logan, the victim, had been married to Harry's cousin. They had a bitter divorce and argued constantly over custody of their son. Logan used to beat her up big-time. The final straw came after one of their fights when she said, "You better be careful, because Harry won't be happy about it." And Logan replied, "Fuck that guinea." He probably could have beaten her up a few more times, and it wouldn't have mattered. But Harry wasn't going to let some Irish goon get away with calling him a guinea.

None of this came out in the trial, but if it did, you had an entirely different case than what I had thought it was. Or what the judge thought it was. There would have been a documented connection between Harry and Logan—along with all the motive in the world.

The last day of the trial, I woke up and packed a suitcase. I knew the judge was reading his decision later in the morning. I wasn't sticking around to hear what he said. I got in my Lincoln and started driving west. I didn't even know where I was going. I was probably twenty miles outside the city, when I clicked on the radio and heard the news: Judge Wilson had found Harry not guilty. I turned my car around and headed back to the office.

When he announced his decision, the judge did all he could to justify the verdict. He mentioned how the neighbor kept changing his testimony. He said you should consider "the first story" to be the one that's "trustworthy." He discounted the other witness, Louie Almeida, because he was an "accomplice." He explained, "According to the law, his testimony is subject to suspicion and to be considered with caution."

Clearly the judge could see the public outrage that would soon be falling on his head. He finished by saying, "My decision may not be a popular one. But for those who disagree, I wish to state that every defendant, and I mean every defendant, no matter who he might be, is entitled to a fair trial and must be proven guilty beyond a reasonable doubt, whether it is a gang-type shooting or the mere stealing of a bicycle."

When I walked into Counsellors Row, there was Pat, sitting at the First Ward table. He got up and I followed him into the lobby, past the elevators and through the door to the stairwell. They had a janitor's closet back there, where he stood a few steps above me. "Wow, great job," he said. "Terrific job."

"Pat," I said, "this judge is in trouble. This case is all over the papers and the rest of the media. Can't we give him more than ten thousand?"

He replied, "Look, he agreed to take it for ten and that's what he's going to get." Pat reached into his coat pocket and took out two envelopes. I knew what a lot of cash looked like and it didn't look like that much in those envelopes. He handed me one and said, "Here's the $7,500 balance for the judge." Then he gave me the other little skinny one. "And this is for you."

I was thinking, "If those are thousand dollar bills in there, it's not a lot." For what I did, I expected to get paid fifty or a hundred thousand. My own expenses were five or ten thousand, just in running back and forth to Florida to see Whalen.

But I didn't say boo. When I got inside my office, I pulled out my envelope and opened it up. He gave me a lousy $3,000. "The bastard," I thought. An extra $30,000 wasn't going to change my life in those days, but it would have told me my efforts were appreciated. I started to see how much money meant to the Mob, and how cheap they were—in so many ways.

However bad I felt about *my* envelope, I felt that much worse about the one I had to give the judge. To smooth the waters, I brought along Cathy Fleming. I knew the judge liked to see her. We met again at that place near his house. At one time it had been a pretty hot Italian restaurant. But it had changed hands, and you would go there now to drink instead of eat. When we walked in the door, the judge was sitting alone at this huge horseshoe bar. He was already getting a load on. I could hardly believe how bad he looked—like he had aged fifteen years in two weeks. His shoulders were stooped. His face was lined. He was a broken man.

Cathy took a seat at the bar, and the judge and I walked into the bathroom. It was a dirty, smelly place. He started talking to me. "The newspapers are going to crucify me. I'm going to lose my judgeship. I can't run for reelection." He was almost crying. Then he looked at me and said, "You did this to me."

"Judge," I said, "before you got involved in the case, I told you what it was. I'm in the same spot you are. I feel terrible, but there is nothing I can do about that."

I then handed him the envelope and said, "Judge, here's the balance."

He looked inside. "That's all I'm going to get?" he asked. "I'm not going to get any more?"

He shook his head and started to limp out of the bathroom. I tried to tell him that *I* would have given him more, but he turned around and cut me off. "You destroyed me," he said, and he walked away.

As I stood in that bathroom, I was truly sorry about what happened to Frank. I should have felt sorry for myself, too.

Although the Harry Aleman fix brought me a lot more business and a lot more influence, it also sucked me that much deeper into the First Ward. I would soon see for myself how Pat Marcy had hijacked the Democratic Party, the city government, the court system, and even the police. Like an octopus, he reached inside each one and pulled the levers of power for the benefit of his cronies and the Mob. Those who got close to him, like I did, lived in fear of his wrath. Time and again, he pushed us into more criminal activity, like the Aleman fix, and time and again, we couldn't back away.

In his supreme arrogance, Marcy never conceived that anyone in his inner circle would ever turn on him. Certainly not me. But while I may have sold my soul to him, I still kept my conscience. It was only a matter of time before the disgust bubbling inside of me boiled over. When it did, I was ready to bring the First Ward machine down around me—even if I went down with it.

COP KILLER

Chicago Tribune, June 16, 1950

And so began a newspaper article about my father, James F. Cooley. Like a lot of stories in the press, this one didn't get all the facts straight. True, my grandfather was shot that "terrible night" in 1927, but he didn't die then. The bullet that hit him between the eyes took another twelve weeks to kill him. It was a slow, agonizing death.

As you read through the clips about my grandfather's murder, the whole story seems so strange but so Catholic, too—with all the drawn-out suffering. The night of the shooting, my grandfather was fifty-one and your typical Irish immigrant cop, walking the beat and chatting it up with the locals. He wore that high Keystone Kops hat. Maybe he was swinging his nightstick, too. Suddenly two men ran up shouting that they had been robbed as they got out of their car. Grandfather walked with them the few blocks back to the scene of the crime, and just then one of the robbers appeared on the steps of a nearby house. Grandfather drew his revolver and told him, "Throw up your hands," but the robber pulled out his own gun and shot him instead. Grandfather, staggered by the bullet, shot back and then fell to the ground. He was bundled into the car of one of the holdup victims, a dentist, so he could be rushed to the hospital. Only the dentist was stone drunk ("confused by his experience" is how one article put it), so he drove around with my grandfather for an hour before they ever saw a doctor. The dentist was later convicted of driving under the influence, but a lot of good that did for my grandfather.

You would think that my grandfather—with a bullet in his brain—never regained consciousness. But three days later, when the coppers dragged a suspect into the hospital for an ID, grandfather raised his head from the pillow and said, "That's the fellow. I'd know him in a million." What a quaint way of putting it. You can hear the Irish brogue and everything. The suspect, Thomas Pemberton, was quite a character himself. They arrested him in the company of a woman described as "colored," but he later admitted to being a card-carrying member of the Ku Klux Klan. When the police searched his home, they found what the press called "an arsenal" of twelve rifles and six pistols.

Poor Grandfather lingered through the winter and into the spring, mostly in a coma. At one point the hospital sent him home, probably so he wouldn't take up a bed for someone they could help. When he finally died in April, he was back in the hospital, surrounded by his wife and six kids. The funeral was a humble affair. A wake in the family parlor. A simple interment in the parish cemetery. A few years before, the neighborhood had sent off Al Capone's little brother in a cascade of roses. All my grandmother got was a pension of $79 a month and the uniform to bury her husband in.

Justice moved a little quicker in those days, and Pemberton was on trial for the murder by October. The state had him dead to rights, positively identified by the victim and bystanders, but when the trial ended, the headline read: "Jury Frees Pemberton in Policeman's Death." Grandmother heard the verdict and fainted away. It was, the prosecutor said, "the biggest surprise I ever had in my career."

However amazing that story sounds, the most amazing part was yet to come.

Dad grew into a tall somber young man, with sleepy eyes and red hair that got darker as it grew thinner. They still called him Big Red, but he was a gentle soul who never used his size to intimidate. He tended more toward the spiritual, much like my grandmother, who never lost her faith despite all the bad breaks that came her way. She was active in the church, and somehow got her sons through Mount Carmel, the South Side's best Catholic high school. Dad took the next step towards sanctification and entered Mount Carmel Seminary, a huge Canadian monastery overlooking Niagara Falls. But after three years, he decided the priesthood was not for him, and no wonder. Within months of leaving the seminary he met my mother and they got married. She was a very pretty brunette, with deep-set eyes. There was a lot more than physical attraction to draw them together. Both were devout Catholics. Both were the children of coppers, and, believe it or not, both of their fathers had died in the line of duty.

And yet, despite all the family history, when Dad and Mom moved back to Chicago with a set of newborn twins, my grandmother "gently urged him"—Dad would say—to join the police department. People may look back and wonder what possessed her to do such a thing. How could she lose a husband to police work and then push her son down the same path? Why would he have let himself be pushed? And why would my mother have let him go?

Obviously, times were different. To some extent their attitude was a sign of their faith with a dash of good old-fashioned Irish fatalism. When your time was up, your time was up and there was not much you could do about it—whether you worked in the police department or a grocery store. But Dad had other matters to consider as well. It was the Depression, and he had to put food on the table for a growing family. One way or another the city was going to stay in business and it would always need somebody to fight crime.

Although the police may have guaranteed a paycheck, it was not a very big one. My parents didn't help matters by being good Catholics and having nine kids—two girls and seven boys. My father always struggled to bring home enough bacon, and my mother struggled that much more to stretch it.

We lived on Chicago's South Side, a gritty area far from the city's skyscrapers. When we looked up, we saw smokestacks and church steeples. Our clouds puffed up from the steel mills like steam from a chugging locomotive. When the wind blew the wrong way, you had a taste like stale bread on the back of your throat.

Dad could only afford one-floor brick bungalows. They were always on the bleeding edge of the "color line," where whites were moving out and blacks were moving in and all hell was breaking out in between. When someone got killed within a block of our house, Dad would say it was time to move. Each of the houses had three bedrooms: one for the parents, one for the two girls, and another for the boys. When there got to be too many of us, we threw a couple of mattresses into the attic.

To make ends meet, Dad juggled a second and sometimes third job, selling mutual funds or insurance. He was almost never home. Mom had to hold down the fort on her own. I remember her working from morning to night, with bottomless piles of laundry, and constant cooking and shopping on a meager budget. She had a whole routine about getting to the butcher or produce stand late in the day, just as they were marking down the prices. The older kids ran interference, so she could get first in line. At the grocery store, she looked for the dented cans and asked for a few cents off. When it came to our clothes, she always found something used, from relatives or the church where she volunteered. All the work wore her down and made her gray before her time. You hardly ever saw her in makeup or fancy clothes.

If needed, Mom could still put on a good show, like the one Sunday in 1950 when our whole family was photographed for that article about my dad ("the sixth in a series describing the bravery and earnestness of typical Chicago policemen"). Mom may have worn a simple dress, but with a baby in her arm she looked as good as Rose Kennedy.

And right there, in the center of the picture, was yours truly, at the age of seven. I was the third oldest, born after a brother and sister who were twins. This day I was decked out in a double-breasted white suit, fresh from my first Holy Communion. Of course, none of my other brothers wore a suit, and I had my hand on my jacket like a little Napoleon—already a hot shit. It's ironic that they took the picture the one time in my childhood when I was dressed so nicely. Even then, I hated being poor and I hated the used clothes most of all. I wanted us to have nice things, and I didn't want to hear my mother keep saying we couldn't afford them. It just made me focus on money that much more—certainly more than other kids my age. I was always out hustling to make some extra change. I delivered papers. I hung outside the corner store and offered to carry people's groceries home. As I got older, I'd ride my bike a few miles to a drugstore that paid me for sweeping up and making deliveries from six to nine-thirty at night. I'd get seventy-five cents, a bottle of pop, and a candy bar. By the end of the week I made five or six dollars, which was a lot of money for a kid. I gave most of it to Mom (although I didn't know it then, she was putting it away for me), but I always kept one or two bucks in my pocket, so I'd have some money for snacks. Because I wouldn't eat my vegetables, I was always hungry. My mother and I went to war over that. She refused to give me more of anything else, and I wouldn't budge on the green stuff—even if it meant starving to death.

The picky eating was just one way I tested my parents. For most of my childhood, I clanged back and forth, between Sin and Sainthood, like the clapper in a church bell. My parents were on the saintly side. Every day they got up at six to go to Mass and then lived out their days in unending sacrifice for all of us. My big brother, the spitting image of Dad, followed in his quiet footsteps and ultimately became a priest. I told the reporter who did the article about my father that I was headed to the seminary too, but my brother and I were cut from different cloth. When kids used to make fun of him because of the holes he had in his clothes, he just turned the other cheek. If kids pushed him around, he never pushed back. It made me sick to see that, and I decided I wasn't going to put up with getting picked on. I was one of the smallest kids in my class, but from the time I was six, if anybody said something I didn't like, I found a way to get him back. I didn't care how big he was. I could always use a brick or a bottle.

Probably the meanest kid in my class was Tommy Dugan. Tall and skinny, he had a perpetual scowl, and little slits for eyes that made him look like a snake. The first time he picked a fight with me, I licked him but good. That actually started a friendship that would continue through much of our lives, with some bizarre twists and turns along the way. As kids, we were like two peas in a pod. Same enemies. Same friends. Always covering the other's back. We were both smart, too, and caught on to our lessons quicker than the guys we hung with. Of course, that was nothing to brag about in our neighborhood. When it came to math, Tommy was practically a genius, but he was so obnoxious, he never got special attention from the teachers. His good grades on tests made them even madder at him.

If my parents were my paragons of Virtue, Tommy Dugan was my mentor in Sin. His upbringing was mostly to blame. His father had a decent-paying job at the gas company, but after work he'd go straight to the bar to drink, and he was a miserable drunk. When he got home at seven or eight, he always found some excuse to start beating the wife and the kids. Tommy grew up hating the bastard and lost his moral compass in the process. He respected no authority, and there was nothing he wouldn't do. When we went into stores, he had me be a lookout and then he would shoplift. At times he picked up a few things for me, too. Tommy also broke into houses to steal. But that was a line I would never cross. I knew it would kill my father if the coppers picked me up for robbery.

I got in enough trouble as it was. Mom could only take so much before she would pull out the ironing cord and start whipping me with it. After a while, I learned how to grab the cord from her. She'd say, "Wait until your father comes home. You'll get it then." But Dad never had the heart for discipline. By the time he dragged in, after some second job, I pretended to be asleep and he was too tired to pull me out of bed. The next day he might say, "God will punish you if you keep doing that." I thought, "Okay," and would keep doing it anyway.

Once, I finally pushed Mom over the edge. I broke a window and we were going to be out some money to fix it. Mom waited for Dad to come home and then marched him over to me. "Now you're going to get it," she said. He took me into their bedroom, put me over the bed and shut the door. Then he pulled the belt out of his pants. For a minute I thought I was in real trouble. But when he started to whack, he just kept hitting the bed instead of me. If this was going to work, I figured, I better do some screaming. Only I yelled too hard, because my mother burst through the door to stop him. When she saw the whole charade, she got really mad and for the first time I could remember, she yelled at Dad. Then he whipped me for real, the kind of beating I never got before. I had to crawl under the bed to get away from him. He felt so bad about hitting me, he apologized for days. I told him to forget about it. He just didn't believe in physical discipline. Maybe I got off easy in the short run, but in the long run I loved him more for it. Later, when it came to committing real serious crimes, I would always think twice—unlike Tommy Dugan. I didn't want to do anything that would break my father's heart.

Dad thought he could stop my fighting by getting me boxing gloves so I could channel my aggression through some supervised outlet. He probably watched *The Bells of St. Mary's* a few times too many. When I started boxing with the Catholic Youth Organization and learned what I was doing, I got to be even more dangerous.

Dugan's family left the neighborhood before we did, but by the time I was in eighth grade, we had to move too, and we both ended up in the same neighborhood again. Tommy's idea of the Welcome Wagon was to arrange fights for me with the toughest kids in his school. We'd go to a vacant lot across the street from a friend's house, and everyone would stand around to see me get creamed. It was like throwing me to the lions, but the fact is, I enjoyed it. Somewhere along the line, I learned that fighting was more mental than physical. I knew that however big the guy, I could go straight up to him and knock him down. It took three fights before everyone in the new neighborhood got the message.

This was the last move of my childhood, and as far as I was concerned, it was where life finally began. When school was out, I caddied at the South Shore Country Club with Tommy and started to make real money. We had a little gang that would get together every night in Avalon Park, a few blocks from our homes. My parents thought I was going to sleep early, but I took the highest bunk in our room and would fix the pillows so it looked like I was still in bed. Then I'd climb out through the window. For a while, I had a ladder hidden behind some bushes on the ground below, so I could climb back in again. Dad saw it one morning and threw it away. He thought a burglar was about to rob us. It never occurred to him that I was the one who was sneaking into the house.

We had wild times in that park. It was near the rail yards, and once we figured out which trains carried the Budweiser shipments, we liberated a few cases of beer. Eventually the railroad police caught on and set an ambush. They pinched me just as I was climbing the fence. I told them I was taking a shortcut to the drugstore and they let me go. I probably looked like too much of a pipsqueak to be involved. Tommy got out of it, too. Some nights I stayed in the park so long, it was too late to sneak home, so I'd just go straight to the golf course the next morning.

I never wanted that summer to end, but when September came, Tommy and I were classmates again at Mount Carmel High School, about three miles north from our neighborhood. It was in a little campus with a couple of sprawling brick buildings surrounded by athletic fields. The administrators and most of the teachers were Carmelite priests and friars. They wore monk-like robes with big leather belts.

I always had to be the class clown. During the first weeks of school, I started in with all my grade-school antics. When the teacher's back was turned, I used a ruler to flick spit into kids' hair. In biology class, I put a wad of bubblegum on the seat of a black guy who sat in front of me. He went up to the board and this long string of gum trailed after him. Everybody broke up. Father Jordan immediately knew who was responsible. He was big and burly, with a reputation for being a strict disciplinarian. He marched me down to the front of the class and had me bend over and grab my ankles. Then he took off his belt and hit me five or six times. He didn't miss like my father did. I must have been in shock, because I didn't realize how hard he hit me until I went to sit back down. It stung so much, I popped up like a jack-in-the-box, which started everyone laughing again. That earned me ten more whacks. This time, I couldn't keep the tears from rolling down my face.

That experience made me behave better in class, but Tommy and I were still slacking off as much as we could. We both had the ability to crack our books the night before a test and get an "A." But then there was homework, and if you didn't do that, you got a beating too. So

Tommy and I would meet at a donut shop around seven-thirty each morning and wait for the "brains" to get off at the bus stop outside the store window. Then we'd drag one of them in and copy his homework. At some point, the Fathers realized we were a dangerous combination. They split us up, so we couldn't be in the same classes—even though it meant one of us would be in a room with the slower kids.

It didn't matter, because we never took the academics all that seriously. What mattered most to us was sports. Everybody wanted to go out for football, because Mount Carmel usually had one of the best teams in the state. I was too small for that. They tossed me around like a feather. Wrestling was different. There I could fight guys my own size, and I loved every minute of it. Some of my most challenging bouts came after school. All the white people had moved out of the Mount Carmel neighborhood and black street gangs were everywhere. During school hours the police were on the street, but after four o'clock, when we left practice, they were nowhere to be seen. We never knew what was going to hit us while we were waiting for the bus. You just had to be unbelievably tough or, if you were alone, know when to run for your life.

Of course, Tommy Dugan had his own demented way of solving our transportation problems. At the start of our senior year, he staked out a used car dealership in our neighborhood, and noticed where they kept the keys for the older cars in the back of the lot. He figured we could take a car for a week and no one would notice. Then we could exchange it for another car. It was quite a racket and not a bad way to get girls, either. We got on their good side by picking them up in the morning, and we could ask them out at night. This went on for a few weeks, until one day Tommy and I were called in to see the dean of students—the chief ass-kicker. He was waiting for us with a police detective. Somebody had ratted us out. The Father told us that even riding around in a stolen car—let alone stealing it—was grounds for expulsion. We could also get jail time if convicted of the crime. But fortunately for us, both the dean and the cop knew my father. "This would kill your dad if he found out," the cop said. As long as we returned the car, no charges would be brought. For punishment, we had to stay after school for the rest of the year. That didn't bother me because I had wrestling practice anyhow.

Despite all of our extracurricular activity, Tommy and I still graduated Mount Carmel with honors. Even though we refused to take what we called the "Genius Classes" that were used to prep the smarter kids, we did well on the college placement exams, and we both got into Marquette University in Milwaukee, two hours north of Chicago. Marquette gave me a wrestling scholarship to boot.

If you looked at the neighborhood where we grew up, and how most of our friends turned out, getting into college was quite an accomplishment. Unfortunately, it also made us a little too cocky. We figured that if we could beat the system at Mount Carmel, we'd have no trouble beating the system in college.

As far as my parents were concerned, with all the trouble I had caused, getting accepted at Marquette was nothing short of a miracle. My older sister had also been accepted there, but she had been a model student. I had gone from juvenile delinquency to the verge of great accomplishment, and they couldn't have been prouder. Even though money was still tight for them, they bought me the first suit I had since my communion.

The story of what happened to that suit pretty much sums up my experience at Marquette. I first wore it in August 1960, the day I showed up for college orientation. They had assigned me to the nicest new dormitory, on the floor with all the jocks. Before long I recognized a tall rangy guy with close-cropped hair like a Marine. His name was Bill Murphy. He played halfback the year his high school beat Mount Carmel and went on to win the Chicago Prep championship. He didn't know me from Adam, but I gave him a nudge and told him to follow me if he wanted a good time.

I had heard there was a brewery only a mile away from the campus. They took you on a stupid little tour, but then they brought you into a room where you got a free sample of the wares. In those days, eighteen-year-olds could drink beer, but weren't allowed in bars. Bill and I went on the tour and had our free beer. We then figured out a way to sneak into rooms where they were serving other tour groups. We did that a few times before the security guy came over and tried to throw us out. I got into a fight with him and they called the police. Bill and I had to run out the back and climb a cyclone fence to get away. As I was going over the top, I caught my leg and tore the pants from the cuff to my knee. Walking back, we passed a bunch of guys on motorcycles. One of them made a crack about my pants, and I picked a fight with him, so there was a little more pulling and tearing on my suit. But I wasn't through yet. We stopped for a hamburger at a joint across the street from the dormitory. Somebody looked at me the wrong way, and we had another fight. I was a little midget compared to Bill, but I was going to prove to him that I was the toughest guy in the world. By the time I got back to my room, the suit was already ruined. I could have rolled it up and flushed it down the toilet.

I had plenty of other escapades in store. Tommy Dugan was no different. Suddenly there were no Carmelite Fathers breathing down our necks to make sure we did our homework. All around us there were constant parties and lots of rich kids who didn't know what to do with their money. It was too much for Tommy and me to handle.

My scholarship didn't cover pocket money or books. I was supposed to get a job for that. I lasted two days at the Elks Club restaurant before I got in an argument with some old fogey customer, but I didn't have to find another job. There was a much better way to make money. I had started poker games in the meeting room on our dorm floor. We bet only a few bucks each hand but those bucks added up. I had been playing poker since I was a little kid, and I quickly realized that the college boys didn't know what they were doing, especially with a few beers under their belts. Besides my winnings, I collected a piece of each kitty for putting together the games and buying "refreshments," although I never drank myself when I was playing. Word got around, and the games went on almost nonstop. There were days I played twenty-four hours straight.

As far as I was concerned, the legit social life on campus was a joke—especially the fraternities. All anyone cared about was their parties. My friends and I decided to put on our own mixers, with everyone invited. The coeds had to pay just fifty cents, but the men paid a dollar fifty. We rented out an apartment near the campus and our only other investment was a keg of beer we'd put in the bathtub. It usually ran out in a couple of hours, but by then we had run out, too. Nobody ever made much of a stink about it, because all the cutest girls would show up. Some guys used to go out and bring back beer on their own nickel.

Of course, Dugan had his own ideas about creative finance. He got guys who worked in the student union gift store to lose a few items on the way from the box to the shelf, like sweatshirts and hats. Nobody seemed to notice that anything was missing. We then set up our own corner to sell some of that merchandise at better prices than the store. It wasn't long before Tommy and I had a reputation—the Irish gangsters from the South Side of Chicago.

Tommy didn't need that kind of encouragement to be bad. After they put him in a different dorm from me, he teamed up with a football player named Gary. He was a muscular Italian kid who hung around the strip clubs and could introduce you to the girls there. He also carried a gun in his belt—the first time I ever saw that. Tommy now had a partner to take him to new heights in crime. They started committing all kinds of burglaries and robberies, mostly inside the dormitories.

As a result, Tommy and I started going our separate ways. The jocks I hung out with didn't want him around, and I couldn't stand Gary. But one day Dugan pulled me aside and promised to cut me in on a great scheme. "If I tell you what it is," he said, "then you're in and you can't back out." I would encounter this trap a few more times in my life, and usually avoided it, but I was dying to know Tommy's brilliant plan. "Gary and I," he said, "are going to rob the drycleaners."

It was a fucking insane idea. I wanted to shoot myself for making the promise. The drycleaner was across the street from Marquette. Tommy had a friend who worked there, so he knew what evening they had the most cash. After the robbery, they would go back to Gary's dorm room and leave the money in his drawer. Then they would sneak into a party and act like they had been there for the whole night. All Tommy wanted me to do was drive the getaway car, and he'd cut me in for an equal share. He set a time to meet me at the dormitory, but I never showed up. I went with some other wrestlers to the Eagles Club, far from campus. They held big dances and had plenty of witnesses to say where I had been. Late that night, as we drove back to the dormitory, we turned on the car radio and found out there was a robbery at the drycleaner. I couldn't believe Tommy had gone through with it, especially without me. But I had to find out for sure. I went to Gary's dorm and climbed through the back window into his room. When I opened his drawer, cash flew out in every direction. I figured they hadn't even counted it. What would it matter if I grabbed a few dollars for myself? It was an incredibly weasel-like thing to do, but I was just robbing a couple of robbers. I shoved a wad into my pocket and headed over to another party.

At four o'clock that morning, there was a banging on my door. It was Tommy and Gary, and I wasn't going to open up. Finally they kicked the door in, but by that time, everybody on the floor had woken up, too, including the resident counselor. They all stuck their heads out into the hall. Tommy and Gary were insane with rage, practically foaming at the mouth. "We know you took the fucking money," they screamed. I acted like I was so drunk I couldn't understand them. They slammed the door shut and tore into my closet, going through all my clothes and pockets. They quickly found the money—three hundred bucks. If the resident counselor hadn't been waiting outside, they would have let me have it then and there, but Gary promised they would get me later.

I couldn't have threats hanging over my head. The next morning I confronted them by myself. "What I did, I did," I said. "But I'm not telling anyone about what you guys did. I'm keeping my mouth shut. If anything happens to me, somebody at school has a sealed letter he's supposed to open. Then the whole story will get out."

Tommy said he didn't want to see me again. I replied, "Good-bye and good riddance."

For the next year or so, I had nothing to do with Tommy, but my life at Marquette had already spun out of control. I was always tired, because I was up all night playing cards. Unlike high school, I couldn't just crack a book before a test and get an "A." My grades were horrible and I was put on academic probation after the second semester. During the summer, I assured my parents I'd get my grades up in my sophomore year. But when school started, I was back to my carousing. One weekend, three of us decided to drive down to Chicago to watch our old high schools play against each other in football. We rented a car and turned back the odometer to hide our mileage. After the game, we got into our car and went to a nearby park to drink a six-pack. A cop snuck up and arrested us.

The patrolman handed us over to some piece-of-shit officer who was working Vice, and he called our parents. Just earlier that week, I sent my parents a letter, telling them I had turned over a new leaf and would be studying through the whole weekend for my first exams. Imagine how they felt when they got a call that I was back in Chicago at a police station. My father came to get me with the two other fathers. "They'll let you go," Dad told us, "but they want us to pay a bribe. That's wrong and I just can't do it."

I had put my father in a lot of nasty situations in my life, but none was worse than this. As I later learned, he had paid a heavy price in the police department for taking the moral high ground. The vice cop was asking the three parents to come up with $500—which was a lot of cash in those days—but the amount wasn't the issue for Dad. Paying off a cop was illegal, and he did not believe in breaking the law. For him, it was as simple as that. The other two fathers didn't know what he was talking about. They were more than happy to buy our way out. Otherwise, an arrest could get us all expelled from Marquette. How could my father let three kids' lives get ruined by a few cans of beer? If everyone didn't go along with the bribe, it wasn't going to happen, so Dad gave in. I knew it wasn't easy for him.

We finally got out of jail late that night, but I didn't go home with Dad. I sensed the turmoil I had put him through, and I couldn't bear to be alone with him. Instead, I talked the guys into driving straight back to Marquette. I didn't call home to talk to him for two or three weeks. By then he had forgiven me.

Even that close shave was not enough to straighten me out. I was tempting fate. I *always* tempted fate. When I got back to school, I still hung out at the bars, even though I wasn't twenty-one. One night while I was in The Stratford, a place right across the street from school, the police raided it for underaged drinkers. We had some phony Wisconsin IDs, but they didn't fool the coppers any. They arrested a whole bunch of us for disorderly conduct and took us to jail in a paddy wagon. We were booked and given a trial date. The coppers let us out on our own recognizance, because we were Marquette students, and told us to stay away from that bar.

But The Stratford was *the* place to go every Wednesday and Friday. I didn't want the people there to think I was under age. As soon as I returned to campus, I went back to the bar and told them that the police checked out my ID and found everything was okay. I figured there was no way they would raid the same place again that night. But two and a half hours later, the police were back. This time it was a different vice squad. I was the only underaged person in the whole joint. They put me in the back of a squad car with a cop named Callahan. As he drove me to jail, we passed an accident scene. When he pulled over to check it out, I bolted through the back door and took off. Good Irish cop that he was, Callahan remembered the name on my fake ID, and now he came looking for me at the dormitory. For three days straight I would get called to come downstairs, but when I saw Callahan's squad car parked in the street below, I would go and hide. A week later, I was called to the resident counselor's office again. This time I didn't see the squad car. I figured that Callahan had finally forgotten about me. I went down to see what was up. There inside the counselor's office was Callahan.

"That's the one," he said, pointing at me like I was in some lineup.

I acted shocked. "What are you talking about?"

"You're the one that took off out of the squad."

"No," I said. "Wasn't me."

Callahan couldn't prove it, because he didn't book me. But the resident counselor knew whom to believe. It was one of the counts they used to throw me out of Marquette. Of course, they had plenty of other ammunition—what with the gambling and the fighting. Then there was the party room we had in the apartment off-campus. For that alone, I could have gotten canned. I wasn't the only member of the class to earn an early exit from the school. They got rid of another forty students, Tommy Dugan included.

I didn't call my parents. I was too ashamed to go home with my tail between my legs. Instead, I moved into our apartment and hatched a crazy plan to go to California. I didn't know anyone there, or what I would do, but I wanted to get as far away as possible.

A few days later I heard a knock on the door. I opened it up and there was Dad. I played dumb. "Dad," I said, "what are you doing here?"

"I know you were kicked out," he said. My older sister was still at Marquette and she told my parents what happened. "You've got to come back home with me."

I didn't fight very hard to stay. I was still a homebody, and once again my father found a way to forgive me. Only this time, I thought, I had learned my lesson. All my little gangster ways—the stealing, the card playing—had been my undoing at Marquette. I was finally ready to straighten out and go absolutely legit.

As far as my father was concerned, there was no question about continuing my education. Dad never forgave himself for not finishing college and he wasn't going to let me make the same mistake. But now I'd have to take a rougher route to that degree: night school, and day jobs to pay tuition.

I applied to Loyola in downtown Chicago. Like Marquette, the college was run by Jesuits. My grades were good enough to get in, but I was rejected when I told them I had been kicked out of Marquette. I needed Dad again. He went to the priest in admissions, and was given an impossible Catch-22. They would accept me only if Marquette would take me back. Dad took me to Marquette and we sat down with the Father who was dean of students. Dad did all the pleading. He said I had learned the error of my ways. I was ready to return home and do penance working my way through Loyola. All I needed was this one letter from Marquette before I could embark on the path to my redemption. The Father agreed to send a letter to Loyola indicating that they would "consider" my readmission to Marquette. But he made it perfectly clear, consideration was one thing, acceptance was another. Marquette wanted nothing more to do with me. As far as I was concerned, the feeling was mutual.

Once I had gotten into Loyola, I had to figure a way to pay for it, and that was no picnic either. I was a nineteen-year-old with a high school degree. The best-paying job I could find was at the Ford Stamping Plant, where they made parts like car doors. Now I would truly understand the value of a college education. Every morning, my father woke me up at the crack of dawn and dropped me off at the plant on his way to work. For the next eight hours I went through backbreaking hell: pushing around slabs of steel, lifting whole doors on the conveyor belt, welding with sparks flying all over my face and hair. I would just get used to one job before they shifted me to another. I went through each day like a dishrag through a wringer. And after I hitchhiked home, I couldn't collapse into bed. I had to change clothes, grab my books, and then take a bus and an El train to Loyola for night school. I didn't get home until after ten. It was, to put it bluntly, a motherfucker.

After two months of this, I was not a happy camper. I was sore. I was exhausted. I was angry as hell—at the world and at myself. One night when I got home from school, my parents were still entertaining another cop who lived a few blocks from us. His nickname was Tiny and he must have weighed 270 pounds. He was a big fat slob and no doubt crooked as hell. How else could he have lived in a halfway decent house and bought a new car every few years? He used to mock my father for having a second job.

I was in no mood to talk to Tiny. My mother put some dinner out for me, and I pulled the plates over to the other end of the table. "Look who's here," Tiny said. "The guy that flunked out of Marquette. You think you're real sharp, don't you?"

"Yeah?" I said. "You're the one who's got a fucking idiot for a kid. *He* flunked out. I didn't flunk out of anywhere."

Getting "kicked out" instead of "flunking out" may have been a fine distinction, but in any case, my dad was not going to stick up for me.

"You have no right to talk back like that to our guests," he said.

"I don't have to take his crap."

Then Dad stood up and pointed toward the door. "If you don't like the rules in my house, then you get out."

Without saying a word, I got up from the table. I packed my suitcase and walked out the door. I was fed up with my job. I was fed up with school. I was fed up with my father for being such a hard-working sucker.

I didn't tell my parents where I was going, which made my exit all the more dramatic. I had hooked up again with my old friend Tommy Dugan. After he got kicked out of Marquette, he couldn't go back home. Instead, he found a shitty little apartment near Rush Street, the city's nightclub district, and a few blocks from Loyola. But this wasn't the same old Evil John. He was going to night school at another college and, like me, working during the day at some menial job.

Dugan and I were back together, like two peas in a pod. Although we were determined to clean up our act, we were still too smart for our own good. One night we got home to find that the electric company had cut off our power. Tommy had forgotten to pay the bill. We could see a light on in the vacant apartment next door to us, so Tommy broke in and we ran extension cords through the windows. The other apartment was not such a bad place. It was still furnished, and since we had gotten inside, we figured we could use it as our study hall. This went on for a few days until one night the door suddenly opened and there was the landlord, trying to show the apartment to a prospective tenant. The guy started yelling like he had caught a couple of burglars. It's not like we had stolen anything. I told him to shut up and the next thing I knew, we were slugging it out.

So much for my attempt at independent living. The landlord ended up calling the cops, and I had to hightail it out of there. I packed the few things I had, and by three in the morning, I was back on the South Side of Chicago. I snuck into the basement of our house and slept there for a few hours, until I heard my parents in the kitchen.

I trudged upstairs with a hangdog expression on my face. The Prodigal Son had returned—after just ten days in exile. Right away my mother asked, "What happened? Did you get thrown out of the place you were in?"

"Oh, no," I said, "I just decided to come home."

My father shushed my mother. "It's great to see you," he said. "Sure you're okay?"

We sat down and had a long talk. He had never expected me to pick up and leave the house that way, but he asked that I not do things that showed disrespect. I promised it would never happen again.

The clapper had swung back toward the Saints. I was home with my parents, more determined than ever to go on the straight and narrow. I really did want to finish college. But getting a good job was the problem. No way would I go back to the factory again. Although office work was easier, it didn't pay enough to make ends meet. I even enlisted in the Marines for an ROTC-type pilot training program during the summer of 1962, but as tensions started to build with the Soviet Union, the program was canceled.

Suddenly, only one occupation made any sense. It was a job that would pay a decent salary and not take me too far from home. It was a job that would pay college tuition as long as I got good grades. It was a job that was as much a part of my family as the Catholic Church and our Irish name.

That July, at the age of twenty, I would become a cop.

Chapter 3

MARCO & THE COUNT

There are incidents in my life that seem so unreal, they play out in my memory like scenes in a nightmare.

One night, in the summer of 1966, I woke up, racked with pain. Through a haze, I saw someone looking at me. His face was bandaged, and the skin that showed through was discolored. He waved arms at me with only bandaged stumps where hands should be.

I was in a hospital bed, and much of my own body was wrapped up in casts and bandages. My ribs and collarbone were broken, my leg crushed. But nothing hurt me more than my left hand. It had been pierced and nearly severed—as though a stake had been driven through the palm. For a while, when I was still semi-conscious, the doctors debated amputation. The guy with the stumps had lost his hands when they melted off in the furnace of a steel mill. Every time he passed my room, he had to look in on me. I guess he figured I was about to join the club.

The doctors did not have to amputate my hand, but it took several more surgeries and months of convalescence before I could leave that hospital room. I had only vague memories of the fight that put me there. I had just arrived home from work one evening. Before I stepped into the house, I decided to go to confession in the church across the street. It was probably the first time I had gone in months. As I left church, I could see the girl who had been in the confessional ahead of me. She was with a bunch of kids from the local street gang, and they were pulling her between the houses across the street. That didn't look right. I ran over and waded into the middle of the pack. When I asked the girl if she was all right, she turned and grabbed me with a look of terror on her face. I put my arm over her shoulder to lead her away from there, and the gang started kicking and punching me. I tried to fight back, but I was getting the shit beat out of me. In the distance, I could hear sirens wailing. Hoping that someone had called the cops, I tried to hold on to one or two of the gangbangers, even as they kept punching me in the head. As I lost consciousness, they pushed me into the street—just as a squad car came to my rescue. The car ran completely over my body. The other cops pulled me out from under the back wheels.

After the doctors decided I could keep my hand, they wondered whether I would walk again without a limp. There were other questions about metal rods, pins, and scar tissue. I had just turned twenty-five, entering the prime of my life. I was not ready to confront these matters of life and limb. Until this point in time, I had felt indestructible. Suddenly my body—and life itself—seemed so fragile.

I wasn't left alone to curse my bad luck. Unlike the guy with melted hands, I had plenty of visitors: family, friends, cops, and even commanders. No one came more often than my dad. He would sit by my bed for hours and talk to me. Perhaps he thought about what happened to *his* father. Maybe he was sorry he encouraged me to join the force. I was off-duty when the fight happened, but I probably would have stayed away if I had been a civilian. Whether or not Dad felt guilty, he still had his faith to fall back on. "God must have had a reason for this," he would tell me. "God must have had some reason."

Not as far as I was concerned.

I had tried to be good. No one could have asked me to work harder as a cop, or to be more fearless. I thought this earned me some measure of redemption for my carousing days in high school and college. If there was any justice in the world, I did not deserve this suffering for trying to help that girl. I had even gone to confession, for Christ's sake.

More than that, I had been a model citizen ever since I moved back with the family and joined the police force. I stuck with night school and got my undergraduate degree from Loyola, and although I had become a cop primarily to earn my way through school, I fell in love with the job right from the start.

Back then, you got just twelve weeks in the Police Academy before they put you on the street with a badge and a gun. They called it "in-service training." In fact, during the early sixties, the crime rate was sky-rocketing and commanders had to throw the rookies into the line of fire. Because I wanted to work out of a station near our house, I first got assigned to the Third District, the roughest in the city. It was home to Chicago's most notorious gang, called the Black Stone Rangers (Black-stone was the street where I lived). With all the drug dealing and gang rivalries, there were constant shootings and stabbings.

My father then got me transferred to the Fourth, not nearly as rough, but still with enough excitement to make the job interesting. I was more suited to police work than breaking my back in a factory or sitting around in an office. Most of my young life I was getting into fights all the time to prove myself. Finally I was getting paid to do it. Better yet, I'd never had a car before. In the police department I could drive around all day.

For the first six months on the force, they wouldn't let me go out in a squad car alone, so my biggest problem was finding other coppers who wanted to ride with me. They all thought I was crazy. With every dangerous call—a shooting or a man with a gun—I raced to the scene. Even when the calls weren't ours, I picked up the mike and said, "Four-oh-two. We're clear to go." I'd crank up the siren, run red lights, anything to get there first.

This got the older cops real nervous. "Relax," they'd say, "what's your hurry?" They wanted to be the *last* to arrive. They would beg me to slow down. "Listen, I got a wife. I got kids," they'd say.

I dumped the partners as soon as I could. When I rode the squad by myself, I had a nose for trouble and made some unbelievable arrests: for robbery, auto theft, burglary, rapes; you name it. I was written up in the neighborhood paper all the time. Most of my pinches came on flukes. I'd see a car that looked out of place, and I'd follow it. If the driver suddenly took off, I'd know something was wrong. When I'd go chasing these guys, I didn't like to lose them—even if I had to run a red light. Twice I had very bad accidents where I demolished the squad I was driving, but each time I walked away without a scratch. The last time it happened was just a week before my beating.

When the district commander came to visit me in the hospital, he didn't pat me on the head like everyone else. He reminded me about the car crashes and said, "It's like you have a death wish. There's more to life than this. You have to start looking out for yourself, too."

It was one of those life-changing moments. I thought, "Yeah. He's right. Here I am, busting my ass for the force, busting my ass for school, and I have nothing to show for it." I was living at home, and I still had to take second jobs to make spending money. Where was the hard work and sacrifice taking me?

There's more to life than this. Now I heard that message loud and clear. It rang even louder with another horrible event that swirled around me in the hospital. Often, so I could sleep, I got an injection of morphine from a young Filipino student nurse. One night she mysteriously missed her shift. A few hours later, she and seven other student nurses, including a girl I had dated, were found dead in a nearby rooming house. They were all the victims of a twisted vagrant named Richard Speck. The murders horrified the nation. Fate could be so insane and so cruel. Sure, I'd had a rotten break, but I was still alive and, unlike that steel worker, I still had both my hands. Friends and family, too. When he looked in my room and saw all my visitors, he probably wished for *my* luck. I had options he could only dream about. As the weeks followed, and my pain lifted, I had no interest in rushing back to work. I needed to make another plan for my future.

For the first time, I started thinking about a real "career." Two years earlier, almost on a lark, I had begun law school at Chicago-Kent College of Law, part of the Illinois Institute of Technology. My major motivation was to get a student deferment from the draft. I never took school that seriously, and would use any excuse to skip a class or drop a course. Although my injuries now meant I wouldn't have to worry about the draft, suddenly the law career looked more promising than before. As a result of the arrests I made, I sat through a lot of trials. Like other cops, I had contempt for most of the gasbags who pranced around the courtroom. But from what I could see, criminal lawyers didn't work that much, and they were certainly making more money than cops. The actual schoolwork wasn't hard for me. I just had to buckle down and do the studying.

It took a year before I returned to police duty, and when I came back, I wasn't so eager to be the crash test dummy. As kind of a Purple Heart for my injuries, the police commanders served me a bunch of plum assignments, and I was not shy about taking them. Finally, in the fall of 1968, they put me in line for the dream job of every cop in Chicago—Rush Street District Vice Squad.

Rush Street was the most happening place in the city. More than a street, it was several blocks of bars, clubs, and restaurants. They were all wedged between the fancy Michigan Avenue shopping district and the townhouses and high-rises of the Gold Coast, the city's wealthiest neighborhood. The lakefront lay just a few hundred yards away, with all its beaches and fabulous people-watching in warm weather.

The sixties' revolutions in sex, music, and drugs all converged on Rush Street's corners. Here were the city's big singles bars, where frat boys pounded beers and tried to pick up coeds. Here were the go-go clubs, where platinum blondes bounced around on pedestals, and where guys with tans and gold chains peeked under their miniskirts. People came to get high. People came to get screwed. On weekend nights there was such a crush of pedestrians, all traffic would grind to a halt. For any red-blooded male cop, whatever your age or marital condition, this was where you wanted to work *and* hang out. After all my years on the gritty streets of the South Side, I could finally spend my days and nights in Club Land. I could even wear plain clothes when I was working. Better yet, my law school was five minutes away.

My first day in the district, they scheduled me for a night shift. I went to roll call with the rest of the guys and shook hands all around. A lieutenant, who was the Vice coordinator, came over and introduced me to another officer and said he'd be my partner. That night we were assigned to cover Old Town, a mile from Rush Street, and more of a hippie place, like San Francisco's Haight-Ashbury. The lieutenant said, "I want you to get the lay of the land, but if you see anything go down, you call me or my sergeant before you take any action. Especially if it's related to a restaurant, a club, or a bar. You don't make any arrests until you get permission."

I thought that was unusual, but Vice was not as cut and dried as robbery or traffic stops. Maybe I had to get my feet wet first.

Then he looked at me out of the corner of his eye and lowered his voice. "At the first of each month," he said, "you'll find five hundred dollars in your locker. If something else comes our way, you get a percentage of that, too."

I just nodded. It didn't take a rocket scientist to figure out where that money was coming from.

I went out with my partner and we walked around Old Town. He took me to see the managers and owners of the bars and clubs, and he introduced me like I was the new fucking beer salesman. It was clear he would never bust these guys, even if we found dope fiends shooting up in their bathrooms. I got bad vibes about the whole thing. I was no Pollyanna. There were times on the South Side when somebody left some cash on my squad seat or picked up my tab at lunch; but if I caught you committing a felony, you were under arrest, and no amount of money was going to buy you out of that.

When we returned to the station house for our break, I pulled the lieutenant to the side. "I'll go along with the program," I told him. "I just don't want any money in my locker. I'm in my last year of law school. If something like this comes back to haunt me, I could lose my license. I've worked too hard for that."

He nodded and said, "All right."

We finished our shift at four-thirty in the morning and went back to the station to check out. When I passed the desk sergeant, he looked up at me and said, "Report here the day after tomorrow at eight A.M. You're back in uniform."

I lasted just one day in Vice. That was probably the world record. But it was okay with me. If they were kissing me off, I could kiss them off, too. As I took the bus home that night, I thought, "Great. My days of police work are over. I'm just going to go through the motions until I finish law school and wave good-bye."

When I showed up at the station the next day, they didn't know what to do with me, so they assigned me to the "umbrella" car. It was shit duty. You were supposed to hang around in case they needed back-up, but nobody wanted back-up from the kind of mopes they assigned to umbrella cars. You just sat in the squad all day until your shift was over.

By the time I got to the car, another patrolman was already behind the wheel. His name was Ricky Borelli. He was a big pudgy guy with walrus jowls and black curly hair. Usually, his hat was on crooked and his tie screwed around. A collar could be pointing up or a button undone. On any other day, Ricky would have been out walking his do-nothing beat. But he had committed some minor infraction, and this was to be his punishment—shoved with me into the umbrella car like two cigarette butts in an ashtray.

After the initial introductions, we cruised around the district. I had trouble getting more than a few words out of him. When we reached the Old Town area, he pulled into a side street and parked the car. He said to me, "Do you want to play some cards?"

"Sure," I said. He pulled out a pack and we started to play gin. He was an excellent gin player (it was about all Ricky could do well), but I wasn't bad either. After a couple of games, he said, "Do you want to play for something?" We spent the next few hours playing for small change. He won some and I won some. He opened up a little more and we had a chat. I let him know I was in law school and would be leaving the force before long.

The next day they assigned me to my own car, but Ricky approached me after roll call and said, "You want to come and have breakfast across the street?" They had a big diner-type restaurant there. I figured, "What the hell?" I was always hungry.

While we were eating, Ricky asked, "Have you ever bet sports?"

"No."

"I do some betting myself," he said. "What I'm looking for is somebody to call in some bets for me."

Over the next few minutes, Ricky explained to me the basics of book-making. He called his bets in to an "office"—really no more than a phone number. Bookies might have more than one office, but they never wanted too much riding on one game. So they limited each gambler to betting $500 per game. Ricky wanted me to call in and pretend I was just another gambler. But he would tell me what to bet and give me the money if he lost. If he won, I would collect his take and turn it over. At the end of the week, I could keep a hundred dollars for my services.

I knew this was all illegal, but it was fascinating as hell. I always had a gambling streak. Even when I was a kid, I pitched pennies. I made much bigger money playing cards at Marquette. I never saw the harm in a little action. Besides, I had a good head for numbers—accounting was my minor in school.

I caught on quicker than Ricky expected. After a few days, I could see that he was an addicted gambler and a terminal loser. He lost on most of the bets he had me place. I knew I could do better. After the third week, instead of putting the entire $500 on a bet I knew he would lose, I would keep $130 for myself.

Making my own bets with Rick's money was not as ballsy as it seems. Early on, I realized that success in gambling had very little to with your knowledge about a particular sport. In fact, that knowledge could be a dangerous thing—especially for a knucklehead like Ricky. He always bet his personal favorites, like Notre Dame. Instead, good bettors played one bookie off against another. If you were smart and you weren't too greedy, you either won a little money or you won a little more money, but you seldom lost everything.

To give myself a cushion, I always gave odds to Ricky that were slightly worse than the ones I was actually getting. When Ricky lost the bet, he paid me more than I had to pay the bookie.

My chance for a big payoff came on the spread—the points separating the winning and losing teams when you bet basketball and football. I could bet on the favorite with a bookie who had them winning by *six* points against the underdog. I could also bet on the underdog with another bookie who had the favorite winning by *ten* points. If the favorites won by seven, eight or nine points, I won both of my bets—a payoff of twenty to one.

The real secret to sports betting was to know as many bookies as possible. I used all of Ricky's contacts to my advantage and started to make bets on my own. At this point, my salary as a policeman was $5,600 a year. One week after I learned to cover Ricky's bets, I won $2,000—what then seemed an unbelievable sum. And the way I was playing with Ricky, there was no way I could lose. I was only concerned that he would come up lame paying off his losing bets. But he didn't. Not for a couple of years.

On rare occasions, the police force still needed our services. The commander would put out an emergency call, and we all had to show up at the station. One time it was to put down a riot at Cabrini Green, a huge complex of dilapidated high-rise housing projects. It stretched over several blocks and had more than 20,000 residents. The squad cars that responded to the first calls were hit by sniper fire from the upper floors of one building. They didn't have SWAT teams in those days. Instead, the commander's response to any crisis was to throw more patrolmen into the fray. A bunch of us were packed into a police wagon and sent over. Before I left, I took my own weapon out of my locker—an automatic carbine rifle. I had plenty of experience with riots and snipers on the South Side, and I wasn't going to get caught in crossfire with just my service revolver. That was like standing in the open with your prick in your hands.

We pulled into one of the Cabrini Green parking lots, and somebody started shooting at us as soon as we got out of the wagon. I could see it was just one guy running along the outer balconies that encircled the building. As soon as I saw the sniper climb the stairs to a higher floor, I raced into the building. He was trying to kill me. I was going to kill him first. I got off a few shots with my carbine, but I didn't hit him. He disappeared into one of the units. When I came back downstairs, I realized I was the only cop who had gone in. All the others had stayed outside, ducking for cover, including Ricky.

It was another of my crazy stunts, but it certainly earned me stripes with Ricky. He wanted me to meet someone. One day at breakfast, he brought along his cousin, Marco D'Amico. Like Ricky, Marco appeared to be in his mid-thirties. He was of medium height and build. Nobody you'd look at twice. The strangest thing about him was his high, arching eyebrows, and his constant smirk. Both made him look almost like Jack Nicholson.

The first few times we met, in the restaurant across the street from the police station, Marco couldn't have been nicer. He was real impressed that I was in law school. Ricky kept talking up how I ran into Cabrini

Green with the carbine and all the balls I had. But mostly we talked about gambling. I figured Marco was a bookie and no more than that.

Now I had all kinds of money in my pocket—for the first time in my life. I hit Rush Street with my friends at least two or three nights a week. I had finally moved out of my parents' house, first to a little studio apartment closer to work. But after I started gambling, I could afford the step up to a one-bedroom apartment in a new glass-wall high-rise that was part of a redevelopment complex. A few of the buildings shared an outdoor pool. It was not as fancy as the Gold Coast, but it was heaven for me. Perched twenty-seven stories above the ground, I had floor-to-ceiling views of the skyline and the sunset. Below me, the western suburbs seemed to stretch out forever, flat as a pool table.

I couldn't have been prouder of my new little crib, and I had my friends over to check it out. Just like in college, I started organizing poker games, only this time the stakes were much higher. I supplied food and whatever booze they wanted. Still, I would never drink when I played cards. To me, the card games were a business that could bring in a few thousand a week, and I didn't want to affect my judgment. It was fine if everyone else got drunk as skunks, because they would just play worse and worse.

Ricky and Marco were up all the time, and they would bring a couple friends of theirs to play. Meanwhile, I started making my own network of friends from Rush Street. These were all people who had money and didn't mind blowing a few thousand. One night, when Marco and Ricky didn't come, a good friend of mine from the clubs brought along a new player named Eddie Corrado. He was kind of a greasy little guy with a big mouth, but he behaved just fine during the game.

As usual, I had a terrific night. When everyone got up to go, Eddie asked if he could stick around and play a little blackjack with me. The way my luck was running, I figured there would be no harm. But my luck quickly turned. Nothing I did was right. We switched decks back and forth. He was the dealer. I was the dealer. It didn't matter. I always lost. After playing less than an hour, I owed him $6,000. I had about $2,500 in cash and I gave him a check to cover the balance.

The whole experience shook my confidence. But something didn't seem quite right. The next day, when I saw Ricky at breakfast, I told him the story, even though it was pretty embarrassing.

"Wait a second," Ricky said. "What was that guy's name?"

When I told him who it was, Ricky said, "Stop payment on that check. He's a card cheat." Ricky called Marco, who told me to arrange for Eddie to come to my apartment when they were there. They would help me work it out.

The next night, Eddie showed up at my apartment, and he was not happy. He brought along some big goon who started giving me a squinty-eye stare from the moment I opened the door.

Eddie strutted into my foyer like a tough guy. "You motherfucker," he said. "You got a lot of balls passing a bad check to me."

I shut the door behind them, and they rounded the corner from the foyer, just as Marco came out of the bathroom. The blood completely drained from Eddie's face. The goon froze, too. In that instant, I realized that Marco was much more powerful than some bookie, and much more dangerous.

Eddie practically fell to his knees. "I didn't know he was a friend of yours," he pleaded to Marco. "Please, please. I didn't realize it."

Marco was calm and matter-of-fact. He made Eddie empty the cash out of all his pockets and hand it over to me. Ricky then walked Eddie and the collector out the door. After they left, Marco counted the cash. It added up to $4,500. He gave me my $2,500 and kept the rest for himself.

It turned out that Eddie had made the mistake of winning a lot of money from Marco a year before. Marco found out that he was a card cheat and arranged for another game at his house. When Eddie arrived, they took him into the basement and beat the living fuck out of him. Marco was still pretty impressed that Eddie cheated me. After that night in my apartment, he put Eddie in card games with wealthy guys and would take a cut of whatever Eddie won.

Eventually, Marco invited me to his "club" to play cards. It was a storefront, with boarded-up windows, on the west side of town—which I took to be Marco's territory. Inside were huge rooms with card tables.

A few booths were up front. Nothing very fancy. They had a kitchen way in the back, but they rarely served food. Still, the place was always full with two or three dozen people. Except for a break on Sunday, the club was open around the clock. Everyone seemed like a bunch of fun guys, just playing cards and hanging out. At first, I thought they were all gamblers or bookies. Only later did I find out that the club members were a who's-who of West Side bad guys—burglars, car thieves, and stick-up men. Some cops and sheriff's deputies, too. Quite a cast of characters.

Eventually I'd come to learn that gambling was literally the life's blood of the Mob. It was their work and their play—almost as much of an obsession with them as making money. Even though they knew better, almost all of them bet, and it was all they talked about. My own love for gambling—whether on cards or sports—got me instant credibility and acceptance.

With the contacts I made through Marco, my sports betting circles grew wider and I started winning all kinds of money. Often Marco knew exactly how much I won. I figured that some of these bookies really worked for him. Before long, Marco asked to be my "partner." He would stake me, so I could make more bets as long as he got a piece of what I won.

This meant I could get action with that many more bookies. I said, "Great. I'll call you each day and tell you what we have going."

"No need to," he replied. "I trust you."

After I started playing with Marco, the bets started to mushroom. On any given day, I could be playing with ten bookmakers. I would meet some down on Rush Street and they would introduce me to some others. Word got out that I was good pay and had big money. It got to the point where bookies from all over the country got in touch with me. On some Saturdays during football season, I had a million dollars in play.

The gambling did not leave much time for police work, but that didn't matter. By this time, I developed a good routine to deal with my extracurricular activity. I started each morning at seven-thirty. I would show up for roll call, pick up a portable radio phone, and off I'd go. My beat was Cabrini Green. Nobody else wanted it, and they stopped letting squad cars go over there because they became targets for the snipers. But I didn't care. I would take my own car, a GTO—I was rolling in money now—and park right against a building, so the snipers couldn't get an angle to shoot at it from their windows. Then I'd grab my radio and just stroll around. They had a school there, and I might wander in and wave at the kids. Maybe help some old lady with her groceries. At most, it would take ninety minutes to do my circuit. Then I would get in my car and drive home, which was less than a mile away. I'd park my car in the underground garage, go up to my apartment, and just keep my radio on as I went about my business. On rare occasions, a sergeant might call in to check up on me. He was supposed to meet me on the beat, but all these guys were too scared of Cabrini to sneak around there. Instead, he'd have me drive to a street corner near the station house. "Is everything okay?" he'd ask.

"Yeah," I'd say. "Everything is okay." Then I was free to go on my way.

During the summer, it was even nicer. I rented a cabana by the outdoor pool my building shared in the complex. Usually the only other residents who hung out during the daytime were stewardesses between flights. I had a little refrigerator in the cabana and an extension for my home phone. The pool area was elevated, so you couldn't see it from the street. It was like my private sanctuary. Ricky would drop by and sometimes he brought along other cops he was friendly with. Even some sergeants. We'd sit around, gab with the stews and drink some beers. In the afternoon, I called in my bets from the pool. Sergeant Bilko never had it better.

I was making plenty of money and having lots of fun, but I was more determined than ever to start my legal career. Through gambling and Marco, I met a lot of people who had trouble with the law. I figured I could build a nice criminal practice around them. In the summer of 1970, I graduated law school and took two weeks off to study for the bar. I never had problems with tests, so I was sure I'd passed, but just in case, I kept my job on the police force until it was official.

One afternoon, when I stopped back in the station to return my radio, the desk sergeant said there was someone waiting for me. At first glance, I thought this was some sort of joke. My visitor was a tall muscular guy in a yellow fishnet leotard and a purple cape. He had a helmet of tight jet-black curly hair and a meticulously trimmed Fu Manchu moustache and beard. He looked like something out of a comic book. In fact, for several years he ran an ad in the back of comic books that showed him scowling and contorting his hands. The ad touted him as the "Deadliest Man Alive," and offered "The World's Deadliest Fighting Secrets" if you joined his Black Dragon Fighting Society.

He called himself Count Juan Raphael Dante, and he claimed to be descended from Spanish nobility. He owned a couple of karate schools and said that he was the master of all the major martial arts and inventor of his own form of combat called, "The Dan-Te (Deadly Hands) System." His materials made a bunch of other wild claims: that he had served as a mercenary for Fidel Castro, that in China he had won three death matches against "the world's foremost fistic and grappling arts masters," and so on and so forth. In fact, Count Dante was another crazy Irish kid from the South Side of Chicago. His real name was John Keehan. "Dante" was the name of a street near where we grew up. From a South Side perspective, he *was* something of an aristocrat. His father was a doctor, and he lived in a wealthy neighborhood, where Tommy Dugan and I would pick fights with the rich kids. It was Tommy who sent him my way. As everyone in the station house stood there gawking at us, Count Dante grabbed my elbow and looked at me with piercing blue eyes. "I have this serious problem," he said, "and I want to know if you can help me."

I took him up to a room on the second floor where we could have some privacy. The Count's "serious problem" was a murder charge, stemming from his invasion of a competing karate studio called Black Cobra Hall. The school's owner had called him a pussy or something like that, and the Count decided he had to defend his honor. Black Cobra Hall was in a strip mall, but they had the outside done up like a castle with a huge wooden door. The Count didn't wait for anyone to answer the bell. According to the police report, he made his entrance by tearing the door off its hinges. Inside, a class was being held with two dozen students, but Count

Dante, with just three of his own students, was ready to fight everybody. One Black Cobra teacher came after the Count with a mace. The Count did that thing with his fingers and ripped the guy's eye out. Unfortunately, Jim, the Count's right-hand man, wasn't that quick and he got run through with a spear. When the Count saw that, he beat a hasty retreat. Jim got a block away before he fell over dead with the spear still inside him.

The Count was arrested and charged with aggravated battery for pulling the guy's eye out. They also charged him with murder under an arcane law known as the Accountability Statute. Since the Count had broken into Black Cobra Hall and started the fight, he was being held "accountable" for his student's death.

The Count wanted no less than a total acquittal on all the charges. "I'm claustrophobic," he said. "If I go to prison, I'll go totally crazy. I can't be confined." He had already hired a big-time South Side lawyer, but the guy would not offer any guarantees. Tommy Dugan told the Count about me: how I was a cop and hung around with mobsters like Marco D'Amico. The Count figured I could pull strings that a straight lawyer wouldn't touch.

I still didn't know if I had passed the bar—I was expecting to hear any day—but as I sat there, listening to this crazy story, I truly believed I could help the Count. "If I can't handle your case," I said, "I'll find a lawyer who can."

He pulled out a wad of bills and paid me a $5,000 retainer on the spot. "I just feel I can trust you," he said, "and that you'll get me out of this."

I have yet to meet anyone else with the Count's amazing combination of talents and flaws. Besides being an expert in the martial arts, he was also a beautician (a supermarket tabloid ran a story about him with the headline "THE WORLD'S DEADLIEST FIGHTER IS A . . . HAIRDRESSER!"). In addition to the karate studios, he owned hairdressing schools. Supposedly, he got involved with martial arts while he traveled through Asia for a wig import business. He did hairstyling for *Playboy*, and somehow that gave him an entree to the whole world of pornography and led to a financial interest in a string of adult book stores. At one moment he could be extremely sophisticated and artistic, and at the next moment crude and ridiculously macho—even more than the Mob guys.

We started to hang out together during the months leading up to the trial. He was living with two different Playboy bunnies, and one was always available for his friends to screw. At night, he took me to parties at the Playboy Mansion, which was just a few blocks from Rush Street. It was a bizarre place, always packed with people. I remember some floors that were a maze of little dark rooms. You would turn one corner and bump into a movie star. You'd turn the next corner and see a couple humping. The Count loved it all, and they loved him. He was a total sex maniac, and he was as flamboyant as anyone from Hollywood. During the day, wearing the cape and leotard, he walked his pet mountain lion along the lakefront. Did that ever attract the girls in the bikinis! He was a babe magnet in every way.

But like Jim—the guy who got the spear in his chest—I discovered that hanging with the Count wasn't always fun and games. One weekend, he invited me to come to his house for a party. Despite all of his money, he still kept a home on the South Side in a pretty rough neighborhood. While the party was going on, we went out to pick up some more beer and wine. He drove a brown Cadillac and on one of the doors, he had this phony crest for the Dante noble family with some kind of Spanish writing. We parked the car in the liquor store lot. As we got out, we saw these two Mexican guys who had apparently been drinking. They pointed at that crest and started laughing. The Count said something to them in Spanish and they said something back. I thought they were all joking around. But when I looked at the Count, I saw this terrifying anger rise up in him. His head became very still. Darkness shrouded his face, and his eyes started to bulge. Then, like a volcano, he blew, whirling first at the biggest of the two Mexicans. Using the middle three fingers of his hand, he made quick raking motions across the guy's face, and in an instant, the Mexican was writhing on the ground, bleeding from his eye and nose. Then he turned on the second guy and took him out as quickly. Behind me, I saw a car door fly open and a guy who must have been their buddy came running over. I decked him myself. Even if I broke his jaw I did him a favor. God knows what would have happened to him if he had faced the Count alone.

In a matter of three minutes, we had the three guys on the ground. I said, "Count, we better go. Remember, you're still out on bond." As we drove away, I tried to explain how delicate his legal situation was. The judge had released him on a murder charge. Virtually any other arrest would put him in jail until the trial was over. But the Count didn't want to hear my legal bullshit. Instead, he kept crowing about how I had clocked that Mexican in the parking lot. He had to tell everyone at the party what a tough guy I was. The next week, when we went out, I didn't want him going to a crowded club. I figured it would only take a few bumps to set him off again. Instead, we went to a real quiet place near his house. Most of the other customers were steelworkers who had just come off a shift. They were caked with grime and sweat. The Count, as usual, was dressed in one of his crazy cape and leotard outfits. He got up to go to the bathroom, and wouldn't you know, one of those hard-hats had to call him a fruit. I heard tables and chairs crashing. I ran back in time to see the Count with one hand on some big lug's throat and the other on his chest. He then literally lifted him off his feet and threw him through the plate glass window. Everyone else just froze in shock. I grabbed the Count and again we ran for the hills. The guy was nothing less than a walking powder keg.

A few weeks later, I learned that I had passed the bar. I had a big party in my apartment to celebrate. I bought a barrel, and inside it mixed champagne with vodka and brandy. Everybody got smashed pretty quickly with that concoction, but if I made a mistake mixing my drinks, I probably made a bigger one by mixing my guests. I invited my friends from the singles bars on Rush Street, who all made their living in perfectly legitimate ways. But I invited Marco, Ricky, and their crew, too, along with some other apes who were always good for a few laughs. One of these guys, John, was in the vending machine business. He liked to act like a big shot and throw his money around. He had his own little entourage, but he was always the biggest loser at our card games. Later that night, when we were both sloshed, John cornered me. Now that he was drunk, all his anger and petty jealousy rose to the surface. He asked what I would do if he took a glass of champagne and spilled it on me. I said, "You do that, and I'll bust your fucking head open."

John replied by tossing his champagne in my face, and I slugged him. His bodyguard pushed through the crowd and punched me, but then Marco and his guys piled on him and beat both John and his goon to a pulp. Then we literally picked them up off the floor and threw them into the hall.

When I walked back inside, I saw that all kinds of things had been smashed during the fight, but worse was the look on the faces of my legitimate friends. They were all stunned. I'm sure they had never seen that level of violence. A few minutes later, every one of them left. Of course John, who took most of the beating, sobered up and approached me at the pool a few days later to apologize for being out of line. But my legitimate friends didn't get over the fight as easily as John. They had seen a part of my life that scared the hell out of them. In the future I would be careful about who I mixed with my Mob friends and clients, and, to the best of my ability, I always tried to keep the two worlds apart.

Literally from the day I quit the police force, I had legal work—clients arrested for gambling, drunk driving, or dope busts. But I figured I needed much more high-level courtroom experience before I could tackle Count Dante's trial. As luck would have it, I got a call from Bill Murphy, my old friend from Marquette. He was now a public defender and he had come across an indigent client named Donald Kristman, who badly needed representation. He had been arrested for robbing and killing a jeweler on the north side of Chicago. Bill had seen enough of the police reports to think Kristman might be innocent, but he couldn't free up the time to take on another client. "Maybe you can get some practice on this case," he said.

I went and met with Kristman in his jail cell. He was a very big, scary-looking guy who had held down a job in the sewers for several years. He just had the bad luck of cashing a check near the murder scene. The wife of the victim picked him out of a lineup. Since he was an ex-con, they got away with pinning the rap on him. I believed his story and took his case for $500, the only fee he could afford.

Marco couldn't believe I would take peanuts on a case with so much stacked against me. In truth, I would have *paid* Kristman to be his lawyer. I wanted the challenge of a jury trial with everything on the line—at least as far as Kristman was concerned. If I had joined a big firm, they would have made me wait years for such an opportunity.

When the trial got underway and the victim's wife took the stand, I wondered what I had gotten myself into. During my cross-examination, she cried and said, "I could never forget the face of the man who killed my husband."

The next day, during the lunch break, I was at a bar near the court-house consoling myself, when I saw a policeman who had been a good friend of mine. He came over and sat next to me. He said, "Bob, they're fucking around with you and withholding a report on this case. I can't tell you exactly what it is, but I thought you should know."

I knew this cop to be a very straight shooter and I trusted him com-pletely. I went right from the bar to the courtroom—finally with a card up my sleeve. I didn't know if it was an ace, but it was something. This judge happened to be Jewish. The victim was Jewish too, and an impor-tant part of his community, so you know the judge was not well dis-posed to my client. But I approached the bench very respectfully, and I said, "Judge, I just found out about a police report regarding this case that the state is not giving me, and the state's attorneys know all about it." I had to bluff if I was going to pull this off.

We went back into chambers and the prosecutors were all upset. They wanted to know who told me about the report. I said I wasn't going to give up the policeman's name, but he was very trustworthy and he had no reason to lie. When the prosecutors kept insisting that I reveal his name, I stood up and said, "Judge, if I have to, I'll go out now and find that policeman, and let him know that they are still hiding that report. Maybe he'll be so outraged, he'll reveal his identity on his own."

This didn't make the judge very happy at all. "You walk out that door," he said, "and I'll hold you in contempt for disrupting this trial."

I kept walking. I didn't know what would happen if I tried to make good on the threat. Suddenly, one of the prosecutors jumped up and said, "Wait, Judge. I think I know what he's talking about." They then went downstairs and came back up with the report. It was the Witness Identification Report that the cops had filled out when the victim's wife fingered my client. I had already seen a *copy* of that, but then I looked at the very bottom of the original. It had a "PS"—the witness called back the detectives a few hours after the lineup to say she had second thoughts about the ID. Somehow that PS got cut off on my copy. The judge wouldn't let me put the victim's wife back on the stand, but I was allowed to call the detective who took her phone call.

This was all I needed for my closing argument. The eyewitness was the only evidence the state had, and if she couldn't be sure about the identity of the killer, how could the jury convict my client? The jury returned with a not guilty.

The Count watched that final day of the trial. I think he was there to check me out, but I kept assuring him that he had nothing to worry about. We weren't going to depend on a jury. With his case we would ask for a bench trial, where a judge would arrive at the verdict. I never said specifically that his case would be fixed, but I definitely gave him the impression that it was. In truth, I couldn't believe that any judge would find him guilty of murder. The assault charge was a different matter.

The Count's judge turned out to be an old, hard-bitten guy who didn't exactly ooze with sympathy or understanding. He spent most of the trial looking like he was having a gas attack. At least he was Irish. Since he was Irish, and I was too, as well as the Count, some luck had to break our way.

Fortunately, the so-called victims were scruffy and unkempt with long greasy hair—not your most upstanding citizens. They looked like the hopheads we picked up on drug busts when I was a cop. They had charges pending against them too, for assaulting the Count and his students with the weapons. During the trial, I kept pointing out to the judge that Black Cobra Hall was not some nursery school. All the evidence photos showed giant axes, clubs, and spears hanging on the wall. I argued, "What else would you use these weapons for, other than to terrorize people?"

In my version of events, the Count didn't invade Black Cobra Hall. Instead, he came over to work out some amicable relationship with the other teacher. Of course, if he did go there to make peace, you had to wonder why he broke the door down. But when you looked at the size of the door, it was hard to believe a human being could have ripped it from the hinges.

My goal was to convince the judge that this was a fight, pure and simple, and that the Count was acting in self-defense. But my real ace in the hole was the state's attorney, Mike. As luck would have it, he was an old drinking buddy of mine from Rush Street. He had as much disgust for the Black Cobra guys as I did, and I knew he wasn't going to hurt me with this judge.

My biggest trouble during the trial was contending with the Count. I put him on the stand to give his side of the story. Although I coached him how to act—humble and unexcitable—he couldn't help himself. Even during my direct examination, he went into all his macho bullshit about how nobody could ever get away with attacking him. The judge kept yelling at him to shut up. Once again, the victims bailed us out. They got on the stand and were as belligerent as he was.

Each day, during the breaks, the judge would go back into his chambers, muttering about the testimony. You could hear him say, "They're crazy. They're all crazy." As I hoped, when he reached a verdict, he put a plague on both their houses. First, and most important, the judge dismissed the murder charge against the Count as a matter of course. The Count, he said, could not have expected his friend to get run through by a spear. That was my argument, and Mike, the prosecutor, did not put up much of a fight on that.

When it came to the charges of aggravated battery, the judge really worked himself into a lather. He screamed, "You're each as guilty as the other. I've never seen such a pack of lunatics in my life. What were you doing with weapons like a mace? What were you doing tearing somebody's eye out? These aren't medieval times. You're both wrong, and I don't see a finding of guilty either way." He dismissed the charges against the Count, and to keep everything even, he dismissed the charges against the Black Cobra people as well.

After the verdict, the Count grabbed me in a bear hug. "You saved my life," he said. "Not even my father could have done what you did."

Meanwhile, I couldn't help thinking, "I may have saved your life this time, but what about next time?" In my bones, I just knew the Count would come to no good end.

My success with the Count's case impressed Marco as well. Throughout the course of the trial, I gave him blow-by-blow descriptions of my client's crazy antics, and I think he was surprised I got him off the hook.

Marco was now ready to throw me a bone. It was a relatively small matter, but it had proved especially difficult to fix. It involved what was then called, "Boys' Court," where they tried cases for defendants between seventeen and twenty-one.

A few months before, a bunch of punks had gotten in a fight with the bartenders and bouncers at Mother's—probably the most popular singles bar in the city. It was a huge place, in a basement. These kids had caused trouble in the past, and they were ready when the bartenders pulled out the little bats they used to break up fights. They took the bats away and started beating the staff with them. They also did tremendous damage to the bar. It turned out that most of their dads were Mob bosses or crew leaders, and they didn't want their kids to have records, since they were all in college. But despite his connections, Marco couldn't make the case go away. The bartenders and the bouncers were determined to take a stand so that something like this wouldn't happen again. Worse yet, the judge was totally straight. There was no way to buy a favorable decision from him.

It seemed like a tough situation, but I felt there was still something I could do. When I was a cop, I hung out in Mother's all the time. I got in a few fights there myself, but I also helped the bartenders put a few fights down, so I became very friendly with everyone in the place. I got in touch with the main complainant, a bartender named Ronnie. These punks had pissed him off big-time, but I explained to him, "Their parents came to me and they have no way out of this. I can be a hero if we get this dismissed, and I'll make sure the little pricks don't come back. Why can't we work something out and let the parents pay the bills for all the damages?"

As a favor to me, Ronnie said he'd try to get the other bartenders to back down. Next I went in to see the judge. He was another tough nut.

He told me he wanted the case to go to trial to teach them a lesson. "Judge," I said, "these aren't bad kids." But we both knew that was a load of crap.

Then I tried to appeal to his sympathy for me. I figured that he was once a young lawyer, trying to start a practice. "Judge," I said, "please give me a chance to work this out. There are some important people involved, and this case could be the foundation for building my business."

The judge decided to give me a shot. He said, "If you can get all the complainants from the bar to come forward and indicate that they don't wish to pursue the case, then I'll dismiss it." I'm sure he never expected it to happen, but my friend Ronnie persuaded the other bartenders to take the money and drop their charges. The case was then dismissed.

My legal career was off and running. The Count sent me great business: celebrity types who got in trouble with a gun or stash of marijuana or something like that. They all paid big fees without blinking an eye. Marco was stingier, but he more than made up for that with the volume of business he could send my way.

Those first few cases taught me the sort of lessons I never learned in law school. The only thing that saved Donald Kristman's neck was my friendship with the cop who told me about the overlooked witness report. The same went for the prosecutor in the Count's case and the bartenders from Mother's. Being a good criminal lawyer in Chicago had very little to do with the law. It was about the relationships you had with your clients and the other people in the courtroom: prosecutors, coppers, witnesses, and judges. For me, there was no line between professional relationships and social relationships. They were both part of the job. I wined and dined clients to get more clients. I wined and dined the court people, so I could do better for the clients. This type of law could be a lot of fun. It could also consume your life.

As far as some people were concerned, there was another reason for my success. "Bob Cooley is a mechanic," the Count used to say. "He can fix anything."

CHAPTER 4

CRIME PAYS

t didn't take me long to find the corruption at the heart of Chicago's justice system. In fact, the very first case I had, soon after I passed the bar, was in Traffic Court—the most corrupt court of them all. My client was up for a run-of-the-mill drunk-driving ticket. I thought the case would be easy to win. First of all, I knew the cop who made the arrest, and he knew I was an ex-cop, so he couldn't play games during his testimony. As for the prosecutor, he was another good friend of mine, and an ex-cop too. And I thought I was on good terms with the judge, Dick LeFevour, the Supervising Judge for the Traffic Court. I put my case on, and, just as I thought, the judge threw the ticket out. But when I walked out of the court, I heard, "Hey, Bob."

It was Jimmy LeFevour, Dick's cousin. Jimmy was a police officer and a notorious drunk who always had the smell of alcohol on his breath. Dick had arranged for him to be assigned to the Traffic Court building. Tall and thin, Jimmy LeFevour lurked around the halls like a ghoul. I didn't have a clue what he wanted from me. "What is it?" I asked.

"The first one is on the house," Jimmy said. "But from now on, any time you have something in here, you come and see me first."

That was Traffic Court. As a cop, I knew funny things happened there, but I had never known the extent of it. Once I became a lawyer, I found out. Either you paid or your client lost. They had a whole routine set up. First you met with the judge's bagman, like Jimmy. You would let him know what kind of case you had. In other words, how serious the charge was. He would then tell you what it would cost. Usually I paid $100 for the judge, $50 for the bagman and $50 for the policeman involved. Sometimes the bagman kept the cop's money, but if he gave it to the cop, almost all the police accepted it. (I did, when I was a cop. That was the system and you were supposed to take the money and shut up about it. As a result, I rarely wrote DUI tickets.)

Each court you went into had a different set of ropes to learn. If you were going to survive, the law you most needed to know was the law of the jungle. Narcotics Court was a perfect example. It was in one of those giant old Roman-style buildings with a huge courtroom—like a coliseum. It was always packed to the rafters with spectators and lawyers. On any given day, they could process as many as five hundred cases. Meanwhile, in the corridors outside the courtroom, you had dozens of lawyers I called Hall Rats, scuttling among the chaos for a piece of cheese. They hung out at Narcotics day after day to hustle clients, and each one had some monetary arrangements with the court sergeant, the clerk, and most of the judges. If a prisoner looked unattached from a lawyer, a presiding judge or a court sergeant might steer him toward a favorite Hall Rat.

I was practicing only a couple of months before I had my first Narcotics case. I had to be in another court first, so I got there late. Just as I entered the building, I saw my client walking out. He had been arrested in a bullshit street narcotics stop, so I was only going to charge him $500. I asked what happened and he said, "Oh, a friend of yours took care of my case." He gave me the guy's card. It turned out to be one of the chief Hall Rats, the son of a judge. The client went on to explain, "I told him I was waiting for you, but he said he was a lawyer and he could take care of it for you. And *he* only charged me $300."

What was I going to do? I wished the client good luck and went inside. Now I had never been in the court before as a lawyer, and this Hall Rat didn't know me from Adam, but I recognized him from my days as a cop. He was a skinny little guy, the sort of slick dresser who wore thousand-dollar suits and fancy little tassel loafers. He was making a fortune from that place and still poaching clients from other lawyers. I approached him and asked, "Do you have a minute?" I'm sure he thought I was a potential client, because I didn't carry a briefcase (I never did).

I walked with him from the courtroom outside into the marble hallway. It had ceilings as high as a cathedral. There were all kinds of people there: policemen standing around, lawyers chatting with clients. First, I asked the Rat if he knew who I was.

"No," he said, "I don't know who you are."

"Funny," I said. "You told my client you were a good friend of mine." Then I pulled out the card he gave my client. "Is this your card?"

When he nodded, I threw him up against the wall. Everybody around us scattered. "Listen you little piece of shit," I said. "You're going to give me five hundred fucking dollars or I'm going to split your head open against this wall."

He shook in his shoes. "But he only paid me three hundred," he whined.

"Doesn't matter," I said. "That's what I was going to charge him."

He counted out five hundred-dollar bills. I could see all the cops looking and laughing. I'm sure the Rat had paid off most of them at some point, but he wasn't so arrogant this time.

Then I put my finger in his face and said, loud enough for everyone to hear, "If you ever steal a client of mine again, there's going to be a fucking problem. And you let the rest of these people know that, too."

Given the nature of my clientele, I probably could have operated my firm out of a phone booth, but I wanted a respectable-looking office in a nice building. For help, I turned to another defense attorney, Allan Ackerman, and he offered to let me share his space and some of his secretary's time. I had approached Allan because he was one of the few lawyers I watched as a cop who impressed me. I especially appreciated his grasp of the technical side of the law—the weak chink in my armor. I practically flunked out of bibliography in Law School. Besides, I hated to be cooped up in a library. For the rest of my career, I paid Allan to do my research and help me write motions. It turned out that he was also a fun-loving guy who liked to play cards almost as much as I did.

When I moved in with Allan at 100 North LaSalle Street, I didn't know how important that office building would be—to my career and my life. As far as I could tell, it was in a great location, right across the street from City Hall, a block from one of the Circuit Courts and a short walk from Federal Court. Otherwise, there was nothing very distinguished about it. The building was a classic twenties-era high-rise with a brick and terra cotta exterior. Inside, it had dozens of small law firms, many with the same smoked-glass doors that they'd had when the place first opened. There was a marble lobby with six elevators, and a restaurant called Counsellors Row.

If not for Allan, I would have never picked out the building. But in a matter of time, 100 North LaSalle became more my home than the place where I slept. It was not just where I worked; it was my club, my hangout, and my personal gambling den—in many ways, the frat house I never experienced in college. Only a year after I started my arrangement with Allan, I was ready to move into a suite of offices with four other lawyers. Just a year and a half later, I had my own suite and two lawyers working for me.

Looking back, it's hard to believe how easily and how quickly my practice grew. The business came to me. I didn't have to go looking for it. I never advertised or promoted myself. If I bet with a bookmaker and he got pinched, I had a new client. If I chatted with a guy sitting next to me at a Rush Street bar, and he found out I was an attorney, I had a new client.

Of course, Marco was a major source of my business. Whenever any of his bookies would get arrested, he would contact Marco, and Marco would get him a lawyer, namely me. I could have six of these cases a week. I'd drop by to see Marco at the Survivor's Club and he'd pay me $1,000 for each one. Later I discovered he was charging the bookies as much as $4,000 for my services.

Even if I had known about Marco's "mark-up," I wouldn't have cared. I was more than happy with what I was making from him. Working for the Mob was like any other business. You had to be productive—churn through as many cases as possible—yet make your customers feel like they were getting better service than they could get anywhere else.

In those days, most of my cases were in Guns and Gambling, a classic "money court." You rarely had trials, just transactions. One of the senior judges in the court was Ray Sodini—a happy-go-lucky guy with a drooping bloodhound face. I didn't deal with his bagman, and we hardly ever spoke before a case. Instead, I would go back into his chambers and the little closet where he hung his suit jacket. I put a hundred in the inside pocket for every case I had in his court. If it was a tough case, and he had to go out on a limb for me, I put a couple of hundred dollars in there. Once in a while, I'd have a real difficult case—what we called an "ink case," because it got a lot of press. Only then would I have to talk to him first. I knew where he had lunch, and I could approach him there and let him decide whether he wanted to throw it out in the preliminary hearing or let it go directly to the grand jury. If he threw it out too quickly, a reporter might notice. I never wanted to put him in a position where the press could embarrass him, and he trusted my instincts. That was the key to my success in working the system. Early on, people realized I wouldn't take advantage of their trust.

For the first eleven years of my legal career, almost every day I gave out bribes—and not just to judges. The other court personnel were equally important, if not more so. On my way into the courthouse, I sometimes stopped to pick up a big bag of donuts or some fried chicken. While the other lawyers lined up to go through the metal detector, I walked past it, and made my rounds before court was in session, dropping off food in this office or that chambers. Along the way, I might shake hands with certain sheriffs or bailiffs. Inside my palm, I folded up a five or ten—sometimes a fifty. We would shake, they would come away with the money and no one else would be the wiser. It's not like I paid them for anything special. It was more like an investment—for a favor they might perform in the future.

For example, when a client was arrested and brought to the Criminal Court for arraignment, he literally entered a zoo—another giant courtroom with the judges and lawyers in the front, a big gallery for spectators, and a cage in the back, where they kept all the prisoners behind bars. A client, say, in a nice suit, would have to sit there among the drug dealers, the burglars, and the drunks still bloody from a brawl. He wouldn't see his lawyer until they were both brought before the bench.

But if I hadn't met a client yet, I wanted some face time before we saw the judge. Lawyers were not allowed in the back of the court, but I'd have a sheriff take my client out of the holding cell and bring him over to a side room, where I would be waiting with a sandwich. I figured he hadn't eaten since he'd been in custody. This had a huge impact on my clients. They realized, right from the start, that I had power in this building.

Paying off the clerks was also important. I wanted to have my cases processed like clockwork—and always before lunch. I didn't like sitting in court on a sunny afternoon when I could have been out at my pool, or at a club taking a massage. I made sure my clients were always the first ones up. If the other lawyers were paying the clerks five or ten dollars for that privilege, I paid twenty. I could walk into a court with twenty lawyers lined up, hundreds of people waiting in the gallery, and I would still be the next case called. It made everybody think I was really connected to all the higher-ups. In fact, the guy who was making me look good was the lowest man on the totem pole.

In my mind, I didn't even consider these little payments as corruption. It was my way of doing business and a leg up on my competitors— just a part of the system in Chicago. And really, what was worse: handing five dollars to a clerk, or writing a hundred-dollar check? That's what you were supposed to do when they invited you to all of those "fundraisers" for judges or prosecutors. They even had so-called benefits for the police. I attended absolutely everything. I'd just walk in and say "Hi," buy some tickets or hand over a check, and leave.

That wasn't the only way to get funny with these people. Sometimes they needed a place for their fundraisers and wanted a deal on the food and drinks. The big Greek restaurants were the popular places in those days, and a lot of the owners also happened to gamble and travel in the same bookie circles I did. I could always help a judge work out a nice deal with them.

If a judge wanted special entertainment for a "stag party," I could help there, too. Early in my career I started representing prostitutes, since I knew what a joke the Vice Squad was. If a working girl was arrested, her only crime was not having friends in the right places. I wouldn't use just any madam to book the judges' parties—only Rosie Armando, because she was a class act, and I could trust her girls not to blackmail anyone, pick their pockets, or talk out of school.

Should a judge ask me to represent a friend of his who was in trouble, I'd never charge the friend or the judge. When the guy got around to paying me, I'd say, "Don't worry about your bill. Just thank the judge. He's a good man."

You still had many legitimate judges—more than there were crooked ones—who didn't take bribes or throw too many fundraisers or ask favors. I kept an eye out for them, too, when I had lunch at a nice restaurant by the courthouse. Before these judges finished their meals, I would get to the waitress and pick up their check. On the way out, they'd say, "I wish you wouldn't do that."

I'd say, "Okay, Judge. That's the last time." Then I'd do it again the next time I saw them. I would do it even before I had cases in their courts. I knew eventually we'd meet up.

At any given time, I had good relationships with about ninety percent of the judges. There were always a few who didn't like me, and I didn't like them either. If I saw one of those guys at some function, I didn't go out of my way to kiss his ass. In Cook County, we could always petition the court for Substitution of Judge. If I had a case that ended up in front of a judge I didn't like, I walked right up to the judge and said, "I want to substitute," and off I would go. I didn't need a reason. In fact, I could also say, "I don't want this other judge either." More than likely I wound up with somebody I did like.

There was no way I could buy myself out of every case. Often, I had to go to a jury trial. Even if I had the judge and everyone else in the court on my side, I still had to win over the jurors. I've never claimed to be Perry Mason, but I would still stake my record in jury trials against any other defense attorney. In fact, my success in these cases, before legitimate judges, only made it easier to pay off the corrupt ones.

Like everything else in my practice, I had my own approach to jury trials. It grew out of my experience as a cop, when I had to spend my days in a courtroom, waiting to testify against somebody I had arrested. I didn't just watch the lawyers. I watched the jurors, learning to see a case through their eyes. Most were working-class people, the sort I grew up with on the South Side. They had no illusions about human nature. Like me, they had a friend or a relative or two who had ended up in jail.

So when I became a lawyer, I never bothered to pretend my client was an angel. Jurors had the common sense to know better.

Instead, right from the start of jury selection, I made it clear that this trial did not hinge on the goodness of my client. I asked each and every juror, "As you sit here, do you understand that my client is innocent?" Most of them would nod "yes." Then I'd ask, "If the state doesn't meet its burden, do you understand that you have an obligation to find him not guilty?"

I repeated this theme over and over in my opening statement. I would never argue that my client didn't do it. I would argue instead that the state has a burden to prove he did it—and prove it beyond a reasonable doubt. In the hands of a good defense attorney, this burden of proof can be a high bar for the state to clear. Even if the prosecutors had a mountain of evidence against my client, I could always count on the prosecution witnesses to bail me out—especially my old friends, the coppers.

I had loads of personal insight into the behavior of the police during a trial. I knew the pressure they were under—from supervisors and prosecutors—to stretch the truth. For some of these superiors, no amount of evidence was ever enough. I also had the example of my own father, who time and again hurt his own career advancement when he refused to perjure himself during big trials. In his mind, perjury was a crime and committing a crime could not be justified, even to get a conviction on a more serious crime—just like one sin couldn't justify another. When I was still a rookie cop, the prosecutors wanted me to testify to something I hadn't seen. I asked my father what to do, and he said, "Regardless of what the prosecutors say, you've got to tell the truth. If they get mad, that's too bad. Let them get mad." That was my father, as honest and straight as could be.

Fortunately for my clients, the cops I cross-examined had different standards. I could see something was fishy just by reading their reports. If the sequence of events surrounding an arrest came off too perfectly, you could smell it. But I never started to cross-examine a cop by challenging him. I took my good old time to set him up. First I played up to his ego. I let him tell the jury how many years he served on the force and what kind of special training he received.

"With all this great experience and background," I'd ask, "do you think you did a good job of filling out your reports in this case?"

He'd reply, "I did a great job. As I always do." Then I'd proceed to point out error after error in the report. For example, if the arresting officer said he chased the defendant and saw him throw his gun to the side, I knew it was bullshit. I had chased a few armed thugs in my time as a cop, and I almost never noticed one do that.

"Exactly when and where did you see him throw the gun?" I asked.

"Well," he answered, "maybe I didn't see him throw it down. Maybe it was after he turned the corner." That was it. That was all I needed. The moment someone misspoke or deviated in the slightest from his report, I had him.

I'd say, "You didn't think this was important?" He'd start to hem and haw, and bit by bit, his whole façade of infallibility would crumble right before the jurors' eyes.

"You just now indicated to the jury that it happened this way. But we see it's not in your report," I'd say, holding up some paperwork. "Either you're lying or you're incompetent." Of course, he wasn't incompetent, because only moments before, he had spent so much time telling the jury that he was so brilliant.

All I needed was that one little slip. I wouldn't let go from there. I knew that the typical juror got real angry when an authority figure was caught in a lie. I could then tell the jury, "We know that this one officer is lying, and that means the other witnesses are probably lying, too. You have an obligation. You took an oath. The state must prove these charges beyond a reasonable doubt, or the defendant is not guilty. Now you have all the reasonable doubt you need to acquit."

To me, cross-examining the state's witnesses was the crux of my entire defense. When I had cases with other lawyers, I always insisted on taking the lead with cross-examination. Even lawyers with more experience than I had let witnesses weasel out of a lie. There was no way I would ever let that happen. I was like a pit bull that locked onto another dog's leg. You'd have to shoot me before I let go.

No matter what I had done to the state's case, I still put my client on the stand. People always question me on that. They see famous trials on

TV, and the defense never puts the client on the stand. I think that lawyers who don't are idiots. If you see the proceedings through the eyes of a juror, you have no choice. The juror looks at the defendant and thinks, "How can you sit in a courtroom, day after day, and have people say all these horrible things about you and not get up to deny it?" The defendant has to get up and defend himself. If he doesn't, it comes off as an admission of guilt, no matter what a judge or anyone else says. That's how the typical juror sees it.

When I started the direct examination of my client, I never tried to gloss over his past. To the contrary, I had him discuss each and every bad thing he had ever done. I had one client get up and talk about his fifty prior arrests. He went on for more than an hour. "I was arrested for this and arrested for that. I was convicted for this and convicted for that." It was like a confessional. But it was still an inoculation against the prosecution. If he could be so forthcoming about how bad he was, then the jury might believe him when he denied the charge in the indictment.

I could also argue that having a record and a lousy reputation made you a target for the cops. I called it my "Jagoff Defense." I used it with a notorious tough guy named Joey Airdo—a pudgy character with close-set eyes, kind of like the short one in Abbott and Costello. Like a lot of mobsters, he owned an Italian beef sandwich stand, and probably ate up his profits. He was a Mob thug from Central Casting, and in this case, was charged with burning out the car and house of a landlord who had evicted him. They found a can of gasoline with his fingerprints and the girl at the store who sold it to him. It was the kind of case I called a dead-bang loser. The prosecutor would not take a plea and wanted a minimum of ten years. Meanwhile, the judge was totally legit and the sort of tough, state-minded sort who would give Joey even more time. I had no choice but to take it to trial. I needed a break from the state's witnesses, and I got it when the investigator testified that Joey's prints were the only ones on the can. The girl who sold him the can and the policeman who found her must have touched it, too. Now I had the fabrication I needed to show that this was a frame-up.

But why would the cops pin a charge on Joey? When I cross-examined the officer from the arson squad, I turned around and asked Joey to stand up. He didn't expect this, so he got up slowly, kind of confused. "Look at my client," I told the officer. "You know why he's here. I know why he's here. We all know why he's here. He's here because he's a jagoff." The whole courtroom erupted in laughter. Except for Joey, who wasn't too happy with this line of defense. I went on with the cross, but when I turned around again, there was Joey still standing. I said, "Would you sit down already?" Then I looked at the jury and said, "See what I mean?"

Now they all laughed even harder until the judge banged his gavel. Later, he threatened to report me for conduct detrimental to my client. But that became moot when we won an acquittal. I would argue that my jagoff routine played a role in the final verdict.

It was fun pitting my wits against someone else. No matter how big the case was or how difficult it seemed. All the bravado and class-clown antics that got me in trouble as a kid now worked in my favor. About the only "homework" I did was to read the police reports the night before a trial. Somehow all the details would burn their way into my memory. When policemen would get up there and testify to something different from their report, I would have my case. It was almost that easy.

After he retired, sometimes my father would come to court to watch one of my trials. He was so proud to see me there. Afterwards he'd say to me, "Son, you have a talent. You have a God-given talent." Of course, he was less than thrilled with the people I was defending with that talent.

I just loved being a lawyer. I loved being in court. I loved being the center of attention. I hated neckties, and I stopped wearing them— before anyone else could get away with it. I'd have a nice sports jacket, but I wore a turtleneck or open shirt with a gold chain. Around this time, I also had a dog I loved—a boxer named Duke. I took him every-where: bars, fancy restaurants, even my office. At one point, the land-lords at 100 North LaSalle threatened to evict me if I kept bringing Duke. I told them to fuck themselves. Duke was part of my image, too.

After a while, I got infatuated with myself and I wanted to win every case—one way or the other. In fact, I went for years without losing. If one of my clients had ever been found guilty, it would have devastated me. I probably cared more about my record than my clients did. If I knew the judge was a money guy, I'd much rather go into his court, make a payment and walk on out. If I had a case that was certain to be tossed, because the cops did something real stupid, I tried to steer it to one of my money guys, so he could get an easy payday. The next time, if I came in with something tougher, he was more likely to help me.

Even in legitimate courts, I usually found an easy way out. If I was on good terms with the state's attorney, I could get him to dismiss the case. Other times, I would offer a plea in return for a lesser charge and sentence. If my client was a burglar looking at six years, I asked for probation. When the judge didn't go for that, then I'd take it to trial, but I made sure to tie up his court for weeks. Even the legitimate judges hated long trials. Like everyone else, they wanted to clear their docket. The next time I came before that judge, he was more likely to give me what I wanted.

Bit by bit, I learned every trick to work the system. Word of mouth about my cases and my results spread. My business grew that much more. But I never treated my job like work, and I never let it affect my lifestyle. Unlike most lawyers, I didn't rush into my office first thing. I rolled out of bed around eight in the morning, took a quick shave, and then went straight to court. I parked right at the bus stop in front of the building. I knew the cops who worked the street and they never gave me a ticket. Inside, I had probably ten judges who would let me use their chambers for making calls to my office and clients. If I walked into a courtroom and saw that the judge was in session, I just gave him a nod and walked back into his chambers.

Unless I had a trial, my cases were almost always over by lunch. After I ate, I grabbed a quick steam bath and a massage. For a few years, during the summer, I'd go back to my cabana and hang out at the pool. But the rest of the year, I went into the office, usually after two. I got my messages from the secretary and might see a few clients, but I never liked too many meetings. Instead, once I had my own suite, I used the conference room for card games. This was something I started when I first shared an office with Allan, but the cards became an institution when I was on my own. Gin was the favorite game during the day. We could usually fit eight around the table. Other lawyers, state's attorneys, and building tenants would drop by, including the two Greek brothers who owned Counsellors Row. I had refreshments for everyone (I still never drank when I played), and if I had a good day, I could win a few thousand bucks. When the prices went up on the restaurant's menu, everyone would laugh and say the owners were losing too much in my gin game.

I stopped the cards around five, so I could start placing my bets for the day. Through my practice and Mob connections, I met a lot of bookies and gambling became practically a full-time job. It could take ninety minutes to call in all my plays, especially during football or basketball season.

There were nights when I stuck around the office and we had huge poker games with thousands of dollars at stake. Sometimes Rosie would send over one of her girls to hide under the table, and if one of the guys was lucky, he got something better than a good hand.

Usually after work, I would go straight to Rush Street where I hung out until the early hours of the morning. Rush Street had grown up from the days of frat-type singles bars. Now there were fancy discos like Faces, swanky spots like the Playboy Club, and huge glitzy restaurants and bars. It was the era when everyone was "swinging" and one-night-stand was no longer such a dirty word. Sort of sexual nirvana for a guy like me. I could keep two steady girlfriends at a time. If one wondered why I had to run, I could always claim that I needed to meet a client at Night Court.

After the clubs closed on Rush Street, I used to bring my dates to the dice games in Chinatown. From the street, you had no idea what was inside. You walked to an abandoned storefront and knocked on the door. You had to know somebody before they let you inside. Then you walked through that abandoned store, across an alley and into another building. If the police ever tried a raid, they would have had the wrong address on the search warrant. You were taken to a big room about fifty feet long with two craps tables and people crowded around them. There were no chairs. Just some tables in the back with free cold cuts and liquor.

There's nothing like the energy at a craps table—people yelling and groaning with every throw. But dice is the ultimate sucker game, and I almost never played. After Marco gave out his Christmas bonus to his crew, he used to have a dice game, just so he could win all the money back. At the game in Chinatown, Mob guys always hit me up for a loan, because they knew I carried a lot of money. If they wanted $500, I would give them $300. I never expected to get it back and didn't even bother to ask. I figured they would ask me to represent them if they ever got in trouble, and it was just a cost of doing business.

After a while, I developed a different sort of reputation among the lawyers and gamblers who hung out with the tough guys. I wasn't a mobster, but I wouldn't let mobsters push me around, either. Once I had a beef with a bookie named Moe Shapiro. He used to hang out at the Playboy Club, and I called him one Friday night to settle the bets I made earlier with him. After I got off the phone with him, I realized I had the wrong score on one of our games. Instead of losing the bet, I actually won, and now he owed me money. By the time I got back to Moe, he had already thrown out his paperwork, and forgot what I actually bet. Instead of hunting through the garbage, he demanded I pay, and I refused.

Moe was connected with the Rush Street group. We used to call them the Jewish Mafia, because so many of their bookies and gamblers were Jews. The following Monday, Moe paid me a visit at my office with his group's top enforcers, Tony Spilotro and Fat Herbie Blitzstein. Tony was a little guy, with the face of a bulldog and a well-known vicious temper. Herbie was easily 300 pounds with a Mitch Miller-type beard and a giant potbelly. He looked like one of those crazy professional wrestlers.

Tony pointed to Moe and said, "He says you lost some money and you owe him some money."

I tried to explain, but Tony cut me right off and barked, "I don't want to hear that nonsense. That's a pile of bullshit. You owe us. We want the money and I'll be back tomorrow to collect the money."

He came back the next day with Fat Herbie, but no Moe. Before Tony even opened his mouth, I said, "I didn't lose it and I ain't fucking paying. That Moe's a fucking weasel."

I then told him that I knew Marco, and Tony backed down. We all agreed to meet later with him. When we did, and I could explain what happened, we agreed to call the whole things quits. They didn't owe me and I didn't owe them.

Tony Spilotro liked the fact I stood up to him. The Chicago Mob later sent him to be their main enforcer in Las Vegas. His temper ended up getting everyone in a lot of trouble, but for a few years he practically owned Vegas. He had a jewelry store near the hotels that he called, The Gold Rush. It came out later that his crew of break-in artists, the Hole-In-The-Wall Gang, used the store to fence some of his best loot.

In Vegas, Tony, Herbie, and I would hang out at Jubilation, a disco that was like Faces, the club on Rush Street. For dinner, we would go to Villa D'Est, a fancy restaurant owned by a Joey Pignatelli, another Chicago South Side guy. I was there with Tony one night when he met up with Frank Sinatra. Tony would never pay for anything in Vegas, so I ended up with the tab—for Frank, his son, and their whole entourage. It came to something like $1,800. The next night I dropped by the restaurant with a girl. When I heard Sinatra was in the private room again, I asked Joey if I could drop by to say hello, but Frank wanted no part of me. I guess he found someone else to pay that night's bill.

By the mid-seventies, it was no exaggeration to say that the cash was coming in hand over fist—easily four to five hundred thousand a year. I had not had an easy road to my law degree. When I looked back on all those dark, cold years, working my ass off to get through college, it was like a very distant memory. Now the money came so easily, I didn't respect it, and as a result, I did silly things with it.

For instance, I bought an old-time gym called Postl's. It wasn't a place to work out, but to relax. They called it a wine and cigar gym, and it was as far from a health club as you could get. Guys went up there for a steam, a rubdown, and a drink or smoke. Charlie Postl had been a wrestling champion at the turn of the century, and when he opened the gym, he had everyone from mobsters like Capone to presidents and mayors show up. My best friend at Marquette, Bill Murphy, was his grandson, and we had stopped by a few times during a break from school. When I told Charlie I wrestled at school, he took a liking to me. He was a crusty old guy, but still a local sports celebrity and they treated him like a king at the fancy steakhouses. He'd let Bill and me eat our fill while he told us crazy stories about his wrestling exploits. After Charlie died, there wasn't much color left to his gym, and the clientele stopped coming. Bill's parents tried to run it, but when Bill told me it was on the verge of bankruptcy, I offered to buy it and bail them out. In some ways it was a toy and an ego boost—to actually own such a symbol of privilege. I also saw the club as an excuse to get my father out of the house. All he did was go to church and watch TV. I hated to see him so idle. He was always willing to help me out, so once I took possession of the club, he showed up bright and early for work. But first thing, he noticed that we were serving liquor without the proper permit. Then he saw some of the old-time mobsters come around, and he didn't like that, either. It took a week before I realized this job wasn't for him.

After two years, I sold Postl's to a couple of young guys who wanted to turn it into a modern health club. Charlie would have had a laugh. By this time, though, I already had my hands full with another crazy investment. But this one worked like a charm. One of my clients, Artie Greco, was a bookie on the South Side. Depending on your point of view, I was one of his best or worst customers. I constantly beat him, but I was also there to represent him when he got arrested. Although Artie was among the few big-time independent bookies, I could see that the Feds were starting to target him like he was a Mafia kingpin. Artie needed a career change, and in 1974 he bought an Italian restaurant in his old neighborhood. Even though he didn't have any experience in the food industry, I gave Artie the cash for the down payment. I thought he had the right bubbly personality for the business. At least, we could have a good time before we flamed out.

The place we bought was called Bruno's, named after the slob who had owned it. The dining room was in a big shed of a building with a little take-out deli in the front. Bruno wanted $50,000 down, in cash, and another $200,000 on contract. I figured he had sold the dump a few times before. The buyers probably gave it back before they could finish the payments. But we had a different plan. We completely remodeled the inside, so it looked like an old-fashioned Italian restaurant with trelliswork and vines. For the chefs, we used Artie's wife and the different Italian women from the neighborhood. They all knew how to cook authentic homemade dishes. Everything was made from scratch. Artie had all kinds of other family to help serve.

We renamed the place Greco's, and it quickly became one of the most popular Italian restaurants in the city. We started busy and only got busier. We had to rip out the deli to make a bigger dining room and a nice bar. Bruno came by during construction and practically had a heart attack. He wanted to know what we were doing "to my restaurant." We told him to get the fuck out. It wasn't his restaurant, and he sure as hell wasn't going to get it back any time soon.

Greco's was always quite a scene. Like I figured, with all the contacts from his previous occupation, Artie attracted both the bookmakers and their customers—the sort of people who are always out looking for a good time. The bookies attracted other shooters in the underground economy—the guys who owned the chop shops and the car thieves who supplied them. Added to that mix were my clients, and crew leaders like Marco and the Mob bosses above them. Then, to make things even more interesting, we started attracting the politicians. Close behind followed the defense lawyers, the prosecutors, and even the judges.

We may have billed ourselves as an Italian restaurant, but looking out on all these different types of customers, I saw a big Irish stew— potatoes, meat, carrots and onions, with nothing quite mixing together. At any moment the whole kettle could boil over and turn one against the other. People were pointing each other out, staring each other down and, in a few cases, getting ready to commit murder.

Major changes were taking place in our local crime world, and they played out right in front of my eyes at Greco's. The Outfit, as they called the Chicago Mafia, was the most powerful organized crime group in America. It didn't get the publicity of the Mafia families on the East Coast, but that was because its bosses weren't killing each other. Instead they ganged up to control everyone else in town.

All of the Outfit bosses were Italian, and they had some Mafia traditions, but their organization was strictly Chicago, and dated back to the time before Capone. They were divided up into five groups, but these were known by the area they controlled and not some family name. There was the Chinatown group, the Cicero group, the South Side group, the West Side group, where Marco was from, and the Rush Street group. If you look at a map of Chicago, you can see that four major freeways radiate out from downtown and cut the metro area into five slices of pie. Each group had control of a slice. The freeways served as their dividing lines.

The five Mafia groups got along very well—like five fingers clenched into a fist. In fact, since they did such a good job of splitting things up among themselves, they decided to organize crime for the rest of the city. If you were doing anything illegal, and lived within a few hundred miles of Chicago, they wanted a piece of it—what they called street tax.

They started with the chop shops and their auto thieves. After that, they put all the bookmakers on the arm. Then they went after the loan sharks and the counterfeiters. They expected the burglars to pay a street tax, and sell all the stolen property through Mob fences so they could get another cut. They got so greedy, they shook down legitimate businesses, too, like go-go clubs and strip joints. Even Italian restaurants. Even Greco's.

To get everyone in line, they killed a few people to make examples. You opened the paper and read that another loan shark or jewel thief had been found in the trunk of a car with his throat cut. The old bosses turned to crew leaders like Marco to organize the shakedowns and, if necessary, the consequences for those who didn't pay. The newspapers called them the Young Turks, and at first the press thought that all the dead bodies piling up were signs of a gang war. The reporters never realized it was the Outfit's war against everyone else.

But that didn't mean there weren't hitches along the way. Early on, the five groups bickered over which one had the rights to which independent criminal. Mob bosses couldn't collect street tax according to their territories. What did you do about a car thief who stole in one part of the city and lived in another? Did the group get the tax based on where the crime was committed, or the location of the criminal? What about bookies? They had clients scattered all over the region and the country. Big bookmakers also had offices in different places, too.

After a few crews got caught in the crossfire, the bosses decided to change their ways. A crew could "grab" an independent criminal, no matter where he was, and as long as they grabbed him first, they could keep him and a piece of his action. This new approach to street tax touched off a Gold Rush, with each group constantly on the lookout for independents and developing their own sources for finding them. The most obvious prospectors for the Mob were the police. Coppers who fingered an independent criminal could get a piece of his tax. Some called in their arrests to the Mafia before they talked to their desk sergeants. A bookie would get pinched, and as soon as he made bail, a goon was waiting for him outside the jail.

Gamblers like me were another way for the Mob to locate independents. The bait was too good for most bettors to pass up—especially if they were already in deep to an Outfit bookie. If you found an independent bookie for the Mob, you could start playing with him. If you won, you split the winnings with your Mob bookie. If you lost, you just let your Mob contact know when the independent bookie came to collect. That's when they "grabbed" the guy and put the muscle on him. As a reward, you got a piece of all the back-taxes they charged him.

I wanted no part of that. The truth is that I liked most of my bookies, and I wasn't about to snitch on them. But one time I did let my guard down, and I got a couple of friends in some big trouble.

They were Ed and Sid, two brothers who had a little law office at 100 North LaSalle. Their father, long gone by this time, had owned some office buildings downtown, which left his sons very wealthy. They showed up at the office each day to do family business, and not even much of that. Mostly, they just sat around. Ed played a terrible game of cards. Sid was an even worse bettor, but he liked to gamble and wanted action in the worst way, so he decided to become a bookmaker. He only booked with me and a few other guys, using betting lines right out of the newspaper. This was the sign of a rank amateur, because the newspaper's lines provide much more leeway than the odds you could get from most bookies. As a result, I loved playing with Sid. He would only let me bet $500 a game, but on a good day I could still win four thousand from him. He was like my safety net.

I never saw Sid as someone the Mob would grab, but little did I know. One night I hung out with Marco at a fancy Italian restaurant on the West Side and watched Monday Night Football. The game was unexpectedly close, and a heavy favorite won by only seven points. Most of the lines had them winning by ten. Marco lost a lot of money and was crying in his beer.

"Believe it or not," I told him, "I was able to lay six points with one book, so I'll make out pretty nicely."

Marco did not share in my happiness. "Who the hell would have a line like that?" he yelled.

I told him it wasn't any bookie he knew. "He's just a square John in my building," I said. "He takes a line out of the newspaper." But I made the mistake of mentioning Sid's name. How many Sids could there be in the directory for 100 North LaSalle?

A week or so later, Sid's brother Eddy came down to see me. He pulled me into my office and shut the door behind us. He was scared stiff. He said his brother had been visited by a couple of Mob goons. They were going to kill him for bookmaking.

"They want him to pay $25,000," he whispered.

All I could do was shake my head. I prayed to God it was a coincidence, but then Ed asked, "Have you ever heard of Marco D'Amico?"

"Yeah," I said. "I know who he is."

"Is he one of the bad guys?"

"Yeah."

Ed turned even whiter at that piece of news. But inside I was boiling—angry with myself for having such a big mouth, but angrier with Marco. How could he do this without talking to me? It was like I put red meat in front of a dog. He was going to devour it first and ask questions later.

The goons told Sid to bring his money to the very same restaurant where I watched Monday Night football with Marco. "We'll pay them what they want," Ed said. "But we want to make sure nothing happens when we give them the money."

I agreed to accompany Ed when he made the payoff. His brother was still so scared, he didn't want to be within a mile of Marco or anyone else from the Mob. They had asked him to continue booking as partner. They would split the winnings fifty-fifty, but if someone didn't pay and they sent out a goon to collect, then they'd keep everything. Poor Sid didn't want to be their partner, or anything else. He had been scared straight. Unlike the real bookies, he didn't need the gambling income. As far as I know, he never made book again.

When Ed and I showed up at the restaurant, Marco himself was there to greet us. I made it look to Ed like I was acquainted with Marco but not too friendly, and Marco played along. We sat down in a booth. Ed gave him the money and got the hell out as fast as he could. Marco counted out $1,000 and pushed the bills toward me. "Here," he said. "That's for the tip." I said, "I don't want that." I stood up and I walked away. I wanted him to know I was pissed, but I wasn't going to get in his face either. I now realized that nothing was too petty for the Outfit. They were always looking for somebody to squeeze. Even if they got nickels and dimes. Most important, I learned that there was no such thing as bullshitting with a mobster. A slip of the tongue could literally end up getting someone killed. Or myself for that matter.

I was determined to do more than ever to keep my two worlds apart. I never dropped names, and if a client wondered whether I knew this or that Mob boss, I would say, "I know him only to say hello." But some of my friends and clients were fascinated by the Outfit and tried to get me to make introductions. None was worse than Count Dante. Time and again, he asked to be introduced to big shots like Marco. He was convinced he could do all these great things with the Mafia, but I knew that even someone as dangerous as the Count couldn't mix with the Mob. They would eat him alive.

Once my law career took off, I didn't see much more of the Count. An incident one night convinced me that there was no way to control the man. We were sitting in my living room, along with our girlfriends from the time. The Count was going on about all of our exploits. He was pretty smashed, and he suddenly jumped up and started ranting to my girl, "This Bob Cooley is one tough motherfucker. I bet you didn't know that he was so tough." Then he turned to me and said, "Go ahead and tell her how tough you are."

He meant to be nice by this, but he was looking a little scary with that curly hair and beard frizzed out like a mad professor. I stood up and tried to settle him down. "John," I said, "just sit a while and relax already."

He got in my face and screamed, "I said, 'Tell her how tough you are.'"

It was stupid, but with the girls there, I wasn't going to back down. "No," I said. "I'm not going to say that."

Suddenly he swung his hand up right alongside my chin. At first it seemed like he barely touched me with his finger, but I felt a searing pain, as though my skin had been ripped off.

I grabbed my face and spun away from him. It would have been suicide to put up a fight, but the Count wasn't about to hit me again. Instead, he leaned over me and blubbered, "Oh, look what I did. You're the only friend I have in the whole world. You saved my life and look what I did to you."

I didn't have to say a word. I'm sure the look on my face said it all: "You crazy motherfucker."

The Count was ready to make amends. He was going to show us a trick. "Go get your gun," he told me. "I want you to point it at me. When I say, 'Now,' you pull the trigger. I'll catch the bullet in my hands."

I replied with the same look I had on my face before. But the Count was serious and that made it even more frightening. He talked to me like he was a magician and I was up on stage with him. "Really," he said and got in front of the floor-to-ceiling window. "Just stand over there and I'll stand here, so no one else will get hurt."

"John," I said, "how am I going to explain this to the cops when I kill you?" I had to shoo him and his girl out of the apartment. From then on, I tried to keep my distance. He would send me business, and call every once in a while, but I refused to socialize with him.

Then one day I got a call from a South Side guy who had been one of the Count's karate pupils. He had made him a partner in his car dealership. He said, "Can you come out here? The Count has got a problem." I drove out, and he told me that a couple of guys came to the lot with a shotgun and were looking to kill the Count. He said their names were Sammy Anarino and Pete Gushi.

Although I didn't know it at the time, they were with Jimmy "the Bomber" Catuara, who ran a crew for the South Side group. The Count had finally met the Mob, and from the wrong end of a shotgun. Since we parted ways, he had built a little empire of adult bookstores. The jewel in his crown was a large storefront in Old Town, still a haven for hippies and headshops. It made him a ton of money. He had intimidated the previous owner, some little Jewish guy, into selling it, but then never paid him what he promised. This Jewish guy had always made his street tax payments to the Mob, so when he complained to them, they promised to get his store back. If it had been anyone other than the Count, the Mob would have tried to threaten him. But they knew they couldn't give him a beating, so they decided to just kill him instead.

I realized I needed a higher authority to save the Count. I went to Marco. To my surprise, he knew the Count and the two guys who were sent to get him. He said, "I'll arrange a meeting and you can straighten this thing out."

A couple of days later, I took the Count to a motel by the racetrack in Cicero. Upstairs on the second floor, there was a bar. When we came in, Pete and Sammy were having a drink, dressed in pullover shirts and slacks, like they were going to the track. I had come from court, but because I wore a suit, Pete was ready to call off the meeting. He said, "What are you, a cop or something?" I had to show him my card, so he could see I was the Count's lawyer.

Pete and I went to a table in the back of the room. I left the Count at the bar with Sam. I knew he would be of no use in any negotiation. It took Pete and me just a few minutes to reach an agreement. The Count could keep the bookstore. He just had to pay the Mob $25,000 and that would be the end of it. Of course the original owner got screwed, but who cared?

When we went back to the bar, we saw Sammy and the Count sitting at a table. At least, I figured, they were calm and acting like adults, but as we got closer, I saw Sammy holding a fork like a dagger. "See this?" Sammy said. "I use this to rip eyes out."

The Count replied, "I don't need that." Then he started making with the hands. "I rip out eyes with these."

Pete and I were both pissed. What did we need this macho stuff for? He grabbed Sammy and I grabbed the Count.

Little did I know that this was exactly the introduction to the Mob that the Count wanted. He agreed to come up with the money and continued to stay in touch with them. A month later, I bumped into Pete when he came to see his lawyer, who was sharing my office. He said, "You tell that crazy Count to stop calling me at four in the morning."

"Pete," I said, "you got no business talking to the Count. You guys are like poison together."

A week later, the Count came up to my office. He wasn't dressed in crazy outfits any more, and he wasn't staying in shape either. He had puffed out, like Elvis did in his last days. But he was as manic and extravagant as always. "You're one of the best friends I have in the world," the Count told me. Then he grabbed my shoulders and whispered, "So I want to cut you in on something I have going. You could pick up a million dollars in cash for your end. But if I tell you what it is, you can't back out. This is going to be the biggest thing in history."

At times like this, when I was worried about him, I didn't call him the Count. "Listen, John," I said. "I've got a better idea. You keep the million and if I need it, I'll borrow the money from you." Whatever this "thing" was, I assumed it had to be illegal. Back in college, my friend Tommy had said something similar about my not backing out and he then tried to railroad me into committing a robbery. I wasn't falling for that one again. I said, "John, I don't want to know anything about it. I don't want to be involved. Besides, in my own experience, a million dollars shouldn't come so easy. Take my advice and forget whatever it is you've got planned."

Three weeks later, I was riding in my car when I turned on the radio and heard that a gang of masked men had broken into the Purolator armored car vault in Chicago and got away with $4.3 million. It was then the biggest cash robbery in U.S. history. Instantly, I knew this was what the Count was talking about. I just hoped to God he hadn't gone and done it with the Mob guys.

Of course, my worst fears came to pass. In a matter of weeks, Pete Gushi was back to see the lawyer sharing my office—to surrender to authorities for the Purolator robbery. To show you how smart Pete was, the FBI agents caught him trying to stash a wad of bills from the job behind a seat cushion in our office just before they hauled him away. He was indicted along with seven other guys, among them a commodities broker from Boston who was accused of trying to launder the cash. I figured he was someone else the Count brought to the party, since the Count had business interests out in Massachusetts.

Only the broker was acquitted; the others took pleas or were convicted. A few weeks after the trial, the Count gave me a call and asked that I drop by that night to see him. He had finally settled down with a very cute little blonde I called Christa. She managed his adult bookstore in Old Town and they were living in a fancy condo on Lake Shore Drive. I brought along a girlfriend, in case I needed an excuse to duck out. We didn't get there until 9 P.M. Christa let us in. The Count ignored my girlfriend and grabbed my arm. With that crazed look in his eye, he said, "Let me show you something."

I followed him back into his bedroom. He opened the closet, and inside was a cardboard box full of money. By this time I knew big money when I saw it, and I figured he had hundreds of thousands, if not a million, in there.

Clearly he was high on something stronger than booze. Sweat was pouring off him, his eyes bugged out, and he was breathing heavily. "You always thought that I was a bust-out and a loser," he said, "but look at this. Look at this." For all of his financial success with the sleazy businesses, and for all of his fame in the martial arts world, Count Dante was still a South Side Irish kid, trying to prove how tough he was.

By now, I had no doubt where he got the money, but I didn't want to hear it from him or be implicated in any way. "Count," I said, "I'm glad for you. I hope you enjoy it. Just don't tell me how you got it." I stayed another forty-five minutes, to be polite, and then I grabbed my girl and left.

Hours later, at four in the morning, my phone rang. It was the Count. "Bob," he said, "you know all that money I showed you? That was just counterfeit. That wasn't real."

"John," I replied, "didn't you hear what I said? I could care less whether it was real or fake," and hung up.

The next evening, I got a call from his girlfriend Christa. "Hurry up," she said, "you have to come over here."

I rushed over to their condo and she let me in, sobbing hysterically. Without saying a word, she led me to the bathroom. There on the floor, slumped against the toilet, was the Count. I didn't have to get too close to see he that he was dead.

"What happened?" I asked her.

She said, "I don't know. He saw some people here earlier in the day, but I can't tell you who they were. They must have done something to him." There was blood coming from his nose, which is supposed to be a sign of poison, but Christa had no interest in finding out for sure.

Like a lot of people who see the dark side, Christa didn't want justice, revenge, or anything else. She wanted to escape with her life and, at all costs, she wanted to avoid a police investigation. I called a friend of mine who owned a funeral home on the South Side and asked him to send over a hearse. Then I called the cops. While we were waiting, I asked Christa if these guys who visited the Count had taken his money. She didn't know what I was talking about. I took her back to the bedroom closet, and when I opened it, the box with all the cash was gone.

Fortunately, I knew the cops who showed up. I said, "This is a good friend of mine. Let the funeral home take the body for now, and they'll do the transport to the morgue for an autopsy." But the Count never did leave the funeral home. Christa asked the funeral director to cremate him instead, and no one was ever the wiser about the cause of death. I never had any suspicions that Christa took the Count's money. A few years later she got married, and I knew she and her husband always struggled to make ends meet. It wasn't as if she had a bundle of cash lying around.

By disposing of the Count the way we did, we only added to his myth for all those martial arts fanatics who idolized him. I'm told that they still think he was knocked off by a rival *sensei* or some such nonsense.

Mystery, too, swirled around the Purolator job, even though Pete Gushi took a plea and agreed to testify against the other defendants. By the time the case came to trial, one of the gang was found dead, and a witness was almost killed by poison in his prison cell. For some reason, the Count's name never came up, even though, from what I could tell, he was the missing link between the Mob, the Purolator guard who let everybody in, and the Boston commodities broker. Still, the Feds never recovered $1.2 million and Pete never fingered anyone higher up in the Mob. He said he dropped a suitcase with the missing money on the lawn of his crew chief, Jimmy the Bomber. Jimmy testified that the suitcase "mysteriously" disappeared, too. It was another Chicago trial that left the press clucking their tongues. People shook their heads and wondered how the Mob could get away with it. By this time, I was not shaking my head. Maybe I didn't know exactly what had happened, but I had a pretty good idea.

INNER CIRCLE
FIRST WARD

CHAPTER 5

HIGHLIFE WITH THE LOWLIFES

F rom the moment Harry Aleman was acquitted in 1977 until 1981, I had the tiger by the tail. People who once had no time for me suddenly looked at me with respect and even fear. Although I never discussed what I had done for Harry, I knew the Mob bosses all found out, because suddenly their crew leaders were coming my way with business. Money flowed into my practice beyond my wildest dreams.

But there was a price for all that raw power and success. At any moment, the tiger could turn on me and, with one swipe of its paw, tear my head off. Very soon after I earned the overwhelming gratitude of the Mafia kingpins for fixing Harry's trial, I needed a favor of my own from them. One of their boys wanted to kill me, and it was none other than my oldest friend in the Mob, Ricky Borelli.

My troubles with Ricky gave me a whole different view of the First Ward and the relationship between John D'Arco Sr. and Pat Marcy. As far as the public was concerned, Senior was the boss in the First Ward, and he certainly looked the part of the Old World politician—always with a laugh and a slap on the back. A First Ward alderman from 1952 to 1962, he was still the Democratic Party's ward committeeman. Over the years, whispers about his connections with organized crime were minimized or ignored. When his son Johnny got elected to the State Senate, it seemed to further sanitize his past. The newspapers made him another "colorful" Chicago character, like a football coach who had been picked up a few times for drunk driving.

I was no smarter than the rest. During my seven years at 100 North

LaSalle, I figured Senior was as high as you could go in the First Ward. My arrangement with his son's firm, Kugler, D'Arco and DeLeo, turned out to be as lucrative as I expected. I got all the work they used to farm out to a dozen other lawyers. Fifty percent of the fees went to me, and the rest went to the firm. Within months of our working together, they moved the firm's office to my floor to make things more convenient for the secretaries. Still, I always insisted on keeping a separate office. Johnny D'Arco was a state senator and Pat DeLeo a Chicago corporation counsel. I thought it would be embarrassing for them to be seen with my organized crime clients.

Senior and son were more than happy with our arrangement. Johnny went to court with me, like his father wanted, but he had no interest in the law or any other line of work. After college, crazy as it sounds, Johnny wanted to be a poet. He even ran away to San Francisco for a while and lived with a bunch of hippies in Haight-Ashbury—until his father sent some goons to drag him back. Senior always wanted his son to be the political success that he couldn't be, but Johnny's heart was never in it.

Still, Johnny absolutely revered his father—to a ridiculous extent. Once we were together in a Vegas casino waiting in line to get our chips. In front of us, unshaven and very disheveled, was the famous University of Alabama football coach, Bear Bryant. When the cashier refused to cash in his chips before he paid off his markers, he got all grumpy and yelled, "Don't you know who I am?" A few minutes later, when Johnny got to the window, the cashier asked him about his own markers and he said, "Don't you know who my father is?"

That was Johnny. I just looked up at the ceiling. Why would some cashier in Vegas know about an old former alderman from Chicago? At times like this, you just wanted to give Johnny a slap and tell him to grow up already.

Usually Johnny's chief concern was getting laid. By lunchtime he was off to the gym to play racquetball or work out. Many afternoons he was holed up in an apartment, getting a blowjob from one of the girls he hired as State Senate interns. With older, more sophisticated women, he was incredibly awkward. That's where he most wanted my advice. Although he regularly skipped appointments with our clients, he was always there to grab a table at a popular outdoor café. If he saw an attractive girl, he asked me to see if she would join us. If I ordered a drink, he ordered the same drink. If I ordered a steak, he ordered that, too.

My only fly in the ointment at Kugler, D'Arco and DeLeo was Patty DeLeo, Senior's son-in-law. I knew from the start that he ran the firm, but I thought he had no reason to feel threatened by me. His bread and butter had always been civil cases, not criminal ones. Patty was corporation counsel for what was then known as the License Court. Meanwhile, a partner in the firm, Dave Kugler, represented bars that were brought before Patty's court for violations like selling alcohol to minors. Before the trial, Patty would find the cop who had filed the complaint and tell him that the accused was going to take a plea. Then, when the cop didn't show for the hearing, the judge threw the case out. It was quite a racket, so Patty should have been fine with just the civil business. Besides, as a corporation counsel, he was strictly prohibited from criminal work.

Still, Patty wanted a hand in referring criminal cases to other firms. As I got to know him better, I understood why. First of all, he was probably getting kickbacks from those criminal lawyers, which meant he could screw Johnny and Senior out of referral fees. But even more important, referring the criminal work gave him an excuse to hang out with the mobsters at the bars and clubs and smoke his fat cigar. Patty just loved to act like a tough guy. He knew that once I became involved, all the crew leaders would eventually gravitate to me.

One Saturday morning, a few months after I started working with his firm, I got a call from Patty asking if I could come to his house. He lived on the West Side of the city, just down the street from Johnny. He answered the door, and I could see he had cuts and bruises all over his face.

"Hey, Patty," I said. "What happened?"

He was still very agitated. "Last night I was at the After Hours Club in Chinatown," he said. I knew the place very well. It was run by the Chinatown group, and was a block from their Italian beef stand, The

Hungry Hound. Drunks with the munchies could chow down on some beef and then stumble over for a nightcap. From the outside, all you saw was a boarded-up storefront. Inside, there was a huge bar that stayed open from 1 A.M. to 9 A.M. After Rush Street closed for the night, all the punks ended up in the After Hours Club. A lot of them were sons of the Chinatown crew leaders, in their late teens and twenties, and they would make their bones by getting in bar fights.

"I mentioned your name to some kid," Patty said. "You know, that we now work together, and he disrespected you. We got into a fight over what he said about you, and look what happened." He motioned around the bruises on his face like Marlon Brando in *The Godfather*. "Can you go straighten him out?"

In other words, Patty wanted me to hunt down this kid and beat the shit out of him—not the typical request one makes of his legal associate. I thought, "This is like we're back in high school."

But to that point in time, Patty had been cold towards me—still unhappy about my deal with his firm. I owed it to Senior to act helpful. I said, "I'll see what I can do."

That night I went to the After Hours Club, and found the manager, Larry, who also ran The Hungry Hound. He was one of my bookies, so we were old friends. I told him Patty's story, and he replied, "That's a bunch of bullshit. I watched the whole thing. DeLeo was trying to pick up that guy's girl and he give him a slap, like he deserved. Your name never came up."

I went back to Patty's house and said, "What the fuck, Pat?"

My relationship with Patty was never real warm and friendly after that, even though I came to respect his intelligence. But it didn't matter what Patty thought of me. I couldn't have been closer with Senior or Johnny, and that's all that mattered. Funny enough, the old man also made a bizarre request around the same time. He was at his beach house in Hollywood, Florida, and he put through an urgent message for me to call him. "I have a problem," Senior said. "Can you come down here right away?"

I jumped on the next plane and didn't even change out of my heavy wool suit. Senior's house was in a beautiful secluded spot overlooking the beach. He came to the door when I rang the bell and was ashen. I asked him what was wrong, and he took me to the front of his house. The picture window had been smashed. He told me his neighbor, who lived a few doors down, threw a rock through it for no reason. Senior saw the whole thing happen, and yelled at the guy. The neighbor yelled back, "Go fuck yourself."

It was an unbelievable story. Even more unbelievable, the perp was named du Pont, John E. du Pont, and he was one of the heirs to the DuPont chemical fortune. As a result, Senior felt powerless to do anything. He wasn't going to call the police, and he certainly wasn't going to sic some Mob enforcer on a du Pont. He figured he would use my services instead. Senior walked to the foot of his driveway, pointed to du Pont's house, and said, "Now you go straighten it out."

"This is an emergency?" I thought. "I had to fly down for this?" But I could see that Senior was really upset. Away from his stomping grounds, he looked like any other helpless senior citizen.

I trudged up the street, sweating like a pig in my heavy suit, and knocked on du Pont's door. I figured there must have been a misunderstanding. How could somebody do something so strange and unprovoked? But then du Pont opened his door, and I had no doubt about what had happened. He was a half-shaven lanky guy with a crazed look in his eyes—not too different from the muttering winos I pulled out of the gutter when I was a cop. "Are you du Pont?" I asked.

He nodded.

"Mr. D'Arco just told me what you did." Then I wagged my finger in his face. "You have no fucking idea who you're messing with over there," I told him. "You better go over and apologize, and then pay for that window or there's gonna be a real serious problem." Then I turned around and walked away. I could hear the door slam behind me.

I went back and told Senior I had taken care of it. Much to my surprise, he called me the next day to say that du Pont had packed up and left town. Some twenty years later, this same nutcase was convicted for murdering a wrestling instructor who lived on his Pennsylvania estate. He shot the man for no apparent reason. Senior never asked exactly what I did to scare du Pont away, but he was very pleased with the result.

From then on, he treated me like another son, and even asked me to drive him to certain high-profile events. Senior always felt better if he had a driver with a gun. Usually it was one of the Mob-associated cops, but he knew I was always packing too, since I carried a lot of cash. When one of his old political cronies died, Senior asked me to drive him to the wake. To be seen with him, at an occasion of such importance, was like becoming a part of the family—at least in the eyes of the political bigshots at the funeral home.

One good turn deserves another, so naturally I went to Senior when I had my problem with Ricky. But Senior did not jump around and show the outrage I thought he would. Instead, he listened with a grave expression on his face, and then picked up the phone to call Pat Marcy.

As far as most people knew, Pat Marcy was no more than John D'Arco Sr.'s assistant. Pat never held elected office and his only title with the First Ward Democratic Committee was secretary. Senior had a huge office in our building. Pat's was a closet by comparison. In public, Senior was the center of attention, while Pat faded into the woodwork. Senior always had a driver. Pat drove himself.

But watching Senior on the phone with Pat that day, I could immediately see who was the boss. Marcy was at home, and he asked that I drive out immediately to see him.

He had a sprawling ranch house in the suburb of Des Plaines. Marcy took me through the house, past an indoor pool as big as any in a hotel, and out to his patio in the back yard. We sat by a grill and wraparound bar. A high brick wall enclosed the entire property, so no one could see inside.

Pat and I still didn't know each other very well, mostly to say hello at Counsellors Row. After I fixed the Aleman case for him, he referred me a few gambling cases from the Cicero group. At his house, he made no attempt to be social. He didn't even bother to get me a drink. Once we were settled, he cut right to the chase and asked me about my problem. I didn't mince any words about Ricky. "I'm sure this guy was going to fucking kill me," I said.

To anyone else, Ricky Borelli looked like the last person in the world to worry about—a big teddy bear in his rumpled cop's uniform with crumbs on his tie. But I knew there was a nasty side to Ricky, and if rubbed the wrong way, he could do nutty things. For example, he told me what he and Marco did to a guy his girlfriend accused of raping her. They beat him half to death with pool cues. When the guy passed out, they threw lighter fluid on him, let it burn until he woke up, and then beat him again. It took weeks for him to recover, and Ricky kept calling him in the hospital room to say they were waiting for him when he got out. The guy left town and was never heard from again.

I also knew that Ricky had the potential to do more than assault and battery. Because he was a cop, he was licensed to carry a gun, and therefore a very valuable asset for the Mob. There were times, he implied, when he paid off his gambling debts to Outfit bookies by doing an "extracurricular." I always took that to mean he whacked someone.

After I began my law practice, I stopped keeping my little book for him. He was always coming up short, and it wasn't worth my time to make him pay. He was like a greased walrus when he owed you money. After a few years, as a favor, I would still place some bets for him, but I tried to keep it to a minimum. We still saw each other frequently. While he was "on duty," in his patrolman's uniform, he came to the office all the time to play gin with me and the other lawyers. Also, he was often around when I hung out with Marco.

Then in 1977, during the football season, he took me aside to ask a favor. For some crazy reason, Marco had let Ricky open his own booking office. "I'm getting real big action," he told me, "and I don't want to get stuck with it if the score goes the wrong way. Can I lay some off with you?" For old time's sake I let him bet $5,000 on certain games. The first week he lost a little, then he won some—which is the worst thing that can happen to a bad bettor—and the following week he lost big, about $30,000. He was supposed to pay me by Saturday, but he was short again. Ricky never changed. He was always coming up lame. I told him I wouldn't take any action until we straightened out, but he said, "Look, somebody owes me a bunch of money. He's in Vegas right now. Just let me play one more time and we'll get straight when he gets back next week."

Like an idiot, I said, "Okay fine," and like an idiot, Ricky bet and lost again. Now he owed me $50,000. I wasn't going to press him for the money. I figured he was broke and there was nothing I could do about it. But he called me the following Saturday night to say he had rounded up $10,000. He wanted me to meet him in Austin Park, on the western border of the city, just off the freeway. I had driven by the place many times. It was rundown in every way, with all the streetlights shot out to hide the dope dealers and hopheads. He said, "I'll be waiting for you outside the clubhouse."

I said, "Sure," but after I hung up the phone I started thinking. Why, with all that cash, would he be hanging outside some boarded-up building in a city park? Why didn't he want to meet in a bar or club? I called him back ten minutes later and said I had a hot date and she wanted to go out to dinner. I told him to call me up on Sunday to set up another meeting.

Usually on Sundays Ricky called after every football game, but I didn't hear from him until after 5 P.M. He told me to meet him at Marco's club. Now I really smelled a mouse in the kitchen. Sunday evening was the only time in the whole week when the place was closed. I called Frank Renella, one of the enforcers from Marco's crew. He was a likeable guy but also very tall and threatening. Frank was not afraid of anybody—especially Ricky. They had beefs from a long way back. Frank owed me a few favors, so he gladly went ahead to the club with one of his guys to see what was what. He called me back a few hours later. "Ricky was in a back room," he said. "He didn't have any money for you, but he had some other guy with him that I never saw before. I think it was going to be a problem."

It was all so unreal. I had never threatened Ricky or even bugged him about what he owed me. But suddenly, I realized my connections with Senior and Johnny made him see me in a different light. I was more than just another guy he owed money. Now he thought I was dangerous enough to collect it. This time I couldn't risk asking Marco for help. Ricky was still his cousin, and there was no telling what he would do for family.

Pat Marcy listened to my story in silence. He knew all about Ricky and Marco. When I finished, he yelled at me, "Why the hell are you gambling like that? You should know better." Like he was my uncle or something. Then he calmed down and said, "Don't worry. I'll take care of it."

The next day at Counsellors Row, I saw Senior, and he said, "You're not going to have a problem with that guy." Ricky then disappeared.

I have no idea where he went. Maybe they just banned him from Marco's club and the places they knew I'd go. I never said one word to Marco and I have no idea whether he was involved in Ricky's vanishing act. People with the Mob often dropped out of sight for mysterious reasons. Most were never seen again, but Ricky did materialize, about a year later. We said hello, and acted as though nothing had ever happened. Of course, nobody ever repaid the $50,000 he owed me, but I didn't care by then.

This whole incident with Ricky made me realize the power of Pat Marcy. Now I paid more attention when I saw him at the First Ward table in Counsellors Row. Pat always sat in the same chair, with his back to the wall and a view of both doors to the restaurant, so he could see everything coming and going around him. The pedestal phone was at his fingertips. No one else sat in his chair when he wasn't there.

Pat liked the fact he could help me, and although he yelled at me for gambling, my little beef with Ricky gave me some street credibility. Pat knew I was not the typical lawyer or, for that matter, the typical gambler. Like Marcy, I skated between the Mob world and the legit world without getting my feet too wet. He could be seen with me in public and not damage the veneer of respectability that was so important to him. He could also hang with me in private and not worry about letting his guard down.

Bit by bit, he brought me deeper into his world. To start, he invited me to sit at the First Ward table at Counsellors Row. If you wandered into the restaurant, you might wonder why that was such a big deal. The table itself wasn't fancy, and the chairs were no different than any others. But for the lawyers, the city workers, and politicians always milling around, it was like a king's court. I started to hear people talk about "Inner Circle First Ward." If you were in it, you had powers other people didn't even know about. It meant you were untouchable. No one dared give up the name of anyone in the Inner Circle—even mobsters who flipped and became government informants.

When Counsellors Row opened for business each morning, usually the first one at the table was Fred Roti, alderman for the First Ward. Fred was not the most impressive-looking guy, very short, with the face and body of a toad. But after the death of Mayor Richard J. Daley in 1976, he was considered to have more behind-the-scenes clout than any other politician in Chicago. If you watched him at breakfast, you knew it was true. He was regularly joined by local officials, like City Clerk Stanley Kusper, other aldermen, and especially Ed Burke, head of the city council's finance committee. He also met with heavyweights from the business community, especially developers and building contractors, who were the biggest campaign contributors. Roti's father, Bruno, had been a Mob boss, so he never completely tried to hide his association with the Outfit. In fact, he made a joke of it. He used to say his election slogan was "Vote for Roti and Nobody Gets Hurt."

When Marcy arrived each day, just after 11 A.M., Roti cleared his guests away, and Pat sat in his royal chair. It was immediately apparent who was in charge and who held his coat. After lunch, Roti headed off to council chambers, and Pat had the table to himself. Then you saw a different cast of characters: not the sort of people who made headlines. Instead, they were judges, police commanders, lawyers, and especially union leaders. The unions were an endless gravy train for the Outfit—a source of do-nothing jobs for mobsters and their relatives. The unions also gave mobsters extra leverage to extort legitimate businesses. A wildcat strike could have devastating consequences to a construction schedule or a crucial service like garbage hauling.

At times, when the topic of conversation got hot, Pat motioned for the visitor to follow him out the door for a "stand-up" conference in the lobby, like he had with me when I fixed the Aleman case. Other people weren't even allowed at the First Ward table. They would walk through the restaurant, catch Pat's eye, and then sit in a booth in a distant corner of the restaurant. This was the treatment he used for lawyers defending mobsters in "ink" cases. It was also how he handled visiting hit men and crew leaders, like Harry Aleman and his partner, Butch Petrocelli, who would drop in on Thursdays. Usually he sat with Butch, while Harry cooled his heels at another table nearby. I had advised Pat never to sit with more than one person when he was talking about something illegal.

After they got to know me, Senior and Pat started coming to Greco's for dinner. One night, I had them at my table when my parents walked in. I loved having them at the restaurant, and it was a major reason I kept my piece of the business. When D'Arco and Marcy got up to leave, I went to sit with Mom and Dad. My father pulled me aside. "Son," he said, jerking his thumb at D'Arco and Marcy as they put on their coats, "I used to arrest those people."

It was hard to believe. Bits and pieces of Dad's memory had started to slip at this point. As it turned out, he was on the road to Alzheimer's disease. If what he said was true, Dad would have pinched Senior and Marcy nearly fifty years before. But in the pit of my stomach, I knew he could be right. When he was a police detective, he had an uncanny ability to match names and faces. His specialty was what they called "cartage thefts," or truck hijackings, and he made some spectacular arrests that were written up in the true crime magazines.

I later found out that Senior and Pat had been arrested for armed robbery during the thirties. Senior was part of a stick-up gang connected to Capone. Once they robbed some women of their purses, and even murdered one of them. In another case, the victim picked D'Arco out of a lineup. His partner in that particular crime was found guilty, but the jury acquitted Senior. Marcy wasn't so lucky, and even served time for his conviction. In those days, he was known as Pasqualino Marchone. As far as my father was concerned, no amount of name changing, wealth, or power could ever erase the stain of armed robbery.

Pat and Senior were not the only ones with records on the First Ward Democratic Committee. Buddy Jacobson, short and stooped and in his seventies, was a constant presence at Counsellors Row. He was a partner with Senior and Pat in the Anco Insurance Company, which had a big office on an upper floor of our building. They used property insurance as another way to shake down developers, building contractors, and anyone else doing business with the city. Pat was a majority shareholder of Anco, but Buddy had started the firm.

Buddy Jacobson may have looked like a harmless old gent, but he had once been a crooked cop and enforcer for Hymie Weiss, the bootlegger who competed with Capone during the Roaring Twenties. One day Buddy was walking with Weiss in front of the Holy Name Cathedral when Capone's men drove by and sprayed them with tommy guns. Weiss died and Buddy barely survived. But he held no grudges and quickly crossed over to Capone's side.

With the money from bootlegging, Capone realized he could put his own people in positions of power to control the cops and the courts. Republican or Democrat didn't matter. He started out by taking over the GOP and then the government in the suburb of Cicero. Crews with tommy guns literally ruled the streets on election day. Capone was convicted of tax evasion and lost his mind to syphilis before the Mob got a foothold in the Democratic Party in Chicago.

After Capone, Tony Accardo was the only real Godfather to rule the Outfit. He stayed in power for nearly fifty years, until his death in 1992 at the age of eighty-six. He was known as Joe Batters for the way he whacked guys for Capone with baseball bats, but he was a lot slicker than his nickname made him sound. He oversaw the expansion of the Outfit into other cities until the Chicago Mob reigned supreme everywhere west of the Mississippi—including Las Vegas. During a half century as the boss of bosses, he never spent a day in prison.

Like Capone, Accardo saw politics as crucial in keeping his stranglehold on criminal activities in Chicago, and the key to that power was the First Ward. The city had fifty wards, but none compared to the First. In terms of power and prestige, it contained both the city's central business district, known as the Loop, and the mansions on the Gold Coast. It had the factories and packing plants on the South Side, and equally important, the slums around them, where the Mob could run its rackets and recruit its soldiers.

Accardo groomed Buddy Jacobson and John D'Arco Sr. to be his front men in the First Ward. Buddy had started out as a Republican and even ran for alderman, but along the way he got convicted of vote fraud, so he gave up any hope of getting elected. Instead, during the forties, he worked behind the scenes of the ward's Democratic committee, and eventually became executive secretary. Because he didn't have a prison record, John D'Arco was chosen to run for office. In those days, he actually bore a resemblance to Capone, not a bad image in the eyes of your typical Italian immigrant voter. Senior was first a state representative. Then, in 1950, he suddenly backed out of his campaign for reelection when he was called before the U.S. Senate's Kefauver Committee on Organized Crime. But two years later, he had no trouble getting elected as First Ward alderman. He ran unopposed in the primary and general election. At the same time, Marcy joined their team as Buddy's assistant. Before long he emerged as the real brains behind the First Ward operation.

Early on, the Mob bosses expected John D'Arco to be mayor one day, but Senior was never the sharpest blade in the drawer and didn't command the respect of his fellow aldermen. In 1962, the FBI tapped the phone of Sam "MoMo" Giancana, then the Outfit's CEO. During one wiretap, they heard Marcy telling Giancana to "dump D'Arco." According to FBI agent and author Bill Roemer, Giancana was reluctant to make a change. But soon afterwards, Roemer barged in on Giancana and Senior while they were having lunch at a local restaurant. Roemer shouted over to them, "Ho, ho, ho, it's Mo." Senior, obviously confused, acted like a politician and shook Roemer's hand. Giancana then stormed out of the restaurant. A day later, Senior checked himself into a hospital, and announced he was too ill to run for reelection. They let him stay on as committeeman, a figurehead for the Democratic Party in the First Ward. A few other Mob lardheads were "elected" alderman until Fred Roti settled in for the long haul, but the real reins of power passed to Pat Marcy.

Pat quickly showed the Mob bosses what a sharp, shrewd guy he could be, and changes in the Outfit's leadership only made him stronger. Throughout the sixties and seventies, Tony Accardo kept trying to kick himself upstairs so he could finally retire. Like in some corporation, he would be chairman of the board and some younger Mob boss would be chief executive officer. But he never found the right man who could take control for very long. A few years after Sam Giancana booted D'Arco, Accardo booted him (and later had him killed). Other choices got arrested or died.

By the mid-seventies, the Outfit was run by committee. Depending on who was in prison, one group leader would become a little more dominant than the others, but most of the time they were in agreement. If some dispute arose, Accardo or another old-timer, Joey Aiuppa, would fly back to Chicago from their retirement homes in Palm Springs. They would hash out the differences and everything would be settled without bloodshed.

This meant that each of the group leaders was like a little king inside his territory, and he didn't have to worry about anyone stepping on his toes. A good example of this was Angelo LaPietra, the boss of the Chinatown group. They called him "the Hook," because he used to hang his enemies from meat hooks when he tortured them to death. He had a big bald head, thick glasses, and the hooded-over eyes of a cobra, but he was only five feet, five inches tall. Maybe for that reason, almost all the guys in the Chinatown crews were also short. I called them the Midgets.

The Hook would have his bodyguard drive slowly through the streets of the Italian enclave in Chinatown while he sat in the passenger seat. The people in the neighborhood looked on in awe. They would point and say, "There's Angelo. There's Angelo." They would then crane their necks to see who else was in the car.

Every summer, the Hook threw a block party right behind The Hungry Hound beef stand on 26th Street. They put up a big tent and had free food. So much smoke came up when they barbecued the ribs and sausages, it looked like the place was on fire. Mobsters and their associates from all over the city would pay something for the Hook's party, even those from the other groups. The whole party, along with the donations, were supposed to be for the poor neighborhood kids. But after you took away the relative pennies the Hook spent on food, he probably had millions left over. Everyone knew it, and they would still contribute. At one point the Hook's son-in-law told me I would have "the honor" of joining their Italian-American Club, which was like Marco's Survivor's Club. Supposedly I was the only non-Italian, but I knew my membership was just another way to hit me up for all their bogus charity tickets.

The Hook's most prized racket was Chinatown itself. The Chinese loved to gamble, and their favorite place to do it was the Chinese Palace, right on the main street in Chinatown. It was like a casino inside, with traditional Chinese games and all the stuff you'd find in Vegas. The On Leong Chinese Merchants Association ran the whole operation. They bribed Fred Roti so the police wouldn't raid it, and they paid the Hook a ton of money in street tax.

Someone as heavy as LaPietra could never be seen with Pat Marcy at Counsellors Row—or any other public place, for that matter. He would just walk through the restaurant to let Pat know he was in the building. Then he took an elevator to an upper floor and walked down the stairs to an unmarked office where they met.

The more I knew about these sorts of arrangements, the more I realized how vital Pat Marcy had become to the Outfit. He was the one link between the Mob bosses and the public officials who helped the Mafia keep a stranglehold on Chicago. Marcy's reach seemed to extend into every nook and cranny of Mob business, like that of an octopus. If he answered to anyone, it was to Accardo and Aiuppa. As far as bosses like the Hook were concerned, he was their equal if not their superior. Pat became so central and so trusted, he was the one designated to receive the army duffel bag full of cash "skimmed" from the casinos in Las Vegas. He counted it, took his cut, and then distributed a share to Accardo, Aiuppa, and each of the group leaders.

A few months after he invited me to the First Ward table in 1977, Pat asked me to join him for dinner on Thursday nights. After work, we met at Counsellors Row, and waited for a big limo to swing up to the front of our building. Inside was Ben Stein, a thin dapper guy in his sixties, with both the style and sharp edges of Sinatra. Stein was another First Ward fixture with a past—an ex-con and one-time union goon who used his connections to build United Maintenance Service, the city's biggest janitorial service. He was renowned for paying off the unions not to organize his workers. He had contracts for the McCormick Place convention center and some of the largest city and federal office buildings. The papers liked to call Ben the "Mayor of Rush Street," because of his constant presence at the nicest clubs and bars. He had the best seats at sports events, too, and was pals with local and national stars from that world. For some of our dinners he brought along Harry Caray, the longtime broadcaster for the Cubs, and Tommy Lasorda, then the manager of the Los Angeles Dodgers.

Stein was married, but he always came to dinner with his girlfriend, Karen Koppel, a petite blonde in her early thirties. She had once been a stewardess. By this time, she was Ben's full-time "kept" woman, living in his Lake Shore Drive condo. Although she was young and cute, she was no bimbo. She dressed in very stylish, refined clothes. She was also smart enough to keep the players straight during our nights out and follow the thread of our conversations. If anything, she was too smart for her own good.

Our other frequent dinner companion, Dominic Senese, could not have been more different. Over six feet tall and 220 pounds, Senese sat at the table like Jabba the Hut. He mumbled just a few words at a time, if he said anything at all. He ran the Teamsters Local that controlled the produce markets and milk trucks, so he had all those businesses by the balls if he ever called a strike. Dominic was one of the few Counsellors Row regulars that Pat invited out to dinner, so he must have had power in union circles. I thought, too, he might be an old friend of Pat's, although I learned differently years later.

I figured I was invited to the dinners for entertainment, sort of the court jester. Of all the people in Pat Marcy's circle, I was the only one who joked with him or talked back in any way. He was never one to laugh, but at least I could get him to crack a smile. I talked a little business, too. I had great contacts in the court and the police force, so I could always share a little gossip. I also gave them legal advice, such as things they should do to avoid a wire, or to minimize the damage if they were caught on tape. One of the biggest reasons Pat invited me was that I always brought a different date. I think he looked forward to checking her out, even flirting a little—especially since he and Dominic came stag. It added a little spice to their evening.

During dinner, while I chatted with my girl and Karen, I listened with half an ear as Pat and Ben talked business. They were deciding how to dole out government contracts or who would run for what office and who would get appointed to what city or county job. Some of the Mob's worst hit men and goon enforcers were on the public payroll. Usually, they didn't even show up to punch in. If there was a strike going on, Pat and Ben talked about how it should get settled and whether the workers or their employers would get screwed. You could understand why Marcy and Stein were friends—from humble beginnings, with prison time between them, they had become two of the biggest power brokers in the city. The influence of the Mob truly extended from the garbage in the street to the lights on top of the tallest skyscrapers. I started to wonder whether there was any place in Chicago where they didn't have a hand. As the meal wore on, Pat would have more drinks of Crown Royal whisky—until he smelled of it. But he never seemed drunk. He was always in command, and everyone else deferred to him.

If you ever asked Pat Marcy about the source of all his influence and power in the Mob, he would say straight away, "Politics." It seemed like a strange answer, because he was so secretive and un-political. Important topics for most politicians, like the economy, totally bored him. But whenever election day rolled around, there was no doubt that he took the vote very seriously. All you had to do was walk by the First Ward Democratic headquarters in our building. On election day it would be packed with people, standing-room only, and humming with activity. Pat set up folding tables with at least ten phones, so there was no way he would miss a call. He got the results from all the precincts in the city before anyone else did, and he demanded nothing less than an overwhelming machine landslide in every First Ward polling place. He would pick up a phone and scream, "What the hell do you mean they got fifteen percent? Wait a second." Then he would shove somebody out the door and the numbers would change by the time the papers came out the next day.

To get their landslides, the First Ward did a lot of old-fashioned organizing, but they did a lot of other things that were not so legit. For example, they used the big housing projects to literally manufacture votes when they needed them. I once went with Johnny D'Arco to Cabrini Green, the rundown complex of apartment buildings that I had patrolled as a copper. He took along bags of "street money" for the party workers. Each voter got five dollars to sign for a punch card ballot and then hand it over to the precinct captain in the polling place. The precinct captain would then punch those cards himself. At the end of the day, he went through all the other cards in the precinct by hand. If he saw holes in the "wrong" places, he punched another hole to invalidate the ballot. Of course, the Republican election judges at the polling place were supposed to keep an eye on the Democrats. But Pat picked the poll workers for both parties in the First Ward. There were absolutely no checks and balances.

At first I wondered why Pat had to win by such lopsided margins. It looked suspicious. But eventually I realized that the appearance of power was more important than the questionable math of any one election. Like a schoolyard bully, if he used the right bluster, he didn't have to back it up. This was especially true with judicial races—the elections that mattered most to the Mob. If a candidate for judge dropped by Counsellors Row to ask for Marcy's support, he always gave it to him. But then, when the opponent came in, Marcy would promise to help him too. In fact, he would do nothing for either side. Merely by promising, he made the judge feel obligated when Marcy would call after the election to ask for favors. These judges had truly sold their souls by asking for his help. This made them that much more vulnerable to intimidation. How could they ever claim that Pat was threatening them when they were the ones who first came to him?

One of my law school professors, who had been appointed an associate judge, asked if I would introduce him to John D'Arco Sr. He was facing his first election and he figured he needed the First Ward's support. He was very straight, and I knew they would chew him to pieces.

"D'Arco won't talk to a stranger," I told him, "but I'll see if I can set something up behind the scenes." I didn't say a thing about him to Senior. The professor went on to win his election, but he never forgave me for not setting up that meeting. He has no idea what a favor I did for him.

To read the newspapers of the day, you would think the late seventies was a time of tremendous upheaval for the First Ward. After the death of Mayor Richard J. Daley in 1976, the Democratic machine picked Michael Bilandic in the special election to finish the term. For the next two years he stumbled through office with the kind of scrutiny Daley never had. Bilandic was too much of a nice guy to bully the press like Daley, and it made him a bigger target for criticism. Decades of corrupt purchasing and bad hires in Streets and Sanitation finally came home to roost in the winter of 1978 when the city was buried by snowstorms. Each blizzard took forever to clean up. The voters blamed Bilandic, and a few months later, he lost the primary to a so-called "reform" candidate, Jane Byrne, the former consumer protection commissioner.

The press treated Byrne's election as some sort of revolution, but at the First Ward table it was considered a total fluke. We knew Jane was no "reformer." She had been a party hack from way back, and if she hadn't gotten into a fight with Bilandic and fired from her job, she would have still been in the fold. I always wondered whether the First Ward secretly helped her, because they thought she would be easier to manipulate than Bilandic.

Her Honor was a real screamer, and like other people who make a lot of noise, it was mostly a sign of her insecurity. I loved to tick her off by parking my car in her parking spot at City Hall. Her bodyguard was a friend of mine, and he used to call and beg me to move it. "She's screaming at me to have it towed," he'd say. He knew the traffic cops in the area were my friends, too, and that none of them would call a tow on me. It was always so obvious that she had absolutely no power.

Roti and Marcy had no trouble letting Jane ride on her little ego trip as long as she didn't screw with any part of the city government that mattered to them—especially the police department.

Besides the courts, nothing was more important to the Mob than the police. Gangs had always infiltrated the Chicago Police Department, usually in the lower ranks; but by the time Jane Byrne took office, the bad apples were in positions of command. For what seemed like a few brief moments, it looked like she would clean up the mess. When the police superintendent unexpectedly retired, Joe DiLeonardi, a truly straight and honest cop, became the "acting" chief. He immediately demoted the top brass with the worst Mob connections. "Joe Di" even let detectives raid Outfit bookies. Over a period of weeks, they made hundreds of gambling arrests.

The acting superintendent and Jane walked into her office one day when Alderman Roti happened to be waiting for her. Joe Di immediately turned on his heels to get the hell out of there. With what he knew, DiLeonardi did not want to be seen in the same room with Roti or anyone else from the First Ward. According to Roti, Jane motioned for Joe Di to come back and when he hesitated, she snapped, "You come in here when I tell you."

But neither Jane Byrne nor the First Ward would bring Joe Di to heel easily. He kept up his raids on the Outfit bookies. According to Roti, he issued an ultimatum to Her Honor: either she got rid of DiLeonardi, or the municipal unions would shut down the city during the upcoming contract negotiations. Just as the Mob thought she would, Jane Byrne buckled. In six months, the Chicago Police Department's reform era came to an end, and crusading Joe Di was sent packing to a station house on the South Side. In his place, Byrne appointed Richard Brzeczek, who had been in my class at the police academy. Dick was strictly a go-along guy.

On Roti's orders, Dick and Jane appointed Bill Hanhardt as his deputy chief of detectives. Bill was probably the most notorious officer in the entire department. He certainly looked the part of the big, bluff Irish detective and had the gift of gab. There was even talk of creating a TV show based on his career. Back in the sixties, he had built his reputation on the Criminal Investigations Unit, kind of a SWAT team, formed to bust Mob crews that specialized in hijacking trucks. Although he made some good arrests, as time went on, he got too close to the people he kept arresting. Joe Di knew that Hanhardt had gone bad and was socializing with crew leaders. To get him out of harm's way, he transferred him to the traffic division. But under the new police commissioner and Jane Byrne, Hanhardt went from the bottom of the barrel to the top of the heap. He then promoted all his cronies under him.

One of the first things Hanhardt did as deputy chief was to order the vice detectives to get their search warrants approved by their supervisors. These officers then reported to Hanhardt. This meant that Hanhardt knew the addresses of all the bookie joints they were going to raid. He then tipped off the bookies so that nothing would be in their offices when the police arrived. He also prohibited vice cops from going outside Chicago, even though he knew some of the Mob bookies were in the collar suburbs just a short distance from the city line. As a result, the only bookies the police would raid were the independents, usually on tips from the Mob.

The police department under Dick and Jane had a whole system for making payoffs. No longer did the criminal lawyers have to deal directly with the detectives involved in a case. There were other more senior detectives who would act as their bagmen. Police payoffs became as routine as payoffs in the Traffic Court.

There was never any secret about Hanhardt's connection with Roti and Marcy. After he was appointed deputy chief of detectives, he showed up at Counsellors Row all the time, and sat with Roti and Marcy at the First Ward Table. He usually came in around 1 P.M., wearing the full officer's uniform with the braided epaulets. He took the next hour for lunch. Occasionally he and Pat got up from the table and went into the building's lobby for a private conference. Marcy told me that Hanhardt was the FBI's liaison with the Chicago Police Department, so he could keep Marcy up-to-date on the Feds' organized crime investigations. Pat arranged for him to meet with the Mob bosses at Counsellors, too. A few times I saw Hook LaPietra walk into the restaurant, catch Pat's eye, and then head straight downstairs where they had a basement bathroom. A few minutes later Hanhardt would get up and follow him.

I had no idea what they talked about down there; but by this point, Hanhardt had become so corrupt, I felt he would do anything for the right price. According to Harry Aleman's partner, Butch Petrocelli, when someone like a bookie or thief was on the run from the Mob, Hanhardt would have him picked up by a squad car. The cops would then deliver him to the hit men.

Personally, I never had too many discussions with Hanhardt. Whenever I looked at him, in his clown-suit uniform, it turned my stomach. My father had given so much to the department and never had a prayer of advancement—precisely because he was so honest. Hanhardt rose to the top despite his corruption, prospered because of it, and, worse yet, actively battled the decent cops who remained. Once, when they returned to the table after a lobby conference, I heard Pat and Hanhardt mention the name of Rich, a friend of mine on the gambling squad. My blood froze. Hanhardt said he was going to take care of him. I didn't know if that meant a transfer, a beating, or death. A little later, I worked up an excuse for my own lobby conference with Pat. Before we turned to go back into the restaurant, I asked if he and Hanhardt were talking about Rich. He wanted to know why I was asking, and I told him that Rich was a good friend of mine. Pat exploded, "That cocksucker is your friend? That motherfucker?"

A few days before, Rich had raided a card game in Cicero. The son of a Mob boss ran it. As the cops pushed everyone into a corner, this kid grabbed a bunch of papers and ran into the bathroom with them. Rich yelled after him, "Don't throw that in the toilet," and when the kid did, he gave him a good crack across the head.

"There's no way," Pat said, "this guy is going to get away doing that to one of ours."

"Wait, Pat, wait," I said. I had to think fast. "You can't let anything happen to him, because he helps us on all of our gambling cases." There was no truth to that, but it was the only way I would get Marcy to show any mercy. "You want to keep him where he is. I'll talk to him, so this doesn't happen again."

Later that day I called Rich and I said, "You got a problem, and I'll take care of it, but in the future, you can't put your hands on these guys."

Even though he did the Mob's bidding, Hanhardt was an outsider. There were other cops who were actually "made" members of the Mafia. Ricky Borelli was one, but a small fry. The supreme example of the Mafiosi cop was Blackie Pesoli, a big muscular guy with the chiseled looks of Sylvester Stallone. You always saw him in a neatly pressed patrolman's uniform with spit-shined shoes. Occasionally he served as Senior's driver, but he was also a regular at Counsellors Row.

I could never figure out why this flatfoot should be so important and, for his part, he didn't pay any attention to me—until I started working on the Aleman case. Then, one day, he approached me at the restaurant. Even when he was friendly, he had an incredibly intimidating manner, like he was just about to hit you. "I hear you're handling Harry's thing," he said. I wouldn't answer him yes or no, and he was impressed that I kept my mouth shut. As it turned out he was incredibly tight with Harry and Butch. In fact, there were times when he drove them on their "errands." Then he said, "If it goes right with Harry, you'll be the biggest lawyer in town, and I can bring you a lot of business."

I just nodded and didn't expect anything more to come of it. How many referrals could I get from one copper? But after Harry was acquitted, Blackie did bring me cases from all over the city and the suburbs. He knew every judge in the metropolitan area and, if a judge was crooked, Blackie also knew how to pay him off.

When most judges started out in Cook County Court, they cut their teeth in Traffic Court, and that's where Blackie ruled the roost—even though he had no official title or function in the building. If the Mob wanted tickets cleared up or reports destroyed, Blackie took care of it. Once we were in Traffic Court together, and Blackie barged into the office of Tony Bertuca, the chief corporation counsel. Tony was having a meeting with four other lawyers. I turned to leave, but in his booming voice, Blackie said, "I need the office. Now get out of here." Without a whimper, Tony cut short the meeting and left his own office with all the lawyers trailing behind him. Blackie sat down and put his feet up on the desk like he owned the place.

Blackie never ceased to amaze me. He had his finger in more pies than a Mob boss. He owned a piece of several different prizefighters, including Jumbo Cummings, who fought heavyweight champ Joe Frazier to a draw (and is now serving a life term for murder). He made deals with the black dope gangs. He also ran the company that provided security at Chicago Stadium. In the eighties, during the height of Michael Jordan mania, if I wanted to see a Chicago Bulls game, Blackie waltzed my date and me right into the building. Sometimes he sat us down in the press box with the reporters. Sometimes we sat in the crow's nest with the cameramen.

But like everyone else in the Outfit, his primary concern was gambling.

He had several bookies working for him, and he always wanted me to bet with them. I discovered there was just one problem. Blackie refused to lose. The first time I bet with one of his guys, I beat him for $5,000. But when I called back to collect, nobody answered the phone. I tracked down Blackie and asked what happened.

"Oh," he said, "that guy got killed."

Four months later, Blackie introduced me to another one of his bookmakers. I told Blackie, "I hope he has life insurance."

I beat this guy, too, the first week we played. The next week, I was down $10,000 on Friday, but hit absolutely every bet on Saturday to go up $20,000. That evening, I called to double-check my figures, and again the line on the phone was dead.

When I saw Blackie, I asked what happened this time. "Oh," he said, "that guy got arrested." If you call in bets to a bookmaker and he gets arrested, all bets are off. I later found out from Rich, my buddy in Vice, that this bookie had *not* been pinched. Of course, Blackie still expected me to pay him the money I owed before the supposed arrest. It was the last time I ever bet with him.

At some point in his police career, the brass offered to promote Blackie to sergeant, but he didn't want any part of that. He was happy being a patrolman. That way he could report each day to his own little desk in the basement of the Greyhound Bus Station, grab his patrol radio and off he'd go. Pity the poor pimp Blackie happened to catch on his way out. This had long been a problem in the station before Blackie came. The pimps would prey on the single girls who got off the buses. But Blackie had no time for filing arrest papers or sitting in court. Instead, he cuffed the guy and dragged him down into the basement, where he strung him up over a water pipe and beat the living hell out of him with his nightstick. I saw Blackie dump one of these guys like a sack of potatoes into the alley. He put a finger in his face and said, "Never come back here. If I even see you driving around the block, I'll fucking kill you."

I always thought I was familiar with the violence that men can do, seeing it firsthand as a kid growing up on the South Side of Chicago and later as a cop. But Mob violence was different from anything I had known. It was truly a depraved indifference to human life—whether friend, foe, or just some hapless stranger.

There were certainly times when I benefited from having the Mob's muscle in my corner. But aside from my beef with Ricky Borelli, I never asked for help; I got it, whether I wanted it or not. Once, I was sitting in Counsellors Row with Marco and Butch Petrocelli when George, one of the restaurant's owners, tapped me on the shoulder. "Somebody's asking for you," he said. He pointed to a big barrel-chested character standing by the cash register. I had seen him a few times at a downtown jazz bar, but never knew what he did for a living. When I approached, he said, in a distinctive British accent, "I'm here to collect the money for Hal Smith."

Hal Smith was one of my independent bookies. The previous week, I bet one way with him and lost. But I covered those bets with another bookie and ended up winning more from him than I lost to Hal. I gave the losing bookie another week to pay me and told Hal that he could wait. When he complained, I told him to fuck himself. "Listen," I whispered to the Brit. "I told Hal that I'll pay him as soon as I get paid by this other bookie."

But the Brit started getting belligerent. He said, "I want the money right away, and I'm not taking no for an answer."

I glanced over my shoulder and could see Marco and Butch craning their necks to look at us. "Believe me," I said, "this is not the right time and place for a beef." The next day was Saturday and I usually spent a few hours in my office, playing cards. I asked for his phone number and said, "I'll call you tomorrow, when it's quiet, and we can get this settled."

I went back to the table, and Butch asked, "Who was that?"

"No one," I said. "Just some guy trying to collect for Hal Smith."

Butch said, "Hal Smith? That rat motherfucker? Are you betting with him?"

Evidently the Outfit had some longstanding beefs with Hal Smith. They believed he stole business from one of their bookies. So Butch wanted to "grab" Hal's goon. I couldn't talk him out of it.

I called the Brit the next day and arranged for him to meet me at the Walgreen's on the corner of Chicago Avenue and Michigan Avenue, in the heart of the city's shopping district. The luncheonette's booths were right next to huge windows that looked out on the busy sidewalks. It was so public, I figured nothing too bad would happen there.

At around nine-thirty that Saturday morning, I pulled into the bus stop outside the drugstore. The Brit was already in a booth and looking right at me as I got out of my car. I walked through the revolving doors and slid into the booth across from him. Casually, I scanned the restaurant, but there was no sign of Butch or his guys. Maybe he had a late night and forgot all about this meeting. "Hey, how you doing?" I said. I motioned for the waitress and ordered a cup of tea.

This guy was so big, he could barely fit into the booth. After a little chitchat, he looked at me and asked, "Have you got the money?"

There was no stalling him. I had promised to bring all the money to the restaurant. I thought, "What the fuck am I going to do now?" At this point the waitress tapped me on the shoulder and asked, "Are you Bob Cooley? Telephone call." She pointed to a phone on the lunch counter. I picked up the receiver and it was Butch, calling from a pay phone on the street. He said, "Get the fuck out of there. Go take a ride."

I hung the phone up, stared straight ahead and walked right past the booth where the Brit was sitting. Out of the corner of my eye, I saw the surprised look on his face. As I pushed through the revolving door, Butch pushed from the other side. Behind him were Bobby Salerno, Fat Mike Bryant, and another hit man. When I got into my car, I saw the four shove themselves into the booth around the Brit.

The next day, I got a call from Hal Smith. "Have you got my money already?" he asked.

"I met your guy yesterday," I said, "and I gave it to him."

"I haven't heard from him since," he replied.

I said, "That's your fucking problem."

The Brit was never seen again. I hope they didn't kill the guy. Maybe they scared him back across the Atlantic. But these people didn't fool around. Not the street guys and not the bosses. You were always playing with fire.

It was one thing for them to beat up on goons. It was another when they mauled innocent people. No one was worse than Marco, who got especially nasty when he was drunk. Once, a policeman stopped him when his car was swerving all over the road. In a rage, Marco tore out of the car and jumped on the cop while he was writing the ticket. During the fight Marco bit off part of the guy's finger. To add insult to injury, the cop got fired, too, since the Mob had influence in the little blue-collar suburb where he worked.

As my business with the Mob continued to grow, and I continued to hang out with the crews, I witnessed more acts of senseless brutality. For the crews, bar fights were just another part of nightlife, like someone else might think of playing pool or seeing a show. The mobsters weren't the only ones in a bar looking for trouble. I got in a lot of beefs myself. Maybe a guy would push me out of a chair or say something to my girl. I was always able to take care of these jokers on my own. But if I was with Marco and his crew, and I knocked someone down, they would all gather around and do a stomp job on him. That's how they operated. If you got in a fight with one of them, you got into a fight with the whole gang. I didn't want their help, but I couldn't stop them either or they would have thought I was weak, and you can never let a mobster think you're weak. For my own safety, I had to walk away, but inside I hated it. I always detested bullies, and now it was like I was one of them.

As far as Marco was concerned, I was his lawyer and social director. Wherever I went at night, he followed close behind. That's what happened when I started to go to the nightclubs in the south suburbs. If I met a nice girl at Greco's, after dinner I would take her to Condessa Del Mar. It had a restaurant in the front and a big showroom in the back for the top Vegas-style entertainment of the day, from Sinatra on down. I became a regular there, and I always got one of the best tables—even if the show was sold out.

Marco decided he had to be a big shot at this nightclub too. He took his crew with him to see a very popular act in those days, Freddy Bell and the Bellboys. While they were all waiting in the bar, Marco ordered a bunch of drinks and wanted to start a tab, but the bartender insisted on being paid first. One word led to another until Marco jumped over the counter and started pounding the bartender. The crew took this as a sign to start smashing up the rest of the place, and after it was totally destroyed, they went into the kitchen, tore the sinks from the walls and turned over the ovens.

That night I was supposed to meet Marco before the show started. When I got to the club, the whole place had been shut down. I was told that the coppers took Marco and his guys off in a paddy wagon. I went to the station, but they were long gone by the time I arrived. It was another police department in the Mob's pocket. Steve, the Greek who owned the nightclub, was stomping around the station parking lot.

"How could the cops let them all go?" he asked me.

I couldn't begin to answer. Worse yet, I realized that I was the one who had brought the Marco plague into his beautiful club. It took Steve a week to get the place back in shape, and the very night he opened for business, who showed up in the bar again? Marco. He just couldn't stay away. At least he apologized and said it wouldn't happen again, but he refused to pay the $40,000 in damages. He told Steve to let his insurance take care of that.

Shortly after this incident, I sold my interest in Greco's. Being a partner in the restaurant business was more trouble than it was worth. Besides, I had moved into one of the ritziest condos in the city, right above Morton's Steak House and just off Rush Street. Now I lived only a block from my favorite hangout, Faces disco.

It would be no exaggeration to say that Faces was the hottest nightclub Chicago ever had. Although it was modeled on Studio 54 in New York, it really did act like a "club" and have some sort of bullshit membership you could buy. I never bothered with it. From what I saw, the doormen were as rude and crude to their members as everyone else. From Thursday through the weekend, people stood behind their velvet rope in lines that wrapped around the block—even in the coldest weather. But if I walked up with the Mob guys, they let us right through.

When you entered Faces, it was like a cave, with a long, low black foyer. But then you came out into a cavernous room with bright lights and glitter balls hanging from the rafters. All around the dance floor, you had booths where people sat and watched the hordes of dancers. Way in the back, behind the dance area, there was a huge horseshoe bar. We would stake out a few booths nearby that could fit about twenty people, and we'd pull over some stools from the bar. The area was literally known as "the Mob corner."

It was only a matter of time before Faces became a hangout for Marco, too. From 1977 to 1979, we met there practically every Wednesday and Friday. The schedule became as regular as my Thursday night dinners with Pat Marcy. Marco always had some of his crew along to drive him home. By this time, he had lost his license and the bosses didn't want him driving anyway. He was always so fucking drunk he was liable to kill himself.

For us, Faces had one major attraction: It was filled with the most gorgeous women in town. We tried to lure them from the bar to our corner by passing out free drinks. Nothing worked better than fancy bottles of champagne. By the end of the night, our tab could run over a thousand dollars. At some point, Marco and I started to alternate paying the bill each week. Once, when it was my turn, I was having drinks with a developer who wanted to get closer to the First Ward crowd. At closing time, the waitress brought me the bill. The developer asked for it and paid without a whimper. None of this escaped Marco's attention—even in his drunken stupor. After the guy left, he came over and said, "This doesn't count. Next week is your turn again."

I had no illusions about Marco's generosity. Like the other Mob guys, money was his god. The major reason he paid the Faces check was to impress the cute girls in our corner. Eventually, though, I had to pop that little champagne bubble. I found out his tax returns showed a minute percentage of his total income. He claimed some Italian beef stands were his sole means of support. I was no choirboy in this regard either, but at least I reported income of a few hundred thousand. "If the government wants to build a tax case on you," I told him, "they can bring in waitresses to show how you're spending all this cash. You have to have one of your guys start picking up these tabs."

No matter when I was at Faces, I almost always saw some of the Chinatown crew. They passed out drinks too, but I never saw one of them pay a bill. I figured that they were somehow connected to the owners. They were also rumored to have a piece of the fancy restaurant next door. On occasion, some poor sap would wander over from the bar and start talking to one of the girls in our corner. Almost immediately one of the Midgets would pick a fight with him. The Midgets worked out at the gym so much that they had wide shoulders, but they were not too impressive at first glance. As soon as the sap lifted a hand, a dozen guys would surround him, like a pack of wolves, and once they pushed him to the ground, they all but stomped him to death. Then, if the people around us got upset at the blood and gore, they dragged the guy out into the street and had him arrested for good measure. One of the Rush Street cops on the take would do the honors.

It got to the point where I couldn't stand the fights any more. But one incident in particular showed me the real animal nature of the crews. It involved Suzie, an absolutely adorable young woman, who came into Faces on a Saturday night with her friend. I was with my girl in the corner talking to two leaders from the Chinatown crew, Larry Pusiteri, who managed the After Hours Club, and Richie Catazone, an older bald guy. Because the young guys treated him with such respect, I always figured that Richie had been some kind of hit man, although he was always pleasant to me. I introduced Suzie as an old girlfriend. I did not mention that she was also a call girl. She lived in a fancy apartment building a few blocks away with Rosie Armando, the high-class madam. They all started talking, and I soon left the club with my date.

Once I was gone, Larry and Richie told the girls about a party they were having later that night at an apartment a few blocks away on Division Street. They assured the girls that I would be there. The address was some junky old brownstone, a place the gang rented for their one-night stands. When the girls entered the apartment, they quickly saw that they were the only females at this party. Larry and Richie crowded around them with some other members of the Chinatown crew. They asked Suzie to "model" a bathing suit. When she refused, Larry and Richie dragged her into a bedroom and raped her.

Somehow, before they were done with her, she managed to escape and run half-naked into the street—just as a police cruiser rounded the corner. By sheer chance, it was one of the few squads to have a policewoman inside. Unlike some of the other Rush Street cops, she would not turn her back on a rape. She followed Suzie back into the apartment to arrest Larry and Richie.

When she got to the station, the policewoman discovered that Larry and Richie had plenty of copper friends. The commanding officer would only let her file for battery and unlawful restraint, but the woman cop said she would go to the prosecutor herself to add a rape charge. The next day, I got a call from Richie. He wanted me to use my connections to head off the policewoman. When I asked him why he had attacked Suzie, he told this whole bullshit story about her being drunk and high. But this was no innocent young girl who misunderstood their intentions. She was literally a hooker. If they had taken their time, everyone would have been happy. Worse yet, they did this to someone they thought was my former girlfriend. "I introduce her to you and you do something like that?" I asked. "Why?"

"Well," Richie said, "it just got out of hand."

I made him and Larry pay her five thousand dollars each in return for Suzie dropping the charges. I explained to her that there was no other justice she would get in Chicago, but I felt horrible. Suzie blamed me for the whole thing. "I thought they were your friends," she said. Some friends.

No matter how violent the Mob was with the rest of the world, they reserved some of their most vicious behavior for each other. Probably their most effective weapon was surprise. Four times, I shared a last meal with a gangster before he went off to his death. Each one was calm and unsuspecting.

The first was Sammy Anarino, a South Side hit man who had been sent to kill Count Dante. After I arranged the deal on the Count's adult bookstore, Sam and I hung out a few times. He needed my help after someone almost shot him to death in his car. He managed to barely escape with his life, but later, while he was in the hospital, the police found a satchel in his trunk. Inside was a bottle of chloroform, handcuffs, surgical gloves, and a gun with anti-fingerprint tape wrapped around the handle. Kind of a hit man kit. The state's attorney brought weapons charges over the bag. Sam asked me to represent him, but his crew leader wanted him to also use another lawyer, Eddy Genson, who

I despised. Sam met me for lunch at Greco's and tried to change my mind, but I politely refused. I wanted nothing to do with Genson. When Sam finally got up to go, he said there were no hard feelings. He left to see "a guy" at a furniture store just a mile away. Not far from the store, someone stopped traffic so that Sam's car was stuck in the middle of the block. He saw the hit men come for him, with shotguns in their hands, and jumped out of his car, but they cornered him on the sidewalk. This time they blasted away until they were sure he was dead.

A few days after Sam died, I happened to walk past Ed Genson. He was so big and fat, he needed a cane to walk. He waddled over and got right in my face.

"You better be careful what you say about me. I heard what you said to Sam Anarino, and Jimmy was not happy to hear that, either." Jimmy "The Bomber" Catuara was Sam's crew leader and one of Genson's biggest clients. He was a dinosaur from the South Side, renowned for muscling the chop shops.

With Sam dead, I figured Ed Genson and his client were in no position to throw their weight around. "Fuck you and fuck Jimmy," I said. "My friends are killing your friends, so don't you ever threaten me again."

Lo and behold, a few days later, the police found Jimmy The Bomber in his car with a couple of .22s in the back of his head—a Mafia-style early-retirement package. The timing could not have been more coincidental.

But for Genson, it was no coincidence. The next time I saw him, outside a suburban courthouse, he ran huffing and puffing to catch up to me. "The other day, when I saw you," he said, "I didn't mean Jimmy *Catuara*. I meant Jimmy *Catrone*." This was total nonsense. Catrone was Genson's law partner—a completely harmless character. But suddenly I realized why Ed was so concerned. He thought that *I* had gotten Jimmy Catuara killed. Worse yet for Ed, with Jimmy dead, he now needed all the friends and new business he could get.

I couldn't get too cocky with the likes of Genson. I had my own clients who were getting knocked off. Little Tony Borsellino was much higher up in the Mob food chain than Sam Anarino, but that didn't make him any safer. He was pint-sized, but his hair was always slicked back, and if he didn't wear a suit, he wore a sport jacket and silk shirt. He was the muscle for all the fancy clubs and bars on Rush Street. We originally met when I defended him on an assault and battery charge for a fight at Faces. After I got him off the hook, we became friends.

He supposedly made his bones as part of an elite ring of truck hijackers and served a few years for a million-dollar silver bullion heist. He was smarter and more ambitious than most mobsters, and although he didn't gamble much himself, he ran a few bookies and card rooms. He would pick my brain about the big sports events coming up and the lines his guys should have. Tony had a large crew, and when I invited him to dinner, he would bring at least five guys with him. I used to host them all at Mama DeLuca's, a family-style restaurant in Old Town. When Butch Petrocelli joined us, it would drive him crazy if Tony had a bigger entourage than he had. It got to the point where Butch would call me first to ask, "So, how many guys is Tony bringing?" It was like the Cold War missile race. One would bring nine and the other would bring ten. All their Mojos would line up at the bar while the busboys kept pulling over more tables and the owner sent out for another leg of veal.

But Tony wasn't like the other crew leaders when we went out with our girlfriends. He was more sophisticated than the rest of them and had a taste for the finer restaurants in the city, like a French place called Le Coq Au Vin, or one of Chicago's most famous celebrity hangouts in those days, Eli's Steakhouse. We would eat dinner there, chat about news of the day, and sit by the piano bar with our girls—usually until the early hours of the morning. We were at Eli's one night in 1979 when Tony got a page. He went to make a phone call. When he came back, he pulled me aside and said, "I've got to go somewhere right away and meet some friends of ours. Can you do me a favor and take my girl home?"

The next day he was found in a field on the county line with five bullets in the back of his head. The FBI had a theory that Tony helped kill some burglars who had been stupid enough to break into Accardo's house. He was supposedly whacked to cover Accardo's tracks. Although I didn't know *why* he was killed, it was the *how* that bothered me. I thought, "I'll never let anyone sit behind me in a car." Borsellino was a very cagey guy, but he still went for a ride without looking over his shoulder first.

Although I truly liked his company, I couldn't shed too many tears for Little Tony. Like Sam Anarino, he was a well-known hit man, and I'm sure he popped a few unsuspecting souls in his time. That was the business he was in.

I felt differently about Karen Koppel, Ben Stein's stylish girlfriend. In the spring of 1980, a few months after Tony was killed, she stopped joining us for Thursday night dinners. There was a mention in the press that she had disappeared and relatives were looking for her. Ben didn't look too concerned. I learned later that she and Ben had split up. Maybe she was trying to break away. Maybe Ben had found another sweetheart. Whatever the reason, when Ben ordered her out of his condo, Karen wouldn't go. This was only a few years after actor Lee Marvin's mistress won her "palimony" suit. Karen probably knew her rights, but a lot of good that did. No trace of her has ever been found.

When I asked Pat what happened to Karen, he told me, "Rick took care of that." Rick Simon was a crooked cop who had been Ben's driver and would one day take over his business. According to Pat, Ben decided to let her stay in his condo, but that wasn't enough. "She wanted $50,000 or she was going to blow the whistle on him," he said.

This was no idle threat for Ben—or Marcy, for that matter. In the years she dated Ben, Karen watched all sorts of people get close to Pat. Just during our Thursday dinners, she heard more than enough conversation to cause serious problems if she ever started talking. The poor kid thought that knowledge put her in a position to bargain. She didn't know it put her in a position to get killed. Pat said to me, "She should have fucking known better."

He was absolutely right. In fact, you could have said the same of me. I should have fucking known better myself. I was foolish enough to think that I could stay above it all and remain protected from the death and destruction all around me. In the next few months, I would find out how expendable I was.

CHAPTER 6

A RUN THROUGH THE GREASE

At the age of thirty-six, Nick "the Salesman" Velentzas was like other Greek immigrants on the fringes of Mob society. He was in the restaurant business—he owned a coffee shop on the northwest side of the city—and he loved gambling. Short and slight, with a pleasant disposition, he was exactly the sort of person Marco and his guys thought they could muscle.

Like the Chinese, Chicago's Greeks were very big bettors. They also ran some of the most happening restaurants in the city, and let the Mob use their back rooms for after-hours dice and cards. One place in Greektown had a whole lamb roasting on a spit right where they played craps. Guys would eat and then roll the dice, their hands dripping with grease.

Besides slinging the hash at his diner, Valentzas ran a card game and kept a sports betting book for a bunch of other Greeks. With each of these operations, Valentzas paid the Mob a street tax. But then somebody caught Valentzas at the racetracks, where he also took bets from his friends. When Marco demanded $300 a month on this action, Valentzas finally reached his limit. He refused to pay another nickel. To show Valentzas the error of his ways, Marco sent three members of his crew: my old friend Frank Renella, Donny Scalise, a former cop and Marco's main man, and Nick Boulahanis, another Greek. They slapped Velentzas around pretty good, and he promised to have their money for them in a few days. When they came back, he paid, but he still complained about all his Outfit taxes. In a heavily accented voice, he said, "All the time I pay, pay, pay, pay, pay."

Donny Scalise didn't feel very sorry for him. He replied, "For the things you've said, and the things you've done, you fucker, you should be dead. I'm gonna tell you something. You're getting the biggest pass of your life."

Boulahanis and Donny both spoke up loud and clear—and right into a wire Velentzas was wearing under his shirt. Nick the Salesman was that rare bird who didn't just get mad at the Mob; he got even. After he was beat up, he went to the Feds and offered to become an informant. Indictments for extortion soon followed against all three slappers. Now Frank Renella, who had helped me smoke out Ricky Borelli, asked a favor in return. He was desperate for me to take the case.

But if I represented Frank, it meant my co-counsel would be Eddy Genson. Marco had already engaged him to represent Donny Scalise. This was like Sam Anarino all over again. Still, I couldn't get too angry with fat Eddy. Ever since Sam and Jimmy The Bomber had been killed, he had done his best to be cordial to me. I still couldn't stand the sight of him, but when Frank Renella kept insisting that I represent him, I said I would talk to Genson and try to work something out. Ed invited me to meet him at the fancy restaurant next to Faces. He sat there, kissing my ass. "Oh, you're a good guy," he said, "and we should let bygones be bygones. You can be lead attorney in this case. You can even use my office whenever you want. I'll have one of the girls there help you."

Through the fall of 1980, Eddy and I worked together on the motions and hearings for the Valentzas case. Then, on Thanksgiving Day, about a week before the trial was set to start, I got a call from Marco. He wanted me to meet him at the Survivor's Club. It was a holiday, but I didn't mind. I could take the opportunity to collect from Marco on my other Mob cases for that week. In those days, it would have been anywhere from $4,000 to $7,000. When I got to the club, nothing seemed out of the ordinary. Guys were at the table playing cards. Ricky Borelli was sprawled out on a couch, sleeping off his turkey. Marco and I had a friendly little chitchat. We didn't see each other as much any more. I was trying to stay away from the Rush Street nightlife with the crews. "Come on," Marco said, "let's take a walk."

We always strolled around the block when we discussed serious business—just in case the Feds had planted a wire somewhere inside his club. As we walked, he said, "Bob, you don't have to worry about the Frank Renella case no more. There's not going to be any case."

I stopped dead in my tracks. "What are you talking about?"

"We're going to whack that little Greek cocksucker," he said.

"Marc," I said, "that's not going to help the case. They already have his Grand Jury testimony. In fact, it will hurt the case. They can use that testimony and we won't be able to cross-examine him."

He said, "I don't give a fuck about the case. No one wears a wire on us and lives to talk about it. We're going to run him through the grease."

This hit me like a ton of bricks. I had already been around too many killings. No way did I want to hear about a murder *before* it happened. I said, "Marc, I don't want any part of this, and you really don't want to do this either." I reminded him about another informant who was killed in the suburb of Calumet City a few years before. The Feds responded to his murder by shutting down the Mob's entire operation in that town.

Marco suddenly got real angry and cut me off. "Listen, you're our fucking mouthpiece," he yelled. "You don't tell us how to run our business. Just do what you're told. We're going to make an example out of him."

I was furious, but there wasn't a damn thing I could do. I couldn't warn the guy that something was going to happen without getting myself killed. Instead, I hoped against hope that Marco was bullshitting. Nick was supposed to be in federal protective custody. I thought, "The bastard's just trying to show off." When we got back to the club, he paid me for my cases. I sat around there a bit longer, talking to the other guys. Then I said, "I'll see you, Marc," and left.

Friday, the next night, Johnny D'Arco and I took our dates downtown to dinner and the movies at Water Tower Place, a high-rise mall and condo which had opened a few years before. Attached to the Ritz Carlton, the complex had marble on the outside and a huge glittering atrium inside. For Chicago, it was considered the height of luxury.

Meanwhile, five miles due west of the Water Tower, in a little row house on the edge of the city, Nick Velentzas met an old girlfriend for a game of cards. Marco's club was just a few blocks away. Later, as Nick walked to his car in a parking lot behind the house, a couple of guys with nylon stockings pulled over their faces came up from behind and blasted him to pieces with shotguns.

The next morning, when I opened up the paper, there was a big story about Nick's murder. It should have come as no surprise. I had been hanging with Marco and his crews for ten years. I knew they were extorting and robbing. I knew they were killing each other too. But none of those other murders hit home like Nick's. These guys had absolutely no concern for the consequences of their actions. They thought they could get away with anything. And by telling me first, Marco had practically made me an accomplice.

Soon, I got a call from Frank Renella. The Feds wanted him in for questioning about Nick's murder. They had us go to a police station in Elmwood Park, where they had found the body. The Mob had plenty of friends in that police department—from the chief on down. We got a warmer reception from the cops than the Feds did. I went into the interrogation room with Frank and listened as the FBI agents grilled him, "So where were you at nine and where were you at ten?"

It was bizarre. I don't think Frank had any idea what had happened, but there I was, sitting around like Mickey the Mope, and I knew exactly who had ordered Nick killed, and I knew about it the night before his murder.

Suddenly it was like the earth had opened up before me. Right there, in the little police station. Somehow, I told myself, I had to back away from the Mob or I would surely get swallowed up in that bottomless pit.

As if my conscience was not bothering me enough, now my father's voice chimed in too. He was getting sicker with Alzheimer's and almost never got out of the house. I tried to drop by to see him at least once a week. More and more, he would be confused about things, but he was always crystal-clear when he first saw me. He would ask if I was still involved with D'Arco and Marcy, and then he would say, "Son, you shouldn't be wasting your God-given talents on these people."

I would nod and say I was doing my best to break away from them, but inside I knew how impossible that was. I just couldn't pick up one day and say to Marcy, "I'm through. Good-bye." I knew too much for him to ever let me go.

Just a month after Nick Velentzas's death, I shared another last meal—this time with Butch Petrocelli. We met a few days after Christmas, at about 2 P.M., in a Greek restaurant called Roditys. It was a bright place with big windows and colorful murals of Greece on the walls. The food was terrific, and it was always so loud and busy that no one else could listen in on your conversation. Butch and Harry loved the place. Butch would bring practically his whole crew there for dinner, especially if he knew I was paying. For lunch, he came alone.

He had just come from a game of handball at his gym and was in a great mood. In fact, from the looks of it, he was on top of the world. The partner in all of his rackets, Harry Aleman, would be indisposed for a while—inside a federal penitentiary. The Feds caught him running a nationwide home invasion ring. Because it was a federal case, Marcy couldn't fix it like he could in the state courts.

With Harry in stir, Butch was the one collecting on all their deals and bookmakers. The Mob even had the gall to charge bettors two percent of their winnings for the Harry Aleman Defense Fund. Imagine how this went over with the bookmakers. Here's a guy who did more than anyone to terrorize them, and now these same people had to collect extra taxes to get him out of prison.

According to rumors, Butch still had the time to do an occasional extracurricular. Supposedly, he was one of the triggermen who'd killed Nick Velentzas. I wasn't about to pop that question over a plate of braised lamb. I already knew too much about the death of the Salesman. Instead, I settled up with Butch on fees he owed me for some gambling cases. Then we sat around bullshitting about nothing in particular. At one point, he looked at his watch and said, "Oops, I gotta run. I have to go meet somebody." Off he went. As usual, he stuck me with the check.

I was the last one to see Butch—or to talk about seeing him—before he disappeared. A few days later, his live-in girlfriend reported him missing. When that happened, you knew to expect the worst.

The pre-trial hearings on the Nick Velentzas extortion case continued right through January 1981. The murder of Nick barely slowed down the Feds. Just as I predicted to Marco, it was now that much harder for us to defend our clients. Every accusation Nick made to the grand jury was sure to ring true. He claimed he was being threatened by the Mob, and look what happened: They fucking killed him.

I prepared Frank for the worst, but he was the one who should have prepared me. He had a little piece of personal history that was far more dangerous to him than a federal case. It came out as Ed Genson cross-examined a policeman during the first day of trial. The cop testified that he had met Frank on a previous occasion.

Genson wanted to know what he had talked about with Frank, and the cop was evasive. Clearly, Genson knew something. He kept pressing, and the cop kept ducking and weaving. When the FBI agent got on the stand, the whole routine started over again. He had met Frank on a previous occasion. He, too, could not recall previous conversations. Something was going on.

When court recessed for the day, I got a call from the assistant U.S. attorney on the case. It was urgent and he had to see me right away. I went to his office in the Federal Building and he shut his door behind me. He said, "It's going to come out tomorrow that Frank Renella informed on some narcotics people a few years ago and got paid for the information. The agent tried to keep from saying it, but he's under oath and he has to tell the truth."

A death sentence would have been better news. As far as the Mob was concerned, once a stoolpigeon, always a stoolpigeon. It didn't matter who Frank Renella had informed on. They didn't care about what, where, or why. They would just kill him—to show what happens to informants.

Now I understood why Frank insisted that I be his lawyer on the case. Genson had a reputation for setting up his own clients when he found out they were informants. A few got whacked while he represented them. I was sure Eddy would tell Marco about Frank as soon as the Feds made it official.

From the Federal Building, I gave Frank a call and told him I had to see him right away. He gave me directions to his house, and I drove right there. He lived in a shitty neighborhood on the second floor of a two-flat. When he answered the door, he was in his T-shirt. Frank was pushing fifty, but he was still very lean and fit, with curly hair down to his shoulders and a strange, craggy face that could be terrifying. Food was on his kitchen table, and it looked like he was getting ready to eat.

"Frank," I said, "tomorrow I think the government witnesses are going to say you were an FBI informant."

Without saying a word, he went over to the kitchen drawer and pulled out a gun. He pointed it at me and said, "If you're setting me up, you're gonna be the first to get killed. If you're not, you're gonna have a serious problem."

"Wait, Frank," I said. "What are you doing? I've come to warn you. I'm your friend."

He asked, "Are you carrying a weapon?"

I unbuttoned my jacket to show him. "No."

He walked over to his refrigerator and opened the freezer compartment on the top. "If you're telling me the truth, then you'll probably need this," he said and pulled out a baggie. Inside it was a gun. A little five-shot. He handed it to me, still wrapped in the baggie, but kept his gun trained on me. He didn't bother to close the refrigerator. He opened up another drawer to pull out some bullets and gave me those, too.

He put on a jacket and looked out the window. Both sides of the street were lined with cars. I had had to park in front of a fire hydrant. Since he couldn't see anyone double-parked, it looked like he was in the clear. He motioned me toward the door. He said, "You go out first. If they're waiting for me, you're gonna get it first."

With his gun in my back, I walked down the steps and outside the building. Nobody was there. He led me down the street to his car. He got in. "You're on your own," he said. "I wish you luck." Then he drove away.

I went back home to have a quiet dinner with a girlfriend at Arnie's restaurant in my building. I had to be in court the next morning for Frank's case, so we went to bed by midnight. I hardly shut my eyes before the phone rang. It was a hit man from Marco's crew. Like a lot of those guys, I had given him money a couple of times to help him out of a jackpot. It was probably the best investment I ever made. He said, "Bob, they're gonna kill you," and he hung up the phone.

It didn't take much time for me to connect the dots. Genson must have already told Marco what he suspected about Frank. Marco must have then sent a crew after Frank. They broke into his apartment and found he had blown town. I was the only one who could have warned him.

Now I realized how serious this was. I knew Marco would be mad. I thought he might yell at me, but killing me was something else. Just a few minutes later my phone rang again. It was another member of Marco's crew. This one owed me some money and he asked that we meet later that night, so he could pay me back. The fucking idiots. Like I was a complete moron. Like that was going to work on me. I told him I was busy and hung up.

For practically the first time in my life I had trouble sleeping. If not for the warning from the hit man, I would have been dead. I couldn't let Marco think I tipped off Frank, so I came up with a crazy idea. I handwrote a statement for Frank, explaining that "he feared for his life," and that "certain persons would make sure he did not, in fact, appear in court," and signed Frank's name.

The next morning, I went to Federal Court and sat there like Mickey the Mope, waiting with everyone else for my client to show up. Court is supposed to start at nine o'clock, but by nine-twenty there was still no sign of Frank Renella.

Out of the corner of my eye I could see Genson smirking like Jolly St. Nick, hands crossed on his big belly. He couldn't have been happier with my predicament.

Finally the judge looked down at me. His name was George Leighton. He was a real straight black guy who did not fool around with the First Ward. He said, "Mr. Cooley, do you have any idea where your client is?"

I told him that some FBI agents went to see him the night before to tell him that he would be identified as an informant. Then I handed the judge the statement. He decided to proceed with the trial anyway. For the rest of the day, I sat in court and watched the proceedings without my client—like a player in a band who forgot his instrument.

The copper and the FBI agent got back on the witness stand and their testimony could not have been worse for Frank. Or me. In addition to saying that Renella had been a prior informant, the FBI agent claimed that he had also fingered Butch as one of the guys who whacked Nick. Maybe Frank figured that Butch was dead, and this would get the Feds off his back.

I knew Genson reported all of this back to Marco. I went straight home after court and didn't even go out to eat. Again I got another call, just before midnight. It was from one of my bookie clients. "We have a guy in custody," he said, "and we need to get him out. If you can meet me, I'll give you the cash for bail." It was another trap to whack me. I said I was too busy, and they would have to find somebody else.

The night before, I had hoped that Marco was having one of his fits and just lashed out in anger. But now one thing was clear: He wasn't going to give me a pass.

The next day, I repeated my little solo act in court and again my client was a no-show. Once court was in session, we all made another show about waiting for my client. Again, after fifteen minutes, Judge Leighton said, "Apparently, he's not here, so it looks like we may have to issue a warrant for his arrest."

"Okay, Judge," I said. "What can I tell you?"

Then the judge asked, "Did you get paid your full fee on this case, counsel?" Clearly he knew what was going on. "If you want to put in a request to get paid from the court, I'll consider it."

I said, "No, that's okay, Judge."

As I left the courthouse, I thought, "Now what?" I knew that Marco's people would be out looking for me. Instead of going to my office, I went back home. I threw some clothes into a suitcase, along with a big pile of cash, and headed to the airport. From there, I caught the next plane to San Francisco.

During the flight, I felt a lot of emotions—mostly anger. Marco had no fucking reason to kill me. I had done nothing wrong to him. I just didn't want someone killed again like Nick Velentzas. I was not going to step over that line.

But I was mostly mad at Marcy and D'Arco. Marco may have been an animal, but he would have never tried to whack me without their permission. I had done so much for the First Ward—things no other lawyer could do. I never crossed them or harmed them in any way. But by this time, I knew them too well to be surprised by anything. If they disgusted me, I had to be that much more disgusted with myself.

In San Francisco, I stayed with an old friend. He had a very successful business and absolutely no connections with the law or the Mob. I explained that I had to keep low for a while. I said, "Something is going on. I can't tell you what." He knew enough about my life in Chicago not to ask any further questions.

I could have hid out with him for a long time; but, after a week, I started thinking, "What am I going to do?" It was only a matter of time before I ran out of cash. If I tried to go somewhere else to practice law, the Mob would be sure to track me down. I couldn't imagine living on the run.

I only had one option: Go back and confront Marco. I had to straighten it out with him once and for all.

I returned to Chicago, but stayed very low. I didn't want any Mob people to know I was in town. I couldn't call Marco to arrange a meeting. It would give him a chance to set up an ambush. Instead, I had to catch *him* off guard. Fortunately, he was an absolute creature of habit. I knew every place he went for lunch and the day he went there. I decided that the best place to surprise him was a small, family-style Italian restaurant. It was in a storefront with big plate-glass windows.

To help me out, I called a good friend who was an undercover cop. I picked him up in my car and parked directly in front of the restaurant. The space had a No Parking sign, but I wanted my friend to be able to look inside and see what was happening there. I didn't tell him the reason for my meeting, but I warned him, "Keep your eyes open. If something goes wrong, I may need help in a hurry." I packed some personal protection as well: a snub-nosed Smith & Wesson Airweight, which I now carried all the time, and, for heavy artillery, a .45-caliber pistol.

I saw Marco's Chrysler Fifth Avenue parked down the block, so I knew he was inside. I got out of my car and quickly walked into the restaurant. There was Marco, in the center of the dining room, sitting at a table with four of the biggest, toughest guys in his crew, including Tony Doty and Donny Scalise. When I walked over to them, they all froze and stared, as though I had come back from the dead. I said, "Marc, let me talk to you for a minute."

I walked with him into the little bathroom and locked the door behind us. I wasn't afraid of him. I knew Marco wasn't packing, because the police could arrest him for carrying a gun. Physically, he was no match for me either. He would have to hear me out. I said, "I'm telling this to your face: Frank wasn't doing anything to cause you people a problem. A few years ago, he worked with the Feds to put away some dope dealers. That was it. He was never cooperating against you. I knew you were going to kill him, but he was my client and I had to warn him. I owed him that."

Marco gave me his squint-eyed stare and said, "What the fuck is the matter with you? You should know better. You were working for us, not your fucking client."

Then, referring to Ed Genson, he said, "The Fat Man did the right thing when he told us about Frank. You report to us first. You, you asshole, had to stick your nose where it didn't belong. What kind of example does that set for the other lawyers? As far as I'm concerned, you'll never get business from us again."

I said, "Marc, that's fine. I don't care about the business. I know you guys are pissed about Frank, but I've done nothing wrong. I did nothing to hurt you people. If you're looking to do something to me, it ain't going to happen. I ain't taking no beating. I'm packing and I'm packing wherever I am. If anyone comes around me, I'll fucking kill him. I got somebody out in front with me right now. He knows exactly what's going on. If I think something is going to happen, I'll kill you right now as we stand here."

When I opened the bathroom door, I didn't know what to expect, but there was Marco's crew, sitting at the table exactly where we left them. Classic mobsters. You took away the boss and they didn't know what to do—like a snake with its head cut off. I walked out of the restaurant, got into my car, and drove off.

The next day I went to court and then drove to my office at 100 North LaSalle. Like the old days, I parked my car in the bus stop, right in front of Counsellors Row. When I walked through the restaurant, I saw Pat

Marcy sitting there at the First Ward table. Suddenly, he was all hale and hearty. "Hey, how you doing, Bob?" he said. "Gee, haven't seen you in a while. Where you been? Vegas?" It was one of the few times I ever saw him laugh.

I nodded and went to my office. Pat may not have known where I was, but he definitely knew why I left. He never once called my office during the entire week I was away. For years he had been calling me at least two or three times a week.

Later that day, I saw Johnny D'Arco and Patty DeLeo. It was like nothing had ever happened to me. Like I hadn't even been gone for an hour. Nobody bothered to ask, "Where were you? What were you doing? Was something wrong?" Obviously, they knew that there was a problem.

Now, more than ever, I just had to get away from these people, but I had to be careful how I did it. If they thought I was totally pissed off or afraid, they might worry about me going to the Feds. I needed some other excuse.

In fact, I still wasn't sure that my problem with Marco was completely over. I carried my guns all the time. Getting shot or even killed was not my biggest worry. My worst fear was torture. These feelings would only be reinforced with the discovery of Butch Petrocelli's body, just a few weeks after my return from California. He was found in March 1981, on the floor of a car parked in some lousy neighborhood on the South Side. The remains were partly decomposed, but they could tell that Butch's mouth had been wrapped shut with duct tape. In that same way, they had bound his hands to his chest. Worse yet, the pathologist said his eyes and nuts had been melted away with a blowtorch, but it was the suffocation that killed him. He literally screamed to death. A few open cans of gasoline were alongside him in the car near some blackened upholstery. The police figured that someone threw a match inside, but then shut the door with the windows closed. The glass got scorched, so you couldn't see inside, but no air was left to keep the fire going.

A few days after the body was found, I happened to bump into Harry Aleman's brother, Anthony, and said, "Geez, that's terrible what happened to Butch."

Anthony's face turned red, and he hissed, "That fucking dirty no-good rat. He was a stoolpigeon cocksucker." Unlike Harry, Anthony was not a real bad-guy type. I never heard him talk that way before. Still, I didn't argue with him. "Okay," I said. "That's a shock to me." But I was thinking, "Butch was no more a stoolpigeon than the man in the moon."

Besides, if Butch had been a stoolpigeon, they would have left his body out in the open somewhere—as an example. They wouldn't have tried to burn the corpse. Eventually we got another explanation for why he was killed, and this one made more sense. At some point, the bosses did the math and figured Butch had kept some of the money for the Harry Aleman Defense Fund. They probably tortured him to find out where he hid it.

I had no illusions about Butch Petrocelli. Like Tony Borsellino, he was a vicious killer. But he was always loyal to the Mob bosses. I saw with my own eyes how he would meet Marcy at Counsellors Row practically every Thursday afternoon. If they could turn on Butch and torture him so horribly for a piece of cheese, they could turn on anyone.

CHAPTER 7

CHICKEN WITH WING

F or a long time after my beef with Marco, I became unbelievably cautious. I always carried at least one gun on me, even
when I went to court (the guards let me walk around the metal
detector). I kept another pistol in the glove compartment of
my car. I became much more careful about the places I went. When I
had to collect on fees or bets, I didn't go anywhere strange; when I met
with people for the first time, I did so only in public. I would never get
into a car with someone sitting behind me. If I was offered a lift, I'd say,
"I'll drive. I have to be somewhere later." I got into the habit of getting
on my hands and knees to check under my car each morning. When I
drove, if I looked through my rearview mirror and thought someone
was following me, I'd take a sharp turn into an alley, or, on the freeway,
would suddenly slow down to see if he'd pass.

My whole lifestyle changed. There were no more Thursday night
dinners with Pat Marcy. I stopped going to Faces and other clubs
where I knew the crews hung out. I didn't want to be with those
people at two in the morning and get caught from behind in a
parking lot.

Now, in the worst way, I wanted to break up my partnership with
Kugler, D'Arco and DeLeo and get my office out of 100 North LaSalle.
But I needed an excuse. Otherwise, they might get suspicious. Fortunately, Patty DeLeo came to my rescue. He asked me to help out a bookmaker and told me it was a "Ward case." This meant the bookie was
someone connected to the First Ward, like a precinct captain, and I
should do it for nothing. I was always happy to help their workers. I

took this bookie to court, and, in short order, his case was thrown out. A few weeks later, I bumped into him at a benefit for Johnny.

Just joking around, I asked, "Are you staying out of trouble?"

"I can't afford to get caught," he said. "You guys are too expensive."

I thought, "What the fuck?" but I didn't act surprised. "We didn't charge you that much, did we?"

"*I* think you did," he said. "A thousand dollars! And you were only in court for a few minutes."

I tried to commiserate and explain the cost of overhead and other such happy bullshit, but out of the corner of my eye, I saw Patty DeLeo walk into the room. I excused myself and went up to him. I pointed out the bookie. "Patty," I said, "I just saw your friend over there and he told me something interesting."

"What's that?" Patty took a quick look at him but was pretty nonchalant.

"He told me he paid you a thousand dollars on his case."

Pat's face took on a surprised look. "But I told you that, didn't I?"

I said, "No, Patty. You didn't. You told me that he was a Ward Case."

Patty pulled a billfold from his pocket and counted out $500—a total admission that he had cheated me. In any other circumstances, I would have been pissed, but now I couldn't have been happier.

The next day, I put on a gloomy face and sat down with Senior. I said, "I think I want to break away from our relationship."

His mouth dropped. "Why?" he asked.

"Patty cheated me," I said. "And I'm sure he's cheating Johnny, too. I just don't want to deal with that."

"What? Are you crazy?" Senior said. "You really want to give up the kind of money you're making with us?"

I said, "I'll work out arrangements with Johnny when he comes back from Springfield. It's time we part ways."

Senior kept shaking his head. "Give it some more thought," he said.

Of course I had to run this by Marcy, too. He suggested I have it out with DeLeo in front of Senior. I replied, "I'm not going to have Senior choose between his son-in-law and me. You guys have to have DeLeo around, but I can't trust him as a partner, so I really shouldn't be involved with the firm any more."

Marcy nodded. What could he say? We both knew that Patty DeLeo could be a snake, but he was also smart and ambitious in ways that Johnny was not. I was sure that they were grooming DeLeo to take over the First Ward after Pat Marcy died.

Fortunately, the lease on my office had just run out. With the partnership dissolved, I had a good excuse to move a block down LaSalle Street to share offices with another lawyer. I explained that I was helping him out and saving on rent in the process. That made sense to everyone and didn't ruffle any feathers. I still did a lot of gambling business, especially with independent bookmakers who were paying street tax. Besides, even after I broke off the partnership, a lot of the other First Ward people kept their cases with me. The only exception was Marco, and I wanted nothing to do with him anyway.

Although my office was not in 100 North LaSalle, I dropped by Counsellors Row for lunch almost every day. I did my best to keep away from the First Ward table when Pat Marcy or Johnny were there. I would say, "Hi," or give them a friendly nod, but would not spend much time talking to them.

My strategy was always two steps forward and one step back. Although I tried to put more distance between myself and the First Ward, I wanted to be visible, so no one would ask, "Where's Bob?" and worry about what I was doing or who I was talking to.

But after a few months of this new life, I was still looking over my shoulder all the time. I knew that people in the Mob had long memories. When they were ready to whack you, they wanted you to think everything was all right so you would drop your guard. In fact, I had seen that happen four times: with the bookmaker Anthony Reitinger, Sam Anarino, Tony Borsellino, and Butch Petrocelli. All were equally clueless when they got up from their "last meal" with me and went to their deaths. Besides, I had already watched Marco in action and how he could lash out in a rage—for no apparent reason.

To feel safe again, I had to know that I was still important to the First Ward. If I worked for them on big cases, no one would be allowed to touch me. It was the only way to find peace of mind. Wherever I moved or whatever I did, everything still circled back to Pat Marcy. Once more, I needed his approval.

It came in July 1981, when I got a call from Alderman Fred Roti. He said, "Pat Marcy wants you to represent some people on a case."

I breathed easier than I had for months. The Marco beef was finally in the past and they were ready to use me again.

The case was only weeks from trial, but it sounded pretty straightforward: something to do with a shooting between two Chinese gangs in Chicago's Chinatown. One group was known as the Ghost Shadows; behind the scenes, they had become the enforcers for the On Leong Chinese Merchants Association in Chinatowns across the country. Among the four defendants in the case was Lenny Chow, one of the Ghost Shadows' top hit men. If he was convicted and started talking to the Feds, he could cause problems for a lot of powerful people in the Chinese community.

"Go meet this guy, Wilson Moy," Fred told me. Moy was like the unofficial mayor of Chinatown, and I knew he paid Roti to keep the cops away from the Chinese gambling parlors. He didn't want to be seen with Roti or Marcy, so close to the Lenny Chow trial. Fred said, "Don't bring him around Counsellors and don't meet him in your office, and when you see him, don't indicate you have a relationship with us."

When I got back to my office, there was a message from Moy and I returned his call. For a minute, I wondered if this wasn't a ploy to set me up, so I arranged to meet Moy for lunch at Arnie's Outdoor Café, just off Rush Street and alongside my apartment building. If they were going to kill me, it would have to be in plain sight of a busy street corner.

But Moy walked in all alone. Tall and thin, in his late fifties, he was dressed in a conservative suit and had the look of a professor. As he filled me in on the case, he was extremely nervous. Up to this time, he explained, On Leong had paid for an experienced criminal defense lawyer, but Moy thought the lawyer charged too much. "If you can guarantee an acquittal," he said, "we will switch our lawyers."

I would *never* tell anyone straight out that I could fix a case, or guarantee a verdict. For all I knew, he was wearing a wire. Instead, I told him that I almost never lost a trial. The real issue was what fee I should charge. Before I could tell him that, I had to look at the police report. If the state had a good case against Lenny Chow, I would charge a high fee. If not, I would charge a lower one. I said I'd call him back after I checked into it.

The next day, I met Marcy at Counsellors Row. Moy did surprise me with one piece of information: Pat had gotten the case assigned to Judge Thomas J. Maloney. Before Pat made him a judge, Maloney had been a criminal defense lawyer, and I bounced him from the Harry Aleman trial, despite Harry's objections.

"There might be a problem with me handling the case if Tom Maloney is the judge," I told Pat. "You know Maloney and I don't get along. He hates me."

Marcy totally dismissed my concern. "That won't be a problem. I'll take care of that," he said. Pat just wanted to make sure Moy would hire me.

"I'm sure I can convince him," I said.

"Then try to get $50,000 if you can," Pat said.

Once again, Marcy used his contacts to get me the police report for the case, and I read it over before I met Moy. The state's evidence against Lenny Chow depended on the testimony of the victim's three fellow gangbangers, who were nearby when he was shot. They were all in a renegade offshoot of the Ghost Shadows, and had tried to muscle protection money from Chicago Chinatown businesses. After they beat up a restaurant owner, the On Leong called in Ghost Shadows from New York to straighten these guys out. When the bad boys pulled their car up in front of the On Leong headquarters, Lenny Chow and the other Ghost Shadows appeared on the balcony with automatics. They sprayed the car with at least twenty bullets. The victim, William Chin, couldn't get out from behind the wheel. Somehow he survived the shooting, but he was still in bad shape.

The whole case looked pretty shaky for the prosecutors. First of all, their key witnesses were admitted gang members who had done bad things. Secondly, they didn't speak English that well. Who knew what words the cops had put in their mouths during translation? This was a classic throw-out case for a bench trial.

I met with Wilson Moy again the next day. I was still careful about what I said. I didn't come straight out and say I would fix the case. Instead, I offered him something like a Chinese menu. I said, "I'll charge you $50,000 for a jury trial. But you know, you can never be certain about a jury verdict. If you go for a bench trial, with just a judge and no jury, that will cost $100,000." I told him that the verdicts were always more predictable with a bench trial.

"That's a lot of money," Moy said. "Can you do it any cheaper?"

I stuck to my guns, and Moy said he would have to check with the national leaders of On Leong in New York. The next time we met, he shook my hand and said, "We're going to hire you, but we want the $100,000 trial."

I told him to give me a check for $10,000 as a retainer. "Is it okay if I give you cash?" he asked.

"Oh, sure," I said.

After seeing Moy, I went back to Counsellors Row and told Pat I could get $100,000 from On Leong. He couldn't believe it. But when I asked for $50,000 as my cut, he said, "Oh, no, no. We can't do that. You know the judge will want a lot, too." I settled for $25,000.

I then started my work on the case. Even if it was fixed, I wanted to give the judge good solid reasons for an acquittal. Moy arranged for me to meet the witnesses. To set everything up, On Leong brought in Chan Kwok Wing, probably the biggest Chinese guy I ever saw. He had a barrel chest and legs like tree trunks. He was supposed to be very proficient in karate, and he walked around with one of those dark martial-arts stares. All the gang members knew about him, and they were scared to death of him. When he showed up, people could die.

They booked a suite for Wing at the Ambassador West, an older hotel just off Rush Street. He could stay in one room and we could meet the witnesses in the other. When I saw the three witnesses, I couldn't believe how young they looked—like three little kids.

Wing gave each one a withering stare, and he spoke to them in harsh barking tones. They were literally shaking in their shoes.

I said, "I know you guys don't speak English that well and when the police interrogated you, they might have misunderstood you."

They all nodded their heads.

"From what I'm told, you didn't recognize Lenny Chow during the lineup, but that's not what the police wrote in their reports."

They nodded again. In truth, they really didn't speak much English and were probably illegal immigrants. The gangs smuggled them in from China to do their dirty work. I told Wing to set up a meeting with a leader of the Ghost Shadows so we could get these three back in that gang and on their payroll.

During the weeks leading up to the trial, Wing and I became good pals. Now that I was working with Marcy again, I wasn't worried about going to the clubs on Rush Street, and I took Wing along. I also arranged for him to stay with Rosie the Madam. He had a thing for her blonde call girls. He ended up saving a lot of money on hotels, but I'm not sure he got much sleep.

Everything seemed to be going smoothly until the victim, William Chin, went back into the hospital and died from infections to his bullet wounds. Now, the charge of attempted murder became actual murder. Typically, a judge would put the defendant back into custody and demand a higher bail. That certainly would have made sense for my client, Lenny Chow, who didn't have ties to Chicago and had never surrendered his passport. But Maloney ruled that we could "transfer" the attempted-murder bond to a new bond for the murder charge. When the prosecutors tried to object, in his typical fashion Maloney barked, "Don't speak up in this court."

No one could believe that Maloney would do something as fishy as transferring the bond. The trial hadn't even started and it smelled like the fix was in. But nothing Maloney did surprised me. In fact, just before the bond hearing, Marcy pulled me aside at Counsellors Row and said, "You have to bring in Herb Barsy on this case."

"Who is Herb Barsy?" I asked.

"He's a lawyer and a friend of Judge Maloney, and the judge wants you to use him. In fact, the judge wants him to be the lead."

This was classic Maloney: a last-minute move to humiliate me. He knew it was too late for me to back out or put up a fuss. I said to Pat, "Okay, I'll hire him." I went to meet Barsy, and, much as I thought, he

was a milquetoast guy who usually carried the bags for the more powerful lawyers in his firm. When I said I would only pay him $2,300, he
quickly agreed. I had my own ideas about who would be the lead
lawyer on this case, but I wasn't going to discuss them with Barsy or
Marcy before the trial.

If you looked at our backgrounds, you would have thought that Tom
Maloney and I might have been friends instead of such bitter enemies.
Like me, he came from the South Side; went to Mount Carmel, where
he did some boxing; and started out as a cop. But from there, all resemblance ended. He was a graduate of the University of Maryland and
John Marshall Law School. Hulking in size, he had flowing white hair
and a ruddy complexion. After he became a lawyer, he put on airs along
with his fancy suits. Unless you were someone who could help his
career, he talked down to you, like you were hard of hearing or mentally
defective. Meanwhile, Mr. High-and-Mighty was defending some of the
worst scumbag narcotics dealers in the city, fucking their girlfriends,
and hanging out in the bars where they did their deals. He was under
federal investigation when Marcy got the state's Supreme Court to
appoint him a full Circuit Court judge immediately after the Aleman
trial (just as Harry predicted).

Once he got behind the bench, Maloney grew even more pompous
and overbearing. He screamed at court clerks and bailiffs like they were
his servants. He had no problem with waltzing into court late and kept
everyone around into the night when that suited him. If defense lawyers
were not paying him off, he belittled them in court and buried their
clients under ridiculously severe sentences. He put as many men on
Death Row as any judge in the system, and held himself out as the ultimate protector of Law and Order. In fact, for the right price, he would
let anyone off for any crime. Absolutely anyone. I couldn't stand his
bullshit hypocrisy. We were bound to be on a collision course—just by
being in the same courtroom.

The state's case against Lenny Chow and the three other shooters
opened with the investigating detective. The coppers had someone
approach me before the trial to see if I would pay them all off to alter
their testimony. Because I turned him down, they decided to embellish

on all the things they put in their reports. When it was time for cross-examination, I got up to tear the detective a new asshole.

Before I could speak, Barsy tapped me on the shoulder. "What are you doing?" he asked.

"The cross."

Under his breath, Barsy said, "But the judge wants me to do it."

"Come on," I told him. "I'm doing this for his own good."

By the time I finished cross-examining the cop, he looked like a total idiot. But later, when I went back to Counsellors Row, Pat Marcy glared at me and motioned toward the rear of the restaurant. "You were supposed to take a back seat in this case," he hissed. "The judge is all upset because you're trying to be a big shot again."

"Pat, I'm trying to give the judge a case," I said. "How can you expect me to sit there and watch it fall apart? If I don't cross-examine the witnesses when they get on the stand tomorrow, there's no telling what they will say."

He waved at me in disgust and walked away.

The next day, another policeman came to the stand again. He testified that in the hospital, shortly after the shooting, William Chin made a "Deathbed Statement," identifying Lenny Chow as the shooter. Usually Deathbed Statements carry a lot of weight with a jury. You tend to think a dying man will be truthful if he knows he's about to meet his Maker.

But Chin did not make the supposed statement on his deathbed. He was released from the hospital and died months later. There was plenty of time in between to take a normal statement. Secondly, there was conflicting testimony about what he actually said in the hospital—from the nurse and copper who were with him. The nurse testified that he mumbled something, but she couldn't make it out. After she left the room, the detective claimed, Chin suddenly spoke up loud and clear, and said, "Lenny shot me." This was quite a feat, since he barely spoke English.

I couldn't let the copper get away with that bullshit, so I got up to cross-examine him. Out of the corner of my eye, I could see Maloney turning different colors of red, once again in a rage that I took the lead.

This time the judge was going to show me who was boss. Against all the prior case law and common sense, Maloney admitted the Deathbed Statement into evidence. I couldn't believe it. He just made it harder on himself to throw out the case.

After he finished reading his decision, Maloney gave me a smirk. This whole trial had become a game of chicken between him and me, but I sure as hell wasn't going to blink first. The gang members were called to testify and, again, I told Barsy I would lead the cross-examination. "These kids recognize me," I said. "If they see you, they may think you're the prosecutor and who knows what they'll say."

When I got up, Maloney looked at me with daggers. He kept staring at me like that for the rest of the day. Meanwhile, Wing, from his seat in the spectator's gallery, was doing his own laser stares right through each witness. According to plan, they recanted the incriminating testimony they had given the police.

I brought Wing back to Counsellors Row to celebrate, but Marcy was in no mood for a party. I left Wing at the bar and followed Marcy as he stormed into the back of the restaurant. This time he screamed loud enough for everyone in Counsellors to hear. "I told you to keep your mouth shut and to sit there and do nothing, and you wouldn't listen."

"Pat," I said, "when I told you last night that I had to cross-examine the witnesses, you walked away. You never told me *not* to cross-examine."

He couldn't argue with that. "This fucking Maloney is nuts," I said. "There was no way any other judge would allow a Deathbed Statement into evidence. He's made a case where there wasn't one. I'm trying to give him grounds to throw it out."

"You're like two fucking kids," Pat said.

I promised him I'd keep quiet the rest of the trial.

Wing and I stayed out late that night, and the next morning we had a nice leisurely breakfast. Maloney had yet to show up for court before 11:00. I was going to be goddamned if I sat around waiting for him again. We walked into court at 10:45, and wouldn't you know, it was the one day the judge was on time. Everybody else—the prosecutors, the witnesses, Barsy—was waiting for us. As soon as he saw me, Maloney started yelling, "Counsel, do you know what time court starts?"

I said, "Judge, the last two days, you didn't come in here until after eleven, and since I had an important matter to take care of . . ."

"Just sit down," he said. As I went to my chair, I could see all the court personnel smiling big-time.

I let Barsy do the rest of the cross-examinations, and the state brought its case to a close. According to the script for your typical fixed bench trial, we then made a motion for a Directed Finding. This was the perfect opportunity for the judge to throw out the case. Maloney had every reason to do so, because the main witnesses to the shooting had recanted their testimony.

But instead, to ram it up my ass one more time, Maloney overruled the motion and told us to put on our case. "Go ahead," he said, "and call your first witness."

Herb looked at me and said, "What are we going to do?"

I said, "Herb, we're not putting anybody on the stand. We rest."

Herb almost died. "What are you talking about?"

"Herb," I whispered, "I'm not calling a witness to let this jagoff judge make a case where there is none." I then stood up and announced to the court, "We rest."

I sat back down and kept my eyes on Maloney, thinking, "Okay, you idiot. What are you going to do now?"

Maloney didn't know what to do. He sputtered and hemmed and hawed.

I truly didn't give a fuck if he found Lenny Chow guilty. We had received only $10,000 up front from Moy. I thought, "Let him face the wrath of Pat Marcy, if he blows this case and $90,000 for us."

Finally, Maloney said, "Well, I'll make my decision tomorrow."

Later, when I saw Marcy at Counsellors Row, I said, "I did what I could to protect the judge. He's a total jagoff. You better straighten him out or he's going to fuck us."

"I've already talked to him," Pat said.

Walking into court the next day, I had no idea what Maloney would do—whether his ego and hatred of me would overcome his fear of

Marcy. Wing let me know we had something else to worry about. He said, "I should tell you. The family of William Chin is going to have all of us killed if the judge finds Lenny not guilty."

We then sat back and watched as Maloney read out his decision. It was almost worth the aggravation of the trial. In essence, he said, yes, he did admit the Deathbed Statement, but no, that didn't mean the dying man knew what he was talking about. How could he have seen Lenny Chow shoot from the balcony if he was behind the wheel of the car? It was the most convoluted piece of bullshit I ever heard.

I had Wing hustle the three witnesses out of the courthouse and into my car. When we drove them back to their hotel, I called some detective friends on the police force. I asked them to take the kids to O'Hare Airport and stay with them until they got on the plane to New York.

From the hotel, Wing and I went back to my apartment. I had a couple of guns on me, but I got another for Wing. I said, "We're going to go to Chinatown and collect that $90,000."

Wilson Moy waited for us in front of his gift shop surrounded by a delegation of other Chinese merchants. It was like a meeting of the Rotary Club. Once we were in his store, he handed me $40,000 in cash in something that looked like a fat FedEx envelope. When I asked for the rest, he said I would have to go to New York and see the On Leong national president, Eddie Chan. "He wants to meet you in person," Moy said.

I took the money back to Counsellors Row. Alderman Roti led me to his City Hall office across the street, where he took out the bundles of cash and counted them. He gave me my $5,000, and stuffed the rest in his jacket and pants pockets. I grabbed copy paper from his desk and put that in the FedEx envelope, so when I took it out of his office, it looked as full as when I brought it in.

Later, when I told Pat about going to New York for the remaining $50,000, he wasn't too happy, but what could he do? Grudgingly he agreed, and he added, "Don't make any stops in Atlantic City on the way back."

I flew to New York with Wing. Ghost Shadow gang kids waited for us at the gate to carry our luggage. Outside the airport, they put us into one Mercedes and a group followed us in another. We drove right to a funeral home on Mott Street in New York City's Chinatown. This was the headquarters of Eddie Chan, national president of the On Leong Merchants Association. We walked upstairs to a reception area where the walls and doors were made of mahogany. Wing went into the office and came out with Eddie's two bodyguards. One was a huge black guy who looked like some kind of weightlifter. The other was a short, dumpy white guy. As I found out later, he was a U.S. Marshal, which meant he was licensed to carry a gun on a commercial airline. Eddie never went anywhere without a U.S. Marshal.

They led me into a huge office, and Eddie rose from behind his desk to give me a greeting. He was a man in his fifties, round-faced and over-weight, with a military bearing—like those Chinese generals you saw in the newsreels. All over the walls, there were pictures of Eddie shaking hands with mayors, presidents, and governors. He had been a staff sergeant for the Hong Kong police force and, in 1975, when the government there investigated police corruption, he moved to New York and brought forty crooked cops with him. Besides investing in souvenir shops, restaurants, and funeral homes, he tried to control the gangs like the Ghost Shadows so he could get a piece of their narcotics and gambling business. A novel and movie called *Year of the Dragon* was based on a character with a similar background. When I sat down by Eddie's desk, he leaned close to me and said, in somewhat broken English, "Give all your money to Wing."

I looked at Wing and thought, "What's this about?"

Wing said, "He doesn't want you to spend any money while you're our guest. I told him how you took care of me in Chicago and picked up all the bills. Now we can do the same for you."

This was a shocker. The Mob bosses in Chicago were so tight, they squeaked. "Can't I have a little money for tips?" I asked.

"No, no," Eddie said. "You don't spend any money here." I emptied my wallet and Eddie put the money in one of his drawers.

We then headed over to a street in Chinatown that was lined with restaurants. We went into one and climbed the stairs to a private banquet room on the second floor. It was filled with On Leong people from all over the country. Like Eddie and Moy, they were prosperous-looking guys in suits. Eddie took me around the room, and I had to shake hands and say hello to each one. We then sat down at a huge round table. Eddie was on one side of me, and Wing on the other. They had a banquet spread out on beautiful china serving dishes, and the whole table spun like a lazy susan. I was probably looking at the finest Chinese delicacies, but there was not a single thing I wanted to taste. I was still the picky eater who drove my mother crazy. Anything with vegetables or funny sauces just turned my stomach. Everyone in the hall sat watching, waiting for me to eat. Finally, I turned to Wing and said, "Explain to Eddie that I'm allergic to vegetables."

This created a whole commotion, and the next thing I knew, they were making a special banquet for me with just steak and seafood. As we ate, and I listened to Eddie, I realized that Wing had laid it on thick about how well I did during the trial and all the connections I had in Chicago—with the cops and the Mob. Later on, Eddie said, "We want you to be our lawyer and travel all over the country for us."

"Sure," I replied. Now this whole event made sense. Eddie wanted to pave the way for me with the other On Leong leaders.

"I would like to come to Chicago some day," Eddie said, "but I can't."

"Why not?" I asked.

"Because some people there want to kill me. If I come, can you make sure I'm safe?" he asked.

"I can arrange that," I said. "I'll have someone pick you up and stay with you the whole time you're in the city."

In fact, I would have never introduced Eddie to any Mob guy for his protection. Instead, I worked out a deal with Gerard, a maitre d' at Arnie's, one of my favorite restaurants. He always carried a little gun in his pocket, and he put on a good show. He was a big, tough-looking Italian with a handlebar moustache. I told Eddie that he was a vicious hit man. Eddie paid him $500 a day whenever he came to town. Eddie usually had a U.S. Marshal with him, and all Gerard really had to do was drive them around.

For the next three years, I represented the On Leong Merchants Association in cities around the country: Boston, New Orleans, San Francisco, and Houston. Usually, one of their kids had killed a kid from another gang. Over that period, I became very tight with Eddie. If something came up during a case, I would fly to New York to see him on it. Every time we met, he had $5,000 in cash waiting, even if all we did was chat.

On Leong gave me the perfect excuse to move farther away from the Chicago Mob. They knew I was out of town a lot, so it was no big deal if I didn't show up in Counsellors Row every day or the clubs at night. Practically no one noticed when I moved to an apartment in the sleepy southwest suburb of Countryside. Just as quietly, I later moved my office to a place near Midway Airport, closer to where I lived. Once, an affluent, flashy image had been so important to me. Now, only my security really mattered.

On Leong also gave me an excuse to be much more picky about the cases I took. Although I still handled gambling arrests, I turned away the other garbage the Mob wanted me to fix, like narcotics cases. I had always refused to work on anything involving rapists or child molesters.

Sometimes, when I turned down a case, and the crime or the criminal disgusted me, I went behind the scenes to make sure it wasn't fixed. Once a drug dealer approached me because he knew the judge was a friend of mine. This judge would have probably given me every break in the world, but only because he was a real good guy. He would never have taken money for it. After I turned down the case, the dealer told me he had found someone else who could get to the judge. I knew that was bullshit, but I didn't want my friend to get a reputation. Before the trial, I called him and said, "I just turned this case down. You should know that the new lawyer says he's a good friend of yours, too. That's why he got the case." Enough said. The dealer got his bench trial, and the judge found him fucking guilty.

In December 1981, I helped stop the fix on another case that really bothered me. The defendants were two cops who beat a vagrant to death at a South Side El stop. They asked him to stop smoking, and when he didn't, they handcuffed him and pounded the living shit out of him. After they dumped him into a squad car, another cop piled on, but the guy was as good as dead by then, and charges against that cop were eventually dropped. Besides being a former mental patient, the victim was also black, so his death got the attention of the Reverend Jesse Jackson, and a bunch of protest rallies followed.

This was a classic "ink" case, but an important part of the story never made it into the press. One of the cops was related to Angelo LaPietra, the little king of the Chinatown group, and Hook wanted to make sure the case was fixed. Blackie Pesoli first approached me at Counsellors Row to handle it. I begged off, explaining I had trouble with cop cases and just didn't take them.

Instead, the First Ward turned to Samuel V. P. Banks, who was, in my humble opinion, the biggest buffoon practicing criminal law in Chicago. He even dressed the part of your Mob lawyer, with crazy shark-skin suits and loud ties. There was only one way to defend this case: Have one cop point the finger at the other for delivering the fatal blow. Each would need his own lawyer for that strategy; but despite this client conflict, Banks represented both cops. Hook's relative was probably the more culpable of the two, so the other cop really got the short end of the stick. Obviously, Banks expected a little help from the judge. That was his one and only ace in the hole.

If there had not been so much publicity, Marcy would have assigned the case to a judge like Maloney. But he would not have wasted Maloney's reputation on these small potatoes. The Mob reserved him for its own murderers or big payoffs. Instead, the case was assigned according to normal procedures and ended up with Circuit Court Judge Arthur Cieslik. Alderman Ed Burke was the political connection who had "made" Cieslik—in other words, he pulled the strings to get him appointed to the court. Burke assured everyone in the First Ward that he could get this judge to do what he wanted.

It so happened that I knew Cieslik pretty well and dropped by his chambers all the time to chat with him. Meanwhile, I also knew Burke, who was a lesser light at the First Ward table in Counsellors Row. Even though I didn't take the case, during the ten days of the cops' trial, I was pretty actively involved.

Once I had been friendly with Ed Burke and his wife, Anne. Along with Patty DeLeo and his wife, the Burkes had had dinner with me at Greco's several times. Ed and I were about the same age, and, like me, he had been a cop for a few years before he passed the bar. But Ed's father had been an alderman, and he had always been groomed for a political career. The second youngest alderman ever elected to Chicago's City Council, Ed was smart and handsome, and had a full head of silvery hair. If it hadn't been for the Daley dynasty, I think he would have seen himself as mayor some day. But Ed was always a little too slick for his own good. On the one hand, he wanted to project a squeaky-clean public image as a churchgoing, devout Irish Catholic, but on the other, he hung out with Marcy, Alderman Roti, and the rest of the First Ward crowd. Behind the scenes, he worked quite a few lowlife deals for the Mob. At least Fred Roti had the decency to stay out of the limelight. Ed Burke always wanted it both ways.

With the cops' trial, Ed tried to pull a typical Pat Marcy. He gave Judge Cieslik a full-court press to acquit the cops. Only Ed didn't know the judge like I did. This guy was no pushover. Short and ornery, with a dark, craggy face and a beetle brow, Cieslik had a knack for rubbing everyone the wrong way. Even though he was a state-minded judge, the prosecutors hated him as much as the defense lawyers. The first time we met, I tried to get a good plea out of him for my client, and when he wouldn't give it to me, I took the case to a jury trial. I got an acquittal. In the bargain, I won his respect too. From then on, he would call me into his chambers and sometimes talk out of school about an ongoing trial or decision he was about to make. I think he appreciated my understanding of juries or how the public might see things. But nothing I could say would ever make him do something wrong. He was as honest and incorruptible as a judge could be.

During an early part of the cops' case, I stopped by Cieslik's chambers to chat. He was amazed that both cops were using Sam Banks as their lawyer. He asked me, "Why didn't they get someone to represent the other one?"

I just shrugged my shoulders.

He then said, "The state has a case. It has a good case."

I said, "Then do what you think is right."

He kept mumbling, "Why didn't he get someone to represent the other one?"

In Counsellors Row, after the first day of trial, I saw Patty DeLeo and Sam Banks at the First Ward table. I went to sit down with them. At that moment, Ed Burke entered the restaurant through the lobby door and joined us. They all started talking about the trial, and Sam whined to Patty DeLeo, "This judge is giving me a hard time."

Burke snapped at him, "Don't worry about it."

But Patty was worried—probably about pissing off LaPietra if his relative got convicted. Patty said to Burke, "Are you sure? There better not be a problem."

"It's only a fucking nigger," Burke said. "I can't see what's the big deal."

By this point, Burke's Fourteenth Ward, on the Southwest Side, probably had more blacks than whites. I thought, "Boy, if some of his voters could hear him now."

The more Banks moaned about the judge, the more my respect grew for Cieslik. The next day, I again popped into his chambers to help keep him strong.

He said, "Ed Burke keeps telling me that this is a First Ward case. That the First Ward will be very upset if I find the cops guilty." He knew about the First Ward's connections with the Mob and was worried they would physically harm him or his family. But I knew the First Ward would never touch a judge, so I lied a little to calm him down.

I said, "I saw Eddie Burke last night at Counsellors Row. He's the *Fourteenth* Ward. He's the only one pushing you on this case. The First Ward is not involved. They have nothing to do with this."

Now I had to see this trial for myself. The next day I watched a few hours of testimony. Witness after witness got up to describe the way the two cops mercilessly beat the victim while he was in handcuffs. Banks tried to claim he was resisting arrest and threw himself to the ground headfirst.

When I went in to see Cieslik later that afternoon, he was pacing around his chambers, his eyebrows practically touching his nose. "The state has got a good case," he said. "And the cops' lawyer can't properly defend, because they can't blame each other."

"Judge," I said, "you just got to do what you think is right."

Cieslik found them guilty of involuntary manslaughter and official misconduct. That night Burke, DeLeo, and Banks were in an uproar at Counsellors Row. I shook my head and clucked my tongue to commiserate, but I thought, "Would they go nuts if they knew what I was telling that judge." Now they started plotting ways to make the judge give the cops probation.

During the sentencing hearing, I continued to see the judge each day after court. He would say, "I just can't give them probation for this type of crime."

I would simply say, "Just do what you think is right." He wound up sentencing the cops to time.

I got more satisfaction from seeing those cops sentenced than from winning my own cases. Cieslik really did do the right thing, and, by providing him some moral support, I may have helped. I liked the way that felt. Now, more than ever, I questioned the life I had made for myself as a lawyer. These feelings grew stronger as my father got sicker.

While I was representing the On Leong, I was out of town a lot and I didn't see him much. I would call and he'd only say a few words before he passed the phone to my mother. He suddenly stopped going to Mass and Communion every day. Sometimes he wandered out of the house half-dressed, even in the middle of winter. Worse yet, his personality changed, and he became mean and violent with my mother. When she told me this, I could hardly believe my ears. His whole life, he had been so gentle. We now know that these are all telltale signs of Alzheimer's disease. But back in the early eighties, it was not as well understood.

When people came to visit my father, he forgot their names, but he always seemed to recognize me. After my mother left the room, he would pull me to the side and whisper, "Son, don't let them put me in a nursing home. I know you won't let them."

But eventually there was no choice. It was too hard on my mother. We put him in a place in the south suburbs. The first time I went to visit, he was strapped to his bed and had crapped all over himself. I went screaming for the nurses. When one arrived, I demanded to know why she had tied him up, and she told me he had been violent. He seemed like a puppy with me. He motioned to the straps and the tubes they put on him and said, "Son, look what they're doing to me."

I sat and tried to chat. He said, "I want to go downstairs and commit suicide." He spoke so clearly and there was no mistaking what he said. For a devout Catholic, taking your own life is a mortal sin. I tried to console him and tell him things would get better, but who was I fooling?

I saw him as much as I could when I was in town. The nurses would put him in a wheelchair, and I would push him around to some corner where we could be alone. I never knew what would come out of his mouth. One moment he made sense, and the next he spoke total gibberish. But one day he looked at me and said, "Son, remember, you have to get away from those people."

"Sure, Dad," I said. "Sure." I told him I had broken away, but the truth was that I had not totally broken away.

Then, out of nowhere, he said, "One of those people. One of Capone's people killed your grandfather."

I had never heard him say that before.

Then he said, "And a crooked lawyer got the killer off. A crooked lawyer."

I knew a jury had acquitted my grandfather's killer, and I knew my grandmother fainted when they announced the verdict. I never figured a crooked lawyer was involved, but it seemed so obvious as soon as the words left my father's mouth. It was why it hurt him to see me associated with Marcy and D'Arco. He was just too nice a guy to come out and say that to me—until his illness took the gloves off.

Dad died in February 1983. It was a blessing when he passed. He had been such a good and caring person, he did not deserve what Alzheimer's did to him at the end. My mother did not deserve to watch him go through that either.

Like other people do after a parent dies, I looked back on my own life and what I had made of myself. I remembered lying in the hospital bed after I was run over by the car, and wondering why I had survived. If God had given me a second chance, I did do something with it. I enjoyed success beyond my wildest dreams. I was generous with the money I made. I used my influence to help friends and family, who were good and decent people.

But as my father feared, I had also become a crooked lawyer. Like the lawyer for my grandfather's killer, I helped murderers get off the hook. And not just any murderers, but professional murderers like Harry Aleman. Could this really be the mission that God or anyone else intended for me?

CHAPTER 8

THE FATAL CORNED BEEF SANDWICH

My work with On Leong soon came crashing to a halt. During one visit to New York, Wing picked me up at the airport. Instead of driving to the funeral home in Chinatown, he took me to the parking lot of a high-rise on the east side of Manhattan. Wing went into the lobby and called up. A few minutes later, Eddie came down to our Mercedes. He handed me an envelope. Inside was a picture of a Chinese guy from Houston standing next to a car.

Wing pointed at his picture and told me, "We want to get this guy killed, because he killed some of our people. We got his partner, but we can't kill him." Evidently their target was always on the lookout for a Chinese hit man, so they couldn't get their people close enough to do the job. They wanted me to find them a white hit man from Chicago.

I just stared at the picture, caught totally off guard. After all these years of working with me, they still thought I was totally Chicago Mob. I realized then that I wanted nothing more to do with On Leong.

Wing asked if he could start meeting with my people to set up the hit.

"That's not how they work," I said. I had to figure a way to get out of this situation without causing them to lose face or get suspicious. "My people have problems doing things like this with strangers," I said. "But I'll see what they say." Of course I didn't contact anyone in the Mob when I got back. I waited a day, and called Wing to say that my contacts wouldn't do it. Wing was pissed. He could probably hear in my voice that I wanted no part of this. Although I continued to call Gerard when Eddie Chan came to town, I did no more legal work for him.

Once more, my law practice was rooted in Chicago, and I tried to expand my base of clients on the southwest side of town where I had my office. My partner, State Senator LeRoy Lemke, was your typical small-time political operator. I had met him when he hired me to get his son out of a jam. Our offices were in a house we shared with a U.S. congressman. With my background in criminal work and his local connections, he thought we could drum up a lot of business together, and he was right. I made a point of showing my face at Counsellors Row, but I didn't need the First Ward. After On Leong, I never went back to them for anything else and, for a while, I got no more calls from Marcy.

If you read the newspapers, you would have thought that 1983 was the beginning of the end for the First Ward. In the spring, the city elected its first black mayor, after Harold Washington beat both Jane Byrne and Richie Daley in a bitter primary. That summer, rumors started to fly about Operation Greylord. For three years, an undercover attorney and judge wore wires to catch fixed narcotics and traffic cases. It looked like the Feds were finally going to clean up the courts. Then, before the year was over, indictments for skimming cash from Las Vegas casinos were announced against fifteen Mob leaders in five cities, including Joey Aiuppa; Tony Accardo's right-hand man, Angelo "the Hook" LaPietra, the little king of the Chinatown group; Jackie Cerone, the boss of the West Side group (Marco reported to him); and Tony Spilotro, the Outfit's enforcer in Las Vegas. The Feds called this investigation "Strawman II." They had already used "Strawman I" to take out Joey Lombardo, the boss of the South Side group.

But despite all these major federal investigations, when I walked by the First Ward table at Counsellors Row, nothing seemed different. There were Roti, Marcy, Patty DeLeo, and Johnny D'Arco, wheeling and dealing as always. Like Byrne before him, Mayor Washington let the same bad guys run the police department. White Democratic machine aldermen, led by Fred Roti, Ed Burke, and Ed Vrdolyak, pretty much controlled city council and the rest of Chicago's government. Johnny D'Arco was more powerful than ever in the State Senate.

As for Marcy, Operation Greylord did not scare him a bit. Even after they were convicted, none of the lawyers or judges nailed by the Feds dared to name anyone who was Inner Circle First Ward. The judges still on the bench may have been more careful, but Marcy went about his business as though nothing had ever happened. In fact, in October, the same month that the Strawman II indictments came down, he fixed a murder case involving Tony Spilotro. His trial featured the usual suspects: Thomas J. Maloney was judge, Herb Barsy the associate defense lawyer. Making a guest appearance as the out-of-town lead attorney was Oscar Goodman. (A flamboyant Mob lawyer from Las Vegas, Goodman was elected mayor of that city in 1999.)

Each day after court, I would watch the same little routine unfold in Counsellors Row. Oscar strolled into the restaurant first, soon followed by Spilotro and his sidekick, Fat Herbie Blitzstein. They would take a booth along the wall and order a couple of drinks and something to nibble. Marcy would walk by and, a few minutes later, Tony Spilotro would get up to follow him.

One night, while I was standing at the pay phone, they passed by me. I don't know what had happened in court that day, but Tony had a pained expression on his face. I heard him say, "Are you sure everything is going to be okay? Are you sure?"

Marcy said, "Don't worry about it." He used the same dismissive tone with him that he had often used with me.

When I saw Pat later and asked him why Tony looked so upset, he said, "He's got nothing to worry about. I've taken care of everything."

It was all so brazen—there for the world to see. If you bothered to look. This was not just any trial. It was probably one of the most notorious cases in Organized Crime history. Although the press called it the M&M Murders, it had nothing to do with candy. Billy McCarthy and Jimmy Miraglia were low-level Mob thugs who got into a bar fight with two brothers. Without first getting permission, they killed the brothers and, worse yet, they did it in Elmwood Park, the western suburb where the Mob controlled the police department. No whacking was allowed there.

To make an example of M&M, the Mob commissioned Chuckie Nicoletti and Milwaukee Phil Alderisio, two longtime brutal hit men.

Tony Spilotro, only twenty-four at the time, tagged along like an apprentice, because he had been friendly with Billy McCarthy. To make McCarthy give up Miraglia's name, Tony tortured him for hours. At one point he put McCarthy's head in a vise and turned it until one of his eyes popped out.

The M&M Murders had happened in 1962. The only reason the state could dredge the charges up twenty-one years later was that they now had a key witness: a man who had made the call that helped Tony trap McCarthy and later heard the details about the killings from Spilotro. This witness, Frank Cullotta, was one of Tony Spilotro's crew, and also a lifelong friend—until Tony tried to whack him. In federal cases to come, Cullotta's testimony would win many convictions. But in the state's M&M case, Maloney did not find Cullotta credible. Surprise, surprise. He acquitted Tony Spilotro of all charges.

The M&M fix was all the proof I needed that the Feds had not come close to Marcy. Even as all the corruption and Mob cases came to trial in federal courts over the next few years, Pat only seemed to get stronger.

At first, I was unbelievably happy about Greylord. All the judges and their bagmen had gotten too greedy. If the whole system changed, I would never have to make another payoff. A state's attorney named Terry Hake set the whole investigation in motion. He got fed up with the corruption he saw on a daily basis. Somebody heard him complain, and the FBI asked if he would wear a wire. Over three years, Hake recorded more than thirteen hundred hours of conversations, first pretending to be a corrupt narcotics prosecutor and, later, a defense attorney who could get cases fixed. In the end, he helped convict forty lawyers and a few dozen cops, deputy sheriffs, and other assorted court personnel. But the investigation team's real targets were the judges (the name Greylord came from the gray wigs the judges wore in England), and they convicted fifteen of them, including Dick LeFevour, who had his cousin Jimmy shake me down in Traffic Court just after I got out of law school.

But for me, Operation Greylord was a disappointment. Despite the body count, it never reached as high as the prosecutors promised. The investigation primarily cleaned up the small-time graft in the narcotics and traffic courts: lawyers and judges at the bottom of the food chain— not the ones working with major felonies or murder cases. It did nothing to change the way judges were appointed or assigned. That entire corrupt system remained absolutely intact. If anything, Greylord helped Marcy. With the conviction of each judge, he had another opening to fill, and if you wanted to be named an associate judge, his charge rose to $25,000.

Operation Strawman was definitely more painful for the Mob. A lot of old bosses went off to prison to die, and important crew leaders joined them. But there were literally dozens to take their place. Territories remained the same. Any differences between the bosses were hashed out. Meanwhile, murder cases were still fixed for the hit men, and the hit men were still killing people left and right.

The Outfit was like an octopus. If you cut off an arm, another grew back. To kill it, you had to go for the head—and that was Pat Marcy. He was the one person the Mob protected at all costs. Like Accardo, he was immovable; but unlike Accardo, he could not be replaced. In the whole organization, he was the only one who held all the strings—to the politicians, to the courts, to the unions, and to the cops.

When all the indictments blew by Pat Marcy without so much as messing a hair on his head, he got even more arrogant than before. It was then, in the last few months of 1985, that he called me again.

Oddly enough, he wanted to meet about a client I already had—a 28-year-old baker from Elmwood Park named Mike Colella, who had been charged with nearly beating a policewoman to death. Although the papers made him out to be a monster weightlifter, he wasn't as big or muscle-bound as all that. Instead, he was maybe five feet, eight inches tall and solid, but did not look so terrifying. However, he was obsessed with weightlifting and that's what got him into so much trouble. He had been referred to me through another kid I represented who was breaking into drugstores. I think he was stealing steroids. Whatever he and Mike were taking, it made them both nuts. At the drop of a hat, they would flip out and fight people. Before the incident with the policewoman, Mike had not been pinched in his life, but suddenly he became notorious. He got into a typical barroom brawl and was arrested for that. Then he got in a shouting match with a couple of suburban cops in an all-night diner, and he was charged with assault and resisting arrest.

Mike came into my office with his father. He seemed high to me and started giving me some lip. I would have thrown them both out, but the father was such a nice guy, I felt bad for him. He reminded me of my dad and the way he saw my good side when everyone else saw the bad. I said to Mike, "I won't even represent you until you're straight." Then I told the father to put him into a thirty-day rehab program.

They returned a month later, and I couldn't get over the difference the rehab had made. When he was sober, Mike was actually a decent kid. He seemed genuine about wanting to straighten out his life. I thought the dad didn't have much money, so I told him I wanted only a $500 retainer and would charge an additional $2,000 for the trial.

According to the press, the police had an open-and-shut case. The policewoman stopped Colella on New Year's Eve for driving the wrong way down a one-way street. When she had him get out of the car, he supposedly jumped her, broke her jaw, and would have killed her if other cops hadn't arrived to pull him off. But according to Mike, the story was more complicated than that. He had been out drinking all night in an Old Town bar, and he was cruising down that street looking for prostitutes. When the policewoman stopped him, he gave her an attitude and said, "I wasn't doing anything wrong."

She had him get out of the car. Then she told him he was drunk, and she was going to arrest him. When she ordered him to turn around, so she could put the cuffs on him, he refused. According to Mike, he was struggling with her when the backup cops arrived and they piled on, swinging away with their nightsticks. I had been in melees like that when I was a cop. You start clubbing with those long sticks and you're as likely to hit another cop as the perp. It was totally possible that's how the policewoman's jaw was broken. There was no doubt that they beat the living shit out of Mike. When they dragged him into the police station, the booking officer sent him to the hospital. They never mentioned his injuries in the police reports. I had medical records as proof, and I could use them to show that the cops were lying. Despite all the bad ink, I thought I had a good chance with a jury.

I had been on the Colella case for just a few months when I got a call from Marcy—the first I'd heard from him since I moved my office to the Southwest Side. He said, "I want to talk to you about something. Can you come down to Counsellors?"

It took me about twenty minutes to drive over. Pat Marcy was at the First Ward table with a guy I had seen around but only knew as Nunzio. Pat motioned for me to follow him out the door.

When we were standing in the lobby at 100 North LaSalle, he said, "Look, you're representing this kid Mike Colella."

"Yeah," I said. "As a matter of fact, I am."

"We'll let you keep him," he said, "but I'm going to make sure the case is thrown out."

Even though I thought the kid had gotten a bum rap, I still wanted no part of fixing a case that involved the police—especially if a cop was supposedly the victim. I said, "Pat, I want to take it to a jury. I can win this case."

He said, "You're not taking it to no fucking jury. We'll handle it."

I said, "It's not a big deal. I've read the police reports. The police are all lying, and I can tear them apart in court. I can win this case."

Now he got pissed off. "Just do what you're told," he said. "You'll take a bench and you'll do what you're told. Can you get ahold of the coppers on this case?"

Actually, I did talk to some cops who knew the policewoman. I told them we could help bring a dram shop lawsuit against the bar where Mike was drinking and make everyone rich in the process, but they did not want the kid to get off the hook. "I tried," I told Pat, "but the coppers are still beefing."

"Then fuck them," he said.

Pat then had Nunzio join us in the lobby. It turned out that he was Mike's uncle, and the one who had told Pat about the case. His full name was Nunzio Tischi, and he was a supervising attorney for the public defender's office. Pat said, "If you need a file or he can help in any way, you let him know."

I drove back to my office pounding my steering wheel all the way. No fucking way would I fix a case with cops. I had to show Marcy that there was another way on this case—that I could take Mike before a jury and win.

I asked Nunzio to get me files on the more recent case against Mike, where the suburban cops charged him with resisting arrest and assault. From what Mike had told me, the police at the diner recognized him from articles about the policewoman. Although they egged him on, he never swung. Instead, he told one cop, "If you ever came to my neighborhood without your uniform, I'd kick your ass." It was not a smart thing to say, but it didn't meet the legal definition of assault either. He did not do or say anything that represented an *immediate* threat.

It so happened that this case was before Judge Adam Stillo, who would have fixed it for me. But I told the judge, "I'll take it to a jury and I'll win." That's exactly what happened.

I went back to see Pat Marcy at Counsellors Row. When we were out in the lobby, I told Pat how I had just won my first jury trial for Mike in the suburbs. I had less to work with than on the policewoman case. I said, "Let me take her case to a jury too. If it's just a bench trial and a judge throws it out, the sky will fall. Believe me."

"No," he said. "You just go before the judge, put the case on, and get rid of it already."

I had asked for a Substitution of Judge, and Pat had the case assigned to Lawrence Passarella, a liberal judge. He must have been as soft as a grapefruit to take on a case like this, but maybe Marcy gave him no choice. Although Passarella did lean toward the defense, no judge could go easy on crimes against cops. In truth, I never liked Passarella all that much. He was one of your classic high-and-mighty judges. When I used to see him at Counsellors Row, he wouldn't even bother to make small talk. Once, he was alone at the First Ward table when I sat down.

"Waiting for Pat?" I asked.

"Pat who?" he said.

Still, even if Passarella was a pompous ass, I figured he couldn't be completely stupid. He might welcome a plea to get out from under this heater case. The minimum sentence for attempted murder was six years in prison. I didn't want Mike to do any jail time. From what I could see, the kid was like a whole new person and finally straightening up his life. If the judge reduced the charge to just aggravated battery, he could get away with giving Mike probation.

I called Mike and his father back to my office. I never said a word about what was going on behind the scenes with Marcy and Nunzio. I told them, "What I can maybe do is work out a plea with this judge and get you probation."

The father said, "Whatever you think is right, I will go along with it."

Once again, I went back to Pat Marcy. I said, "I talked to the kid and his dad and they're willing to take probation. Let me work out a plea on this."

Marcy did not want to hear about a plea. "Just go and do what I told you to do." Obviously, through Nunzio, someone had offered a lot of money to the judge for a not guilty.

But whatever Marcy said, I was still determined to work out a plea. Since Pat wouldn't let me talk to the judge, I tried to go first to the assistant state's attorney. They had a special prosecutor on this case because of all the publicity. I said to him, "I'd like to work out a plea if you can reduce the charge from attempted murder to just the battery."

He said he needed to check with his superiors. He came back the next day and said, "No. We're not going to reduce it. Either you plead guilty to attempted murder, or we go to trial."

I wanted to say, "Listen, you fucking asshole, you're not going to win this case, and you don't even know it." But I bit my tongue and said, "Okay. We'll go to trial."

I approached Pat one last time about working out a plea, but Marcy refused to listen. "Just go in there," he said, "and stop with this."

But I didn't go to trial. Three times before our date came up, I went into court and asked for a continuance. I avoided Pat, so he wouldn't ask me about the delay. I hoped against hope that something would develop to get me out of this.

By February 1986, I realized I couldn't stall the Colella case much longer, and I did everything I could to distract myself. I stayed up late, I drank more than usual, and I gambled like a demon. Because I wasn't thinking clearly, I made silly bets—violating all of my own rules about covering both sides of a line. When the year started, I was on a winning streak, but now it was like I had been cursed. All my numbers went the wrong way. In the first few weeks of February, I went in the hole for $350,000. On just one day, I lost eighteen out of twenty college basketball games, where I bet from $5,000 to $10,000 a game. Never in my life did I have a day like that. Maybe it was the Catholic in me, or just plain superstition, but I started to think I was being punished.

My biggest mistake was playing with Bob Johnson, an independent bookie from the south suburbs. He was big and burly, more than six feet tall, and had been a boxer, so he thought he could throw his weight around. I had nearly had a fight with him once before. Worse yet, he was a cokehead, and had his own debts piled high. At times it made him desperate. I owed him $55,000, and he started calling me several times a day to collect. He'd tell my secretary, "Your boss is a bust-out fuck. Tell him I want my money, or I'm coming there to get it." At one point he called me at home and, to get him off my back, I told him, "I can't talk now. I'm being raided by the IRS." That kept him quiet for a few days, but then he started calling again.

I had been in the hole to bookies before and, with enough time, I played my way out of it. But Johnson and the approaching fix started throbbing away like a cavity. I had no desire to save the tooth. I just wanted it out and done with.

Finally, I had to let the Colella case come to trial—on the last Wednesday of the month. The case was heard in the criminal courthouse on 26th and California Street. Spectators were kept behind bulletproof glass, so they heard the testimony through speakers. As I expected, the gallery was filled with reporters, cops, and officials from the Fraternal Order of Police. This was the sort of trial my father would have attended when he was a union officer.

The whole proceeding lasted no more than three hours; but, for me, it seemed to go on and on like a slow-motion nightmare. It started with the testimony from the policewoman. She described how Colella reached into his car before he turned on her. She said, "He came up with this bar of cold, rolled steel. He said, 'That's it. I'm going to kill you.' "

This quote appeared in the newspapers the next morning. They did not bother to report on my cross-examination of the policewoman or the other cops. As for the steel bar, the cops said they found it behind the car. How did it end up there, if Colella was under a pile of cops? Also, they never bothered to dust it for fingerprints. Clearly this so-called weapon and her claim about his threat to kill her were ways to trump up the charges to attempted murder. When I asked the cops about beating Mike, they wouldn't even admit he bled, let alone that he needed all the stitches and had all the contusions listed in his medical report.

Unfortunately, the evidence—or lack of it—would have mattered only if I had had a jury focused on a verdict, but this entire proceeding had nothing to do with the law. Instead, I was stuck in a crazy charade. On the inside, I had a judge who knew his ruling before he ever took the bench. Meanwhile, on the outside, reporters and the rest of the public had their minds made up too, before they had heard one word of testimony.

But the worst part of the trial did not come until the very end—when Passarella announced his ruling. He switched off his microphone and whispered to the court, "Not guilty," and then all but ran out of the courtroom. He never gave any further explanation for his verdict.

At first, the spectators thought he was going to lunch, or needed a bathroom break; but when they saw the prosecutors jump to their feet and get all pissed off, there was pandemonium.

As I walked out, the policemen started yelling at me: "You should be ashamed of yourself. You should be ashamed of yourself."

I just ignored them and pushed my way through the crowd, but inside I was seething. Every day of my life, I looked at the hole in my hand from the beating I got as a cop. How could anyone give *me* crap about a police beating? But then again, I had allowed myself to be associated with a total travesty of justice. All of my feelings were twisted inside-out like a pretzel.

As I drove to Counsellors Row, I thought about Passarella. No matter how much I disliked the man, I felt sorry for him. I thought, "This is an exact replay of what happened to Frank Wilson in the Harry Aleman trial. This fix will be his ruin."

When Marcy saw me enter the restaurant, he got up from the First Ward table and walked into the lobby. Once again, he led me past the elevators and through the door to the staircase. He stood above me on the steps leading to the janitor's closet. Again, he reached into his pocket and took out an envelope.

He said, "Here's the other $2,000 you have coming." I had never told him about my fee arrangement with Colella's father. Obviously he had been talking to them, or someone close to them.

As I took the envelope, I said, "This judge is going to have a serious problem. The media is all over this. This guy will probably lose his job."

He said, "That's none of your business. It's not your concern what happens to him."

"But what if he beefs on us?" I asked.

"Nobody would dare fuck with us," he said.

I thought, "Maybe you're looking at someone who will."

The moment I had the thought, I looked away. As crazy as it sounds, I wondered whether he could read my mind or see something in my eyes. That was the kind of power he had over me.

After I left Counsellors Row, I tried to get the trial off my mind and go about my business, but I didn't sleep well. I had bad dreams. I saw dead people out of my past. The innocent ones, like the bookie Anthony Reitinger, and the not-so-innocent, like Butch Petrocelli, who were killers themselves. I kept hearing my father say, "I used to arrest these people." Or "You shouldn't be wasting your God-given talents on these people." These people.

I also heard Marcy's voice. Over and over again, I heard him say, "Nobody would dare fuck with us." Then I started thinking: "Maybe, after I was almost killed so many times, this is the reason I was left alive—to fuck with Marcy and the First Ward."

My father used to say, "The Lord has a plan for all of us, and there's a reason why things happen." Now at night, I started thinking: "This is my destiny: to take down this horrible organization."

But then the next morning, with the light of day, I said to myself, "Why would I pick a fight with Marcy? It would be like committing suicide, and I have a fantastic life. I worked my ass off to get a law license.

TOP: My family in 1951. In the center of the picture stands yours truly at the age of seven, fresh from my first Holy Communion—already a hot shit. (*Chicago Tribune* photo by the *Chicago Tribune*.) **ABOVE (LEFT):** Count Dante in his famous comic book ad. I have yet to meet anyone with his amazing combination of talents and flaws. **ABOVE (RIGHT):** Marco D'Amico, 1994. He once said to me, "Nobody wears a wire on us and lives to talk about it."

LEFT: The four major freeways sliced the Chicago metro area into pieces of pie—one for each of the Outfit's main groups. **BELOW RIGHT:** Tony Spilotro in 1974, then the Mob's main enforcer in Vegas. He liked the fact that I stood up to him. Later, we had one of my "last meals" together.

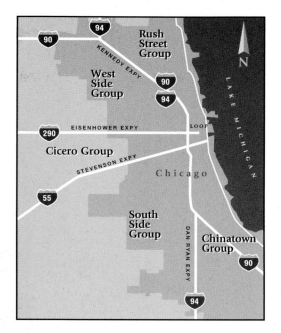

BELOW: Tony Accardo (center of photo, wearing glasses) and Joey Aiuppa (far left), have a sit-down with some of their bosses in 1978. The five Mafia groups got along very well—like five fingers clenched into a fist.

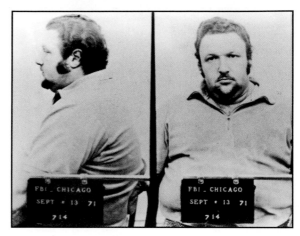

ABOVE (LEFT): Angelo LaPietra, the little king of the Chinatown Group. They called him "Hook," because he used to hang his enemies from meat hooks when he tortured them to death. ABOVE (RIGHT): Herb Blitzstein, Tony Spilotro's sidekick. He looked like a combination between Mitch Miller and a weird professional wrestler. RIGHT: The First Ward table itself wasn't fancy, but for the lawyers, city workers, and politicians always milling around, it was like a King's Court. (*Chicago Tribune* photo by the *Chicago Tribune*.)

ABOVE (LEFT): John D'Arco, Sr., 1952, in Council Chambers. The resemblance to Capone actually helped his career. The Mob bosses expected him to be mayor one day, but Senior was never the sharpest blade in the drawer. (As published in the *Chicago Sun-Times*, Inc. Copyright 2004 by *Chicago Sun-Times*, Inc. Reprinted with permission.) **ABOVE (RIGHT):**

Johnny D'Arco in 1990. He yelled at the prosecutors, "Slander my name all over the world—you!" Then he marched out of the courtroom, leaving his wife behind to bawl her head off. (As published in the *Chicago Sun-Times*, Inc. Copyright 2004 by *Chicago Sun-Times*, Inc. Reprinted with permission.) **LEFT:** From left to right: Yours truly, wearing a hat and sunglasses, with Alderman Fred Roti, John D'Arco Sr., and Sam Banks on our way to criminal court in 1978 during my heyday. I loved being a lawyer. I loved being the center of attention. (As published in the *Chicago Sun-Times*, Inc. Copyright 2004 by *Chicago Sun-Times*, Inc. Reprinted with permission.)

TOP (LEFT): Pat Marcy (right), 1990, with lawyer Terence P. Gillespie. "Nobody would dare fuck with us," Marcy once told me. I thought, "Maybe you're looking at someone who will." (Photograph by Brian Jackson. As published in the *Chicago Sun-Times*, Inc. Copyright 2004 by *Chicago Sun-Times*, Inc. Reprinted with permission.) **TOP (RIGHT):** Harry Aleman in 1977. He bore in on me with that Evil Eye and asked, "Are you sure you can handle it? Are you sure this judge is going to throw the case out?" **ABOVE:** Judge Frank J. Wilson, running from reporters after he acquitted Harry Aleman. When I paid him off, he said, "You destroyed me." (Photograph by Larry Graff. As published in the *Chicago Sun-Times*, Inc. Copyright 2004 by *Chicago Sun-Times*, Inc. Reprinted with permission.)

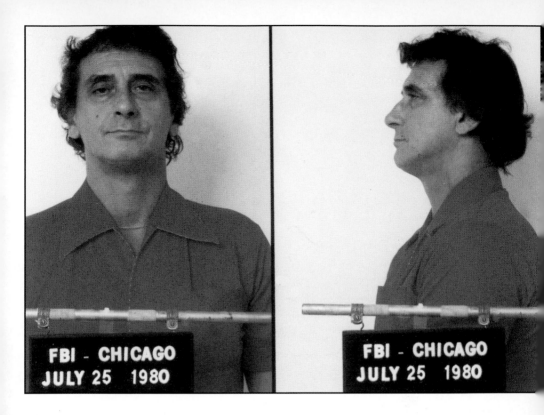

ABOVE: Frank Renella in 1980. He went over to the kitchen drawer and pulled out a gun. He pointed it at me and said, "If you're setting me up, you're gonna be the first to get killed." **RIGHT:** Judge Thomas J. Maloney in 1977. The arrogance of the man knew no bounds. For the right price, he would let anyone off for any crime. Absolutely anyone. (Photograph by Jim Frost. As published in the *Chicago Sun-Times*, Inc. Copyright 2004 by *Chicago Sun-Times*, Inc. Reprinted with permission.)

BELOW (LEFT): Tony Borsellino in 1978: a very cagey guy, but he still went for a ride without looking over his shoulder first. **BELOW (RIGHT):** Alderman Fred Roti, 1996, never ended his association with the Outfit. He used to joke, "Vote for Roti and Nobody Gets Hurt." (As published in the *Chicago Sun-Times,* Inc. Copyright 2004 by *Chicago Sun-Times,* Inc. Reprinted with permission.)

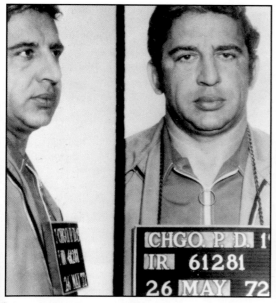

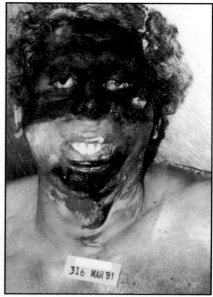

ABOVE: Butch Petrocelli, living in 1972, and dead in 1981. If they could turn on Butch and torture and burn him so horribly for a piece of cheese, they could turn on anyone.

ABOVE (LEFT): Alderman Ed Burke and his wife Appellate Judge Anne Burke (2000). I wanted the Feds to look at two cases they were involved with: a wife stabber out for insurance money and a high school principal who abused his students. (Photograph by Brian Jackson. As published in the *Chicago Sun-Times,* Inc. Copyright 2004 by *Chicago Sun-Times*, Inc. Reprinted with permission.) **ABOVE (RIGHT):** John DiFronzo in 1992, when he was CEO of the entire Outfit. As I walked through his showroom, I wondered if he had installed a sophisticated device to detect wires. **LEFT:** Attorney Ed Genson in 1998. He staggered to the judge, pointed at me, and said, "This man is a legal assassin. Every time he opens his mouth he plunges a dagger into my client." (Photograph by Bob Black. As published in the *Chicago Sun-Times,* Inc. Copyright 2004 by *Chicago Sun-Times,* Inc. Reprinted with permission.)

Why would I want to give everything up for nothing? I don't want to give it up."

The day after the Colella trial, when I got back to my office, I got another crazy call from Bob Johnson. He was screaming, "I want my money! I want my fucking money!"

I slammed down the phone and got in my car. I had a lunch meeting scheduled at Counsellors Row, and got angrier as I drove. If I was going to stomach a fix like Colella, the least the Mob could do was get these fucking bookies off my back. When I walked into the restaurant, I passed Marcy, going in the opposite direction.

"Pat," I said, "can I talk to you a minute?"

"I'm busy," he said. It was an absolute brush-off—maybe his way of getting back at me for beefing about the Colella fix.

As I sat through my meeting, I couldn't get my mind off Marcy and the "injustice" of it all. One way or another these people were going to help me with *my* problem.

I had another idea. With all the bosses in prison, the Mob had given Marco control over most of their gambling operations in the Chicago area. I figured he should have clout with any bookie—even the independent ones. After I left Counsellors Row, I drove to his Survivor's Club—for the first time in years. Marco was there playing cards. I asked to talk a few minutes, and when he got up from the table, I told him about my problem. He couldn't be bothered, either. He said, "Put the names down and come back and see me in a day or two."

Now I was really pissed. I figured: "Fuck it. If Marco won't help me, I'll just go over his head to Johnny DiFronzo." After Jackie Cerone was convicted in Operation Strawman, DiFronzo had become the head of Marco's West Side group. Accardo also anointed him the boss of the other bosses—the latest in the Outfit's long line of acting CEOs. John was a different breed from the other Mob bosses. He may have done some dirty work to make his bones, but over the years he had polished up his act considerably. Fit and trim at fifty-eight, he always wore a suit. He had razor-cut hair with a distinguished patch of gray at the temples. He spent most of his time at his Chrysler dealership on the West Side, and he definitely looked the part of a wealthy car dealer. When I walked into his office in the back of the Chrysler showroom, he gave me a warm greeting and asked, "What can I do for you?"

I said, "I'm sorry to bother you with this, John, but I have a problem. I owe a few people some money on bets I made. If I can get a little more time, I can straighten out with them. I just need a little more time."

Like I thought he would, John took a real interest in my problem. I had recently represented his kid on a case, got the charges dropped, and never even sent him a bill. He said, "Give me a list of the people who are bothering you, and I'll have someone look into it. Then get back to me tomorrow."

When I went back to the dealership on Friday, DiFronzo told me his people had contacted all the bookies on my list, except one. He asked, "Who is this Bob Johnson?"

I said, "He's a guy on the South Side."

"Who's he with? Nobody knows who he's with."

I said, "I don't know." I realized Bob Johnson was not paying the Mob his street tax. I had just gotten him into a lot of trouble.

John then sat me down, and he said, "Bob, I don't want you paying Bob Johnson—or anybody else, for that matter. You don't pay anybody anything. As far as I'm concerned, you are now clear." Then, just like Marcy did years before, he scolded me. "And I don't want you gambling any more, either. You get yourself in trouble. You've always been a big gambler and you should know better already."

I nodded my head, but some day I fully intended to pay my debts so I could start gambling again. All I needed was enough time to win back everything I had lost. I thanked John for his help and promised to mend my ways. By the end of the day, two of the bookies called to assure me that they would not collect. One of them, Dominic Barbaro, said, "I never threatened you. You make sure you tell your friends I never threatened you." For the first time in a long time, I didn't hear anything from Bob Johnson.

But the bookies were not my problem. I still didn't sleep well. I still couldn't get the Colella case off my mind. Just as I expected, the papers crucified Judge Passarella. Only a week after the trial, Passarella met with the chief judge of the Circuit Court and asked to be transferred out of the criminal division. Richie Daley, then the Cook County state's attorney, charged that the verdict showed "total disregard of the facts of the case." But Daley put all the blame on Passarella's judgment and said he had come up with similar bad decisions in the past.

The press figured something else was going on. I got a call from John Drummond, then Chicago TV's premier crime reporter. He brought a crew to my office to tape an interview. Right in front of the camera, he asked me if the Colella case was fixed. I replied that the state had no case, and I truly believed that. "The police got up on the stand and they all lied," I said. "The judge did the right thing." Of course, he did the right thing for the wrong reason, but I didn't say that.

When Saturday rolled around, ten days after the Colella trial, I was still in turmoil, just boiling inside. That morning, for a little fun, I went downtown to play gin with my old lawyer pals at 100 North LaSalle. The group included Allan Ackerman, the first attorney I had shared an office with. We had our laughs, and it was like the good old days again. I totally forgot my troubles. We finished up early in the afternoon, and I wanted to grab some lunch before I went home. My favorite deli, the Dill Pickle, was only a few blocks away, so I decided to take a stroll. Getting a corned beef sandwich was my only purpose in life. When I turned the corner onto Dearborn Avenue, I happened to pass the Federal Building. It seemed to draw me like a magnet. Suddenly I thought, "Maybe I should see who's up in the Strike Force office."

The Organized Crime Strike Force was a federal agency set up specifically to go after the Mafia. I figured that the attorneys and FBI agents reported directly to the U.S. Attorney General in Washington, D.C., with no local stops in between. That's all I knew. I didn't even know anyone who worked there.

I walked into the lobby, and there was a security guard behind a little desk. When I asked if anyone was in the Strike Force office, he called and got an answer. I told the guard my name and that I was an attorney, and he was told to send me up.

Only one person was in that day—Gary Shapiro, chief attorney for their entire Chicago operation. He was in his shirtsleeves, probably catching up on paperwork.

"I'm Bob Cooley," I said.

"What can I do for you?" he asked.

"I'd like to help you destroy the First Ward," I said. "I'd like to help you destroy Pat Marcy."

ON
THE
WIRE

CHAPTER 9

IN THE WEEDS

Once I walked into the Strike Force office and opened my mouth, it was like I had stepped off the ledge of a sky-scraper. There was nothing I could do to save myself. Eventually I would hit the ground. I just didn't know how long it would take.

What do you want?

That was the question Gary Shapiro kept asking. It was the question all the Feds would ask. He said, "If you're coming here to help us, what do *you* want in return?"

Immediately I had second thoughts about the whole thing. I was talking to a federal agent—a stranger—about illegal things I had done or known about. "What *am* I doing here?" I thought. "Have I gone crazy?"

"Do you need money?" Gary asked. "Do you need protection? Do you need anything?"

I said, "I don't want anything. I don't need anything. But I think I can help you people. I think I can help you people take down the First Ward. That's the cancer behind the courts and everything else in this city."

In my own mind, I didn't have a clear picture of what I could do. I imagined they would want me to wear a wire, like Terry Hake, who developed all the Greylord cases. But that meant I would be a witness, too, and I knew the defense would attack my testimony by claiming that I had come to the authorities for personal reasons—to get myself out of a jackpot. That's how *I* would destroy a government informant:

first get him to discuss his motives for cooperating—such as a lighter sentence or money—and then destroy his credibility in the eyes of the jury. How did I know that the Feds or the state didn't already have me on tape or have me as a target in one of their investigations? If I was coming in to save my own neck, I'd be a stoolpigeon and my testimony would be worthless.

I said to Gary, "What I want you to do is check that I don't have any problems of my own. If I'm under investigation already, then I can't help you."

"But what do you know about the First Ward?" he asked. "What can you tell me? I'm sure we don't have any investigations against you."

I wouldn't take his word for it. I said, "I want you to check with all the federal agencies and really make sure there's nothing out there." I gave him my card. "If I have no problems, then get ahold of me and we'll sit down. Maybe we can do something."

Only a few minutes passed while I was in Gary's office, but after I walked out of the Federal Building, I was in a different world. Once again, I looked over both shoulders when I walked, nervous as a cat. I realized what a stupid thing I had just done. What if Gary was connected to the First Ward? He'd be calling Marcy or Roti at that very moment, and I would have just signed my own death warrant. Meanwhile, I had given him a reason to make *me* the target of an investigation. There were plenty of reasons why the Feds never went after the First Ward, but there was nothing stopping them from coming after me. My case could be bundled up with all the attorneys they indicted in Greylord.

A week went by, and I was relieved that Gary Shapiro didn't call. I figured he had forgotten the whole thing. That was fine with me. I now had no interest in helping him.

On Tuesday, March 18, I spent the morning in court and drove back to my office after lunch. When I walked into the reception area, I could see by the look on my secretary's face that something was wrong. "Bob," she whispered, "are you in some kind of trouble?"

"Why?" I asked. "What's wrong?" For all I knew, Bob Johnson had paid a call.

She said, "I think there are some FBI agents in your office."

My heart sank. I walked back and saw them sitting there: a man and a woman; very square types with neat hairstyles and conservative suits. In other words, they looked exactly like FBI agents.

They got up to greet me, and we shook hands all around. When we sat down I could see them giving my office the once over.

The man, Steve Bowen, did most of the talking. He wanted to know why I looked so surprised. "You told Gary we should check if you had any problems and then come see you."

"I'm surprised," I said, "because I thought I would get a call from Gary first."

"Well, we did all the checking and you don't have any problems," Steve said. "So what can you tell us? How can you help us?"

"I thought I could do something," I said, "but now I'm not really sure."

But with the two of them sitting in my office, I couldn't tell them to get lost. They already checked into my background and knew about all my notorious cases. I had opened a Pandora's box. If I kept my mouth closed, they had reason to stay focused on me until they found something to make me talk. There was no stopping now.

Then Steve said, "Are you sick? Do you have some kind of terminal illness?"

"No," I said. "I'm feeling fine." At first it seemed like an odd question, but I realized that he was totally mystified by my motivations.

He asked, "So why do you want to talk to us?"

"Because it's something I feel I have to do," I said. I was too embarrassed to mention my father. Besides, how could I talk about something so personal when I had just met them? I said, "The average citizen in this town doesn't have a prayer when he goes into court. You had this Operation Greylord and it just made the First Ward more powerful. It's business as usual for the court system. Somebody has to stop it. Nobody else has the balls and nobody else will."

Then again, Steve asked the question: "But what do *you* want for this? We don't have cases on you anywhere."

I said, "Fine, then all I want is 'use' immunity." This meant they could not use anything I told them to bring charges against me. "If you can build cases some other way, so be it." As a next step, I asked that they arrange another meeting with the U.S. Attorney to make sure I had the protection I was looking for. I said, "Just tell Gary to get ahold of me."

Gary called back and set up a meeting with me two days later at the Holiday Inn in the western suburb of Oak Brook. I had no idea why they picked that location. With its fancy golf courses and big new subdivisions, Oak Brook was the new "residence of choice" for the Mob bosses. Marcy himself had just bought a home there.

When I walked into the lobby, I saw Steve Bowen, one of the FBI agents who had come to my office. I was supposed to pretend I didn't know him and go upstairs. He followed, and then led me to one of the rooms on the second floor. Inside was the other agent who came to my office, Marie Dyson, with Gary Shapiro. They brought along another agent, Jack McCoy, a bull-necked drill sergeant type. We had to pull the chairs near the bed so everyone could have a seat.

Gary then said, "I had a conversation about you with Anton Valukas." He was the U.S. Attorney for the Northern District of Illinois. "We decided that 'use' immunity for you would not be a problem."

Although I was glad to hear about the immunity, I was not happy he had talked to Valukas. Evidently the Strike Force had to work with the local U.S. Attorney. Although I didn't know anything about Valukas— he had just been appointed a few months before—I did know something about his predecessors. After they left office, almost all of them ended up working for one of the two big Chicago firms that the Mob bosses and politicians used when they got into trouble. It was a revolving door. One month they supposedly investigated the bad guys, and the next month they defended them. If Valukas saw that same career path for himself, would he want me to take down his future clients?

But Gary wasn't finished with the bad news. He went on to say, "We want you to understand that if you work with us, you can no longer do anything illegal. You can no longer fix cases, and you can no longer gamble. . . ."

Crazy as this sounds, I never thought my gambling would be an issue for them—maybe because I didn't consider gambling to be *that* illegal.

I held up my hands and said, "Whoa. Wait. My problem is that I owe some money to some bookies. I had a few real bad weeks. If I can just keep playing a little longer, I'll win back enough to straighten out."

But Gary wouldn't hear of that. He said, "You can't gamble any more. Period. If you are going to be a Cooperating Witness, there are certain rules you have to abide by." Then, he went on to give me *more* rules. I could no longer do any work in Federal Court whatsoever. Also, I couldn't handle any serious case where a client might get a lot of time, because later he might complain that my government work interfered with his defense.

I let them know they were cutting out a big chunk of my income. Gary said, "If you need money, we'll give it to you in return for the business you're turning down."

"I don't want your money," I said. "If I take money from you, then it looks like I'm a stoolpigeon, just doing something to help myself. Juries will never believe me."

When they asked how I would get along without their money, I said, "I'll handle it myself. I can build my civil practice."

As far as the gambling debts were concerned, Gary wanted to give me the money to pay those off. I told him about Dominic Barbaro, Bob Johnson, and a few others. "We want to build cases against some of these bookies," he said. "Will you make payments to them?"

"I saw John DiFronzo about Bob Johnson," I said. "He specifically told me not to pay Johnson back."

Jack McCoy jumped up from the bed. "You saw *who*?" he asked.

When I explained what had happened at DiFronzo's dealership, McCoy laughed. "You've got to be kidding."

McCoy had been a hard-ass from the moment I met him, and now he all but called me a liar. I said, "If you don't believe me, let me put on a wire and I'll confirm what I'm telling you."

I did not expect to start this relationship by wearing a wire on *the* top boss in the Mafia (Accardo was mostly retired by this time). But now my honesty was at stake. I had to prove myself, or I'd never get off on the right foot with the Feds.

Then, for the next few hours, I told them the story of my life: my youth on the South Side, my years as a cop, how Jimmy LeFevour tried to shake me down in Traffic Court my first few days out of law school—even about Count Dante. At first, I thought they only wanted to hear about the courts, but when I told them how Marcy fixed the cases for Colella and Lenny Chow, McCoy acted skeptical again. "You really think you can take down Marcy?" he asked. Evidently he specialized in organized crime for the FBI, and he knew how hard the First Ward was to crack. He asked me what I could tell them about Fred Roti, John and Johnny D'Arco, Patty DeLeo, and Marco D'Amico. I still wasn't ready to talk about the Harry Aleman case, but I told them how I fixed a case for Harry's brother-in-law, Richie Kimball, when he kicked an FBI agent in the head during a bar fight. I thought they'd enjoy that story.

But there was one name McCoy did *not* want to hear. At one point I said, "Next to Marcy, no one is more dangerous than the police department's chief of detectives, Bill Hanhardt."

I started to explain what he was doing to protect the Mob bookies, when McCoy interrupted me and said, "You don't like him, do you?"

"Sure I don't like him," I said, "but what does that have to do with anything?"

Then he asked: "Is that why you're making these things up about him?"

I said, "I'm not making anything up. I'm here to help. You asked me what I knew and I'm telling you." Hanhardt had been the Chicago Police Department liaison with the FBI. In the process, he might have become McCoy's friend, too. (Hanhardt retired from the police force a few months after this meeting.)

If McCoy was against me, he was the only one in that hotel room. Gary Shapiro and the other two agents looked pretty excited. After that meeting, McCoy faded out of the picture. The next morning, when it came time to get ready for my meeting with DiFronzo, just Steve Bowen and Marie Dyson showed up at my apartment.

In time, I got to know Steve and Marie pretty well. They were two of the straightest arrows you could ever find. Steve was slim and bald, and he carried himself like a Marine. Marie had dark short hair. She was very proper and reminded me of a no-nonsense teacher you'd have in grade school. They always did everything strictly by the book. Each and every time before I put on a wire, I had to sign my own consent form saying that I put on the body recorder "voluntarily" and without receiving threats or promises. Only after we completed the paperwork did Steve take me into the bedroom so I could "attach" the wire.

The FBI used a body recorder made by a Swiss company called Nagra Audio. It came in a silver metal case the size of an old-fashioned whiskey flask. Inside was a mechanism as precise as a Swiss watch: two tiny reels with thin tape that threaded through a series of gears and posts.

Steve wrapped an Ace bandage around my thigh with a pocket for the case. From there, he ran two wires under my shirt. They had microphones at the tip, and he taped each one under my collarbone. Everything still seemed so unreal; it was like I was watching him do this to someone else. Once Steve left the room to let me finish getting dressed, I grabbed my Smith & Wesson Airweight and attached it to a holster on my belt. I would need more protection than an Ace bandage if DiFronzo caught me with that fucking Nagra.

Steve and Marie wanted to follow me in their car and then wait near the dealership in case I had a problem, but that was too risky. I didn't want anyone strange to be seen around me in that West Side neighborhood, since it was crawling with Marco's crew. Instead, we agreed to meet in a nearby park after I saw John.

If I had been in a daze up to this time, once I got in my car and drove to DiFronzo's dealership, the full impact of what I was doing hit home. My entire body broke out into a sweat. Marco's words rang in my ears: "Nobody wears a wire on us and lives to tell about it." After I wore a wire on DiFronzo, there would be no turning back. I was a registered informant, and the Mob would kill me if they ever found out.

As I walked through DiFronzo's showroom, I started to wonder if he had installed a sophisticated device to detect bugs or wires in the building. John was sharp enough to do something like that. The Ace bandage on my thigh felt like a cast. I kept glancing down to make sure there was nothing funny about the way my pants hung.

A guy in a suit sat at a desk outside John's office door. He was supposed to look like a salesman, but he was really one of DiFronzo's bodyguards from a West Side crew. I'm sure he was packing, too. He recognized me and let John know I was there. DiFronzo chased some people out of his office and had me come in.

I half-expected a bell to go off when I walked through the door, but nothing happened. Instead, once again, John gave me a warm hello, and that put me at ease. All I had to do was thank him, I thought. There was nothing suspicious about that.

I told John how quickly some of those bookies got back to me and how scared they sounded. He got a kick out of that. But then I said, "I appreciate what you did, but I'm going to make a couple of payments to these guys."

That got John upset. He yelled, "What the fuck are you making payments for? I told you not to. You're not afraid of them, are you?"

I said, "Bob Johnson has been calling and harassing me."

He said, "You're not afraid of him, are you?"

I said, "No."

He said, "Then I don't want you paying him. You're not supposed to. He's not with anybody."

I didn't really say I would *not* pay the bookies. I just told John not to worry, shook his hand to thank him again, and got the hell out of there.

Later, I met Steve and Marie in the park. I delivered the Nagra, and my little tape sure delivered the goods. Once the Feds listened to it, they couldn't believe their ears. For the first time, they had ample evidence that John saw himself as the top Mob boss. Meanwhile, the tape gave me a future "inoculation" in case a Mob lawyer ever questioned my motives for coming in. DiFronzo made it clear that I didn't have to pay the bookies back, so no one could say I helped the Feds because I owed money on my gambling debts. Most important, the tape proved to Gary and the agents that I wasn't some idle bullshitter—like McCoy made me out to be.

But still, the Feds were in no rush to put a wire on anyone in the First Ward. Instead, they kept my sights lowered—as far as they could go— and had me focus on the bookies. The first one I called was Dominic Barbaro. He was still scared by the warning he got from DiFronzo's people to stay away from me. I told him I would pay him back, so we could start playing again. Poor Dominic couldn't help himself. He was scared of DiFronzo, but he really wanted that money. We arranged to meet at an Italian beef joint a few blocks from my apartment in Countryside.

Steve Bowen and Marie Dyson showed up again at my place to get me ready. First they counted out fifteen hundred-dollar bills and noted the serial numbers of each one. Although I owed Barbaro $24,000, we were going to pay him a little at a time. The Feds used each payment as a separate count in the indictment. This time, they brought a special Nagra recorder for me. Compared to the first model I wore, it held more tape—enough for three hours—and included an on/off switch that came up through a hole in my pants pocket. Although Barbaro had not been my client, I had represented a bookie who worked for him. On the chance I might bump into him or any of my other clients, I could reach into my pocket and shut off the recorder, so I wouldn't violate attorney–client privilege. But this new, bigger recorder didn't fit in the special pocket of the Ace bandage. Instead, Steve used the bandage to wrap the Nagra to my leg.

I drove the few blocks to the beef stand. Inside this joint, you ate at a counter that ran along a plate glass window. I pulled into a parking spot right in front of the place where Barbaro sat and stuffed his mouth with a sandwich. He was a little, skinny guy with a ferret face. He could see me through the window and gave me a nod. I opened my car door, but when I put my leg out, I felt the bandage give way. The Nagra fell through my pants and clattered to the ground. I was still behind the wheel, but when I looked up, there was Barbaro staring at me. I had no idea how much he saw. Immediately, I pointed to my right. When he turned his head, I pulled my leg back into the car and the Nagra came up with it. I slammed the door shut and backed out of my parking spot. Barbaro watched me pull away, frozen like a statue—with his mouth open and the beef sandwich in his hand.

Steve and Marie had parked up the road, and they were equally shocked to see me drive off. I'm sure they wondered where I was going with their $1,500. I drove straight back to my house. Soon after I walked inside, they rang my doorbell. I told them what had happened and for a few minutes, we were all in a state of panic.

"I don't know if he saw it," I said.

"If he did," Steve said, "you have a serious problem."

Then my phone rang. It was Barbaro, calling from the beef stand. "What happened?" he asked.

I said, "Didn't you see those coppers sitting in the gas station parking lot? I pointed to them. It was like they were staking you out."

"Oh," he said. Dominic had just gotten pinched a few weeks before. In fact, he wanted me to represent him in that case. Then he said, "Do you have my money?"

I told him I'd meet him behind a restaurant down the street.

After I got off the phone, Steve said, "Are you sure you want to go through with this?"

I said, "I'm not worried about him." Barbaro talked like a tough guy, but I could break him like a twig. Still, before I left, I pulled the Nagra and the Ace bandage off. When I saw Barbaro, he didn't have a clue that anything was wrong, and I handed him the money. Although I couldn't record the transaction, we had him set up to receive future payments. For the next meeting, I had him come to my office. Besides my wire, we also had a hidden video camera filming him through a hole in an attaché case. But during this visit, he said he didn't want my money. He wanted me to pay him back by handling his case. There was no way I could do that, but I told him, "I'll think about it."

He said, "Remember, you tell your friends I never threatened you, and I never will threaten you. You're a nice guy."

Then he asked me if I had heard from Bob Johnson. "I was told they're going to kill Bob Johnson," he said. "They're going to kill him because he threatened you. And he ain't paying street tax, either."

This was more information than we wanted to hear. Now the Feds had to pay a visit to Johnson and warn him that someone from the Mob might be looking to kill him. The next night, Bob Johnson called me at home. The FBI had attached a recorder to my phone, and I turned it on as soon as I heard his voice on my answering machine. I picked up the receiver and he was practically crying. "Your friends are going to kill me," he whined. "You got to help me. You got to put a stop to it."

I said, "Bob, I don't know what you're talking about. Why don't you meet me in my office and we can talk about it?"

He said, "I'm not coming anywhere near you," and hung up.

Then he called a day or two later. This time he was loud and belligerent, slurring his words together like he was high on something. "Where's my fucking money?" he screamed. "I want my money. Where's my fucking money?"

"Bobby," I said, "if you come on down to my office, I'll give you some money."

There was no way he'd come to my office. Instead, he sent someone else to collect for him, an ex-con who was involved with the South Side group. Like I did with Barbaro, I only gave him $1,500 each time he showed up. A few days later, Johnson would get high, and then call again to threaten me. This helped build a case for extortion in addition to bookmaking.

Bit by bit, as I dug myself deeper into this double life, my habits and my surroundings had to change. I became sensitive to the fact that my apartment was on the ground floor with big windows, so I moved to a place on an upper floor without a view. My longtime secretary was a sharp young woman, who would eventually figure out what was going on, so I had to let her go. State Senator LeRoy Lemke was not so sharp, but I didn't want him to suffer collateral damage, either, so I forced him out of our partnership.

The hardest change was to stop gambling. It was such a huge part of my social life, my relaxation and my recreation. Just a week after I got my instructions from Gary, one of my best buddies, a crazy dentist, asked me to put some money on a big game for him. When I called in the bet, I couldn't help but place one for myself. As soon as I did, I realized what a mistake I made. One stupid bet could destroy the entire investigation. I said to myself, "If I'm going to do this, I can't lie to the Feds." The next time I saw Steve Bowen, I told him I had something to say. It was as bad as going to confession when I was a kid. "Steve," I said, "I gambled." I gave him the name of the bookie and the amount I gambled, and I never did it again.

But I didn't go through all these changes just to nail a bunch of bookies. I wanted to go after big game already. During the spring of 1986, I continued to brief the FBI agents about all my activity with the First Ward, so I could start wearing a wire on Roti and Marcy. One story always led to another. I would start talking about the Lenny Chow fix with Judge Maloney, and the next thing I knew, they were picking my brain about the On Leong Chinese Merchants Association.

We now met at a more convenient place for me, a Countryside motel near my apartment. In May, Gary Shapiro and another assistant U.S. attorney attended the session, and I expected they would finally have the written agreement for my "use" immunity. But once again, Gary started our meeting by saying he had had a discussion about me with the U.S. Attorney, Anton Valukas. "When we told him about all these different things you were involved in and that some of them were illegal acts on your part, he said it might be a good idea if you pled guilty to a misdemeanor." Gary then stopped and asked, "What do you think of that?"

I was so angry, the blood was pounding in my ears. I said, "What the fuck are you talking about?"

Gary said, "He just thinks that because you've admitted to all these things, it might be a good idea if you plead guilty to some misdemeanor."

I said, "You fucking people have got to be kidding. I came in to help you. I'm giving up my life. All I asked for was 'use' immunity. Now you're telling me to take a plea and maybe go to jail. If I go to jail, I'm a dead man. Besides, I can't plead guilty and be of any help to you. It will negate all I'm trying to do. It will totally destroy my credibility. It will look like I was in trouble and that's why I came in to you." I got up from the chair and said, "I made the mistake of my life." Then I stormed out of the room.

I walked the few blocks back to my apartment, kicking myself all the way. I had been too trusting. I ate all their bullshit about not gambling or practicing criminal law. I wore a wire on the most powerful mobster in Chicago. And what did I get in return? The jackpot.

When I got home, I was still so hot that I decided to go cool off by the pool. I grabbed my portable phone, stomped downstairs, and had just settled into a lounge chair, when I got a call. It was Gary. "Why did you leave?" he asked. "What's the matter?"

I said, "Fuck you. I don't need this bullshit. I better get myself a lawyer. I'm going to need one." Then I hung up and called my old friend from Marquette, Bill Murphy. He had become a very successful defense attorney. I said, "Bill, I met with the Feds and I was going to cooperate with them."

He couldn't believe it. Bill was always warning people to stay away from the Feds. He said, "Bob, are you crazy? You know you can't trust them."

"You're probably right," I said. "I think now I'm going to need some representation. I thought I had a deal with them, and now they're backing out."

"But what did you do?" Bill asked.

"I can't even tell you," I said, "but now I don't know what I can do."

Bill and I arranged to meet the next day, but before I even left my apartment that morning, Gary called me again. I told him, "You people have really wronged me. I got myself a lawyer and now you have to talk to him before I say another thing."

Gary said, "But we changed our mind."

"What?"

He said, "I told you '*Valukas* thought it was a good idea to take a plea.' But if you don't think it's a good idea, we'll just forget about it. If you have a lawyer, that's fine, but be careful. It's dangerous for you to talk to anyone else."

"Okay," I said, "I still want something in writing." In fact, I didn't get my "use" immunity in writing for another year and a half. But what was I going to do? I had already crossed the line, and like I told myself in the parking lot of DiFronzo's dealership, there was no going back.

A few hours later, I got together with Gary and the rest of the team at the Countryside motel. It was probably the most productive session I had with them. I put together a list of all the judges I had paid off— either "hand to hand" or through a conduit, like Pat Marcy or a clerk. Also, for the first time, I gave them the details behind the Aleman fix.

But even after all I told them, the Feds would still not let me go after the First Ward. Instead, they pointed me toward another distraction. This one involved a defense attorney named Joe Ettinger, one of my professors in law school and one of the city's leading experts on ethics. He was representing Big Bill Hill, probably the city's biggest dope dealer at that time. Evidently, he had gotten Hill to come up with $25,000 to pay off the judge. One of Ettinger's cop friends was going to be the conduit, but the bagman suddenly died of a heart attack and the judge never got the money. Ettinger was now in a fix himself. He couldn't ask the client for another payoff, and if he didn't deliver the expected results during the trial, Big Bill could get very mad at him. Mr. Ethics went to Blackie Pesoli for help, and since Blackie knew I was a friend of the judge, he sent Ettinger my way. I notified the Feds. Although they authorized me to wear the wire on Ettinger, they didn't want me to do anything to help fix the case. I had Ettinger meet me in my office, so we had him on tape and on the hidden video camera. I couldn't help but find the whole scene amusing. Here was a lawyer everyone thought was legit, trying to buy the sort of fix he condemned from his media soapbox. I got him to tell me the whole story all over again. Ettinger was clearly terrified of Big Bill. He said, "It's very important. Whatever you want, I'll pay you. I have to get a not guilty."

By the time Ettinger left my office, I thought the Feds had a rock-solid case against him. But they asked that I meet him again and get him to tell me what he would pay for a fix. We met at one of my favorite Greek restaurants. I pretended that I had already talked to the judge, and that he was afraid the Feds were watching this trial. I told Ettinger what strategy he could use if he took the case to a jury, but he cut me off and said, "I don't want to take it to a jury."

I had a lot of trouble getting him on tape that day in the restaurant. Maybe he suspected something or thought we would be overheard. He talked in whispers, so even I barely understood him. When I asked what he would pay, he decided to be cute, and wrote the figure on the back of a napkin. I kept my eye on the napkin, and when he wasn't looking, I put it into my pocket. It was an airtight bribery case. When FBI agents later questioned him, he out-and-out lied to them, which was another felony. But like so many of my other investigations, for some mysterious reason this one never resulted in charges.

By June, it looked like the Feds wouldn't let me do anything but chase these small fry. I decided to take the bull by the horns. I went through the old files in my office, looking for something that might get Marcy to talk to me about one of the cases I had fixed. I found a grand jury transcript from New York. It had been sent to me by another lawyer who worked on On Leong cases. One of the witnesses repeated a story he had heard about how we fixed the case for Lenny Chow.

This time, I wasn't going to ask the Feds for their permission *before* I talked to Marcy, so they could tell me, "No." Instead, I first went down to Counsellors Row without a wire and had Marcy come out in the lobby with me. I said, "Pat, somebody's going to send me a copy of a grand jury transcript. It's supposed to say something about On Leong and that the case was fixed with Tom Maloney."

He said, "You're kidding."

I said, "Yeah. When I get it, I'll show you."

"Oh, yeah, do that," Pat said. "Most certainly."

Now that the door was open, the Feds had to let me walk through. I called Dave Grossman, one of the FBI agents assigned to me. He then had me meet with Tom Durkin, an assistant U.S. attorney. Tom was a big hefty guy with glasses. He had been an accountant before he went to law school, and from the outside he looked like a fairly mild-mannered CPA, but he was an absolutely ferocious trial lawyer and an expert on racketeering. He quickly became my strongest ally among the federal prosecutors. I told Tom, "If you can just let me wear the wire when I show Marcy this transcript, I can get him to implicate himself in the On Leong case."

Somehow Tom and Gary Shapiro got the permission for me to wear the wire on Marcy. I waited a few days and on Thursday, June 5, went back to Counsellors Row with my Nagra. I took Marcy into the lobby to look at the transcript. Not until I pulled it out did I notice—for the first time—that there was a date on the upper corner of each page, and it was from years before. I pulled it back from him and held my thumb over the corner of the transcript, and acted like I was helping him flip to the important pages. "Look here," I said to Pat. "I got a copy of the whole transcript this time."

Then I showed him some of the testimony and said, "This little fucking punk is saying I told him the case was fixed. I never told anybody that we fixed the case. In fact, everybody thinks I'm enemies with Tom Maloney. Nobody knows that he or you were involved and nobody is going to know you were involved."

I was laying it on thick. Too thick. But so much was at stake; I couldn't help but overdo it. Pat looked at me and he looked at the page for a minute. Then he said, "Bob, didn't you go down there? You went to New York, didn't you?"

"Uh-huh," I said. Marcy had told me exactly what I wanted to hear. He confirmed he knew all about the On Leong fix down to my trip for the final payment.

"Who was the judge?" he asked.

"Maloney," I said. "Maloney was the judge." Later I asked, "Don't you think you should warn him?"

Pat shook his head no. He said, "If there's a problem, he'll get ahold of me. He knows how to handle himself. I ain't going to shake him up."

I walked out of Counsellors on a cloud. The statute of limitations had long since passed on the On Leong fix, but if we made a new case, we could link it with On Leong and show a pattern of racketeering. Now, I thought, we were ready to rock and roll. I could stop spinning my wheels on bookies and build a case against the First Ward.

After they heard the Marcy tape, all the prosecutors and the FBI agents on the Strike Force were finally convinced I was telling them the truth, and they could see the potential of my investigation. There were no objections when I asked to put a wire on Alderman Roti to show that he was also involved with the On Leong. The next week, unannounced, I dropped into his office at City Hall. The secretary told me he was in the city council chambers. She called him there, and he told her to have me come over.

I went back down to the second floor of City Hall, and as I turned the corner, I saw that they had installed a metal detector right in front of the council chambers. There had been some raucous protest the day before and the police didn't want to take any chances during the city council meeting. I would have turned around, but Roti was on the other side of the metal detector, talking with a couple of people, and he spotted me. He waved for me to come on in. I walked towards him down the long hall with its cathedral ceiling. As I got closer, I looked to see if I knew one of the coppers by the metal detector, so he would let me walk around it, but I didn't know any of them. I got a few feet away when I just stopped in my tracks, turned on my heels, and walked back down that long, long corridor. I could feel Roti's eyes on me each step of the way.

I went right from City Hall to my car and pulled the wire off. Then I went across the street to Counsellors Row and left a message at Roti's office that I would be waiting for him to call me at the restaurant.

After an hour or so, when I didn't hear from him, I left Counsellors Row. I met the agent and handed my Nagra back to him, and then went to my office. I still didn't get a call from Roti. I couldn't stand waiting to hear from him or wondering what he was thinking. The next day, without the wire, I went to Counsellors Row when I knew he'd be eating lunch. He was sitting at the First Ward table with Marcy and a few other people. When he saw me, he said, "Why wouldn't you come through that metal detector yesterday?"

I tried to laugh, and then bent over to whisper, "What do you think? Because I was wearing a piece. I can't walk through those things and have them find that."

"Oh," he said. "So what did you want anyway?"

I came up with some excuse to ask for a bullshit favor. He acted like he'd be happy to help. I waved good-bye and left.

Now even I was spooked. I wondered if he really bought my explanation. Out of the corner of my eye, I saw Marcy give me a funny look—or what seemed like one. The Feds didn't have to keep me away from Counsellors Row any more. Until I was sure where I stood with the First Ward, I wouldn't go back to the restaurant—with or without a wire.

If I was edgy that summer, I had a good excuse. One week after the incident in City Hall, I had another of my last meals—this time, dinner with Tony Spilotro and his younger brother Mike. Earlier in the year,

Tony had survived another prosecution when he was acquitted for the burglaries committed by his Hole-in-the-Wall Gang. Oscar Goodman represented him again, and a "surprise" witness for the defense was the recently retired chief of detectives for the Chicago Police Department, Bill Hanhardt. He discredited the Feds' chief witness, Frank Cullotta, who had been Tony's old pal. Spilotro got another break—or so it seemed—at the start of the Strawman trial for casino skimming. He developed a legitimate heart condition. His case was then severed from that trial. His co-defendants, including some very top Outfit bosses, were found guilty. As I looked at Tony across the table, he looked much older than his forty-eight years. His hair was now gray and his bulldog face had gone puffy. I thought, "No fun being a tough guy. Not any more."

Little did I know. Tony thought he was in town for a sit-down the next day with his new crew leader. Instead, he and his brother were beaten to death with baseball bats and buried in an Indiana cornfield. A farmer found the bodies a few weeks later. Evidently, the bosses were not happy about the trouble hotheaded Tony had caused in Vegas. Worse yet, his behavior may have touched off the Strawman cases, but then he got off the hook when so many of his elders went away. The use of the bats said it all. The Outfit did not play games. They played for keeps.

I climbed down from the mountaintop, and was back in the weeds with the Feds as they tried to build more bullshit cases. In the middle of the summer, they asked me if I would fix a "contrived case" before Judge Adam Stillo in the Maywood branch of the Cook County Circuit Court. I said, "Sure."

The Feds used to call Maywood the Mafiosi court. A lot of the Mob's cases ended up there, because it was smack in the middle of the Italian suburbs. There were as many Italians inside the courthouse as outside— judges, lawyers, and court personnel. Terry Hake, the mole in Operation Greylord, broke his pick trying to crack it. The place was too damn insular. Johnny D'Arco had introduced me to Judge Stillo at a fundraiser and, as I told the FBI agents, I had paid him off dozens of times. He was a jolly old guy, always pleasant, but no dummy either. He was very careful about how we exchanged money, and I was sure he'd be extra-careful after Greylord.

In August, wearing my wire, I approached Judge Stillo in his chambers to see if he would still work with me. He said he might—as long as it wasn't a gambling case. I told him I wouldn't bother him with bullshit. "Unless it's real important, I won't even talk to you," I said.

So what did I get as my "real important" case? The Feds concocted the most bullshit traffic stop I could imagine. Supposedly an *off-duty* state policeman pulls a guy over after he sees him drive erratically. (He had to be off duty, so the Feds would not have to wrongly account for a state police car.) When he looks in the car, he sees an open can of beer. Then he finds a few grams of marijuana in the glove compartment. Worse yet, to play the part of the driver, the Feds used some corn-fed blond FBI agent from Oklahoma and gave him the name James David Hess. When I met the guy, I said, "You look just like an FBI agent."

Later I told Tom Durkin, "This isn't going to work. It just doesn't ring true. Why would a guy who looks like this have the open beer *and* the dope?"

I suggested they put a gun in the glove compartment instead. But for some reason the Feds weren't allowed to fake a gun charge—even if it had a broken firing pin. Against my better judgment, I decided I should be a team player. At least they were trying to make a case. "Okay," I said, "we'll try it."

Two months later I put on my wire and went back to Stillo's chambers. He wanted to gossip a bit about the D'Arcos and some of the Mob figures I used to see in Senior's Florida beach houses. I told him that I had no idea why Senior would sell those beautiful homes. The judge joked, "Bugs in them."

At some point, I slipped in the news that my "important" case had been scheduled. "I got something coming up in about two weeks," I told him. "It's some guy with some 'grass' in the glove compartment of his car." I explained that he'd have no trouble throwing it out, because the arresting officer made an illegal search. But then he said, "You know my nephew Joey? Talk to him."

That was bizarre. Judge Stillo never had a bagman before. I always paid him off directly, but it was another sign he was trying to be careful. His nephew, Joey Stillo, was a tall thin snake of a guy—almost the polar opposite of his uncle. They both lived in the suburb of River Forest, but Joey was a criminal defense lawyer, and he loved hanging out with the bad guys in the Italian restaurants and bars on the West Side. After I broke up with Johnny D'Arco's firm, the First Ward started steering Mob cases toward Joey.

I took Joey to lunch, and he, too, wanted to chitchat about Johnny D'Arco. We finally got around to the "Hess" case, and I explained why it would be so easy for his uncle to throw out. I didn't ask outright for a fix. I would never have done that in the old days, and I wasn't about to change my habits while I was wearing a wire. Instead, I said, "You tell me what's fair and we'll take care of it then."

Joey said, "All right."

"As I say," I said, "I never complain about the numbers."

Before I left, Joey assured me that he'd work things out with his uncle. "Don't worry," he said. "I'll make the call."

The Hess case went to trial November 5, 1986. Just the day before, we had elections in Cook County, and three judges were thrown off the bench—including Lawrence Passarella. The press and everyone else blamed his downfall on the Mike Colella case. Judge Stillo must have seen that in the morning papers. Not the best timing for a fix— especially with me.

The trooper who was supposed to have arrested Hess was the state's most important "witness." I tried to coach the guy beforehand. In our twisted world of make-believe, I wanted him to say things that would make it *easier* for Judge Stillo to throw the case out. "Testify that you used your flashlight," I told him. "Then we would have an illegal search."

This trooper got pissed off with that suggestion, because he knew the law. "I *never* use a flashlight," he said. "I'm not going to lie."

"But you didn't really arrest him, either," I said. "This whole case is a lie."

When he got up on the stand, the trooper ignored my coaching and said exactly what I told him *not* to. It was like he was going in for the kill on a real case. I didn't think it mattered much. But Judge Stillo ruled that the search was legal, and he found my client guilty. He gave him a $50 fine and a year of supervision. Maybe he thought he was doing me a favor, because the sentence could have been as much as $1,000 and a year in prison.

But I was stunned. I had never lost a case before this judge. After I left the courthouse, I regrouped with the FBI agents and the prosecutors. We were all in shock. I wondered whether now, after Judge Passarella's defeat, I was too hot for another fix. One of the prosecutors suggested I should still pay off Joey in return for the light sentence. I rejected that idea. Then the Stillos would know for sure I was trying to set them up. "Let me go see Joey anyway," I said, "and see if I can turn this around."

I put on the wire and went downtown to Joey's law firm. When we were alone in his office, I started to beef about the state trooper's testimony. I told him I could understand why the judge found Hess guilty, but then Joey cut me off. "That's not why he did it."

"Then why?" I asked.

"Something about this guy coming from Oklahoma," Joey said. "He looks like an FBI agent."

I tried to laugh it off as Greylord paranoia. "This judge is seeing FBI agents in his soup."

But when I turned over the tape, the Feds didn't see the joke. They thought I had to leave town. If Stillo had figured out I was working with the FBI, they said, my cover was blown. It was a matter of time before everyone knew.

I wasn't leaving town—not over this stupid case. I said, "Let me see the judge and see what I can do with him." That very afternoon, I put on the wire and went back into Judge Stillo's chambers and caught him right after lunch. When I asked what happened with my "client," he said, "He didn't sound right. He sounded like a plant. I just started having bad vibes out there." When the judge ran a check on Hess's license plate, no name or address came back, which is usually what happens with a law enforcement vehicle.

Inside, I was seething. How could the Feds be so careless? But on the outside I kept acting like this was one big joke. "Judge, you have to be kidding," I laughed. "This guy's a bookmaker. I've known him for years." Thinking fast, I said he was with the Rush Street group. I figured

Stillo wouldn't know any mobsters from that part of town. I explained that Hess wanted to be a commodities broker, but now that he was on supervision for this offense, he couldn't get his license.

The judge bought my explanation and offered to make it up to me. I went back to him a few months later to get the supervision terminated, just to keep my story straight, but at this point he didn't ask for money, and I didn't give him any.

Even though no money changed hands with the Stillos, their intentions were clear on the tape. The Feds had been too quick to give up on the case and me, I thought, when all it took to seal the deal was one more wire on the judge. His comments alone about "the plant" gave the Feds enough ammunition to bring charges against him and the nephew. But I didn't care much either way. The Stillos were strictly penny-ante, like something out of Operation Greylord. But while we were playing around with this bullshit case, we did get our first big break—totally out of the blue—and it would lead to none other than Judge Thomas J. Maloney.

CHAPTER 10
THE WORST FUCK

Everything in the Maloney case started with an "innocent" phone call from Billy Swano, a criminal defense attorney. When I had first met him years before, Billy was a public defender and a real sharp lawyer. We started going to the same places at night, and sometimes we would hang together. He had dark good looks and a frat-boy mentality about partying, but then he started to dip too much into the cocaine and would do crazy things when he got high. Once, his girlfriend called me to say he was beating her up and stalking her. I straightened him out, and Billy left her alone. Not a totally bad thing, since she became my girlfriend for a while. Another time, a client asked me if he could trust Billy to buy some dope for him. Again, I had to confront Billy and get angry with him. I said, "Are you fucking nuts?" But he would listen to me like I was a big brother.

After he left the public defender's office, Billy became a private criminal attorney. When he put his mind to it, he could be an effective lawyer. He won some high-profile cases and I sent a few lowlife clients his way. But when he called me in September of 1986, I hadn't seen him for a year. He said, "Can I meet with you?" Coincidentally, he lived in an apartment complex close to my own in Countryside.

In my bones, I felt this could be important. I called Steve Bowen, and when I mentioned Billy Swano's name, he said, "Are you kidding? Will you wear a wire on him?" Evidently something was up with Swano, but Steve couldn't tell me.

By the time Billy appeared on my doorstep, Steve had dropped off the Nagra. This time I tried to put it inside one of my cowboy boots, but that turned out to be another fuck-up. Every time I moved, my boot squeezed the metal case and shut down the recorder. It didn't matter, since Billy didn't say anything too earthshaking. He mostly wanted to talk about Paul Baker, a client I had pawned off on him. Baker was a weird violent guy who ran with a bunch of hick thieves and drug dealers called the Hillbilly Mafia. The last time I saw him, he was lying on his couch with a needle sticking in his arm. I never wanted anything to do with him after that. Whenever you turned around, Paul Baker had another murder or attempted murder charge against him. To escape the latest rap, he started talking to the Feds. An assistant U.S. Attorney showed Swano what Paul said about him and me—about how he wanted to gamble with me, how he paid Swano in cocaine and so on. Most of it was a bunch of bullshit, but some of it was true. Billy started talking like a tough guy. He wanted me to find someone who could "whack" Baker.

"Whoa, Billy," I said. "You don't even want to think like that or you're just gonna make more problems for yourself."

He decided to withdraw from Baker's case the next day. First he would see the judge and then he'd break the news to Paul, who was in Cook County Jail. He asked me to go with him when he saw Paul. I couldn't believe Swano was so scared of him. But Baker did have a cross-eyed psycho look. I had made him wear thick glasses when I defended him before a jury in a murder case. He smashed the glasses on the table as soon as he heard, "not guilty." But Billy didn't need me to protect him from Paul. Baker was already in jail. What could he do to Billy there?

I got the wire and met Billy the next day at the Criminal Courthouse. They were holding Baker in a cell behind one of the courtrooms. We went in together to see him. I told Paul, "I found out you gave the Feds some information about me. Why would you do that, after all I did for you?" Of course, Baker denied it. I said, "Swano indicates you have a beef with him. You better work it out in a nice way." Then I left the two of them alone.

When Billy came out, he said, "I have to go upstairs to see Judge Maloney. You want to walk with me?"

I figured, what the hell. I didn't have anything better to do. Besides, I could see Billy was stewing over something. We got in the elevator, and he said, "He fucked me."

"What?" I replied. Was Maloney the one who fucked him?

Then Swano asked me, "What's the worst fuck that somebody can do to you?"

To bust his balls, I said, "Steal your girl?"

He said, "No. Worse than that." Then out of the corner of his mouth, he added, "He takes the money and still finds them guilty."

"On a case?" I asked.

"A murder case," he said.

"You're kidding."

"But I got the money back," he said.

I thought to myself, "Is he really talking about Maloney?" Just to make sure I got this on tape, I repeated back what I heard him say: "He takes the money, finds them guilty, and then gives the money back?" I asked. "What good does that do you?"

Now I remembered. He had just worked a big case in front of Maloney that was in all the papers. It involved a contract killing for the city's most notorious street gang, the El Rukns.

We got out of the elevator, and Swano left me for a minute. He poked his head into Maloney's chambers, but then came back when he saw the judge was out. I asked Billy if he was talking about the El Rukns trial.

He nodded and said, "Listen, I mean Maloney and I have been like this for years." He held his two fingers together. "He always thought I was a great lawyer. I've always won up there." Then rubbing his thumb over his index finger, he added, "His track record has always been excellent. But now he's nuts. He's not to be trusted."

When I kept telling him I couldn't believe it, he shot back, "Just trust me. It just happened."

At that very moment, the elevator doors opened, and who got out but Judge Thomas J. Maloney himself. At first he looked shocked to see me standing there with Billy boy, but then he gave me his usual scowl and went huffing off down the hall. Billy chased after him.

Now I understood why the Feds were so interested in my meeting with Swano. Later, they went nuts when they heard the tapes with him. Evidently they had a few high-placed snitches in the El Rukns, along with some wiretaps on their phones, and knew a fix was coming down. During the entire trial, they had watched behind the scenes, hoping to catch Swano and Maloney in the act. At the last minute, with all the press that the trial was getting, Maloney must have gotten cold feet. He found Swano's two clients guilty. Then, to add insult to injury, he held their sentencing hearing before a jury, and they both got the electric chair.

It didn't matter that Maloney gave back the El Rukns' money. He had still originally intended to fix the case. Swano knew more than enough to implicate him. Meanwhile, my tape with Marcy about the On Leong fix could help build a racketeering charge against Maloney, too.

Suddenly, the misery I had gone through to wear the wire seemed worth it. Next to Marcy and Roti, Maloney was the symbol of all that was wrong with Chicago's criminal justice system. He wasn't fixing traffic cases and misdemeanors like Stillo. He was fixing *murder* cases, and no judge in America had ever been caught doing that.

Still, to get anywhere on Maloney we needed Billy Swano, and just hours after I left him outside the judge's chambers, he called to say he wanted to meet again that day. I told him to come to my office.

I put on the wire, and we set up the hidden video. Once he sat down in my office, I told Swano I had heard things about the El Rukns trial. He knew I had sources in the police department and the FBI—he used to see me hanging out with agents in the bars on Rush Street. "Billy," I said, "they're investigating this case. They know about the El Rukns and the money being transferred. You may find yourself with a problem. You should try to get yourself immunity and work something out."

He said, "I never said anything about fixing the case or passing money."

Now I knew why he had come to my office. He was trying to "clean up" and throw cold water on everything he told me in the courthouse. Maybe after I left him, Maloney had mentioned to Billy how much we hated each other. Maybe Billy had seen a lawyer. Before he said another word, I cut him off. "You're talking in a strange way for some reason," I said. "I think we better end the conversation right here, because you're talking into a microphone or something now if you're talking like that."

Here I was, accusing *him* of wearing a wire, but it calmed Billy right down. He almost apologized. "I'm not talking into a microphone," he said. "I appreciate your help." We shook hands and I showed him out of my office.

Nothing was going to come easy for us. I would need a lot of time before I could turn Billy around. The most important thing was not to bug him about it, or he would get suspicious. I had to wait for him to call me again to check out my "sources."

When I first started working with the Feds, I had fantasies about making cases for them one after another, and being done with the whole investigation in a year. But now, winter was rolling around again, and I hadn't done shit.

Then, I got a call from one of the FBI agents on my case. Anton Valukas, the U.S. Attorney for Chicago, was finally ready for a meeting. He asked that I go to the Palmer House, an old hotel in the center of the city's business district. When I got there, I went through the usual routine: I saw Steve Bowen in the lobby, and he followed me into an elevator. We went to a room on an upper floor.

Valukas was waiting for us there, wearing his suit and tie like he was ready for court. He had reddish hair and a pinched, pale face with a stern expression. He never extended his hand. He only said, "I'm Anton Valukas."

I said, "I'm Bob Cooley."

So much for pleasantries. He then said, "You paid off Judge Sodini, didn't you?"

"That's right," I said. I had given the FBI agents Ray Sodini's name along with a list of other judges I had bribed. I used to pay Ray for guns and gambling cases by going to his chambers closet and leaving money in his jacket pocket. He had been indicted the year before as part of Greylord, and his case was coming to trial. Valukas made himself the prosecutor—probably because the case would be a slam-dunk conviction.

"I want to know what you can tell me," Valukas said. "I want to use you as a witness."

"What?" I couldn't believe my ears.

He repeated, "I want to use you as a witness."

If he used me as a witness, my cover would be blown and the whole investigation would be over. I said, "I haven't done anything yet."

"I need you on this case," he said.

"But please don't call me as a witness on this case," I said. I was practically begging him. "If you give me a chance, I can do so much more than Sodini. I can destroy the whole First Ward. I can take down all the Mob people."

But nothing I said seemed to matter to him. "To assure a conviction on this case, I need you as a witness," he said.

He needed me like he needed a third eye. So many lawyers had paid off Ray Sodini, Valukas could have lined them up around the block. He kept me in the room for another half-hour, asking when I had paid Sodini and how much each time. I could feel the steam coming off the top of my head.

As soon as he let me go, I found a phone in the hotel and called Gary Shapiro. "This is bullshit," I told him. "I've given up my law license. Once I'm exposed, I'll have given up my life. All this, to be one more witness against Ray Sodini?"

I was told that Gary had to go to Washington to keep Valukas from putting me on the Sodini witness list. They could still have called me to testify during the trial; but then, in January 1987, Sodini pled guilty. Who knows? If poor old Ray hadn't thrown in the towel, my whole investigation could have come crashing down around him.

Still, over the course of 1987, I wondered what I could ever accomplish with the Feds. They just kept me busy on bullshit assignments that never went anywhere.

At the beginning of the year, it looked like they wanted me to make a gambling case against DiFronzo and some of the crews. I went to a couple of Super Bowl parties with a very cute young woman, who was an FBI agent from the East Coast. We were both wearing wires. Marco and his crew hosted one of the parties at a West Side Italian restaurant.

John DiFronzo was there at one of the tables with the chief of the Elm-wood Park Police Department. At one point, they sold "squares" for point combinations in the upcoming game. You paid $1,000 and picked a square. If your square contained the last number of the win-ning team's score, you could make a lot of money. To determine the numbers that went with each square, they picked cards from a deck. Marco's right-hand man, Donny Scalise, pulled my "girlfriend" over and said, "To make this honest, we'll have her shuffle the cards and cut the deck."

I thought, "Donny, you have no idea how honest she can be."

Later, the agent and I attended a similar party at Faces, run by the Chinatown group. There, too, I bought a square.

We had enough to shut down both places, but the Feds didn't make a case against anyone for the Super Bowl parties. They also refused to let me put a wire again on any of the First Ward heavyweights. Mean-while, the ropes they wrapped around my practice were starting to rub me raw. I was now careful to report my income to the IRS, but I had to pay my back taxes, too. I was getting chopped down to size an inch at a time.

Even more frustrating, when I knew a case was about to be fixed, the Feds wouldn't let me do anything about it. The first time was a child abuse trial that started just after I came in. The molester was a wealthy car dealer from the South Side who had abused a grandchild. I used to see him eat at Greco's all the time. I notified the Feds, but they told me, "You can't interfere with a live case." Just as I predicted, it went to a bench trial before a bad judge. He threw out the confession and acquitted the bastard.

Late in 1986, Blackie Pesoli approached me to see if I would "handle" another, more notorious child abuse case. This one involved a Chicago high school principal named James Moffat. He was accused of molesting five students (four boys and a girl) at least eight times. I told Blackie this sort of case turned my stomach, and he didn't bug me any more about it. But then I saw that the case ended up with Alderman Ed Burke's wife, Anne, and a high-priced lawyer named Lawrence O'Gara. It was to be decided in a bench trial by Francis Mahon, one of the Circuit Court judges Ed Burke had made. Everyone thought Mahon was straight, and maybe he was, but this time I didn't ask the Feds for permission to intervene. Instead, I called the judge's personal bailiff and disguised my voice. I said, "The Feds know that Eddy Burke is behind fixing this case, so they're paying real close attention." The judge found Moffat guilty and called the evidence "shocking and ugly."

Of course, Anne Burke screamed to high heaven about the verdict, but this was no flimsy case. The state had the school's staff testify about how Moffat kept taking the kids into his private office and then went to their teachers to change their grades. I got some small measure of satisfaction from that outcome, even though there was nothing else I could do with it.

But meanwhile, Mr. and Mrs. Burke were working on another disgusting case—this time with Pat Tuite, another of the First Ward's high-profile criminal defense lawyers, and also their good friend. The Feds would let me use my wire on this one, but once again there was nothing I could to do affect the eventual verdict. The defendant, Herbert Cammon, was a social worker accused of stabbing his wife to death to collect on her life insurance policy. There was all kinds of circumstantial evidence against him: He married the woman after a "whirlwind romance" and she would be killed just a few months later; despite the marriage, he kept his gay lover; he insisted on a $250,000 policy for the wife when the insurance agent advised him that $50,000 was enough; a janitor saw him in their apartment building just before the killing, but he later told police he had been nowhere near; there was even evidence that Cammon called the insurance company to see if the policy was in effect shortly before the wife's murder. When the case went to trial in 1984, the jury deadlocked, voting ten to two for conviction. After that close call, Cammon was evidently willing to pay *anything* to make sure he wasn't convicted in the retrial.

Pompous Pat Tuite liked to think of himself as a great lawyer, but nobody—not even Clarence Darrow—could have saved Cammon in a legitimate retrial. To acquit this character, Tuite needed a bench trial and plenty of help from the judge. He had just one problem— the judge on the case was ornery little Arthur Cieslik. After his experience with the killer cops case, Burke knew he couldn't trust Cieslik to give him the verdict he wanted. Instead, he pushed Cieslik to recuse himself.

But Cieslik dug in his heels. He didn't know why the case should go to another judge. Then, Tuite brought in Anne Burke as his co-counsel. She told a reporter that working with Tuite on this case was her law school "graduation gift." Since Cieslik had "political ties" to Burke's husband, Tuite and Anne Burke filed a motion asking the judge to withdraw.

Still, Cieslik wouldn't let go of the case, and the appeals courts agreed with him. He could sniff out what the defense intended to do, and for the next three years he fought their motions. At one point, he got an angry visit from Alderman Burke. Cieslik told him that there was a lot of evidence that Cammon had killed his wife. According to the judge, Burke then said, "It's only a fucking nigger." (Both Cammon and the wife were black.) I heard Burke use that same line when he talked about the vagrant the cops had killed.

Cieslik said he replied, "She was a human being, Ed. She was a human being."

A few times during 1987, I went to visit Cieslik in his chambers while I was wearing a wire. Although he didn't know it, I got his version on tape and hoped Cammon would be the basis for a case on Burke. I tried to keep the judge strong, but I could see they were wearing him down. He was convinced that Burke and Tuite were orchestrating a campaign against him in the press. An article appeared about him in the *Chicago Tribune*, charging that he used harsh sentences to punish defendants who chose jury trials. Later, he was reprimanded for "disparaging" comments he made to female attorneys. Finally Cieslik had had enough and he let the Cammon case go. If there really was a campaign against Cieslik, it succeeded. During the next election, he was thrown off the bench—with the help of the *Tribune* editorial page. No one could ever call the judge "politically correct," but as I knew too well, he had far more honesty and integrity than most of the judges the paper endorsed.

Once Cieslik let go of the Cammon case, it was assigned to none other than Thomas J. Maloney. Now, I thought, the Feds had all the necessary pieces to follow a classic fix as it developed: first, how Burke maneuvered behind the scenes to get an honest judge off the case, and then how the First Ward machine could rig the so-called random assignment to Maloney. The final piece would come with Maloney's ruling, which was sure to be a not guilty. To pull Burke, Marcy, and Maloney into one indictment would have been a Strike Force trifecta.

In my mind, we already had a good case against Maloney with the El Rukn trial. As I hoped, Billy Swano finally did give me another call, in March 1987 (six months after I threw him out of my office). We met in a diner parking lot near where we lived in Countryside. Billy got into the passenger seat of my car. Since I had seen him last, the El Rukn prosecutors had put on more pressure. For legal help, Swano turned to Ed Genson and his partner, Jeff Steinback. As he sat in my car, Swano told me that Steinback had approached the prosecutor directly and asked if the Feds had Swano on tape. The prosecutor said, "No."

I had to bite my tongue. Obviously, the prosecutor didn't know about *my* tape with Billy. But how could he have answered that question at all? He pissed away all of his leverage. "Billy," I said, "the prosecutor is lying."

They were building a case on him, I said, whether or not they went after Maloney. Again, I told him, he had to make a deal. Billy wasn't ready to go there yet. "I would never roll over," he said. Clearly, he was scared to death of Maloney and the First Ward. Also, if he did prison time, he could meet up with some El Rukn inmates, and that wouldn't be fun either. As far as he was concerned, his only option was flight. "If they give me a lifetime in jail," he said, "I'm gone."

I shrugged my shoulders and wished him luck, but I did everything I could to seem disinterested. It's not like we were close friends, and I didn't want him to think I was pumping for information. He would have to get in touch with me again.

Almost three months went by before he called. He asked if I was going to be in my office for the next few hours. As soon as I got off the phone with him, I called Steve Bowen. He rushed over to bring me the Nagra. By this time, I knew myself how to set up the hidden video camera inside the attaché case. I liked to have both the video and the wire running in case one or the other broke down. I had a feeling that the third time with Swano would be the charm.

He arrived only a few minutes after we had everything set up. I could tell he was under enormous pressure and maybe a little high. The whole time we talked, he kept sitting down and standing up, rubbing his face or twirling his sunglasses. I got the impression he had just come from his lawyers and that they had gotten more calls from the U.S. Attorney.

One more time, Swano wanted to know how my sources got their information. I told him, "Somebody was telling them what was going on, step by step: what happened, how it happened, when it happened, where it happened."

"I wonder who that is," Swano said. "Are they saying that they have somebody tight with Maloney that was talking to me? If I fixed the case, who did I bribe?" Realizing what he said, he backtracked a bit and added, "Just, you know, hypothetically?"

"They have information that you bribed Maloney," I said.

"That's wrong, that's ridiculous," Swano said. "Maloney would have to say, 'Swano gave me money.' Right? Maloney ain't gonna do that. They'd have to have proof that I gave Maloney money."

For some reason, this didn't make sense to him. He said, "I wonder if they had Maloney wired. His phone might have been wired."

Clearly there was something else missing in what I told him—and it gave him hope that my "source" didn't know shit. Then he said, "They'd have to have somebody between Maloney and me."

Suddenly I realized what he was talking about—a bagman. Maloney would have never taken a payoff directly from Swano. There must have been someone else who took the money from Swano and gave it to the judge.

Now Swano got even more specific. He asked, "There was no mention of another lawyer involved?"

I answered, "There is somebody else."

Swano got up from his chair and, without knowing it, stared directly into the attaché case camera. "Well, that would be a liability," he said. "That'd be a real liability right there." He then let loose with a sigh—a sigh like all the air had been let out of his lungs. Billy could see his future, and it wasn't looking too good. You had to feel sorry for the guy.

As far as I was concerned, right there we had all we needed to make a case on Maloney. Once Swano knew I had him on tape, he would have no choice but to cooperate with the Feds and testify about the cases he had fixed with the judge.

After his close call with the El Rukns, you would think that Maloney would have sworn off fixes for a while, but the arrogance of the man knew no bounds. In January 1988, the Cammon murder case came before him in a bench trial. In another of his infamous convoluted rulings, Maloney called Cammon "a schemer, crooked, ignorant and callous," and then acquitted him for murdering his wife. Cammon died soon after, from AIDS. The only justice in this case was to come from the insurance company. After reviewing the evidence in the trials, the examiners refused to pay on the policy. If nothing else, I hoped that Tuite, Maloney, and the Burkes never saw an extra nickel for their fees.

I didn't know if I had enough evidence for the Feds to go after Ed Burke on this case, but Maloney was a different story. One way or the other, I thought, his day would come.

CHAPTER 11
CANDID CAMERA

By the start of 1988, I still had not managed to do anything of substance against the First Ward. I kicked myself for putting the wire on Marcy so early without having much of a case. Now I needed to have Pat, Roti, or Johnny D'Arco approach me on something current. Otherwise, I would never get permission to tape them.

For the first few months of the year, I tried to make something happen just by showing up in the right places. It was like trolling. In January I went to Florida and called Johnny D'Arco to let him know I was in town. We had lunch with Larry Oberman, the developer who picked up my bills at Faces to get closer to the First Ward. A few years before, in a truly bizarre incident, he was arrested for a plot to assassinate Mayor Harold Washington (who died from a heart attack in 1987). Although Larry first asked me to represent him on the case, Oberman was eventually steered to another First Ward lawyer. Maloney acquitted him in a bench trial.

After lunch with Oberman, Johnny asked that we get together again when we were both back in Chicago. I made a point to look for him the next time we were both in Counsellors Row, and he told me he did have a case for me to "handle." A chiropractor friend of his had been caught in a billing fraud. But Valukas wouldn't let me follow up with a wire. He told the assistant U.S. attorneys it was too "dangerous." That was such bullshit. I had already worn a wire on John DiFronzo. Was a state senator more dangerous than a Mob boss?

At one point, while I was in Counsellors Row with Johnny, Pat Marcy walked by. He acted a little more friendly than he had been in the past. Still, nothing developed from these chance meetings. I was trying to make a fire by piling up twigs and waiting for lightning to strike.

Meanwhile, Valukas decided to make my personal life that much more miserable. He said I had to stop doing criminal work of any kind. He had cut off my arms when he stopped me from taking on big cases or federal cases, and now he cut off my legs too. This all came about because of a case totally unrelated to me. A witness to a murder had approached me and offered to change his testimony for $200,000. I wasn't the lawyer, but I knew the defendant's father, a state senator. I could have kept the whole thing to myself and no one would have been the wiser. But I did the right thing and informed the Feds. Valukas saw the incident as a reason to go to Richie Daley, then the Cook County State's Attorney, and let him know I was working with the government. Just talking to Daley could have put me at risk, since Marcy had friends and relatives working assistant as state's attorneys (I reported one of them to the FBI). After Daley and Valukas spoke about me, they decided that *any* criminal work was now a "conflict" for me.

I had been making a decent living with the nickel-and-dime misdemeanor work. Once they took that away from me, I needed extra income. Although I built a civil law practice, I brought in another attorney full-time to help. I couldn't pull more money from him. Now when the Feds offered to make up for my lost business, I had to say yes. I took just $1,800 a month—enough to cover basic expenses—but I hated to take *any* government money. Down the road, when we finally got to trial, I could see it coming back to haunt us.

One day, while all of this was going on, Dave Grossman, one of the FBI agents, appeared at my door. He said, "You have to leave town. We have to get you into Witness Protection."

I said, "What are you talking about?"

"We just got information that your life might be in danger," he said. "You've got to go right away. I have some people coming by in a short while to help."

He was trying to save my life, and at the same time he was giving me a death sentence. That's what leaving Chicago meant to me. "I can't leave," I told him. "I haven't done anything. I haven't done what I set out to do. The least you can do is tell me why you think I have a problem."

"Someone came to a grand jury and testified that he did something illegal with you," he said. "The only other person he mentioned was just killed. We think he's giving you up because he knows you're next on the list."

"Let *me* worry about that," I told him. "I'm not going anywhere on that basis. End of conversation."

Whenever threats like this popped up with the Feds, I always laughed them off; but inside, I did know the risk I was taking. Now, I carried two guns with me at all times—the five-shot Airweight and a .45 with nine rounds. If Marcy had even a suspicion I was working with the Feds, he'd have me killed. I had no doubt about that. If I needed an example to keep me on my toes, I could look at our old Thursday night dinner companion, Dominic Senese. In January 1988, he got out of his Lincoln to open the security gate to his Oak Brook subdivision. Two guys walked up to him and one emptied a shotgun into Dom's face. He was 71, but still as big as a horse. After they ran off, he somehow crawled back in his car and managed to drive home. Over the next few days, the papers were full of stories about the failed whack job in Oak Brook. Supposedly Dom had fallen out with the Mob over control of his Teamsters local. Whatever the reason, Dom didn't talk—in fact, his jaws were wired shut—and he never cooperated with the Feds. Instead, he quietly stepped down from office. Of course, none of the reporters mentioned Marcy in their stories, but I knew who was responsible for the hit. Just a few months later, Johnny D'Arco had a fundraiser in the ballroom of a Gold Coast hotel. I saw Dom come in, his face covered with bandages like a mummy. He walked right over to the table where you handed in your donation. When he saw me, he stopped to say hello in a strange, strangled voice. Even through the bandages, I could see that the lower half of his face had been blown away. Then, I watched him shake hands with Johnny. Pat Marcy sat right nearby, but Dominic—who I once thought was Marcy's best friend—kept his back turned to Pat and then left the room.

By the spring of 1988, I realized that my time in Chicago had become very short. I had to make something happen soon. If some other Mojo shot his mouth off to a grand jury, Valukas would just as well be rid of me. I could no longer wait for a phone call, like the one I got from Swano, or a chance meeting at Counsellors Row. Instead, I had to brainstorm with Tom Durkin and Steve Bowen to get the investigation off the dime. If they could concoct some stupid traffic stop for Judge Stillo, why couldn't they come up with something a little more elaborate to catch Marcy and Roti in a sting? If they had restrictions with criminal cases, why couldn't they try civil ones? I suggested they fabricate a lawsuit for the Chancery Division of Cook County Court. That's where disputes were settled over huge amounts of money—even sweeter honey for a sting.

In early April, I put on a wire and met with Marcy at Counsellors Row. We went into the lobby, and I told him some bullshit story about two partners in a tax shelter racket. They now hated each other, and my client was suing to get $350,000 out of the bank account of their busted business. I wanted to make sure the case got in front of Judge Anthony Scotillo. I had bribed him in the past, and I knew Pat kept him on a short leash. When Pat heard about all the money involved, I could see his eyes light up. He told me he'd look into it and I should get back to him in a week. But when we met again, Pat wasn't his arrogant old self. He had spoken to the top judges, and they didn't want to screw with Chancery assignments. Greylord trials were still in the papers. "These guys are scared to death," Marcy said, "and I'm not gonna fuck around with them. I know they're gonna flip if they squeeze their neck a little. I don't need that shit."

Like it or not, we had to enter the lawsuit in the Chancery computer and wait for it to randomly assign the case. "There's no way to get around the machine," Marcy said. "I tried that a year ago."

We decided to take our chances with the computer. It was like throwing dice, but that was always fine with me. For the next few weeks, the Feds put flesh on the bones of our contrived case. My "client" was named Jim Nichols and they called his ex-partner Paul Wilson. In fact, everybody involved, besides me, was really an FBI agent with a pseudonym, including the lawyer for the other side. In July, I filed the complaint for Jim Nichols. The assignment came back a month later and bang, I rolled craps. Instead of a real corrupt judge, like Scotillo, we got David Shields, presiding judge for the entire Chancery Division. Every lawyer who was ever in his court held him in total esteem—including me. I had tried a dozen cases in front of him. He never found my clients guilty, but he never asked to be paid and I never thought of paying him. He was the last judge I considered to be a money guy. In fact, he was supposedly on track to be Chief Judge for the entire Circuit Court of Cook County, one of the largest unified court systems in the world.

But there was nothing I could do about the assignment. I had to tell Marcy. The subject came up while we were having lunch at the First Ward table. As long as we didn't speak about any illegal act, Marcy often brought up topics of previous conversations while we were eating. He asked who we got for my tax shelter case, and I said, "We got Shields."

"I wouldn't go near him with a ten-foot pole," Marcy said—just as I thought.

At that very moment, Patty DeLeo was sitting down for lunch. As usual, he couldn't help but overhear our conversation. A few minutes later, he pulled me aside and asked why I mentioned Shields to Marcy. I told him about my bad luck with the assignment, and that we couldn't work with Shields.

"No," Patty said, "he'll do whatever we want." He rubbed his thumb over his index finger. "All he's worried about is this."

I couldn't believe it. Of course, Patty DeLeo did his fair share of bullshitting, but he seemed totally confident. If he was right, my only regret was dragging Judge Shields into the investigation. But it was too late. Patty was on tape, and like it or not, I was committed to follow through. If he could make this happen, I told Patty, there would be $5,000 in it for him.

Three days later, on the morning of my hearing with Judge Shields, Patty and I walked into a bathroom in the Daley Center, the main office tower and courtroom complex for the Circuit Court. First I checked to make sure no one was sitting in one of the stalls. Then Patty said, "Give me the money, and I'll give it to him."

Into Patty's hands I counted out fresh, government-issued hundred-dollar bills. I said, "One, two, three. . . ." When I wore the wire, I always made a practice of counting out loud. If I got killed before we went to trial, I wanted the tapes to speak for themselves.

Patty was only too happy to play along. During one $2,500 payoff, after I counted out the hundred-dollar bills, he asked, "Was that twenty-five?"

From the bathroom, we went up to the 24th floor, where Patty ducked into Judge Shields's chambers for a moment, and then came out. Judge Shields told Patty he couldn't take the money until he granted the temporary restraining order (TRO) during our hearing. Shields would take a bribe, but he was being honorable about it.

When the Feds got my tapes back, they were ecstatic. The fact that Shields was a presiding judge made this a very big catch for them. I felt horrible that he was involved. He had always been such a fine and decent person. But if he had to suffer, at least it was for a good cause. With a case against Patty DeLeo, I was finally putting a crack into the foundation of the First Ward.

As it turned out, the first Shields payoff was not enough for the prosecutors. They always wanted one more nail in the coffin, and then another. They had tailed DeLeo after the hearing, when he went back into Judge Shields's chambers with the cash, but they were not sure he actually handed it over. To get the judge himself to confirm the payment, they asked me to wear a wire on him. I refused. I had never paid Shields in the past, I said, and for me to ask now would be suspicious. In truth, I didn't want to make things worse for him. Besides, I was hoping against hope that Patty kept all the money for himself.

But the Feds cooked up another excuse to bribe the judge. At the end of the month, at their urging, they had me ask Shields for more hearings. First, I requested to turn the TRO into a preliminary injunction. Then, when my client's ex-partner filed an emergency motion to release some funds, I asked the judge to stall the case, so we could force him to settle. After the second payoff, Patty told me the judge "was like doing somersaults."

Patty DeLeo and I never got along better. But then, during all this action, rumors about me cropped up in First Ward circles. One of my judge friends tipped me off that Pat Tuite, the criminal defense attorney, was telling people, "Cooley can't be trusted" and that they should be careful around me. Tuite had a lot of reasons to give me shit. If nothing else, he knew I had bucked up Judge Cieslik during the Cammon case. But problems for the Mob were happening wherever I went—and for good reason. I had taken undercover FBI agents to the racetracks and pointed out bookies there. That summer, the Feds raided their booking offices and held people for questioning at the tracks, including the Cicero group's top boss, Joe Ferriola. He had just had a heart transplant, and he didn't appreciate the anxiety.

I couldn't take the chance that Patty would hear stories about me from Tuite or someone else. I had to take the offensive. After one payoff to Judge Shields, while we were riding down the elevator, I mentioned what Tuite was saying about me.

Patty acted like it was funny. "Maybe you are a beefer," he said.

"Huh?" I said.

"It's possible," he said. "Better men than you have gone down that drain, haven't they?"

For a moment, I didn't know if he was being funny or calling me out. I replied that this wasn't something for Tuite to be "joking about."

Patty agreed. "You should never say anything like that. That's one of the worst things you can say about someone."

From then on, I never worried that Patty would be suspicious of me. He went along with each twist and turn on the Shields case, so he probably didn't suspect a thing. At the end of September, when we were done with all the proceedings, I gave him $6,000—$5,000 to keep and $1,000 to pass on to the judge for future services.

We never knew if Patty made the final payment to Shields, but the Feds had all they needed for an indictment. In fact, unknown to me, they had planted a bug in Shields's chambers, which helped lock it down that much more. This one case vindicated all the FBI agents and the assistant U.S. attorneys who supported me. More important, it got Valukas to back off and let my investigation run its course.

After more than two and a half years on the wire, I was finally on a roll. With the contrived cases and a little luck, I could do some real damage. In the next twelve months, I helped build four more major indictments and contribute to several others. Two of those cases were textbook examples about how closely the Mob was tied to Chicago's elected officials and court system.

Johnny D'Arco became the glue for a couple of those cases, after I finally figured out how to get a wire on him. I was in Counsellors Row with the Nagra to see Marcy. When Johnny approached me, I simply left the tape running and recorded him as he asked me to fix a case. With this totally unsolicited request, I got permission to wire Johnny directly. But I didn't want to just fix a case with him. I wanted to do something much bigger than that. I wanted Johnny to help me pass a state law.

Despite all his laziness and screwing around, Johnny had become one of the most powerful politicians in Springfield. By this time, he was assistant majority leader in the State Senate and chairman of the Insurance Committee. As far as I was concerned, his influence throughout the state capital was directly related to the First Ward back in Chicago. This meant he had the clout to push a bill through the legislature *and* get the Republican governor to sign it into law. In those days, the governor was Jim Thompson, another former U.S. attorney and a guy with a reputation for being super straight, but Johnny seemed as close to him as any Democrat. I had watched them meet on a couple of occasions at the health club and sit together in the steam room when they had to talk about something confidential.

In the fall of 1988, Johnny would have breakfast with me at a newly opened restaurant near his South Loop townhouse. Believe it or not, the place was decorated in a Capone-era gangster theme with tommy guns on the wall. Whenever we ate together, Johnny was always critical of my diet. In the morning, I liked eggs and ham, which I would wash down with a Coke. He would be picking at granola or fruit and telling me about his cholesterol count. He looked too fucking skinny, if you asked me. He had recently divorced, and when we met at this tommy gun place, he left his new girlfriend at home to watch his kids. Sometimes he would use our breakfasts as an alibi, and then cut out early to see another girlfriend. Even in his mid-forties, Johnny was up to his old tricks.

On Monday morning, October 31, I wore my wire to breakfast with Johnny. After a little chitchat, I told him I had a big client from the East Coast looking to pass some insurance law. About ten years before, when we were in Vegas with another state senator, Johnny said he would pass legislation in return for a fifty-fifty split of lobbying fees. When I asked if I could take him up on that offer, he said he would be my "co-counsel." He told me that insurance companies paid lobbyists $50,000 to get bills passed. I said I could probably get that and promised him $5,000 up front. Johnny suggested a "tax dodge" he had used in the past. We would sign up a licensed lobbyist as our front man, and pay him a nominal fee. In return, he would report to the IRS that we paid him the entire $50,000. That way we wouldn't have to pay taxes on our cut. He gave me the names of lobbyists who could "keep their mouths shut," including Arthur "Ron" Swanson. (In 2003, the Feds indicted Swanson for various kickback schemes involving the administration and friends of Governor George Ryan, who was later indicted as well.)

Just a few weeks after our breakfast, on December 23, I was counting out fifty hundred-dollar bills to Johnny as he sat in the passenger seat of my car outside Counsellors Row. I didn't even know what law I was bribing him to pass. The Feds were debating that question. They didn't want him to ram through legislation that could actually affect the state's insurance industry. Eventually, they came up with something silly: a law to permit one specific travel agency to sell trip-related insurance. Why would anyone have paid $50,000 for that? Fortunately, Johnny was never one for details. He just complimented me on my car and shoved the money in his pocket. Before he left, he wished me Merry Christmas.

While I was building a case on Johnny, I was putting something together on Marco D'Amico, too. For obvious reasons, I did not want to leave him out of the picture, but I was forbidden from walking into his Survivor's Club with a wire. Now the Feds told me I was too valuable to take that risk—or some such bullshit like that. But I didn't give up hope. Almost every night, I went to the Maywood Park Racetrack and hoped to see Marco or his people there. One night, in March 1989, while I was watching the races, I saw Tony Doty. He had become Marco's top guy. He said, "Hey, Bobby, how you been?"

I said, "Okay."

He said, "Gee, how come you're not playing with us any more?"

Of course, the Feds didn't allow me to make sports bets any more, so I told him, "I don't have to gamble any more. I've got my own book."

He said, "You do?"

I said, "Yeah. I've got a bunch of guys from the commodities exchange and some lawyers. I'm picking up around $10,000 a week doing that."

The next day, I called Steve Bowen and told him to get the paperwork ready for a wire on Marco.

Steve got upset. He said, "We told you, you can't do anything against Marco."

I said, "But I have a feeling either he or his people are going to call me first."

That's exactly what happened. Only a few hours later, Tony Doty called and said Marco was looking for me. I put on the wire and went to see Marco in his club. He took me outside and we walked around the block. I acted like a dummy; like I didn't know I really had to pay street tax for my little book. Marco was only too happy to spell out exactly what he wanted and why. He said, "Bob, even I can't protect you. You gotta pay tax if you got a book. No matter how small it is. You know the rules. If you don't pay, something is going to happen and I can't help you."

A few days later, I returned with my first weekly payment of $2,000. Marco took me to the back of the club. While I was counting out the money, I had an idea.

I said, "Marc, I need to borrow $50,000. Can you get me some money?"

At first, he balked—like he was afraid I'd gamble it away.

Then I said, "I need it for Johnny D'Arco. He's going to pass a law for us in the State Senate, and he has to grease the palms of all those senators."

I could see the wheels turn in his head. He nodded and said he would think about it. I thought, "What could say more about Chicago politics than this? You take juice money from the Mob so you can bribe a state senator to pass a law."

But the street tax and the juice loan were just the beginning of the case I built on Marco. One day, when I was in the club counting out cash, Marco asked, "How come you're not betting with us any more?"

I said, "Remember, Marc. I have my own operation."

He said, "Why don't you move some money our way? You must be overloaded on some games."

I needed some bullshit answer to distract him. If I really did have a book, I *would* want to move money. "Maybe I could," I said. "But I'm involved in a big card game."

"Where's the game?" Marco asked.

Again, I had to say something. "It's over at the Water Tower apartments."

"How much money is in the game?"

I said, "Oh, you got to bring $10,000 to sit down. I make real good money at it."

He said, "We can hit the game and you'd get twenty-five percent."

"No, Marc," I said. "It's too dangerous."

He said, "What do you mean?"

I said, "It's at the Water Tower. That's a fancy building. They got all kinds of security."

He said, "No. We hit a game there before. My guys come in with shotguns. What are they gonna do? Nobody's gonna balk. Do any of your guys have weapons?"

I still put him off. "Let me think about it, Marc."

In fact, this idea was my dream come true: a phony card game as a sting, with FBI agents as the players, so we could catch Marco's crew in the act of armed robbery. Still, I had to be careful about entrapment. I never wanted the tapes to show that I was eager for something illegal to happen or that I was encouraging it. Instead, I wanted to show that I tried to talk him out of it first.

For the next few months, Marco and I continued to talk about the card game. In my bones I could sense that my investigation would be drawing to a close before the end of 1989. If I played my cards right, Marco's raid on the card game could be my grand finale.

While things were picking up with Marco, I got another break to get me back inside the First Ward. This one came from my younger brother—a totally straight lawyer who knew nothing about my work with the Feds. He had clients who owned property in a gentrifying First Ward neighborhood, and they wanted to change the zoning from manufacturing to commercial. Like everyone else in Chicago, my brother's firm took the request to the alderman, in this case Fred Roti. As soon as he heard the name Cooley, Freddy asked my brother's partner if the "Cooley" in the firm was related to me. He then said I should call to follow up with him on the matter.

This mystified my brother, because he knew I didn't do much real estate work. But when he asked for my help, I immediately understood where Roti was coming from. Old Freddy knew the zoning change would make the property valuable, and he wanted a bribe in return. Coincidentally, that very week, the Feds wanted me to meet some FBI agents who had investigated Roti for three years. They still hadn't gotten to first base on him. Now they wanted to buy a trucking company for $200,000 and then bribe Roti to put up No Parking signs by the entrance. I said to the agents, "I can save you guys a whole bunch of money."

I arranged with Freddy to have our zoning chat during his morning hours at Counsellors Row on June 5. By the time I got to the First Ward table, around eleven o'clock, he had already been holding court for a few hours. I sat down across from him. Like this was all new to me, I pulled out a pen and a little notebook from my pocket. I said, "Freddy, tell me what the procedure is now."

Freddy grabbed my pen and pulled my notebook over to his side of the table. He then wrote the numbers "75" on a corner of the page and underlined it. Then he slid it back at me.

"Hmmm. Okay," I said.

"You know what I'm talking about?" Freddy asked.

"Yeah," I said. "Little ones, not big ones."

Freddy got a kick out of that. "Nooooo," he laughed.

"Okay."

Then he just came out and said, "Seventy-five hundred."

"Hmm?" I said. I wanted to make sure I got that on the tape.

"Seventy-five hundred," he said, even louder.

I motioned Freddy to follow me into a quiet corner of the restaurant. We sat down at an empty table. He had his back to the door.

I pulled out some money and said, "Let me give you five hundred now so you got some lunch money in your pocket."

As I was counting out the bills, who should walk into the restaurant but Uncle Pat. He saw the two of us sitting there, away from the First Ward table, and immediately knew something was up.

He marched over and barked, "What's going on?"

Fred went bolt upright, like he had just gotten a jolt of electricity, and shoved the money into his pocket. "Oh, Pat," he said. "See, you weren't here, so I figured I'd start it."

As soon as Pat found out we were talking about zoning, he sat down and jumped right in. He said, "Tell me who the fucking owners are."

I mentioned the name, but he didn't recognize it. He wanted to know if it was a big project. I told him it wasn't, but he waved me off. He said he'd find out more about it on his own, and let Freddy know what they should pay us.

Three days later, I went back to Counsellors Row, to give them the first installment on the bribe. Marcy saw me enter the restaurant and then led me to the back. When I asked if Roti's figures were right, he said, "The figures are okay."

"Let me give you thirty-five hundred more now," I said. Again I counted the bills out, but Marcy then recounted to make sure.

A week later, I made my final payment on the zoning bribe to Freddy. Again, we went to an empty table in the back of Counsellors Row. "Let me give you the rest of this," I said. "Did you talk to Pat?"

"Yeah," Roti said.

"Okay," I said, "Because I gave Pat thirty-five. Here, check it. Those are fifties. There should be fifteen."

After I was done counting it, I said, "Here's two thousand more. That should be the whole thing then." A few months later, when my brother and I had to make a presentation to the city council, Roti didn't even bother to show up for the meeting. He had his lackey, Alderman Bernie Stone, get up and say that Freddy thought it was "a good project."

From beginning to end, the zoning bribe was the most rock-solid case I built against anyone. There was absolutely no doubt what Marcy and Roti wanted or what I paid them. The Feds were very happy. Still, for me, it was all just icing on the cake. Zoning kickbacks were a dime a dozen in Chicago. The First Ward's control of the courts was something entirely different. That's what I really wanted to expose.

Ever since we finished the Nichols case with Judge Shields, I had been after Tom Durkin and the agents to cook up another civil suit for Marcy to fix. But this time it had to be assigned to Judge Scotillo. As far as I was concerned, he was the most corrupt judge, and practically Marcy's precinct captain inside the Circuit Court. When Pat put up candidates for associate judge, Scotillo lined up the votes from the other judges.

To get the case to Scotillo, the FBI agents just kept entering it in the computer—over and over again. We called it *Eldridge v. Carr* and used another bullshit story about battling partners. This time, my "client," Alan Carr, was the defendant and quite a little weasel (played once again by an FBI agent). Eldridge (another agent) caught him stealing $210,000 from their business. If these Chancery Court judges had ever talked to each other, they would have wondered why this one stupid case was on so many dockets. It took about twenty tries, and several months, but it finally popped up for Scotillo at the end of June.

In some ways, the delay worked out for the best. Only the week before, I made my last payment on the zoning bribe and was back in the good graces of Marcy and Roti. I dropped by Counsellors Row to let Pat know about the Chancery case. We went into the building lobby to talk, but it was full of people. Pat didn't like the looks of it. Maybe he was starting to feel nervous about things. When I made my last payment to Roti, Patty DeLeo took me aside to say that the FBI had questioned Judge Shields about my previous Chancery case. This was news to me, but Patty wasn't concerned in the least. "They got nothing on him," he said.

Marcy might have thought differently. He pushed through the revolving doors and led me out to the street. We talked just a few moments. I let him know I had a new case to handle with Judge Scotillo and that something would be happening any day now. He nodded, happy to hear it, and we then walked the few steps to the front doors of the restaurant. I held my arm out for him to go first, but for some reason Pat decided to be the gentleman that day. He stepped back and pushed me ahead of him. With the warm weather, I was wearing the Nagra body recorder in a harness over the small of my back. Pat put his hand right on the unit. The moment I felt him touch me there, a complete shock went through my system. I kept walking into the restaurant. I had no idea if he felt anything or had a surprised look on his face, and I couldn't turn around to see if he did.

Normally, I would have left Pat and gone about my business, but now I couldn't walk away or show any concern about what happened. I followed Pat back to the First Ward table and watched him take his seat. All of the other chairs were taken, mostly with Mob-connected union people. I stood there for a few minutes and then arched my back. To no one in particular I announced, "Wow. I strained my back and now it's killing me." Then I said good-bye and walked away.

The next day, I made a point to go back to Counsellors Row—but without the wire. I bought a back brace and walked around stiffly, hoping someone would notice, so I could make another explanation. But no one said anything, and I just sat around bullshitting.

Once again I debated with the agents about leaving town. But after a week of hanging around at Counsellors Row, I saw no change in Marcy's attitude towards me. We agreed I should go forward with the *Eldridge v. Carr* case.

By now, the tension became second nature for me. Even if I was scared as hell, I got it out of my head by thinking, "This is something I have to do." I was mentally prepared to die. At one point, I thought about getting cyanide capsules. I did not want to be taken alive and put on a meat hook. I could deal with the idea of poison, or a sudden blast from shotgun or .22. If it was time to pay the price, so be it.

For the first time in two weeks, I put on the wire and went back to see Marcy. I told him that my Chancery case had now heated up. Eldridge had discovered the bank account where my client, Carr, had hidden $210,000. That morning, Eldridge's attorney (actually an agent) had filed an emergency motion with Judge Scotillo to stop Carr from withdrawing the money. I opened up a folder and showed Marcy the motion. If Scotillo could stall for two days, I told him, my client could get back to town and withdraw the money.

Marcy went to his phone by the First Ward table and called Roti to join us. A few minutes later, Freddy came running over. As we stood in the lobby, Marcy opened the folder and showed the papers to Roti. I tried to fill him in on the background, but Marcy cut me off. "Just tell him what you want," he barked.

They knew that Judge Scotillo's court was in session and only someone important could interrupt him while he was on the bench.

I said, "I want the judge to stall tomorrow when the other lawyer comes in."

"Hold it, hold it," Freddy piped up—like a kid raising his hand in school. "Why don't I go see. . . ."

"Call our friend Buck," Marcy said, finishing the thought for him. They meant Pasquale "Buck" Sorrentino, presiding judge of the entire Cook County Circuit Court's Law Division. "All right," Marcy told him. "Go see Buck."

Freddy grabbed the folder from me and waddled off to the Daley Center. In the span of just a few minutes, I had seen Marcy, the Octopus, in all his glory—first reaching to pluck the seniormost Alderman from City Hall, and then using the chief judge as his errand boy to fix a Chancery Court case.

I hung around Counsellors Row for a while and waited for Freddy to come back. After my scare from the previous week, I was still a little antsy. I walked over and said hello to George, one of the brothers who owned the restaurant. I chatted with some lawyers having breakfast. At one point, I glanced at the First Ward table. Pat had caught the eye of someone who had just entered the restaurant. But instead of Roti, it was Rocky Infelice, probably the most feared crew leader in the Cicero group. He was big and bear-like with a bald head and deep, close-set eyes. He went straight downstairs where they had a bathroom and a party hall that was usually closed. Marcy hurried after him.

Rocky was not a guy with a sense of humor. I never tried to pal around with him. I knew the Mob bosses reserved him for their most vicious and important hits. The Feds believed he had organized Tony Spilotro's baseball-bat execution—if he hadn't in fact done the deed himself. He was later convicted for the torture murder of the independent bookie, Hal Smith.

I went back to my schmoozing. When I looked again at the First Ward table, Marcy was standing there next to Roti. Freddy had a big grin on his face. Evidently the mission was accomplished. They motioned for me to go out in the lobby with them.

According to Freddy, he pulled the chief judge off the bench while he was working on another First Ward case (FBI agents shadowed Roti every step of the way and then followed the judge). After Buck got his instructions from Roti, he went directly to Scotillo's courtroom. Roti said, "He walked over there in person and he gave him a piece of paper."

It seemed we should all be happy. But Marcy looked pissed off. He then motioned for me to follow him outside again. I chased after him down the sidewalk toward the old city parking garage in the middle of the block. In all the years of our secret meetings and payoffs, he had never taken me there before. I suddenly realized I had not seen Rocky Infelice leave the restaurant, and I looked over my shoulder. Were they on to me?

Pat walked through the entrance of the garage and up some steps. I stayed just behind him. He pushed open a rusty metal door. There was a dark, stinky bathroom inside. In the moment before I followed him, I thought, "That bastard Rocky is waiting in there. They're going to grab me and check me for a wire." All this time, Pat had not said one word to me. I walked in after him and the door shut behind me. Pat just opened his fly, stepped over to the urinal, and took a piss. I had already reached for one of my guns. After he zipped up his fly, he turned around and said, "We're gonna have to take care of Scotillo *and* Buck now."

But we still didn't know what Scotillo would do. "Is he going to help us for sure?" I asked.

"Positively," Marcy shot back. The next day we had our emergency hearing with Scotillo. The judge played his role to the hilt, barking at me like I was the biggest idiot in the world. But he refused to grant a temporary restraining order to the plaintiff—just as Roti ordered—and continued the case.

On Thursday, I was supposed to meet Roti to discuss what to pay everyone, but this time I walked into Counsellors Row without a wire. I was still spooked by my walk to the garage with Marcy. If he had been testing me, I did not want to push my luck for a second day.

Roti led me to a table in the back of the restaurant. First he wanted to know my fee for the Chancery case. I told him it was $25,000 and asked what the judges would want. He grabbed a napkin and wrote "2500," and then circled it. When I asked what he and Marcy wanted, he put "7500" under the other number. Then, he added them up to "10,000" and underlined the total. "That's what we need," he said.

I told him I had just $2,500 on me. I counted it out and handed it to him under the table. I crumpled the napkin with his numbers like I was going to throw it out. When he turned away, I shoved it in my pocket. That would have to do for evidence on this payoff.

I made the next payment on Friday, a week later. By this time, I felt better about wearing the wire, so I caught Roti on tape asking me, "You got an envelope?"

I said, "Yeah. I'm gonna give ya thirty-five hundred more today. I don't want to take too much out of the bank at one time."

I arranged to make the final payment to him or Pat on Monday, July 10. I was hoping I'd wire Marcy for at least one payment. As usual, Steve Bowen met me at my apartment that morning to bring the Nagra and paperwork. While I was driving downtown, I called Counsellors Row from my car to see if Pat was in. George, the owner, answered. I asked for Marcy, and the next thing I knew, Roti was on the phone. I said, "I'm just checking to make sure somebody's there for me."

He said, "Pat's here, but I'll meet you outside."

As soon as he said that, I knew something was wrong. I parked my car in the alley next to the restaurant and called Steve. I said, "Steve, something is wrong."

He said, "What do you mean?"

I said, "Because Roti got on the phone and he wants to meet me outside. Something must be going on."

I hung up the phone and got out of the car, and there was Steve standing right behind me. For the first time in a long time, he had followed me into town. He said, "Are you going to make the payment?"

I said, "I guess so, but something must be wrong."

As we stood there in the alley, Mike, the beat policeman, who happened to be nearby, walked up to us. "Guess what?" he said to me. "They found a bug in the restaurant."

I couldn't believe it, but from the look on Steve's face, I saw this wasn't news to him. It was why he followed me.

At that moment, I heard someone call, "Bob."

It was Roti. He spotted me from the sidewalk and motioned for me to come right over. Fortunately, Steve was wearing a suit that day, so he looked like just another lawyer. I said to Mike and Steve, "I've gotta go."

I hustled over to Freddy, who had a frown on his face. He made a little circular motion with his hand—as if to say we couldn't talk around there. "They found something in the booth right by our table," he said. "Come on. Let's go across the street."

As I followed him, I was still trying to digest the news. Why did the Feds need a bug when I was getting all we needed with the wire? This could blow my last payoff.

Roti led me through the side door of City Hall. "I know you're careful," he said.

"You gotta be," I said.

We took the elevator to his office on the second floor. It was a set of massive rooms with pillars and high ceilings. I'm sure most mayors didn't have anything as big. Usually his secretary was in the reception area, but today she was gone. I followed him into his inner office. As soon as I went through the door, he turned around and locked it.

My first thought was, "This is a fucking setup and I got a wire on." I expected to see some muscleheads come from behind the corner. I reached for my gun, ready for a battle. But Roti walked over to each of his two windows and lowered the blinds. Then he turned and said, "What have you got? Four?"

He was talking about my last payment of $4,000. Now I was at ease. "Yeah," I said. "Four. That's the end of it."

He took the money from me and started counting it.

"Well, there are no other problems, are there?" I asked.

Fred shook his head.

Later, I heard how a busboy had found the bug the previous Friday. It was actually a tiny camera, mounted in the booth across from the First Ward table. At first, the owners didn't know what to make of it. They waited through the weekend, and finally decided to call the FBI on Monday morning.

For me, the camera was total overkill, and it certainly put my investigation—if not my life—in jeopardy. I had clearly told the Feds that Pat Marcy never talked dirty at the First Ward table. Worse yet, nobody told me about it beforehand—or even after it was found. The FBI agents knew I was walking into Counsellors Row with a wire to make my payoff exactly when everybody would be most paranoid about surveillance.

For the next few days, the papers were full of stories about "the bug in the soup" at the First Ward table. They even had a diagram in the paper that showed the view from the hidden camera and the placement of various microphones.

But after the smoke cleared, it was pretty much business as usual. Marcy found some expert to sweep the restaurant and all of his offices to make sure there were no other bugs. The next time I sat down with Roti at the restaurant, I asked if he was worried about anything that the camera picked up. He shook his head. He rubbed his thumb over his index finger to indicate cash and said, "It never changes hands here." In fact, I had paid off Fred in the restaurant several times—although not at the First Ward table. It seemed so obvious to me: At the very time I return to Counsellors Row to start fixing cases again, a bug shows up. But fortunately nobody put two and two together.

Although we had good evidence against Roti and Marcy for the Chancery fix, the Feds were still not satisfied. Once again, they were concerned about their case against the judge. They wanted me to wear a wire on him, so we could hear Scotillo confirm that he had gotten paid. But I knew this judge pretty well. He was very, very sly, which is why he survived Greylord without a nick. You couldn't meet him for lunch or give him a call and expect a straight answer from him. To try to put the judge at ease, I had another idea. I knew where he lived on the Gold Coast and how he walked to work. One August morning, I "accidentally" bumped into him on the street.

"Oh, hey, hi, Judge," I said.

He was a big distinguished-looking guy with a full head of black hair. He had gotten a little soft around the middle, but he always wore an immaculately tailored suit. "Oh, hi, Bob," he said. I asked him if he had time for coffee, but he said he was in a rush. I said good-bye, but then turned back and said, "Judge, wait a minute. Let me talk to you a second."

I told him that the *Eldridge v. Carr* case worked out great for me, and he confirmed that the chief judge "delivered a message" in time to help. But when I asked if Buck took care of him, he said, "Just between you and I, no. He just took a pass on me. He didn't do anything."

"Oh, no," I said. "That's terrible." I told him how I had given $10,000 to Roti and Marcy, and that $3,000 was meant for him and the chief judge.

"You know how they are," Scotillo said.

I thought, "You bet I do."

I could see the judge's sixth sense kick in, and he started to pull away. As we said good-bye, I laughed about him getting angry with me during the hearing.

"Oh," he said. "That was just an act."

I left there thinking we had all we needed to indict Scotillo. He clearly indicated that he knew the case was fixed and he helped it go our way. But the Feds still felt we didn't have enough evidence because the judge got no money. We had to come up with a new excuse to bribe him, which meant another episode in the story of the dueling partners, Eldridge and Carr. To add some spice to the situation, we brought in a new character, my client's girlfriend (another of those cute FBI agents). According to this twist in the plot, she still had access to the account and Eldridge was suing to block it.

This time, to play the role of bagman, I turned to our distinguished state senator, Johnny D'Arco. I knew Scotillo was tight with Johnny and would feel more comfortable taking money from him. I had been seeing Johnny throughout the summer, and despite all the uproar over the camera at Counsellors Row, he wasn't worried one bit. On one of my wires, he laughed that the only thing the bug would pick up at the First Ward table was some political gossip and "dirty jokes." In September, I gave him $2,500 more for my bogus law. He promised that when the legislature had its spring session, "I'll slip something in and nobody will know the difference." I thanked him again and mentioned how much it cost me to get the zoning change from Roti. Johnny said, "You shoulda came to me. I would have done it for ya a lot cheaper."

He was only too happy to help bribe Scotillo—for a piece of the action. Once again, I wanted the judge to stall a temporary restraining order—this time against the client's girlfriend. I told Johnny how Marcy or Roti stiffed the judge the last time I tried to pay him off.

At first he laughed, "Roti would stiff his own mother." But Johnny understood what had happened. "They feel they made him," he explained. Still, if he was going to help me make a payoff to Scotillo, he said, I shouldn't tell Roti or Marcy about it.

Johnny then had me drive him directly to the judge's apartment, so we could talk about it with him in person—which would have been a wet dream for the Feds—but the judge wasn't home. Johnny had to handle it without me. In October, I handed him $2,500 while he was eating his Cream of Wheat at a downtown hotel. I told him to give the judge $1,000 and keep the rest for himself.

To confirm that Scotillo got the money, I prepared another "accidental" meeting with the judge two weeks later. I went to the restaurant where I knew he had lunch, and I made sure to bring two very attractive young ladies with me. Scotillo walked in, along with the chief judge, Buck Sorrentino. As soon as they got a load of my guests, they came running over to say hello. In between the chitchat, I slipped in a question to the judge: "Now, Johnny took care of you this time, right?"

He replied, "Yeah. He did." With that reply, I thought, we had a solid case against Scotillo and a new case against Johnny.

My investigation had not gotten serious until the spring of 1988, but by the end of October 1989, I knew we had all the evidence we needed to bring down the Octopus, Pat Marcy, and the rest of the First Ward—Fred Roti, Patty DeLeo, and Johnny D'Arco. In the process, we also pinched the Circuit Court's most powerful judges, including David Shields, Anthony Scotillo, and, worst of all, Tom Maloney. I even thought we had enough to make a case against Chief Judge Sorrentino and possibly Ed Burke. If nothing else, I figured, Illinois' court system would have to be overhauled from top to bottom when all this came out.

For reasons that weren't made clear to me yet, the Feds let me know that there was only a few weeks left before I had to leave town. But at this stage, even if we did have the First Ward locked up, I still had some unfinished business: I wanted one more stab at making a case on Harry Aleman, and I had a few scores left to settle with Marco D'Amico.

Chapter 12

PARTING SHOTS FOR
HARRY AND MARCO

O f all the bad things I had ever done, the one I most wanted to undo was fixing the murder case against Harry Aleman. The whole idea of putting him on trial again for the Logan murder was like an impossible dream throughout the investigation. When I first started talking about it with the agents and prosecutors, everybody laughed at me. They said, "What? Are you nuts? He was found not guilty. That's double jeopardy." The Fifth Amendment says you can't be tried twice for the same offense. On the other hand, a defendant can't tamper with the jury either, and as far as I was concerned, that's exactly what Harry did when he had Marcy get me to bribe Judge Wilson.

I said to the Feds, "We can go on the basis that there was no jeopardy because Harry knew ahead of time that the case was fixed."

But there was no way to connect me with Harry Aleman—there was no proof he even knew me—and there was no evidence to connect me with his case. My first ploy was to get help from Judge Wilson. Earlier in 1989, the Feds let me visit Frank where he retired, in Scottsdale, Arizona. They still had no hope of building a case against Aleman. At best, they told me, we could add a few counts to Marcy's federal racketeering charges for fixing another trial.

To be honest, I had one more reason to go. I wanted the Feds to give me a nice warm-weather vacation. To make the experience complete, I hooked up with Cathy Fleming, an old girlfriend, who had moved to Lake Tahoe and was working as a cocktail waitress. She had been with me when we met with the judge and his wife before the Aleman case. I remembered that the judge's wife liked her, and I thought she could help put them at ease. The FBI had no problem with my bringing Cathy along. They figured she made it look like a vacation for me. To play it up to the hilt, they put us in a luxurious resort. For a few days, it was like old times.

After we settled in to our room, the agents gave me Frank's home number. He answered the phone and I told him I was in town on vacation. I invited him to bring the wife and have dinner with us, since the hotel had such a fabulous restaurant.

When the judge met me at the bar, he looked like his gruff old self, only his limp had gotten worse. I said it must have been six years since we last met. "No," he said. "It's been nine years. I've been here dying for nine years."

Cathy didn't have the effect on him that I expected. At the sight of her, he seemed to stiffen, and then he practically clammed up for the evening. Our plan was for Cathy to go to the ladies' room during dinner, and we figured the judge's wife would follow. But Mrs. Wilson stayed rooted in her chair the whole time we were there. Meanwhile, as we ate, I could see the judge sip wine, but not the hard liquor he used to drink. He seemed on guard.

My only chance to speak one-on-one with Frank came after dinner while we were walking to his car. Cathy stayed back chatting with Mrs. Wilson, so the judge and I could put some distance between them. I told him that subpoenas were going out to people involved in the Aleman murder trial. If I was called, I said, "I'm gonna testify. I'm not gonna take the rap on this. The only way I can get in trouble is by perjuring myself." It was my way of telling him to cooperate. I truly didn't want him hurt even worse by this case. "What are you gonna do?" I asked.

"Don't worry about me," he said. Even with his horrible limp, he was walking faster and faster, trying to stay away from me. I was practically jogging to keep up with him.

"I'm sure they know the whole story," I told him, "but they can't do anything to us. See, the five years is long gone. This statute [of limitations] is long gone."

But whatever I said, he replied, "I don't know anything about anything."

Then he got in his car and, with the window down, started backing out and pulling away—even though his wife and Cathy were still far behind us.

Only later, when I was alone with Cathy, did I discover why the judge was so upset to see her. She was with me at the bar when I gave the judge the final payment for the Aleman fix. After I went to pick up the tab, he said to her, "Stay away from that Cooley. He's a bad man."

In 1989, he had to wonder why she was still with me after what he said, or why she had come with me to see him. It must have smelled like a setup. But Cathy's memory alone made the trip to Scottsdale worthwhile for the Feds. Later she could testify about my connection to the judge, and that he did something with me that Frank considered "bad."

But we still had to prove that Harry knew about the fix. When I found out that Harry was hanging around Maywood Park Racetrack during the day, I wanted to approach him there with a wire and get him to implicate himself. Some agents tried to talk me out of fooling around with Harry. This monster was certifiably dangerous. But by October, I wasn't so concerned about the risks. The whole investigation had been a death wish. How could I deny myself one more score, so close to the end?

That morning Steve met me at my apartment with the Nagra. He and Jim Wagner wanted to follow me around the racetrack, but I told them to stay away. Harry was sure to have people looking out for him. I figured he'd stay out of public areas, so I went to an upper level of the clubhouse, where they had private boxes. I walked past the party room. Most of the lights were off, but I could make out someone sitting alone in the corner. It was Harry. I wandered into the room, like I was lost and looking for the sky, and then I bumped into his table.

"Hey, Harry," I said.

He looked up and gave me his evil eye. Maybe thinking I was a cop, he said, "Who the fuck are you?"

"Harry," I said. "Don't you recognize your old pal? I'm Bob Cooley."

A light came on in his eyes. "Hey, Bob. Yeah. How ya doing?"

I took a deep breath and sat down with him. I said, "Harry, you're looking great." It was true. His hair was gray, but the weightlifting he had done in prison left him pretty fit for a guy pushing fifty. "Doing the time did you some good."

Harry didn't think that was so funny. He gave me his stare again. "I ain't never going back in," he said.

"Not if I have something to say about it," I thought.

Out of the corner of my eye, I could see Harry's brother-in-law, Richie Kimball, walk in. He was the guy I once represented for kicking an FBI agent in the face at a nightclub. I hadn't seen Richie in fifteen years. He squinted as though he didn't recognize me and left the room.

I had to be quick before someone else barged in on us. I said, "Listen, Harry, let me talk to you for a second." And I walked him back to the far end of the room, where they had a bar and some stools. I sat down at one and he sat down next to me.

He seemed to be looking at me kind of funny. Maybe he could tell I was nervous. I said, "Some lawyer said you were pissed at me about something."

He said, "What are you talking about?"

While he was in prison, Harry asked me to give a job to his kid, who was a law student. The cocky little shit used to show up drunk or high, so I had to fire him. I said, "I thought maybe because of your son."

"No, Bobby," he said. "That ain't the case. If I was mad at you. I would tell you."

I thought, "Sure, Harry. You would tell me with a .22 in the back of the head." I said, "That's good to know. I wouldn't want to be on your wrong side."

He said, "Oh, Bobby, no. You're a great guy."

Then I took a deep breath. "You know who I just bumped into?" I asked.

Harry leaned closer to me.

"The judge," I said.

Harry pulled away. "What do you mean, 'the judge'?"

"The judge on your case," I said. "Frank Wilson."

As soon as he heard the name, Harry jumped off the stool. "I don't want to talk about it," he hissed. "Don't ever mention that name again. Don't ever say nothing again."

"Motherfucker," I thought. I once instructed this guy to never discuss anything illegal from his past. What could be more illegal than fixing your own murder trial? "If someone brings it up," I used to tell him, "assume you're talking into a wire."

Richie and two buddies came back into the room. Harry sat down at a table by the wall, but he never took his eyes off me. With his arms folded, he gave me an absolutely evil stare.

I couldn't leave now and get Harry even more suspicious. Instead, I walked over to Richie and started to shoot the breeze. All the time we talked, I could feel Harry staring at me. I had my two guns, but I had the wire, too, and I felt like it was burning a hole right through my leg.

To explain why I was hanging around, I told Richie I had a horse in the next race. When I went to make the bet, I looked back and saw Richie hiding behind a pillar to watch me. Now I had to blow a few hundred bucks to show I was serious. I went out to the track to watch the race. After it was over, I wandered back into the party room with Harry one more time. I wasn't going to run and hide. I wanted to show I had no reason to be afraid. I stuck around until no one seemed to notice me, and then I left.

Even though I didn't get much out of Harry, I got enough to make the wire valuable. First of all, it showed, beyond a doubt, that he knew me. Also, the way he acted when I mentioned Judge Wilson's name showed that he was hiding something. I still had no illusions about how difficult it would be to retry him. But at least I had done all I could. To take him to trial for the murder, I would need to convince state's attorneys instead of federal prosecutors, and that couldn't happen until I left town.

As I kept building cases against Marco, I pushed my death wish up another notch. If I was going to go out with a bang, it would come with his raid on my card game. But I wanted to make sure I was there when it happened. It would have to be the very last act of my investigation, and then I could leave town.

In November, with everything else winding down, the Feds realized they should let me start betting again. I was in Marco's club each week to pay my street tax. I might as well do double duty and help them make a few last gambling cases against some bookies. The day they gave me the go-ahead, I zipped over to the club to bet. When I walked in, there was Ricky Borelli, the fat slob, lying all over the couch. Marco had let him have his own book again. I thought, "This is payback. This is double payback." Either I would beat him for serious money or, if I lost, I would never have to pay him. But when I put my mind to it, there was no way I could lose to Ricky. In a matter of two weeks, I won $40,000 and managed to collect half. I started betting with two other West Side offices: one run by Marco's right-hand man, Tony Doty, and the other by his brother-in-law Bobby Abbinante. Marco had just sold the beef stand Bobby used to run for him, and Bobby was desperate to make some extra money.

With the okay to gamble, I had another excuse to hang around Marco's club. Whenever Marco saw me, he wanted to go outside and walk around the block. He had moved his club out of the West Side storefront and into a nicer building in a residential neighborhood of Elmwood Park. We would stroll around a little park across the street or walk in the nearby schoolyard. Just like I thought, he couldn't get the robbery caper off his mind. He kept asking, "What about the game?"

When I first approached the Feds with the idea of staging a card game for the robbery, they went ballistic. They said, "It's absolutely too dangerous to have you in a room with these guys swinging shotguns." They didn't want to cause problems in a fancy place like the Water Tower or any other apartment building, for that matter, even if all the players were SWAT team FBI agents. Too much could go wrong in a confined space.

I then asked, "What if we can do it somewhere that's totally under our control?" I suggested the resort town of Lake Geneva, Wisconsin, just an hour from Chicago. Marco and some other mobsters would vacation up there and were trying to take over the dog track nearby. They knew about all the wealth in the area. We could find a house with plenty of land all around it, so no innocent bystander would be in harm's way.

To set this up for Marco, during one of our walks I said, "Lately, Marc, when we have our games, we don't just go to one place. We're going to different people's places."

"Like where?" Marco asked.

"Last week, we went to Lake Geneva. What a great place." Then I acted like an idea suddenly dawned on me. I said, "But wait. The more I think of it, the more I think something could be done there. It's right out in the open. It's pitch black, and they only got local nitwit cops running around."

Marco got all excited about this idea. Then the next time I saw him, I mentioned that sometimes we had a couple of dope dealers in the game, and how they would bring briefcases with one or two hundred thousand in cash.

It was like we were writing a movie script together, only he didn't know it. Meanwhile, I had to deal with my nervous Nellie producers back in Washington.

Marco had some concerns himself when he heard about the drug dealers, because he knew they carried guns. He wanted to make sure "there would be no heroes."

I told him, "No, as long as your guys don't get nervous."

"They don't get nervous," he said. "They're professionals." He claimed they were real experts at this sort of operation and worked all over the country. Getting these guys out of circulation would be another bonus.

A few days before Thanksgiving, the Feds told me I would have to leave town the following week. It was like they had given me my date of execution. Valukas had decided to step down as U.S. Attorney. Just as I thought, he was going back to his old firm of Jenner & Block, and would soon be representing the same scumbags we were looking to lock up. During the press conference announcing his replacement, Valukas wanted to break the news about me. The Feds even thought about having U.S. Attorney General Dick Thornburgh come in for the occasion. By this time, nothing Valukas did could surprise me, but the irony of it all was beyond belief. At every turn he tried to squash my investigation. Now he had finally succeeded in shutting it down, so he could tout it as the greatest achievement of his term.

Like it or not, my time would be up in just a matter of days. Before I left Chicago, I had to break the news to my family. At the time, my mother, four brothers, and a sister lived in town. I invited all of them and the in-laws downtown for dinner at a nice new restaurant. My mother was in her seventies, still sharp and active, and I loved seeing her have a good time with everyone. As far as they were all concerned, this was just another of my dinner parties, so no one imagined anything was up. As the evening wore on, I took each of my brothers aside. I told them, "I've been working with the government for three years. I'm going to do what I can to change things, but it means I have to leave, and I won't be able to contact you for a while." They took it really hard. I promised each one that I'd figure out a way to tell Mother before the dinner was over, but I couldn't bring myself to do it. We were all laughing and joking, and she was having so much fun. After she left, my brothers stayed behind and wanted to pound me for not breaking the news to her. I couldn't blame them.

It's hard to describe my feelings during those last days in Chicago. There was a great sadness inside of me, and a dread about my future, but also a tremendous anger. All of these emotions combined to put me into a frenzy to tie up every loose end that I could. I chased down Ricky Borelli and the other bookies to collect on my bets. I also arranged to pick up the juice loan from Marco that I was supposed to use for bribing Johnny. Marco had Tony Doty deliver the $50,000 in the parking lot of a West Side White Castle. He got into my car and handed me a paper bag stuffed with cash. I wasn't wearing a wire, but I left my car phone on. Jim Wagner listened in from his car around the corner. This whole scene smelled like too much of a setup for the FBI, and they wanted to make sure no one grabbed me.

At this stage, I truly didn't care if I got hit. I kept priming Marco for the robbery, and I set things up so the FBI couldn't leave me back in Chicago. But with all the arrangements being made in Wisconsin, and Valukas screwing around with his press conference, I still didn't have an exact day for the game. Then, on the morning of Wednesday, November 29, I was told they were ready to go—that night. Right away, I went to see Marco at his club. I pulled him outside and said, "It's going to happen tonight."

Marco was pissed. "Those guys are out of town," he said. "I can't get them back in time."

We needed a Plan B. "What about Bobby?" I asked, referring to Bobby Abbinante, Marco's brother-in-law.

Marco shrugged his shoulders and then nodded okay.

Ever since Marco told Bobby about our plan for the card game, Bobby was pitching me to rob it. He told me that he did home invasions, too, and that his crew was as fast and efficient as the one Marco wanted to use. Bobby was a weightlifter, more than six feet tall and probably the toughest guy in Marco's gang. He was ambitious, too. Besides making book, he had some kind of job as a tow truck driver with the City of Chicago.

I was expecting Bobby to meet me at the club with the money I won betting with him. He didn't show up until two o'clock in the afternoon. I told him, "Marco has decided to let you do the card game, but it's tonight."

Bobby said, "I'll get ahold of the boss." He didn't mention a name, but it was probably a guy I would have recognized.

After I left the club, I called the agents on my cell phone. I said, "You should put a tail on Bobby. He's rounding up the crew for the job." But he was off before they could follow him.

I drove from the club back home to pack. The plan was for me to leave for the airport as soon as we were done in Wisconsin. The Feds warned me not to bring any suit or clothing with a label that could identify where I was from. I could only take two suitcases. Everything else I left behind.

I drove up to Wisconsin with Jimmy Wagner, the FBI agent on my investigation who specialized in organized crime, and the one who coordinated a lot of the details for the sting. I had told Bobby I would come up with some excuse to leave the game around nine o'clock and go back to the hotel where I was staying. He could call my room and I'd give him directions to the house.

I checked into the hotel, and when I went into my room, there were five FBI agents waiting for me. They were all with the Milwaukee SWAT team. The supervisor was a hard-ass, and he didn't want a civilian like me anywhere near the action. But I hadn't come all this way to sit on my ass by the swimming pool. When the phone rang, Bobby was on the other end. He told me that they had come up in two cars. One would be the "work" car, which was probably stolen. They would drive that to the house and then ditch it after the robbery.

The agents had put a wire on my phone, and as I spoke with him, I tried to be the voice of reason. I said, "I don't want anyone to get killed."

He said, "Nobody's going to fuck with us. We've got these big shot-guns and carbines. We're all set." This was really all we had to hear. Even without an actual robbery, we could build a case against him just for taking automatic weapons across state lines to commit a felony.

When I asked him where he was, he told me he was right outside the hotel in the parking lot. He wanted to follow me back to the house. He said, "We'll see you when you're coming out."

I said, "I'll be out in about twenty minutes."

After I hung up, the supervisor got angry with me. "What did you tell him that for?" he asked. "You're not going anywhere."

I said, "Sure I am."

He said, "No. We'll have somebody put your clothes on."

Bobby wouldn't fall for that. He knew what I looked like. I said, "I have to go."

Jimmy Wagner agreed with me. He said he would get in the car with me to make sure I was all right. Besides, the supervisor was not about to pull the plug on this whole operation, given all the resources they had already put into it. We let the Milwaukee agents get a head start. Then Jimmy and I left the hotel and got into my car.

Wagner had picked the perfect place for the raid. It was a big A-frame post-and-beam house on a dirt road cul-de-sac. To one side there was a trail leading into the woods. Another house was in the distance on the other side of the subdivision. A bunch of Jaguar-type luxury cars were lined up in the road as additional bait. You had to park your car in the cul-de-sac and then walk a few dozen yards across the lawn to get to the house.

It was pitch black out there, just like I told Marco, but the agents had planted flash grenades all over the grounds, and were ready to light everything up as soon as the bad guys made their move. Curtains were drawn over all the big windows in the house, but you could see lights and smoke coming from the chimney, so it looked like something was going on inside.

The front door opened for us, and we walked into a huge split-level living room crammed with agents. They were all in bulletproof vests and armed to the teeth with machine guns and rifle barrels sticking out everywhere. Clusters of agents had set up to shoot in practically every direction.

Now the supervisor barked at me to go upstairs to the master bedroom and lock myself in the bathroom. If shooting started he didn't want me to catch any stray bullets. At this point, I couldn't argue with him, but I left the door open, and I could hear the reports from all their lookout points. They must have had some agents with night vision hidden along the trail. They also had a surveillance plane making sweeps overhead.

At one point I heard, "Here comes the car. It might be them. There are four males in the car. They're slowing down. Someone got out of the car. Now, the car is speeding up and taking off again."

There was a circular drive that went all the way around the subdivision. They didn't come back for another hour. They shut off the headlights and slowed down.

I heard someone say, "They're probably ready to come in."

But then the guy they let off got back in the car and it drove away. After two more hours went by, there was still no sign of the car. We thought, "What the fuck?"

It was probably 4 A.M. Jimmy Wagner knew I had a 7:30 plane to catch. He said, "Let's get out of here."

The agents figured that the robbers had seen something suspicious and then ran off. But I could never let something go that way. I had to find out what happened and see if there was anything more to salvage from all this. At around 5:30, when we got closer to the city, we stopped at an undercover FBI office. Using a monitored phone, I called Bobby's house. I got his wife and she woke him up for me.

"What happened?" I asked.

"Oh, fuck," he said. "We were all set and ready to go. It looked perfect. We were going to come in through the sliding doors on the porch. But after we dropped a guy off, we drove around a little and we saw a fucking copper sitting there." Later, I found out that the FBI had warned the local sheriff that there might be a ruckus. His asshole deputy got curious and parked nearby to rubberneck.

Bobby and his crew parked behind him and watched for a while. "We give him a chance to leave and he's still there," Bobby said. "We figure he's sleeping or fucking something, so we decide we were going to do it anyway. We went to get the work car, but when we start it, a hose broke."

Bobby said they even tried to find a mechanic in town to fix the work car, but everything was closed at that point. Now, he wanted to use the other car, but the boss of the crew was more careful and he called it off.

Even though they didn't go ahead with the robbery, Bobby's description to me over the phone was corroborated by the surveillance. Together, along with the weapons violations, it made a good case against them all. Still, I could get Bobby and his crew to try again. I said, "Then maybe we'll do the game next week."

He said, "All right."

After I hung up, I said to Jimmy, "We can do this thing next week. We can find out who these stickup men are." I was concerned about getting that group off the street. Besides, it would give me more time to collect the $100,000 the bookies owed me.

But Jimmy told me I wasn't doing anything next week. "You have to leave town today," he said. "Valukas has everything arranged."

We went straight to Midway Airport. Jimmy handed me my ticket and watched me get on the plane.

For some reason, Valukas never got his press conference with the U.S. Attorney General. But a few hours after I left town, FBI agents fanned out across Chicago to serve subpoenas. It soon became common knowledge that the requests for information stemmed from wire recordings I had made for the last three and a half years. One of the agents went to City Hall and happened to see State Senator John D'Arco Jr. as he talked in a lobby phone booth. The agent would later tell the court that

Johnny heard something over the phone that made him drop the receiver. "He gasped like he was in pain, almost as if the wind had been knocked out of him," the agent testified. Then Johnny stumbled backward out of the booth, fell to the floor and, holding his head in his hands, cried, "Oh, my God."

LEGAL
ASSASSIN

CHAPTER 13

WITNESS DEJECTION PROGRAM

N ovember 29, 1989. One life had ended for me, but if you asked what would come next, I couldn't have told you. When Jimmy Wagner took me to the airport, I literally had no idea where the Feds were sending me until I looked at the ticket and saw that the destination was Fort Myers, Florida. I was in a daze the whole flight. All I had to my name were those two suitcases and about $5,000 in cash.

Jimmy told me that another FBI agent would be waiting for me at the airport, but when I got off the plane, there was no one at the gate. As I went for my luggage, I saw a sign that read: "Turn left to Marco Island." This was just not some funny coincidence. Marco D'Amico and a bunch of the other Mob bosses and crew leaders had started to buy land in Marco Island, about fifty miles south of Fort Myers. That was their new hangout. What were the Feds sending me here for? Once again, I had to ask myself if they knew what they were doing.

I went to a pay phone to call Jimmy. He said, "Go to the motel by yourself. Just give me a call and let me know when you check in."

They put me in a decent place near the airport, where I could lie around by a pool. When I got to my room after I checked in, I flipped through the channels on my television and saw they carried WGN out of Chicago. The noon news was on and the next thing I knew, I saw John Drummond, the crime reporter, with a breaking story. He was talking about me, and they flashed one of the tapes with me on the screen. He announced that I had been exposed as an undercover agent, working for the federal government, but then he started in with all this bullshit about me being involved with cocaine and having gambling debts that drove me to become an informer. Immediately I could see what was happening. Once the big criminal defense attorneys like Pat Tuite and Ed Genson got a look at their clients' subpoenas, they realized they would be facing me in court, so right away they had to cut me down in the minds of potential jurors. They had to make me look like somebody who got caught by the government. Then they could argue that I would say anything to get off the hook, just like a rat.

I grabbed the phone and called John Drummond at WGN. I said, "John, what they're saying is a bunch of bullshit. That's not the way it is. These lawyers are trying to smear me and ruin my credibility before I give any testimony. I wasn't forced to come in. It was just the opposite. I'll call you back later, and tell you the true story."

I always knew the criminal lawyers would try to crucify me. I just didn't think it would happen this soon. My mother didn't even know I'd left town, and I didn't want her to find out this way. Fortunately, when I called, she still hadn't seen anything on TV. I tried to prepare her for what would come out. "Don't pay attention to the stuff about me in the media," I said. "Most of it won't be true."

But then I told her I had left town. "I'll be gone for a while, but I'll stay in touch and let you know I'm okay," I said. I promised that over the next few days, I would be calling the reporters. "I'll straighten it out with them and make sure they don't destroy the family name."

Of course, this all seemed so strange to my mother—it was almost like telling her I had a terminal illness. There were times when I heard her crying on the other end of the line. As soon as I hung up with her, the phone rang again. It was Dave Grossman, the FBI supervisor. He said, "Valukas wants to talk to you," and he transferred me to another line.

The next voice I heard was Anton Valukas. He only had a few hours left in his stint as U.S. Attorney. That was still plenty of time to make my life even more miserable. He said, "We heard that John Drummond was on television earlier today, saying you would be talking to him."

I said, "Yes. That's right."

"Please don't talk to anybody," Valukas said. "You might affect the cases."

"But wait," I said. "My family is back there, and the defense lawyers are dragging my name through the mud with all this stuff about drugs and gambling debts."

He thought that was funny. "Oh, don't worry," he laughed. "All the truth will come out when you go to court. Let them say whatever they want right now."

"Can't you have someone come forward and deny these things?" I asked.

He said, "No. We can't do that now. But if you want your investigation to be successful, you can't say anything. You'll have your day in court, believe you me."

And, like a jackass, I listened to him. I never called back John Drummond or anyone else from the press. The next morning, the *Chicago Tribune* article about my investigation had the following lead: "A Chicago lawyer who feared for his safety because of gambling debts. . . ." Nobody from the government ever came forward to defend me during this period, and the defense lawyers were left alone to dirty the jury pool.

Judge Cieslik used to tell me how easy it was for lawyers like Pat Tuite to manipulate the press. To some extent, you can understand it. When stories break, reporters are desperate for any information they can get. Prosecutors are as much to blame as defense attorneys when it comes to leaks, but prosecutors come and go. The high-paid, high-profile criminal lawyers stick around, and they're the ones with the crime reporters in their pockets. I had a few myself. But I never floated gossip in the press that I couldn't back up in court. I didn't want jurors to walk into court thinking one thing to find out another. They tend to take that out on your client.

To make matters worse, the Feds called my investigation, "Operation Gambat"—for Gambling Attorney. I certainly don't deny that I gambled, and loved doing it, but that name turned everything back onto *my* activities and *my* motives. As a result, whenever the newspapers wrote about me, my first name was always "crooked" or "corrupt." One reporter created a whole new adjective for me: "corrupt-lawyer-turned-government-informant." Meanwhile, they had different descriptions for Pat Marcy, such as "businessman" or "an influential member of the First

Ward Democratic Organization." In all the months leading up to his trial, no one ever wrote that he was an ex-convict. For that information, the reporters had to look as far as their own newspapers' clip files.

From the start, almost all the press reported that I was in the Witness Protection Program, but nothing was further from the truth. First of all, I always thought Witness Protection was something for stoolpigeons and rats—people who informed for the money and had nothing better to do with their lives. A year before I left Chicago, the FBI had someone from the program come to talk to me to change my mind. He told me how four people would pick me up and stay with me at all times; how we would keep moving from hotel to hotel; how I wouldn't be allowed to call home. That sounded like jail to me. I asked him very nicely to leave my apartment and never come back.

Those who knew the truth thought I was brave to opt out of Witness Protection, but to be honest, I had to wonder how much protection the program would give me. Most people think the FBI or the Secret Service run the program. In fact, it's the U.S. Marshals Service. My life would have depended on a bunch of guys who weren't making all that much money—under $30,000 in those days. What would they do if the Mob put a huge bounty on my head?

After I had been in Fort Myers for a few days, I got a visit from another agent. He told me that Tony Accardo, the grand old Godfather of the Outfit, had come out of retirement to fly back to Chicago and deal with the fallout from my investigation. One wire caught another old boss saying, "They ruined the First Ward." The FBI was more convinced than ever that the Mob would have me killed, and once again this agent pleaded with me to go into Witness Protection.

But I wouldn't change my mind. The FBI didn't like it much, but they decided to work out their own special program to keep me in hiding until my trials were over. When the agent asked where I wanted to live, I didn't have a clue. He told me that the Denver area was nice, and I decided to give it a try. Steve Bowen met up with us and I flew with him to Colorado. Before we looked for an apartment, he took me to a Denver courthouse. There, we legally changed my name and they gave me a new Social Security number to go along with it.

I chose to live in Littleton (now known for the student shootings at Columbine High School), a very picturesque town outside of Denver. After I signed the lease for my apartment and my car, I sat down with Steve and figured out my monthly expenses. Whenever it came to government funds, I always gagged a little. I didn't want to take too much and have the defense lawyers throw that back in my face during a trial. It was like my Vow of Abstinence. I let Steve add only $150 a week for spending money. My total income came to $3,200 a month. There were nights at Faces when I had spent more than that for the bar tab. Eventually, when I had to show up in court and needed to buy some suits, they gave me a raise to $3,400 a month. Because of some silly government regulation, it was easier to do that than write up an expense report for clothing. I never let them raise my monthly allowance beyond that amount. Before he left town, Steve introduced me to the Denver-area FBI agents. I would meet them once a month to get my pay in cash.

My apartment was in a nice new subdivision. I had no complaints about it, but obviously I felt totally isolated in a very strange place. The first night I was there, the temperature was sub-zero, weather that was much colder than anything I had experienced in Chicago. Inside, it was warm, but I still had trouble getting to sleep. Then, at three in the morning, there was a knock on my door. My first thought was: "Who could that be? I don't know anybody in this town."

But the knocking got louder, and then I thought, "Good Christ. They found me."

I tried not to panic. How stupid would a hit man be to knock? Typically they just burst in, but because of the weather, the front doors in these apartments were too big and thick for that. When I looked out through the peephole, I saw a guy standing there, and it looked like he had some kind of rifle cradled in his arm.

I no longer carried my guns, so now I had to scramble to find something I could use as a weapon. I don't even remember what I grabbed, just that it was big and solid. As the guy kept pounding, I quietly took off the chain. Then I suddenly yanked open the door to brain him.

It was the maintenance guy with a crowbar and a sledgehammer. He must have thought I was some kind of crazed paranoid psycho, but I couldn't have been happier to see him. He said, "The pipes are frozen and I may have to knock a hole in your wall. Is that okay?"

I said, "Fine. Fine. Go ahead and knock down the wall if you want."

About the second day I was there, I decided I would go out and hit the nightclubs. I wanted to make some friends and see what life was like in my new hometown. I was sitting in the bar, minding my own business, when a guy came over and sat down next to me, smoking. I quit smoking when I was a kid, and I just hate cigarette smoke. I said, "Excuse me, could you move the cigarette so the smoke doesn't keep blowing in my face."

He said, "Why don't you move?"

The next thing I know, we're exchanging words, and he's asking me outside to fight. As soon as we reached the parking lot, the guy waved me off and left. When I went back into the bar, people came up to me and said, "This guy's always causing trouble, and we were hoping to see him finally get a beating."

But then, as I sat there, I started thinking, "Am I fucking nuts?" With the mood I was in, who knows what I could have done to him? If I got arrested in this strange town, it could have caused some serious problems. I was supposed to be in hiding. I had to learn to take a little shit and keep a low profile.

The FBI wanted me to spend my days going over the hundreds of tapes I had recorded with my wire. Their secretaries tried to transcribe them, but had every other line marked "IA" for inaudible. They gave me earphones and a little steno machine. Often, I had to listen to the same thing over and over again. It was incredibly tedious and boring work—especially for a guy like me who has trouble sitting still.

When Christmas Eve rolled around, did I ever feel alone. I couldn't even call my family. The Feds were still concerned the Mob might find a way to trace calls to their numbers. When I turned on the radio or the TV, all I heard was holiday music, and it made me even more homesick. I finally decided I had to get out of the apartment.

I got in my car and drove into the mountains. When the road ended, I turned off on one of the trails. I went as high as I could go, and then backed up to turn around. I had leased a cheap car with front-wheel drive, not like the big Chryslers or Lincolns I had back in Chicago, and it got stuck in the snow. No matter what I did, I couldn't push it out. I waited to see if anyone would drive by, but no one did. I remembered passing a volunteer fire station on the way up, so I got out of the car and walked back down the mountain. The station was much farther away than I thought, maybe four miles, and when I finally reached it, it was closed for the night. I had to keep trudging through deep snow and bitter cold without boots or a heavy coat. After a few hours of walking, I wondered if I would ever get back without freezing to death. I really started to feel sorry for myself. Like everything else in my life, I had taken this stupid outing without any regard for where it would take me, and once again I was paying the price. Finally, I reached the road and flagged down a car to give me a ride.

If I needed something to make me feel even worse, it came a few weeks later when I got a call from one of the FBI agents. On the day I left town, he went to Arizona to interview Judge Frank Wilson. He told Wilson, "Bob Cooley has been working with the government and they have you on tape. You may be called as a witness."

But Frank was no more forthcoming with him than he was with me. He kept up with the same line, "I don't know what you're talking about." But then, in February, they called him again to say that he'd be granted immunity if he testified before the grand jury. After he put down the phone, the judge went into his back yard with a handgun and blew his brains out.

When I heard this, I just felt horrible. He was the most decent of all the people involved in my cases, and the bribe he took for Harry Aleman was probably the worst thing he ever did in his life. Still, he wouldn't have gone to jail if he cooperated. He was just too embarrassed and humiliated to do that. Of course the family claimed he was depressed over health issues, but the timing told me otherwise. If I hadn't gone to the Feds, he would have been left alone to live out his years.

I also felt badly for my family. They didn't deserve the infamy I brought to our name, or even my father's story. When I took on the zoning change for my brother's clients and turned it into a sting, I never thought about the impact this would have on my brother's law firm or his career. Neither he nor the clients knew about the bribe, but their names and the property were dragged into the papers with news about the Roti and Marcy subpoenas.

That whole winter was like a black hole for me. But eventually I realized I had to get over it. If my investigation hurt good people, at least it was something I had attempted for a good cause, and it was that much more important for me to make successful. As for myself, I had already jumped off the building when I became an informant. The life I had once loved so much was over, and there was nothing I could do about it. Instead, I had to find a way to enjoy what was left to me.

I decided to stay in touch with family and friends back home—even after I learned that the Mob had put a million-dollar bounty on my head. I actually let one buddy come out to visit me. His name was Bobby Whitebloom. He had been a lawyer for the secretary of state's office, and I originally met him through Johnny D'Arco. After he retired from the state job, Bobby worked for an insurance company. During my last years in Chicago, he became one of my closest friends. He was short and slight, and very quiet, but he loved to hang around me and watch the crazy crowd I attracted. Sometimes he'd join me when I'd have a group of people at a Greek restaurant. He always left early, but he usually picked up the check on the way out.

I became Bobby's entire social life, and he was devastated when I left town. After we talked on the phone a few times, I decided that Bobby could fly to Littleton and see me. I totally trusted him to keep my location a secret. But shortly after he got back to Chicago, he called me and said, "Johnny D'Arco came to see me at work. He said, 'I'm sure you know where Bob Cooley is. Tell me or you're going to have problems.'" Johnny said he would be back in a week.

I was furious. D'Arco knew that Bobby had health problems, but the kid also had brass balls, and was not going to knuckle under to anyone. I called the Feds and told them that D'Arco was intimidating Bobby. I knew that agents had already gone out to Mob leaders like M and warned them that there would be consequences if anyone harassed my friends and family. But now the Feds figured they might have another count against Johnny if they could get Bobby to wear a wire. Like an idiot, I agreed, and helped talk him into it.

Bobby did get Johnny D'Arco threatening him on tape, but we'll never know what could have been done with his evidence. Bobby already had a weak heart, and after this incident, he had more problems with it. A few months later, he wound up in the hospital and the doctors wanted to operate. The night before surgery, we talked and Bobby was nervous. I tried to assure him. I said, "Bobby, you're going to be okay. You have great doctors and you're in a great hospital." But what did I know. He died on the operating table. I felt partly responsible for dragging him into my situation, but now I lost any pity I ever had for Johnny D'Arco. He deserved everything he had coming.

Back in Littleton, I kept going out to the nightclubs to meet people. My best friends were one couple from the area. She was going to law school and, without revealing my identity, I could regale her with stories about my years as a criminal attorney. She had to go to Chicago for a conference, and her boyfriend asked me to pick her up at the airport when she returned. I met her at the gate. First thing, she said, "I thought I saw you on TV." The FBI had me wearing a toupee to change my appearance, but it didn't fool her any. Coincidentally, flying on the same plane was the Cook County State's Attorney, Cecil Partee. I had known him for years, but he walked by me at the gate like I wasn't there.

Obviously, it was a matter of time before word got back to Chicago that I was in the Denver area. The FBI yanked me out of there, and I moved next to Richmond, then Charleston, Charlotte, and Atlanta. Each time, the Feds got a tip that the Mob knew where I was and that the hit men were coming to get me. I stopped buying furniture or too many nice clothes, because the warnings would come so suddenly, I would have to leave everything behind.

Even when I was on the run, I couldn't help but build new cases for the government. I had just been in Atlanta for a few days when I heard about the Buckhead area, and I walked into one club there. It reminded me of the places back in Chicago where the mobsters used to hang. I struck up a conversation with a guy at the bar. "I'm just here from Denver," I said, and gave him my new name. "I'm an attorney." One thing led to another, and I realized that my new friend was a mobster who specialized in fixing traffic cases. The judges and lawyers would come to this club to meet him. He also did some bookmaking and gambling, so he loved my advice on betting lines.

The next morning, the Atlanta agents assigned to help me couldn't believe who I had met at the bar. He was a crime boss on the level of Marco D'Amico. They had been trying to make him for years, but the last informant who got close to him ended up dead. They asked me to build some cases on him, and I was only too happy to help. I thought this was great. Here were all the mobsters in Chicago looking for me, while I was working on these other bad guys in Atlanta. I went back to wearing a wire and hosted dinners for the crime boss and his friends. I started to meet women through the local singles ads, and I had them come along, too. A few more agents were added to the mix as my associates—two males and a female. One of those agents was a single guy who liked to show off for the woman. One night, when he was drinking with her at the bar, he started to brag to her about his exploits. Later, the bartender took me aside and asked, "You're not an FBI agent, are you?"

"What are you talking about?" I said. "Who gave you that crazy idea?"

"Your buddy over there," he said. The bartender pointed at the single-guy agent. "He's been talking all night about making raids with a SWAT team."

That was the end of my Atlanta operation, and now I had to ride out of town again. Too bad, because I had really started to love Atlanta.

But I couldn't let any of these detours distract me from the investigation in Chicago. My main purpose in life was to convict everybody I had made cases against. That's why I had to stay alive and why I had to move if there was ever a hint that the Mob knew my whereabouts. If they got me, then they won. I wasn't going to let that happen.

In September of 1990, I made a trip back to Chicago to testify before a grand jury. They took me into the Dirksen Federal Building through a basement garage and up to a room that looked like a lecture hall. Grand jurors sat where the students would be. Tom Durkin, the assistant U.S. attorney, asked me questions, and most of my answers were "yes" and "no." After this went on for a couple of days, I realized the sheer number of charges that were lining up behind my testimony—like freight cars at a rail crossing.

Finally, a few days before Christmas 1990, the Feds had the big press conference that Valukas thought he would get. Fortunately, in his place was the new U.S. Attorney for Chicago, Fred Foreman, along with U.S. Attorney General Dick Thornburgh and FBI Director William Sessions, who both flew in from Washington for the occasion. They announced three indictments. There was one against Patty DeLeo and Judge Shields, and another against Johnny D'Arco. But by far, the biggest case was against Pat Marcy and Fred Roti and their "enterprise" known as "the First Ward." The charges included fourteen counts and six acts of racketeering that touched on everything from the phony Chancery case of *Eldridge v. Carr* to the zoning bribe and the fixes for Harry Aleman, Lenny Chow, and Mike Colella. There was only one charge in the indictment that I didn't develop—a bribe Marcy took from someone who wanted his brother to be an associate judge. (The Feds found out about it when they tapped Marcy's phone at Counsellors Row.)

The next day, the *Chicago Tribune* front-page headline read: "Five Indicted in 'Corruption Feast.' " It quoted Fred Foreman when he said, "Whatever type of corruption you wanted, you could get, and this movable feast went from the First Ward to Springfield, to City Hall, to the Circuit Court of Cook County; even to the highest levels of the Chancery Court."

With just these three indictments, the paper said, "The charges in Operation Gambat surpass in both money and scope the corruption unearthed in the infamous Operation Greylord investigation into judicial corruption."

When a reporter asked whether the investigation would produce any more indictments directly tied to organized crime, Attorney General Thornburgh replied, "Stay tuned."

But I had a few questions about the indictments myself—especially about the unindicted. If they could accuse Marcy and Roti for fixing the Eldridge case, why wasn't there a charge against the judge, Anthony Scotillo? What about all the cases I had against Marco and his crew?

What bothered me most was that they didn't indict Maloney—and, according to my grapevine of FBI agents, they didn't plan on doing it in the future, either.

A few months after the press conference, the Feds brought me back to the Federal Building in Chicago to start our preparations for the first trials. As usual, the FBI agent took me in through the garage and let me off by the elevator while he parked the car. At that moment, the U.S. Attorney, Fred Foreman, walked by.

At first, he was startled to see me. He thought I was in protective custody like everyone else. I had dealt with him years before, when he was the DuPage County State's Attorney. I always thought he was a straight shooter and we got along just fine.

Fred said, "Bob, what are you doing here?"

I said, "I'm waiting to go upstairs."

He said, "Are they taking good care of you?"

"Sure," I said.

As he started to get on the elevator, he added, "If there's anything I can do, you let me know."

Then I said, "Fred, wait. There is one thing you can do."

"What's that?" he asked.

I said, "You can indict that scumbag Maloney."

"We had a meeting on that," he told me. "The assistant U.S. Attorney who had the case indicates he doesn't have enough evidence for conviction."

I said, "This man is probably the worst judge we ever had in the system. It would be good to indict him even if he gets acquitted, so people realize you can't get away with that behavior. If we indicted Shields, we can indict Maloney. The case on him is better."

He said, "I'll take another look at it."

I knew his real problem was not the case but the prosecutor who got the assignment. So far, all the Gambat indictments had come through Tom Durkin. He was bright and aggressive, but he couldn't prosecute all of my cases. We needed another sharp attorney to go against Maloney. I told Durkin and Foreman that my favorite candidate was another assistant U.S. Attorney, Scott Mendeloff. I was already working with him on one of the last Greylord cases, involving a sheriff's deputy named Lucius Robinson, who had been bailiff and bagman for some very corrupt judges. Although Robinson took a guilty plea for accepting a bribe, he lied during his grand jury testimony to protect all the judges he helped pay off. Now the Feds were coming after him for perjury. Since I had passed money through Lucius a few times, Scott asked me to be a witness.

In June 1991, I was in a hotel in Wisconsin, working with Scott on the Robinson case. I hated preparing for a trial. I had hated it when I was a lawyer, and I hated it just as much when I became a witness. When I was the attorney, I used to read the police reports just once and was ready to go. Now, I would read a transcript from my wire just once and I was ready to go. But that wasn't good enough for Scott. He's very methodical, and he wanted me to go over everything again and again. One day while we were doing this, it just started to get on my nerves, and I said, "What's happening with Maloney? The statute must be coming close." I figured it would soon be five years since his El Rukn trial with Swano.

Scott said, "That's really none of your business. Why don't you concentrate on this case?"

I said, "Why am I wasting my time here on this bailiff, this go-fer, when Maloney—the worst scumbag of all—may skate because he's politically connected with Ed Burke?"

That got Scott really mad. He said, "You can't take these cases so personally. You're not supposed to push for prosecution. You're not a prosecutor. You're only a witness."

We went back to a transcript and started to bicker again about a word on the tape. I was frustrated, but I could see I had raised an issue that got him equally frustrated. Finally Scott said, "Either you're going to work with me and do what I tell you, or I might not call you as a witness."

One of the agents was there, and I said to him, "Maybe you should change my airplane reservation to tomorrow." I got up and started to walk out the door.

Scott said, "Come on. Stop it already. Let's go back to work."

Soon afterwards, he got paged and went to another room to make a phone call. He came back a few minutes later. "Now you can be happy," he said. "We just indicted Maloney."

It turned out that the statute of limitations for the El Rukn trial was closer than I thought. The indictment against Maloney and Swano came on the very last day that the government could bring charges.

CHAPTER 14

"SLANDER MY NAME"

n the days after the first Gambat indictments were announced, the papers and TV stations went back to speculating about my motives for becoming an informant. I knew this was really audition time for all the stories that the defense attorneys would tell the jury. Once again, they trotted out the bullshit about my gambling debts and that I was afraid of Bob Johnson and Dominic Barbaro. Pat Marcy hired Genson to represent him, and fat old Eddy was quick to dismiss all my cases by saying, "They are the ravings of a sick mind, and Mr. Cooley will be shown as such in court."

But in the same article where this Genson quote appeared, *Tribune* reporter Ray Gibson added some new perspective. He found out about my beef with Marco and my disgust with the Mike Colella fix. He also mentioned that my brothers served with distinction as police officers, and my father's reputation for honesty. He wrote, "Friends say reports that [Cooley] was in fear of his life because of gambling debts are untrue. . . . He had simply become fed up with corruption."

Who was the real Bob Cooley? A lot of people were waiting to see, but my debut on the witness stand would not come with an Operation Gambat trial. Instead, I was asked to testify in a wide-ranging case the Feds had brought against the On Leong Merchants Association. Originally, they had more than thirty-three defendants from all over the country, but most of the counts involved the gambling operation that the Chicago On Leong ran out of their headquarters on Wentworth Street in Chinatown. From the balcony of that building, Lenny Chow had shot William Chin.

I had known for some time that the government was investigating the On Leong. After I came in, the Strike Force had me wear the wire on Wilson Moy to confirm that he had paid to fix Lenny Chow's murder case. We also got evidence that he was paying off Roti to keep the police from raiding his games. The Feds even paid me to go to an On Leong convention with Moy in Taiwan. While we were still in Taiwan, Moy and I met up with Wing and Eddie Chan, the former national leader of the On Leong. Eddie fled the U.S. as soon as he found out the Feds were on his trail. I tried to talk Eddie into coming back, but he knew better.

A few weeks before I was supposed to testify at the trial in Chicago, I went to an Iowa hotel to meet the assistant U.S. Attorney leading the prosecution. His name was Stephen Anderson, and he looked to be a young guy who might have bitten off more than he could chew with this case. When I first walked into his room with the FBI agent Steve Bowen, Anderson went overboard with all the compliments. "What an honor it is to meet you," he said. "I realize what you've done and all the sacrifices you've made." He laid it on so thick, it was embarrassing. Finally, I said, "Okay. Let's get started already."

I was with him in the hotel for two days, going through all the details of the Lenny Chow trial. When we were ready to leave town, Steve Bowen dropped Anderson and me at the airport. I said good-bye and we went our separate ways. I'm sure Anderson thought Witness Protection was picking me up (the FBI never wanted me to tell anyone where I was going). But while I was walking around the airport, I saw Anderson again at a phone booth. I remembered something I forgot to tell him. I walked up from behind just as I heard him say, "How would you feel if you were stuck in a room with a stoolpigeon for the weekend?"

I spun around and walked away before he could see me, thinking, "What a phony piece of shit." I was supposed to call him before I came back to town to testify, but I was still so fucking mad, I never did.

While the Lenny Chow fix was an important charge in the On Leong indictment, it was still a small part of the whole trial. There were dozens of other charges against eleven defendants, and I could only testify about two of them, Wilson Moy and Wing. But as far as the media was concerned, On Leong was all about me. Throughout their coverage of the trial, the reporters called me the star witness. It was like the sideshow had taken over the circus. When I made my first appearance, July 1, 1991, the case had already dragged on for three months, but the *Chicago Tribune* front-page headline read: "Cooley's Credibility On Trial."

The article made it clear that the defense lawyers saw much more at stake in my testimony than the verdict for the On Leong trial. The reporter, Matt O'Connor, wrote: "If defense lawyers have their way, Robert J. Cooley, the lawyer turned government informant, will be on trial as much as the defendants when he testifies Monday for the first time in federal court." Because of my "corrupt behavior," O'Connor predicted, my "character and credibility are expected to come under blistering attack" by the defense attorneys.

You didn't have to read too much between the lines to see what he was driving at. The lawyers saw this trial as a just a first skirmish. For them, the most important battles—over the First Ward—were yet to come, and anything they could do to weaken me would help.

In fact, prior to my arrival in Chicago, various court documents had already been leaked to the press to muddy me up in advance. One was the "proffer" that the government submitted in which I listed my illegal acts. An article on that leak had the headline: "U.S. Says Informant Bribed 20 Judges"—actually, it was 29. The other leak was a motion filed by Ed Genson for Johnny D'Arco. It tried to stop me from testifying in his case, because I was "simply [and] inherently unreliable." Genson filled the motion with every negative thing about me that he could find. It was clearly written more for the press than the judge. He dragged in bullshit charges made against me by my ex-client Paul Baker (who was also Swano's client) when he talked to the Feds—the sort of stuff that would never be allowed in court. He even dug up the time I was arrested in Milwaukee back when I was going to Marquette.

You couldn't look at the papers or watch TV without seeing this crap about me, and I knew it had to be getting through to the jurors. They probably expected me to show up in court covered in slime like the Creature from the Black Lagoon.

My first day of testimony, I entered the Dirksen Federal Building through the basement garage. I had no idea about the commotion this was causing on the street with the news trucks or with all the reporters in the lobby. I went up through the judges' elevators and then down the halls past their chambers. It was like entering a theater from the backstage.

The government held the case in what was called the Ceremonial Courtroom, because of all the lawyers and defendants involved. It was probably the biggest place for a trial in the city of Chicago. When they brought me through the side door and out into that huge room, it was standing room only. Besides the press and all the spectators, I saw a whole aisle full of lawyers who were waiting to pound me in the upcoming Gambat trials. Johnny D'Arco, Patty DeLeo, and Eddy Genson were crammed in among them on a gallery bench.

I could see by the looks on their faces that they weren't expecting the new Bob Cooley. In the words of the *Tribune*, I was "distinguished in a dark blue suit and striped tie." No more turtlenecks and gold chains. My demeanor changed as well. As a lawyer, I was a bantam rooster as soon as I stepped into a courtroom. But as a witness, I was a little nervous and shy. I even spoke in a softer voice, and tried to answer, "Yes, sir," and "No, sir," when a lawyer asked me a question.

To start off the direct examination, the assistant U.S. Attorneys would lead me through a confessional—just like I used to do with my clients. I went over each and every bad thing that I had done: from the little cash tips I got as a cop, to the bribes I gave out as a lawyer, the cases I fixed, and my IRS problems during the investigation. I even explained how I withheld information about certain people and activities when I started talking to the Feds and only fully disclosed later. This part of a trial is never easy—the legal version of a rectal exam. Unfortunately, I had to go through it for the first time with Steve Anderson instead of Tom Durkin, a prosecutor who knew me well. Anderson went along like he was reading a laundry list. The *Tribune* would sum up my first day's testimony with the headline "Bribes Were My Way of Life, Informer Says." Meanwhile, anything I said about the Lenny Chow fix was practically reduced to a footnote in the press coverage.

Representing Wilson Moy was pompous Pat Tuite. From the moment

I appeared in the courtroom, he made a big deal about my security and complained that it would bias the jury into thinking, "This witness has to be afraid of somebody." From then on, I always entered before the jury did and was sitting at the witness stand when they arrived.

As I went over my litany of bad acts with the prosecutor, Tuite sat ramrod-straight at the defense table, mugging and tsk-tsking for the jury. The night before he was to cross-examine me, I saw Tuite on the TV news. He used to hold his little press conference in the hall of the Federal Building. He kept telling the reporters how he couldn't wait to get me on the stand. Boy, did that charge me up. I couldn't wait to see him, either.

The next morning, when they brought me into the Federal Building, Steve Anderson asked to meet with me first. The other prosecutors told him I had developed information on the Cammon case that Tuite had fixed with Ed Burke and Judge Maloney.

Anderson said, "When you go into court, I don't want you causing a disruption during the cross-examination. This trial has been going on for a couple of months, and we can't afford a mistrial if you make any charges about Pat Tuite."

I said, "Then you better protect me and keep that piece of garbage from playing games with me."

But Tuite played every game in the book and Anderson hardly lifted a finger. He spent hours going through my proffer, while he took on all these airs and made little comments along the way, like: "I'm disgusted to be a lawyer in your presence." Or at another point, when I explained again how I detailed my illegal activity to the Feds, he said, "That took an awful lot of time, I bet."

At one point, he asked if I admitted taking tips when I was a policeman. When I told him I did, he said, "You became a five- or ten-dollar whore; isn't that right?" He continued in that vein, saying again: "As you look at it now, weren't you whoring your profession as a police officer by taking those five and ten dollars?"

Now this would have been hard enough to take from a straight lawyer, but not someone as rotten and corrupt as Tuite. Through all of this, Anderson sat with his finger up his ass, hardly ever making an objection.

Later, Tuite handed me something to read. I didn't hear his instruction to read it to myself. When I started to read out loud, he shouted, "Are you trying to pull some shots, Mr. Cooley?"

I started to apologize, but then he shouted again, "Judge, would you admonish this *snake* to listen?"

I couldn't look angry or flustered, but, by the end of the day, I decided I wasn't going to take it any more. Tuite got close to me and said, "I doubt that you ever knew an ethical lawyer if you saw one."

I replied, "That's two of us."

Tuite spun around like I had punched him, and a hush went over the courtroom. Then he pointed at me and said, to the judge, "I resent the comment. He made a comment to me, and I resent it."

But the judge hadn't heard what I said. When he asked, another defense counsel yelled out, "Judge, I heard the comment. He said, 'That makes two of us.'"

Now everyone laughed, and of course, this exchange became the lead for the TV news shows and the next day's papers. When he left the court-house, Tuite ran the other way when he saw the cameras coming.

The other big bombshell of the day came when Tuite asked if I had gone to the Feds because I was afraid of my bookies. I told him that they had been contacted and told to do whatever I wanted them to do.

He laughed. "Who did you contact to contact them?"

"John DiFronzo," I said.

Again, everyone—even Tuite—was stunned. Then he laughed me off like I was bullshitting. "And he supposedly talked to these people, right?" he asked, his voice dripping with sarcasm.

I answered, "I know he talked to these people."

Tuite mugged some more for the jury, but he knew better than to challenge me. It would only give the prosecutors a chance to play another tape.

The On Leong trial continued long after I finished my testimony. Finally, facing open rebellion from the jury, the judge forced it to a close. The jurors returned a split decision, acquitting the defendants of all the major charges, and finding just Wilson Moy and a couple of the restaurant owners guilty of tax evasion. Of course, I mostly testified against Moy, but as far as the papers were concerned I was the reason the government lost the case. According to the *Tribune*, the jurors "divided over the credibility of Robert Cooley, the corrupt-lawyer-turned-federal-informant who is a key witness in the government's Operation Gambat probe of First Ward corruption." The article quoted one juror as saying that someone put "the Snake" next to my name on a bulletin board in the deliberations room. When asked about me, the jury foreman said, "I don't think much of him."

From what little I saw of the case, the Feds tried to pack too much against too many people into one trial. Jurors even had trouble keeping the names straight. But I learned some things from those juror comments about me. In future trials, I tried to make eye contact with each and every juror at some point in my testimony and otherwise try to build a rapport with them.

Fortunately, by the time the On Leong verdict came out, we were already deep into the first real Operation Gambat trial, against Patty DeLeo and Judge Shields. This time, I was totally confident about the prosecution. In addition to Tom Durkin, who had just been promoted to first assistant U.S. Attorney, we had Mike Shepard, another long-time federal prosecutor and a tough trial attorney.

As for the defense, you couldn't have had two more different lawyers. Representing Judge Shields was Dan Webb, the former Chicago U.S. Attorney during Operation Greylord. He was renowned for taking apart Ollie North in the Iran–Contra hearings. Like so many before him, when he left the Justice Department, Webb had pushed through the revolving door to Winston & Strawn, another Chicago-based firm that specialized in defending wealthy white-collar criminals. He was considered the finest trial lawyer money could buy.

But then, sitting at the other defense table, representing Patty DeLeo, was a lawyer as far removed from Webb as I could imagine—the clown prince of the criminal courts, Sam Banks. He was just an idiot in every way. I suspected that he charged Patty no fee for the case, because so much of Sam's business came out of the First Ward. But this was no time for DeLeo to be a cheapskate. He had a lot at stake—like years in prison. I thought, "How stupid can Patty be to use an incompetent like this?"

Despite the presence of Banks, this case was no slam-dunk for the government—even with my tapes and the recordings from the bug in Judge Shields's chambers. First of all, Patty DeLeo was the only person who saw the judge taking the bribe, so Dan Webb could argue that Patty pocketed all the money I gave him and that the judge only ruled in my favor because my "client" was in the right. In fact, the FBI agent who played my opposing lawyer in the case did not put up much of a fight during the hearings. Supporting this line of defense was the sterling reputation of Judge Shields, and I was not about to tarnish the man with my testimony.

When Webb asked if I had ever bribed Shields in the past, I told him "No." When he asked if the judge had ever indicated he wanted money, I also said, "No." Like a good trial lawyer, Webb sensed my positive feelings about Judge Shields, and he milked them for all they were worth. I ended up saying that Shields was always a gentleman to me, and very professional whenever I dealt with him.

This part of my testimony did not thrill Tom Durkin and Mike Shepard, and they ripped into me after court adjourned for the day. They didn't want me to lie, but they didn't want me to be so complimentary, either. "Don't worry," I told them. "You watch what happens when Sam Banks cross-examines me. I guarantee he'll mess it up for Judge Shields."

That's exactly what happened. Banks started off by asking some silly questions about my "sordid past." First, whether I took money as a cop. Without mentioning his name, I told him how Alderman Edward Vrdolyak left some cash on my passenger seat after I let him go in a traffic stop. Then he wanted to know how much I spent gambling. When he asked me about the bribes I paid in Traffic Court, I gave him my standard reply: "It happened every day I was in there. Anyone who worked in the courtroom on a regular basis either paid or lost."

But as I talked, I could see the wheels spinning in Sam's head. He knew that if he wasn't careful, I could testify about the murder case *he* tried to fix. I was in Counsellors Row all those nights he worked with Ed Burke on the killer cops trial. Like I thought, Sam didn't probe too much into this area.

Then, Banks committed the cardinal sin for trial attorneys: He asked me an open question and had no idea about my answer. "Now you had no problems paying judges, did you?"

I replied, "There were some judges I couldn't pay personally."

Thanks to this moron's question, the jury realized that a corrupt judge might take money from one lawyer, but not another. It followed that maybe DeLeo was the only lawyer Shields trusted to be his bagman.

Dan Webb almost had a fit. He pulled Judge Shields and their table away from Patty and Banks to literally put space between them.

For me, the best part of Banks's cross-examination came with his final questions. Previously, he had me estimate my income as a lawyer. I told him that in my good years, I could make two to three hundred thousand a year. When he asked about my current income from the government, I answered, "$3,400 a month."

With a furrowed brow, he did the math. You could see him realize that this added up to a lot less than what I used to make. Clearly I did not cooperate with the government to increase my income. Finally, Sam sputtered, "And that is by your own choice, is it not?"

"Well, yes," I said, "it is my own choice."

One episode during the trial most defined the character of Judge Shields. Webb tried to pound home that Patty was slippery enough to take my bribe and never turn it over to the judge. Of course, I had several stories to support that theory. I could start with the time I caught him red-handed, cheating me on what I thought was a Ward case. That incident gave me an excuse to break from his firm. Before I could start the story, Sam Banks jumped up and down. He demanded a separate trial.

The judge, Ilana Rovner, was a no-nonsense lady who didn't stand for this kind of commotion. First she rejected Sam's motion, and then she excused the jury. I told her the story, and she decided that the jury could hear it, too. During this time, I could see Judge Shields talking with Webb. Then, before the jury returned, Webb got up to say his client had instructed him to withdraw the question. Even though it was in his interests, Judge Shields would not trash Patty's character any further.

As the trial came to a close, Webb put Shields on the stand—a desperation move for a lawyer like that. The judge came off very well in the direct examination; but during the cross, he opened the door for Tom Durkin to ask about the time he was stopped for drunk driving. He had shown the arresting officer his judge's card. A year after this arrest, as head of the National Conference of State Trial Judges, Shields wrote that judges "cannot use their judicial office for the purpose of advancing a personal interest." This embarrassing story may not have seemed like a big deal compared to the other charges, but I believe it did plant seeds of doubt with the jury: namely, that the defendant was pretending to be something he was not.

The jury deliberations went on for four days. According to the papers, most of the time was spent listening to the tapes. First they listened to what was recorded on my wire when Patty DeLeo confirmed what I wanted from the judge. Patty had said, "We want to stall it till next week."

I replied, "Fine, that's all we need."

Then, a few minutes later, the bug in the judge's chambers picked up Patty saying, "Stall it till next week, and the case will be settled."

Since the bug was installed in an old radiator, the sound would go in and out with the steam. But after listening over and over, the jury became convinced that Patty really did say the word "stall." The judge clearly replied, "All right," and stall is exactly what he did for me when he presided over the hearing a few minutes later.

"The jury was probably sorry to hear it," Mike Shepard later told the reporters, "but it's there." Evidently they liked the man as much as I did, but they had to do their duty. They found both Shields and Patty DeLeo guilty.

When it came time to sentence them, the Shields personality did not win over Judge Rovner. She sentenced the judge to 37 months and said, "What you have done has shamed many honest judges, but more importantly impaired the public's belief in a fair, impartial judiciary." It was exactly Judge Shields's reputation, she said, that made his conduct "particularly tragic," because "all over Cook County, lawyers and litigants are saying, 'If Dave Shields could do this, then any judge is capable of doing this.' And what is being said is, 'Who is there left to rely upon, when those who are so trusted prove themselves to be so untrustworthy?' "

Shields may have hurt himself most with her by continuing to deny responsibility. I guess that was his pride talking. Judge Rovner pointed to the evidence from the wires and the bug. She told him, "As much as you wish it otherwise, those words are on that tape. You were convicted by your own words—and once again by your false denial at trial."

Surprisingly, she sentenced Patty DeLeo to a few months less than the judge, but she gave him a tongue-lashing too. She told him to listen to the tapes with Shields as they plotted to stall the case in his chambers. "Listen to them," she said, "and it is obvious to all that it is simply business as usual going on there in that locked chambers. The citizens of Cook County have unfortunately seen this scenario played and replayed. And, Mr. DeLeo, we are all tired of it."

To his credit, Patty took it like a man. Instead of denying it, he told the judge that the trial was a "very devastating experience." He said, "If there are lessons to be learned, believe me, I have learned them."

Patty may have learned lessons from the convictions, but none of those rubbed off on the political or legal establishment in Chicago. Harry Comerford, chief judge for the Cook County Circuit Court, called Shields and DeLeo an "isolated case." He claimed that the court system had already gone through enough reforms after Greylord and didn't need any more.

In October 1991, the trial began for Johnny D'Arco—only two weeks after we finished with Shields and DeLeo. As far as the press was concerned, the jury was still out on my credibility. Reporters kept pointing to the bug in the judge's chambers as the crucial piece of evidence in the first Operation Gambat conviction.

Normally when my testimony was over in a trial, I was supposed to leave town, but a couple of times I didn't. After the FBI agent dropped me off at an out-of-town airport, I would rent a car and come back to Chicago and spend time with family or with girlfriends. I felt secure, because I figured nobody would think I'd be in town.

Sometimes I did crazy things during a trial, too. I'd tell my girlfriend where I was staying, and have her wait for me in the lobby with a little champagne and other party favors. She'd pretend not to know me when I walked in with the agents after dinner. They took rooms on either side of me. Once I could hear their doors close, I'd call down to the desk and have the receptionist send my girl up to join me. I'm sure the Feds would have gone nuts if they found out about this. Still, I needed something to make me happy at night, since my days were spent hearing what a lowlife scumbag I was.

Of all the trials, none was more vicious or personal than Johnny D'Arco's. I was the source of almost all the evidence, either through the tapes from my wire or through my testimony. As a result, Ed Genson decided to turn the entire defense into an attack on me.

In his opening remarks, Genson dismissed the tapes. "There was nothing here but talk," he told the jury. "A lot of smoke, a lot of fantasy." Then, waddling around the courtroom and gesticulating with his cane, he dismissed me. "The man is a paragon of corruption," he said. "The man is walking slime. And this is the man who is going to explain the tapes?"

After the defense attorneys were done with their opening statements, court was adjourned. Usually, I came in before the jury did, so they wouldn't see me enter the courtroom through a side door or with security guards. When I first took the stand, all I could think about was Bobby Whitebloom, and how D'Arco had hounded him to death. I made sure to catch Johnny's eye. He started to glare at me, but then I gave him a wink and a smile, just to bust his balls. From that moment on, as even the *Tribune* noted, he "looked toward the gallery, and avoided glancing at Cooley."

Meanwhile, as the jury filed in, Genson walked right up to me at the witness stand, like we were the best of friends. He said, "You're looking pretty good, Bob. Are you feeling all right? Are they treating you okay?"

This was not only the guy who had just called me "walking slime." He had also nearly gotten me killed when he told Marco I warned my client Frank Renella about being named an informant. "Ed," I said softly, with a pleasant little smile on my face, "go fuck yourself. Just go and fuck yourself."

My direct examination by Mike Shepard took four days. Again, we went through my confessional. Again, I explained why I came in. I said, "I offered my services to help put a stop to some of the corruption in the court system and some of the organized crime corruption here in Chicago."

Once more I was careful about my demeanor, and tried to be polite and soft-spoken at all times; but throughout my testimony, Genson would jump up and make objections or call for sidebars—especially when I explained what some of the tapes were about. As I told the jury, I never mentioned the words "fix" or "bribe" outright. Instead, we all spoke in code.

At one point, when Mike Shepard asked me what it meant when I said, "Go shake some hands," I explained that it meant passing bribes. Suddenly, Johnny's voice piped up and, making some lame stab at sarcasm, said, "You're the best, Bob. You're the best." Genson put his arm around Johnny's shoulder and told him to shut up. Then, for the rest of day, when I said something he didn't like, Johnny would put his face in his hands and shake his head.

I thought the tapes had enough incriminating statements from Johnny to seal a conviction. But according to the media, the verdict would hinge on my cross-examination by Genson. The *Chicago Tribune* headline said it all: "Focus Still On Cooley's Motives." Like Tuite before him, Eddy had promised in his opening statement to take me apart on the stand.

I had no fear of Genson. I knew how lazy and sloppy he was. Still, in the first few minutes of his cross-examination, I came the closest to breaking down in Federal Court. He was going on about all the oaths I took and violated. He went through the ceremony I had gone through in Springfield to become a lawyer. He asked if I raised my hand to swear in, and when I told him I did, he added, "With your father standing next to you, a Chicago policeman?"

"He was there," I said.

As soon as he mentioned my father, my eyes clouded over. I got so incredibly angry, but I couldn't show Genson that he had hit a weak spot. Instead, I tried to focus on giving him the shortest answers I could. If I kept thinking about my father, I knew I would choke up.

That was the roughest patch, even though Genson had me on the stand for weeks during his cross-examination. I could have told you what questions he would ask before he asked them. At one point, he said, "You tried [jury cases] with some success. Isn't that correct?"

Immediately, I realized that this was a trap. If I bragged on myself about being a great lawyer, why would Johnny or anyone else need me to fix trials? Or so Johnny's jury might think.

I answered, "I won some. I lost some."

If Eddy had asked for specific numbers, I would have answered that I probably won forty-eight and lost two. Instead, he didn't press any further. He just turned over a bunch of pages on his legal pad and started another line of attack.

In each of my Operation Gambat cases, the defense always looked for some magic bullet to explain why I went to the Feds. For Genson, it was Operation Greylord. I had admitted bribing Judge Wayne Olson, who was convicted as part of the Operation Greylord investigation. He then became a government witness, and Eddy argued that I expected him to rat me out.

But the opposite was true. "I was told he wasn't naming any of us," I testified.

"Who were you told by?" Genson asked.

"By some friends of yours," I answered.

I could see Eddy choke on that. Of course, he had to ask a follow-up, and I got to mention Pat Marcy. Later, I explained to the jury that I was never worried about the Greylord witnesses. "I was in the inner circle of the First Ward," I testified, "and I knew they wouldn't name me." When I came in, one of the first assistant U.S. Attorneys to interview me was Charles Sklarsky. Coincidentally, he also interviewed Judge Olson. Later in the trial, Sklarsky was called to the stand and confirmed that Olson had never named me, and that I was not under any government investigation when I walked into the Strike Force.

Genson's other big argument was that I went to the Feds because I was desperate for money: a drunk, a loser, and a bust-out. But Johnny, he claimed, was my opposite number: sober, successful, and influential. This became Eddy's theme throughout the trial; that I was a photo negative of

Johnny. The reporter for the *Chicago Daily Law Bulletin* played right along. She described me as "pink, bald, overweight," with "yellow-tinted glasses." On the other hand, she wrote that D'Arco was "dark, handsome and slightly built. He likes to read and go to the gym."

Eddy made a big deal about Johnny's wife, Maggie, who sat behind him in court, and the fact that I never got married. Of course, I could only chuckle inside, knowing how Johnny used to screw around and ask my advice about women. In fact, one of the last conversations we had had was about Maggie. I asked him why he didn't marry her already. He said, "I'm not going to marry her. Why do I have to marry her?" At some point, Johnny must have realized I had this conversation on tape. Who knows if that got him to finally pop the question?

According to Genson, Johnny only humored me out of pity, because I was "shabbily dressed" and "driving an old car." I have no idea why Genson picked on my clothes or my car. But I do know one thing for sure: He never bothered to read all the transcripts from my wires. The prosecutors later reviewed tape transcripts that showed Johnny complimenting me on my sports jacket, and asking where I got it. In another tape, after he got into my car for a payoff, he asked me who made it and said it looked just like a limo.

But even without those tapes, Genson's arguments were nonsense. "*I* was passing out money to *him*," I testified. "I had my pockets full of money all the time, so I would not assume that made me out to be a bust-out."

In fact, the longer Eddy kept me on the stand, the more problems he made for his client. He kept asking open-ended questions that let me introduce other illegal things Johnny had done that were not part of the indictment. At one point, he went over a discussion we had had, during breakfast, about my bribe for passing the state law. Genson charged that I was using "double-talk" and had no reason to believe Johnny wanted a bribe for passing the law.

I replied, "I know what he's done in the past."

When he asked what that could be, it was like he loaded the gun and then handed it back so I could blow his brains out. I answered: "Sir, I was present in Vegas when he talked to Richie Guidice how he was going to work this deal." Giudice was a state senator Johnny talked into becoming a lobbyist. I went on to testify that Johnny explained how he would split our lobbying fees fifty-fifty, and then told us how to avoid paying taxes on our share.

Eddy started to sputter, realizing what he had done. He demanded to know why I didn't bring this story up during my direct examination. I answered, "I was told I couldn't, unless I was asked on cross-examination."

Before long, Eddy was whacking the defense table with his cane. "This is totally improper," he shouted, "and I move for a mistrial."

Now Johnny was on his feet and yelling, "This is ridiculous. He's absurd."

Judge George Lindberg sent the jury out of the courtroom. But Johnny still wasn't done with his tantrum. He slammed his chair against the table and yelled at the prosecutors, "Slander my name all over the world—you!" Then he marched out of the courtroom, leaving his wife behind to bawl her head off.

Eddy next staggered over to the bench, one hand clutching his chest and the other pointing at me. "This man is a legal assassin," he hissed. "Every time he opens his mouth, he plunges another dagger into my client."

I was dismissed, too; but later, when I went over the trial transcripts, I could see all the comments Eddy would make during the sidebars. As far as the judge was concerned, Genson took "risks" when he asked his open-ended questions, but Eddy blamed me for how things were unraveling. He told the judge, "I have known Robert Cooley for twenty-five years. He is as crafty a human being as there is. This is no accident. We are not dealing with some street guy that likes to talk. He's taking shots. . . . I've been doing this a long time, and I don't get these shots pulled on me."

But before the judge brought me back into the courtroom, he admonished Eddy, "Mr. Genson, I am going to ask that you restrain yourself. I realize that there is a certain amount of gesticulation associated with your presentation . . . but I don't think you are entitled to belittle the individuals who are representing the government. . . ."

Poor Judge Lindberg. This was only his second criminal trial and, as he admitted, "I am a very mild-mannered judge." But he was presiding over a madhouse. We adjourned for the weekend and when we returned, he tried to take back some control. He told me that I was "not a lawyer in these proceedings" and should keep my answers to "yes" and "no."

But then he said to Genson, "Next time I see that cane misused, it's going out the door." He warned both Johnny and Eddy that if there was another outburst, "I am not beyond arranging different housing."

Genson finished his cross-examination a few days later, but he had helped me open a Pandora's box filled with Johnny's other illegal activities. The prosecutors needed three more days of redirect to go into everything. Before I left the stand, Eddy still had to give me one more shot. "Is there any lie you won't tell to win?" he bellowed.

I calmly replied, "Do you expect me to perjure myself and put myself at risk?"

By the time I finished, I had spent fifteen days of testimony as a witness. Usually, after I was done with a trial, I would go to another floor in the building and wait for an FBI agent to take me to the airport. This time, when I walked into that room, it was full of agents with submachine guns and flak jackets. During the trial, someone had called in a tip to a reporter. He said that the Mob knew I was living in Richmond and planned to kill me before Christmas. I pulled up stakes again.

Meanwhile, back in the courtroom, Johnny and Eddy still had a few more dramatic moments for the jury. The day after I wrapped up my testimony, Genson put Steve Bowen on the stand. Eddy accused the FBI of pursuing Johnny as part of a vendetta against his father. At the mention of Senior's name, Johnny burst into sobs and "shook with emotion," according to the *Tribune*. I read that and had to think how Senior had started this all, when he pulled me aside in Counsellors Row and asked me to help his son. Johnny was never cut out to be the player his father wanted him to be. Who knows what Johnny would have become if Senior hadn't tried to live his dreams through him?

Like Judge Shields, Johnny, too, had to take the stand in his own defense, but then the defense got even more inane. First, Johnny testified that he never knew I had asked for a bribe. "Many times I didn't understand what he was talking about," Johnny said of me. "A lot of times I would not listen to what he was saying or just not pay attention."

Still, Johnny had to explain away the times I gave him money. In the beginning of the trial, Genson argued that I pocketed the money and never paid Johnny off. As proof, he played the tapes when I counted money to pay Marcy, Roti, and DeLeo. When I gave the $5,000 to Johnny in my car, I didn't count out each bill. It was crazy for Genson to bring up all these other payoffs, because it only confirmed the things I said about First Ward corruption.

But now, with Johnny on the stand, Genson totally reversed course. They would no longer deny that I paid off D'Arco. "Unfortunately," Johnny testified, "I took his money." With the Scotillo bribe, he claimed that he pocketed the $2,500 I paid him, and never intended to give the judge a $1,000 bribe.

"You lied to Cooley for a thousand bucks?" Mike Shepard asked.

"I lied to him because he kept bothering me," Johnny replied.

He told the court that he considered my $5,000 payment for the state law to be a "retainer" from my client, which Johnny described as a "national or international corporation."

Shepard then asked, "You were going to be paid by this national-international corporation in cash? In a car?"

"That's correct," Johnny answered.

In a bizarre appeal for sympathy, Johnny blurted out to the jury that he expected to be indicted for paying off Scotillo. Tom Durkin and Mike Shepard objected, but as far as I was concerned, he was just banging more nails into his own coffin.

In his closing argument, Mike Shepard told the jury: "You learned all about bills, Senator D'Arco-style. You learned how he takes in dollar bills, you learned how he puts through bills in the legislature, and you learned how he tried to sell you a bill of goods when he got caught on tape."

But in his closing statements, Genson acted like I was the one on trial. He called Johnny a sensitive poet and a "family man," who rose above his roots. But I was a "drunk," a "gambler," and a "womanizer," who was still mired in the gutter. "You can't reform a sewer rat," Genson told the jury. "The attempt to make [Robert Cooley] look like a reformed sinner was pitiful. He has been a trial lawyer for twenty years. He is as slippery as an eel."

Genson's description of me made the TV news, but it didn't have much effect on the jury. It took them seven hours to find Johnny guilty.

Again, when the newspapers discussed the case with the jury, they had to ask them about *my* credibility. But this time, the *Tribune* reported: "Because of the strength of the tapes' contents, forewoman Connie Kelly said, the jury did not even discuss the credibility of Cooley, formerly a longtime crooked lawyer.

" 'I wouldn't date him,' Kelly, a nurse from the west suburbs, said of Cooley. 'But I think he was a credible witness.' "

Judge Lindberg gave Johnny three years. Also, as part of the sentence, he ordered him to "never seek employment by any state."

Johnny didn't cry in court this time, but his response was typically wacky. "Somehow," he told the judge, "I must learn to live with myself." Evidently that meant living someplace else. He had already relocated to Florida with his wife. Just before he got out of prison, they let him take a plea on bribing Judge Scotillo. In return, he only had to serve another six months for that crime. For reasons I don't understand to this day, Scotillo was never indicted.

The day of the D'Arco verdict, the Feds finally decided they couldn't let defense attorneys like Tuite and Genson continue to smear me without some official response. Chicago U.S. Attorney Fred Foreman—in total contrast to Valukas—held a press conference to set the record straight. Tom Durkin and Mike Shepard joined in as well. Foreman praised me for having "opened a window to corruption."

Tom, for the umpteenth time, told the reporters that I had not been under investigation when I approached the Strike Force. In terms of my motives, Tom explained, "He was sick of what he was doing and sick of what he saw."

Only a few reporters attended this press conference. At least one of them was Matt O'Connor from the *Tribune*. He picked up their comments in the bottom of the story about Johnny's verdict, and the paper set the tone for future coverage with the next day's headline: "D'Arco Conviction Has Probe On A Roll."

CHAPTER 15

THE HARDER THEY FALL

I could not wait for the case to begin against Pat Marcy and Fred Roti, but the trial didn't start until December 14, 1992—just about a year after Johnny's conviction. Some of the delay came from the typical back-and-forth over evidence, but most of it was related to the defendants complaining about their health, first Roti and then Marcy. By this time, Fred was seventy-two and Pat was seventy-nine, but I thought they were faking it. I knew the old Mob bosses had this deathbed stuff down to a science. There were even certain clinics they used to get phony diagnoses. Still, even the government doctors agreed that Pat had a "terminal" heart condition. To lessen the strain on him, the judge agreed to keep court in session only four hours a day and four days a week.

With all the counts in the indictment, the prosecutors needed the first day just for their opening statements. The defense took half of the next day for theirs. To my utter and total amazement, Eddy Genson represented Pat Marcy. I figured Marcy must have been getting a First Ward freebie from Genson—like Patty DeLeo got from Sam Banks. Eddy had failed so miserably in the D'Arco trial, I didn't see how anyone could use him for another Gambat case. Maybe money really did mean more to Marcy than life itself.

Once more, from his opening statement, Genson made me the focal point of the trial. "Other than Cooley, no one else will testify that Pat was any way involved in this case," Genson said. "It is only the word of Cooley regarding Aleman, regarding Chow and regarding Colella, the word of a lawyer who has prepared witnesses to lie and prepared himself to lie in this case. It's a word of a liar, a drunk, a bribe giver, a bribe taker, who took and gave money to let the drunk driver drive again, the killer kill again and the dope peddler sell dope again."

If Eddy was trying to play to the press, it wasn't working so well any more. In fact, the papers were not just referring to me any more as the "corrupt lawyer." Sometimes I was also the "government mole"—not yet your sterling citizen, but at least a few rungs up the animal kingdom ladder from snake and rat. Meanwhile, the media wasn't referring to Marcy as just a businessman. Both major papers finally reported that Bill Roemer, the former Chicago FBI agent, had identified him as a "made member" of the Mafia during a U.S. Senate hearing.

But Genson argued in his opening that if Marcy had done anything wrong, it was not criminal—it was political. "This case does not involve fixes," he told the jury. "It's about old men, brought up in a different system. It involves favors that are clearly political but not against the law. That's all politics is—favors. This, ladies and gentlemen, is old-time politics."

Engineering the acquittal of hit men was just politics? I had to hear how Eddy worked that one out with the jury.

When I entered the courtroom on my first day of testimony, I really looked forward to seeing Pat. I expected that with all the talk of illness, he might be shriveled or frail. But when I took the stand and glanced over at the defense table, there he was, sitting next to Genson, and he looked exactly as I remembered him—even with the pissed-off glare. I stared back as if he wasn't there; but when Genson looked the other way, I flashed Pat a wink and a smile. His glare got even darker, but then something caught in his throat, and he started to breathe more heavily.

Tom Durkin took me through the direct examination for the rest of the day. Once again, he was brilliant at laying out a complicated case in very simple terms for the jury, with great charts and photos. Counsellors Row had gone out of business shortly after Marcy and Roti were indicted, but there it was again, up on the easels. The prosecutors marked out the location of the table and the path Pat would take into the lobby of 100 North LaSalle and back past the elevators into the janitor's closet. Whenever I made a reference to organized crime or hit men, Genson would jump up with an objection. But what other words could I use to describe Johnny DiFronzo, Marco D'Amico, or Harry Aleman? Out of the presence of the jury, the judge instructed me to refer to anyone associated with organized crime as First Ward or First Ward associate. I thought that was a laugh. The judge didn't know how right he was.

We skipped the next day, a Wednesday, as part of the judge's shortened schedule for Marcy, and then returned after lunch on Thursday. Although I spent most of my testimony looking at Tom or the jury, I could still see Pat out of the corner of my eye. He kept bringing his hand to his mouth, like he was ready to cough. By late in the afternoon, I was up to the fixed case for Mike Colella. Suddenly, Pat started coughing again, in two long jags. At first, I tried to ignore it, thinking he was trying to distract the jurors, but after the second fit, the judge called a brief recess. When Pat came back, he was still sucking wind.

We adjourned less than an hour later. That was the last I ever saw of Pat Marcy. He went straight from the Federal Building to the intensive care unit of a suburban hospital. The doctors reported that he had suffered a heart attack at some point in the previous twenty-four hours. They predicted that he would need another half year before he could return to trial, but he didn't live that long. He died three months later. Still the guy with the upper hand—right to the very end. He was going to deny us the chance to see him humbled, even if it killed him.

The remaining trial against Fred Roti was an anti-climax—like seeing the shadow instead of the monster in a horror movie. At least I was done with Genson. Roti's lawyer, Tom Breen, was much more slick and competent, and he knew where he was going in the cross. He wasn't out to score points in some bigger battle against Gambat and me. He was trying to reduce the sentence for his client. The tapes with Freddy were too damning for a not guilty across the board.

Eventually, Breen admitted that Roti took the zoning bribe and claimed the Chancery fix was one of those "old-fashioned" political favors. But when it came to the On Leong fix, he denied everything. Of course, the Lenny Chow trial happened before I became a government informant, so I never had Fred's voice on tape from back then. I'm sure

I could have gotten him to talk about the case when I was wearing the wire, but the day that I had approached him, he was behind the metal detector in City Hall. I only mentioned Roti's name in passing to Pat Marcy when we discussed the On Leong grand jury transcript outside Counsellors Row. Our best evidence was a tape I made with Wilson Moy. He told me that he had been paying Roti off for other things as well. Moy said, "I found out, with him, money first, money first, money first." But with his accent, Moy's comments did not come across clearly on the tape—especially when he said, "Alderman Roti."

For this trial, Tom Durkin gave his most powerful closing statement. "You can get away with murder in Chicago," he told the jury, "if you have a fix in the First Ward and the money to pay for it." During the course of the trial, he assembled a chart with pictures of all the judges and politicians involved in the cases that were fixed. Pointing toward the chart, he said, "At the top of this chain of corruption, this rogue's gallery of photos, stood Pat Marcy and Fred Roti. They pulled the strings."

Breen used his closing to attack me. Because I was "sly and treacherous," he said, I could trap Roti into committing a couple of minor offenses. But with the On Leong fix, he suggested, I kept all the money I got from the Chinese. He then described me as "a dishonest, conniving manipulator, who had not done a decent thing in his life."

Mike Shepard picked up on that line in his rebuttal and said, "He caught Fred Roti. That's a pretty decent thing."

The jury deliberated two and a half days, and Breen's strategy paid off. Freddy got a pass on the On Leong charges—a potential nine-year sentence. But he was found guilty on eleven other counts for the zoning and Chancery bribes. After the trial, the jurors explained that my tapes on the murder fix were not as clear-cut as the ones for the other charges. Maybe we had just set the bar too high with all the other evidence we had.

But the judge, Marvin Aspen, had no doubts about Fred Roti's guilt, and he threw the book at him during sentencing, giving him the maximum term of four years, an additional three years of supervision, and fines over $125,000. For Judge Aspen, the case didn't have to do with the specific illegal acts, but the holes in the system that permitted them. He said, "The power of the First Ward to effectuate that kind of corruption in the judicial system . . . was not an isolated case." Commenting on Marcy's influence on the appointment of judges, he asked, "What does that judge do down the pike when that judge receives a telephone call . . . from Mr. Marcy or the First Ward? We know what that judge does, because we've seen it in this case. Whether it's Judge Wilson, Judge Maloney, or other judges who have been implicated in this case as being the order-takers from the First Ward. It is truly a chilling spectacle."

In asking the judge to go easy on Roti, Breen described him as a "role model" to other aldermen. Judge Aspen replied: "The specter, Mr. Breen, of Mr. Roti being a role model, of counseling other aldermen in the City of Chicago . . . is not a very happy one. Mr. Roti's corruption and greed spread over many years. Whether it's courts or zoning, or other types of activity, Mr. Roti has committed serious crimes. . . ."

The judge went on to explain that the crimes were not "against individuals alone," but also against the reputations of honest judges and city officials. Then he added, "But there is a bigger victim, and that's the whole democratic process. When you have courts of law that are fixed, when you have city government that is fixed, what you're doing, really, is attacking the core of democracy. You're saying that this democracy . . . is the same as any other banana republic or corrupt regime."

During the trial and the sentencing hearing, nothing was more pathetic than the slavish little lackeys who showed up as witnesses and boosters for Roti. Prime among them was Alderman Bernie Stone from the 50th Ward on the northern tip of the city. Many times he had joined me, Marcy, and Roti for breakfast at the First Ward table. I had several of those chitchats on tape. Bernie is Jewish, but Marcy and Roti hated Jews—even more than they hated blacks. It seemed like every time Bernie was at the table, they found a reason to start badmouthing different Jewish people or start telling "cheap Jew" jokes. Bernie Stone just sat there and listened. He never said a word. This wasn't accidental or just insensitive. They intentionally wanted to insult him to put him in his place. Those were the sorts of people that Roti and Marcy were. To later watch Stone jump up to vouch for their *character* turned my stomach.

I wanted to say to him, "Those people never had an ounce of respect for you." But a guy like Bernie probably had no respect for himself either.

The trial against Judge Tom Maloney started a month after the Roti conviction. The indictment had him fixing five cases—three of them for murder, including the Lenny Chow trial. As we went on from one Gambat trial to the next, there was always some new hurdle to clear. This time, we had no incriminating tapes with the judge on them. Instead, we had tapes and testimony of the people around him. After he was indicted, Swano finally decided to cop a plea and cooperate with the Feds against Maloney. After the court bailiff, Lucius Robinson, was convicted for perjury, he also agreed to testify against Maloney for a lighter sentence.

The judge's co-defendant was Robert McGee, a lawyer the government accused of being the bagman on some of the fixed cases. He was a Casper Milquetoast, like Herb Barsy, the attorney Maloney had forced down my throat as the co-counsel in the Lenny Chow case. I had to believe he was terrified of Maloney, or he would have flipped too. The government would have gladly cut him loose, like they did with Billy Swano. Instead, McGee was like a ghost in the courtroom. Nobody paid much attention to him one way or another. Whenever there was a sidebar, he'd go to the coatroom in the back of the court and pace back and forth.

At sixty-seven, Maloney was as big and beefy as ever. He sat behind the defense table like he was still on the bench, with his arms crossed over his chest. As one reporter wrote, he "scowled." He scowled at the witnesses. He scowled at the prosecutors. Even at the judge and jury— almost like he was telling them, "What right do *you* have to judge *me*?" He had retired just a few months before the Marcy and Roti indictments, so he must have known something was up, but he also believed that Swano would never flip on him. According to Billy, the last time they talked, he asked, "Are you standing tall?"

Swano replied, "I hear they are trying to put a tax case on you."

He said Maloney got "red-faced" and then replied, "Don't worry about me. You take care of yourself."

After Swano heard that I had him on tape, he did take care of himself, and agreed to cooperate with the government. I certainly wasn't the central witness in this trial, but I was the one who got Swano to flip, and without him the government had no case. When I took the stand, Maloney's eyes narrowed, his faced turned red, and he kept mouthing the words, "Motherfucking liar. Motherfucking liar." Sometimes he said it loud enough for me to hear.

His brother, a retired copper, sat behind him, and he glared at me the whole time too. It was quite a sight to see these red-faced Irish guys with white hair jawing at me—like some kind of "motherfucking" choir. When no one was looking, I'd give Tom a big wink and a smile, and watch his face get redder.

In his opening remarks, Maloney's lawyer, Terry Gillespie, called me, Swano, and Robinson "three rotten eggs." He said, "They're con men extraordinaire, three of the best in the business, and they're going to try to con you."

"Con man" was about the nicest thing any defense lawyer had called me. But Gillespie, who was a good lawyer, put his finger on the problem for the prosecution. Swano and Robinson—who were closer to Maloney's illegal activity than I was—really were stoolpigeons. They testified in this trial to reduce their own sentences. What they said about Maloney *before* they flipped had more credibility than what they said under oath, because it would help corroborate their testimony. Terry Hake, the mole in Operation Greylord, came in to confirm that Robinson had fingered Maloney as one of the judges who could be "approached" for a fix in criminal court. My job was to walk through my tapes and videos of Swano, as he told me what happened behind the scenes in the El Rukn trial.

When it came time for my cross-examination, Maloney tried to run the show with his defense team. I was told later that he wanted his lawyers to take me over the coals and smear my family. Evidently they talked him out of it. Gillespie didn't even do my cross-examination. He left that to the co-counsel, Tom Breen. He was businesslike, just as he had been in the Roti trial, and smart enough to realize that they shouldn't make me their focus. That had to be Billy Swano, and the defense couldn't have asked for a more tempting target. As Gillespie put it, he not only represented the El Rukns, "he did dope with them." He also went back and forth a few times with the Feds before he decided to come in. I was told he seemed shifty on the stand—not able to look anyone in the eye.

Besides my tapes, the government had other evidence to corroborate Swano's testimony, but there was one missing link. At a critical point in the El Rukn trial, Swano exchanged phone calls with Robert McGee, Maloney's bagman. According to Swano, McGee called the judge in his chambers to discuss the fix and then called Swano to tell him the fix was off and that Maloney was giving "the books back." The government had records for Swano's calls to McGee, but not McGee's calls to Maloney.

The day the prosecutors were winding up their case, we learned that McGee's phone records still existed. Most big phone companies throw those out after eighteen months, but the apartment complex where McGee lived used a little local firm. When that company sent someone to testify to McGee's home number, he brought along the records for every call McGee had made. An assistant prosecutor noticed them in his briefcase and, bang, the Feds suddenly had very important new evidence.

In the words of the *Sun-Times*, the phone records fit Swano's story "like a long-lost glove." The calls from McGee went out to Maloney's chambers exactly as he had said in his testimony. With this unexpected corroboration, Billy's credibility got a huge boost with the jury.

There was also one other piece of circumstantial evidence that really clinched the case for the jurors. Over several periods of time, the Feds observed Maloney buying money orders. Later, during deliberation, the jurors asked themselves, "Why would a big-shot like Maloney stand in line for a money order?" They figured he must have had something to hide.

This is the common sense at the heart of our jury system, and it's more important than any fancy arguments or high-tech evidence. Juries are what the First Ward tried to avoid at all cost. And a jury finally took down the high and mighty Maloney. For fixing four of the five cases in the indictment—including all three murder trials—they found him guilty of racketeering, racketeering conspiracy, conspiracy to commit extortion, and obstruction of justice.

For the sentencing hearing, prosecutor Scott Mendeloff practically staged another trial to make sure the judge threw the book at Maloney. In his opening remarks, Scott said, "It is the view of the government that this is, simply, the most pernicious course of judicial corruption in the history of this state." Scott then explained that the hearing would help "complete the picture of Tom Maloney's life of corruption." In addition to testifying on cases Maloney fixed as a judge, witnesses would testify on cases he had had a hand in fixing as a defense attorney. This included what Scott called "one of the most notorious case fixes in the history of the county, *People vs. Harry Aleman.*" Maloney had been Harry's attorney, until I had Marcy replace him with the out-of-town lawyer, Frank Whalen.

In many ways, this hearing was our dress rehearsal for retrying Aleman. Scott even brought in my former girlfriend, Cathy Fleming, to corroborate my relationship with Judge Wilson. Also, for the first time, I testified about the things I saw at Counsellors Row during Tony Spilotro's M&M murder trial, and how Marcy indicated the fix was in for that case.

After Cathy and I were done with our testimony at the sentencing hearing, Scott brought in a bunch of other witnesses, including a former cellmate of Harry and a former client of Maloney who was in Hook LaPietra's crew. The whole proceeding took more than two days, and, at the very end of it, Judge Leinenweber gave Maloney a chance to speak. He went on for two hours.

Remembering that the old windbag had once been a boxer in college, the *Sun-Times* wrote, "Thomas J. Maloney went down swinging." Although he hadn't testified in his own trial, Maloney went through the evidence, point by point, and denied everything. Along the way, he had some choice words for everyone involved in the case—even some reporters who followed it, like Carol Marin, the investigative reporter and anchorwoman for WMAQ-TV. Of course, the choicest words were saved for the three people who put him in this jackpot: Swano ("a conniving slime rat"), me ("a corrupt, inept slob"), and even Scott ("devious, and I don't think the truth is in him").

By the time he was done, Maloney stamped out any shred of sympathy that might have remained for him. There he was, an arrogant piece of shit in all his glory. To have him say something bad about you was like a badge of honor.

After listening to all of this Maloney baloney, Judge Leinenweber said, "What you told us here today is too little too late." He explained that they would not retry the case during the hearing, but then he added: "I personally agree one hundred percent with that jury verdict. I don't know what caused you to go wrong . . . whether it was money or whether you have ties to organized crime, I don't know. But you did agree to fix these particular cases."

Scott was hoping the judge would give Maloney twenty-five years. Leinenweber gave him fifteen instead; but, with federal guidelines, he had to serve at least thirteen—practically a death sentence for a guy pushing seventy years old. All in all, I couldn't have asked for too much more.

The Stillo trial opened in July 1993, just three months after Maloney's conviction. By this time, Gambat had such a head of steam behind it, there was no stopping us. The timing could not have been worse for Judge Stillo and his nephew, Joey. On the surface, this seemed like our weakest case. The judge did find my "client," the FBI agent, guilty, and no money ever did change hands.

Joey had attended almost all of the previous Gambat trials, and tried to stare me down each time. He probably watched me every day that I testified against Johnny D'Arco. Besides giving me dirty looks, he apparently didn't watch anything else going on in the courtroom, because he ended up choosing Ed Genson as his lawyer.

True to form, Ed went on to bungle the case for Joey and Judge Stillo, too. Once again, he tried to put me on trial, except now he called me "the most corrupt attorney in the history of Cook County." He took bits and pieces that came out in our previous cases (some involving his previous clients) and tried to tie them together like cans on a dog's tail. The On Leong fix, the Colella fix, the money I owed to the bookies, the money I owed to the IRS—for all these reasons, he charged, I went running to the Feds.

By trying to tar me, he just reminded the jury that all my cases had ended up in convictions. When he cross-examined me, this time for seven hours, he only boosted my credibility. The government had two other lawyers testify about paying off Judge Stillo, including Billy Swano, but the jury only convicted him for the charges that involved me—even for cases I fixed with the judge long before I wore the wire.

The prosecutors wanted a sentence of ten years for Judge Stillo, but Judge Leinenweber told them, "I'm dealing with a 77-year-old man," and gave him just four years. He only served a third of that before his parole. Joey got just two years, and served eight months at the federal pen in Oxford, Wisconsin, where all his Mob friends used to go. Then, after he did his time, he came home and suddenly died. Very strange, right to the end.

As we were wrapping up the Stillo trial, I was in the papers for another hearing—my own. A few years back, when I first appeared on the stand, the state's Attorney Registration and Disciplinary Commission opened an investigation into my conduct. This was usually the first step in getting you disbarred.

It was nothing less than a kick in the teeth. Even though the government had *indicted* Johnny D'Arco, Judge Shields, Patty DeLeo, and Maloney, the Disciplinary Commission had not opened an investigation into their conduct. Just mine. I had already suspended my license and I never planned to practice again, but for me, this was a matter of justice, pure and simple. I petitioned the Illinois Supreme Court to let me surrender my law license, so there would be no need for a hearing. But the court declined my request and told the Disciplinary Commission to proceed with their hearing. The Illinois legal establishment was clearly looking to slap me down. When asked about the Disciplinary Commission's actions, Barry Miller, the head of a Chicago legal reform group, put it this way: "A series of circumstances have created the appearance that the system may be 'punishing' Robert Cooley for cooperating with federal authorities in exposing judicial corruption."

To add insult to injury, the Disciplinary Commission scheduled my hearings in the middle of the Maloney trial. For evidence of misconduct, their investigators submitted the transcripts of my testimony in previous trials. The proceeding was like a kangaroo court. The board took less than an hour to recommend disbarment. I sent the commission a letter asking for another hearing. I explained that I had no desire to practice law again. Instead, "This concerns whether my legal career should be allowed to end with some salvage of dignity, or as an exceptional example of professional disgrace."

When my letter leaked to the press, the *Tribune* thought it was very funny. Their article began, "Poor, misunderstood Robert Cooley." It said that I was crying because: "The criminal-defense bar is focusing on his past career as a bribe-paying lawyer and a fixer. . . ." In my letter to the commission, the paper said, I was "peddling" a "message" that "we should be filled with admiration for his work as an undercover informant and key prosecution witness in the federal Operation Gambat investigation."

Actually, there was another message I was peddling. What about looking at *all* the lawyers and judges in the Gambat investigations who were caught doing unethical and illegal things? Like Alderman Ed Burke, Judge Anthony Scotillo, Chief Judge Buck Sorrentino, Joe "Mr. Ethics" Ettinger, and Judge Lawrence Passarella. For whatever reason, the government didn't indict them, but why didn't the Disciplinary Commission open up investigations on them? I sent a letter that offered to provide the necessary information, but never got a response. The Feds told me they would hand transcripts of my wires over to the Disciplinary Commission for further investigation, but I knew that would never happen. It would raise questions about why the government never brought charges.

Clearly some of these people were protected, either because of their personal connections or because of the lawyers they chose. A couple of years after I left Chicago, the FBI had me fly in to Milwaukee to help develop a case on Ed Burke. Cammon had just died of AIDS, but obviously Maloney was a hot topic for the Feds, and now they were willing to take a second look at all of his bench trials. They put me up in a hotel and even got a conference room for the day. The agents told me they were finally ready to investigate Burke. I just laughed at them. "Why are you wasting my time?" I asked. "Nothing is going to happen to him."

"Oh, no," one agent said. "We're here to build a case."

"Then call Judge Cieslik," I said and gave him his phone number. "You have to get to him right away. He's getting up there in years."

Two months later, I got a call from a new FBI agent on the Burke case. "Do you have that phone number for Judge Cieslik?" he asked. "We lost it."

After the Stillo case, I realized that Gambat had reached as high into the political and judicial establishment as it was going to go. I had to get resigned to that, and turn my attention back to the lower-level hoodlums—especially Harry Aleman.

In the early nineties, the Feds had done their best to make life difficult for the Outfit. They convicted Johnny DiFronzo and some other Mob bosses for trying to take over an Indian casino in California and collect on Tony Spilotro debts in Vegas. A few months after I left town, they went after Chicago-area gambling operations by arresting Rocky Infelice, Harry Aleman, and seventeen other muscle guys—mostly from the Cicero group. The charges related to the street-tax racket and how they killed off independent bookies like Hal Smith to keep the others in line. I was ready to testify about the time Harry wanted me to find independent bookies for him to grab. But Harry was not about to risk a jury trial—especially if I was going to testify against him. Despite his tough talk at the racetrack about never going back to prison, he copped a plea. It was a smart move. Rocky Infelice went to trial, got convicted, and the judge sentenced him to life. With good behavior, Harry expected to be released by 1998 or, worst case, the year 2000.

But I had other ideas. I kept after Tom Durkin and Gary Shapiro to share my testimony about the Harry Aleman trial with the Cook County State's Attorney. Finally, the Feds arranged for me to meet with Pat Quinn, an assistant state's attorney in charge of the Organized Crime Unit. We had a little rendezvous in Arizona. He was my kind of lawyer— a big, balding, round-faced Irish guy who loved a good joke. We ended up in a bar that was a hangout for some Chicago Mob people. The place had a little gimmick where you would sign a dollar bill and they would post it on the wall. Pat had me sign one "Bob Cooley," just to bust the balls of any Outfit guy who happened to pass by.

Pat told me that he had discussed retrying Aleman with the lawyers in the state's attorneys' appellate office. These were considered their best legal minds, and they told him that there was absolutely no way to beat double jeopardy. But Pat was convinced otherwise. He had the theory that Harry had never had *any* jeopardy during the first trial, because the bribe assured him of a not guilty verdict.

On December 8, 1993, the Cook County State's Attorney, Jack O'Malley, held a press conference to announce that the state had indicted Aleman again for the murder of Logan. "Justice took a hit in 1977," O'Malley said. "A murder case was fixed." O'Malley was one of those rare Republicans elected to office in Cook County, and at first I thought he was a gutsy, independent guy, but he turned out to be a politician like the rest of them. When Mike Wallace and *60 Minutes* wanted to do a story about the case, O'Malley gave the go-ahead—until he found out that Mike Wallace had no intention of interviewing him. He then prevented me from talking to Wallace, which killed their story. Funny enough, they already had the interview with Harry in the can.

Harry's lawyer was my old gin-playing pal, Allan Ackerman, and a technical battle like this was right up his alley. When the press asked him about the indictment, he quoted from the Fifth Amendment provision—"nor shall any person be subject for the same offense to be twice put in jeopardy of life or limb." Typical Allan. Then he told the reporter, "The public prosecutor cannot subordinate constitutional protections for political gain."

Putting Aleman on a pedestal of constitutional protection was like dressing up a pig in a tuxedo. But I'm sure Allan had to tell himself something to justify defending a monster like Harry.

The *Tribune* called the indictment "Mission Impossible," and quoted a "double-jeopardy authority," from the University of Chicago law school. "There might be some hope if the state could show that the defendant was really a prime mover of the bribery effort against the judge," he said. "Even then, it would be a very difficult case to win."

But we got an important break when the case was assigned to Circuit Court Judge Mike Toomin, a super-smart guy with the guts to back a tough decision. In a forty-five-page opinion, he ruled that a fix really did negate double jeopardy. If the defendant knows a judge has been bribed, he argued, then "the claim of jeopardy is more imagined than real." In reaching his decision, Toomin said he researched common law back to the Magna Carta.

But next, we had to prove to him that the Logan case really was fixed—and that Harry had a hand in it. I don't think any preliminary hearing was ever more important. You could even say it was more important than the trial.

The hearing was held in the judge's courtroom in the old Criminal Courthouse on 26th Street and California. To protect me, it was held in secrecy. Allan Ackerman and Aleman didn't know about it until the last minute. When I took the stand, I didn't bother to smile or wink at Harry. You can't play games with a stone-cold creep like that. But when I did look at him, I was surprised to see that he had gone completely gray.

The whole proceeding was very businesslike. Judge Toomin did not allow any grandstanding from the lawyers or digressing by the witnesses, and he hurried us all along. I had already told the Aleman fix story so many times, I could have done it in my sleep, but for the purposes of the hearing, I gave more details about Harry's personal involvement: my first meeting with him when Marco brought me to The King's Inn motel; how Harry gave me his wife's number to relay a message; how he and Butch met with me about bribing a witness; and how they took my business cards after his acquittal and referred me a bunch of new business. Also, I discussed how Cathy Fleming was with me when I paid off the judge. Her presence that night had become crucial in connecting me with Frank Wilson.

In his cross-examination, Allan Ackerman zeroed in on our biggest obstacle in proving the fix and getting a conviction—the passage of time. One after another, he asked about the key people in my story: John D'Arco Sr., Pat Marcy, Judge Wilson, Butch Petrocelli, and Harry's out-of-town lawyer, Frank Whalen.

"Living or dead?"

The answer—for all of them—was dead. As Allan later joked in his closing argument, the trial would be like a "séance." Which would make me the medium. I was the government witness who would do most of the talking for the deceased.

The only other government witness at the hearing was Vincent Rizza.

During the first Aleman trial, he had been a Rush Street vice cop. And also an independent bookie, a drug dealer, and a cokehead. Harry "grabbed" him and became a fifty-fifty partner in Rizza's book. He saw him practically every day to collect the street tax, and sometimes they would chat. Rizza testified that Harry had once said, "Committing murder in Chicago was okay if you killed the right people."

During the murder trial, Rizza remembered, he had seen Harry and told him that "it looked bad" and "the newspapers were crucifying him."

But Harry was unconcerned. According to Rizza, Aleman said, "It wasn't a problem. It was taken care of."

Of course Rizza was not your most upstanding witness, and Allan went to town on Rizza's rap sheet, which included perjury. But Harry could not deny that he knew Rizza or me. When he copped a plea on the Rocky Infelice street tax case, Harry admitted his association with Rizza and that he had asked me to help him find and grab independent bookies like Rizza.

The only defense witness at the hearing was the nephew of Frank Whalen. He had helped his uncle prepare Harry's case and, as expected, he testified that he never saw me. But during the cross, Pat Quinn brought out the fact that this nephew was only a few years out of law school. Why would Whalen have stayed in Florida and relied on this kid for a murder case if he didn't know the fix was in?

Assistant State's Attorney Scott Cassidy gave the closing argument. He summed up our testimony, plus all the incriminating circumstantial evidence: how Harry first asked to substitute for Judge Wilson, and then turned around and accepted him; how Whalen was incredibly lazy in preparing for the trial. Based on this record, Cassidy argued, the trial "shouts of impropriety. The stench reeks."

It smelled for Judge Toomin, too. One month later, he ruled that Harry was not protected by double jeopardy and should be retried for the murder of Billy Logan. In most other preliminary hearings, judges only need to find probable cause. But this time, Toomin had to find that a fix actually had taken place and blame Harry in the process.

In his ruling, Toomin made a judgment about me, too, because my testimony was central to the state's case. The judge wrote: "I find [Cooley] to be a credible witness. He was persuasive. He had a good memory. There was clarity to his testimony, and there was very little contradiction."

Speaking for his client, Ackerman said that Harry was "utterly amazed that any sworn judicial officer could believe an informant like Robert Cooley."

Again, the *Tribune* turned to its so-called "double jeopardy expert" for his opinion, and he predicted that the Appeals Court would overturn Toomin's ruling. "Bribing a judge is an extreme case," the so-called expert said. "But once you start creating exceptions to double jeopardy protection, you undermine a great deal of its value."

Well, this joker was wrong again. A panel of the Appellate Court unanimously affirmed Toomin's ruling, which went all the way to the U.S. Supreme Court and beat back every challenge. From the time the State's Attorney first issued the indictment, it would take more than four years to finally get Harry's trial under way.

In the meantime, we were able to clean up the leftover mobster garbage from my investigation. There were the bookie cases against the likes of Dominic Barbaro. (We never indicted Bob Johnson, because he was arrested on another charge and supposedly hanged himself in the federal lockup.) We also brought an indictment for perjury against Blackie Pesoli. While I was wearing a wire, he had asked me to help him fix a divorce case for an insurance executive. He copped a plea and got an eleven-month prison sentence.

In November 1994, just as the statute of limitations was running out, the Feds indicted Marco D'Amico and nine other members of his crew, including Bobby Abbinante, Tony Doty, his brother Carl, and my old copper pal Ricky Borelli. Besides charges for bookmaking, extortion, and racketeering, the indictment also included conspiracy to commit robbery—Marco's little plot to rob my card game in Wisconsin. According to the papers, at the time of his arrest, Marco was "second-in-command" to Johnny DiFronzo.

Marco had once said to me, "Nobody wears a wire on us and lives to talk about it." Fortunately, I lived, and I was more than happy to talk about it, but I knew that Marco wanted no part of me in that court-room. Five months after his arrest, he copped a plea. Although he admitted his guilt, his agreement with the government stipulated that he "refused to cooperate with the government." Marco knew what happened to stoolpigeons.

During the sentencing hearing, Marco's lawyer talked about his "devotion" to his family and then introduced "his wife—of 35 years—and four daughters." I guess all the mistresses couldn't show up for the occasion. According to the *Tribune*, the lawyer then told the judge that Marco "had visited Skid Row dressed up as Santa Claus, sponsored youth baseball teams, had a restaurant he operated give free food to poor children and anonymously left boxes of basketballs at playgrounds."

The judge was not impressed. She gave him twelve years and three months. Ricky got off much easier, with ten months of prison and two years of supervision.

Besides my work in the courts, during the mid-nineties, I testified at hearings about the Mob's influence in the unions. Bit by bit, the Justice Department was trying to take back the Chicago locals from the Mafia, especially for the Teamsters and the Laborers' International Union of North America. If the government's hearing officer could make a credible link between a union official and organized crime, he could throw him out of office and replace him with a trustee.

The Laborers Union represented the lowest level of unskilled workers. Most of the members were ditch diggers and street sweepers who worked for the city. For decades, their local had been the personal property of Hook LaPietra and the Chinatown group. Frank Caruso and Bruno Caruso, the brothers who ran the local, took down six-figure salaries. No-show laborer jobs and union positions were filled with Mojos, their family and friends.

I had no trouble linking the Carusos with LaPietra and the rest of the Chinatown group. They were like fixtures at all my favorite places on Rush Street and in Chinatown. The Laborers Union hearings were usually conducted in a hotel ballroom, but for me they had a special session in an FBI conference room. For hours I talked about the old days, hanging out at Faces, making bets at the social clubs and race-track, or dropping by the late-night dice games in Chinatown. It made me remember how much fun I had once had.

I'm sure my testimony did a lot of good for the unions and the city, but I was still biding my time until I was back in court with Harry. This would be the final curtain—on Operation Gambat and my life in Chicago.

Finally, on September 22, 1997, the State of Illinois took its second crack at Harry Aleman. In the words of the *Tribune*, the trial opened "a new chapter in the history of American jurisprudence." Pat Quinn, the prosecutor who had done so much to get Harry retried, had been elected to the Appellate Court, but we still had Scott Cassidy on the case, along with another veteran state's attorney, Neil Linehan. Oddly enough, for his lawyer, Harry reached out of state to a guy from Kentucky named Kevin McNally. Evidently he had just reversed a death sentence for one of the killers in Harry's old crew, and Aleman was convinced he could work a miracle for him, too.

I had never had security like I did for this case. Months before the trial, the guards at the federal prison caught Harry slipping a note to his stepson. It read: "The two will be taken care of if this goes to trial, one after the other." The Feds considered me to be one of the "two." An FBI agent on my cases, Vic Switski, spent two weeks preparing special pro-tection for my route in and out of the courtroom. This time, when we drove to the city from my out-of-town hotel, it was in a motorcade with cars in front and in back. As we got closer to Chicago, they shut down traffic on the freeway and then the surface roads leading to the old Cook County Criminal Courthouse. Since there was no basement entrance like at the Federal Building, I was surrounded by SWAT TEAM FBI agents with flak jackets when I got out of the car. Inside the courthouse, they had another two dozen agents with machine guns, and they led me to the judges' elevators. All the courtrooms were locked down while I walked through the halls. To get into Judge Toomin's court, you were searched and then had to go through a metal detector.

Still, when I walked into the courtroom, it was standing room only. I saw FBI agents, lawyers from my other trials, and family members of the victim, Billy Logan. The first witness had been Logan's sister, and she remembered how he had died in her arms. Harry sat there at the defense table in a brown sport jacket over a polo shirt—like some guy eating lunch at a country club. He had his family there, too. Reporters wrote that he blew kisses to his wife each day. He also had some other friends as spectators. One goon kept staring daggers at me. He looked familiar, and I pointed him out to Vic. When the FBI ran a check on him, they found out he was a hit man for the Mexican Mafia. He still had an outstanding warrant, so they could lock him up.

Aleman's lawyer, McNally, referred to me in his opening statement by saying, "The only reason we are here is because of a corrupt lawyer."

Boy, was that ever true. In every way.

He went on to argue, "This is a murder case. This is not a bribery case. . . . Mr. Aleman did not bribe anyone. Mr. Aleman does not know anything about a bribe. Frank Wilson was an honest judge."

In just those few words, he had set up the challenge for my testimony. I had to convince the jury that Judge Wilson had not been honest, that he did take a bribe, and that Harry knew all about it. Unlike my other Gambat trials, this case was not built on tapes and transcripts. Absolutely everything I said—about things that had happened twenty-five years ago—would have to come from my memory with very little corroboration from other sources.

But by this time, after all the testifying I had done, remembering was not such a big deal. I had a way of putting myself back into those moments the lawyers asked about. When the assistant State's Attorney, Neil Linehan, asked me about Counsellors Row, I could see the First Ward table in the corner and then the lobby outside, where Senior introduced me to Marcy. I heard Pat tell me about an important case and ask, "Do you have somebody that can handle it?" It was like the whole scene materialized before my eyes.

It was the same when I described The King's Inn motel and my meeting with Harry. He walked into the room and pumped my hand, "Hey, how ya doing? How ya doing?" And then bore in on me with that evil eye, and asked, "Are you sure you can handle it? Are you sure this judge is going to throw the case out?"

When I got to the point in my testimony where I made the final payoff to Judge Wilson—in that stinky bathroom—I saw him, too. Right in front of me in the courtroom. Standing there, rumpled and half-drunk, a little off-balance on his gimpy leg.

"I gave him the money," I testified.

"What money?" Neil asked.

"The seventy-five hundred," I said. I started to break down.

"What was his reaction?" Neil asked.

I could see Judge Wilson looking at me and I put my hand up to my eyes. Tears were running down my face. "He was . . . He was . . ." I cleared my throat. Then I said to the court, "He was a broken man."

I looked again at my vision of the judge, and saw him standing there with the envelope. I heard him ask, "That's all I'm going to get?"

I saw him turn his back on me when I tried to explain. I saw him start to walk out of the bathroom, and then turn around to say, "You destroyed me."

He was right. I destroyed him.

And I destroyed myself, too.

Harry's lawyer didn't put up much of a fight during my cross-examination. He kept me on the stand for a few hours, and then I was gone.

The surprise witness for the defense was Billy Logan's ex-wife, who is also Harry's second cousin. She had already said that Logan beat her, but now she had something new to add. She testified that she had dated Harry's old partner in crime, Butch Petrocelli. She told a story about a time when Logan tried to break into her house while she was with Butch. She said that the two guys went out into the alley, and she heard Butch threaten to kill Logan.

You had to laugh. Harry probably had been the one who asked Joe Ferriola to have Petrocelli tortured and killed. Now, to get himself out of this jackpot, he was ready to dig up Butch for help.

The jury didn't buy it. After four hours of deliberation, they found Harry guilty. According to the *Tribune*, Logan's brother and sister were weeping with joy. Harry blinked a couple of times.

With this case, the prosecutors did more than beat double jeopardy. It was also the first time a hit man had been convicted for murder in the history of Chicago. Some record for the town that Al Capone made famous. Scott Cassidy, the assistant state's attorney, said, "It's a great day for American justice."

When it came time for the sentence, Judge Toomin did not take any chance that Harry Aleman would ever get parole. He gave him from one hundred to three hundred years. As important as all that time is the fact that it's state time. Once Harry completed the sentence for his street tax charge, he had to leave the cushy federal pen in Oxford, Wisconsin, and go back to a nasty state prison in Dixon, Illinois, where he'll serve out the rest of his days.

The moment Harry's guilty verdict was announced, I should have been as happy as the Logans. Instead, I felt a terrible void. It was like I had nothing more to live for.

The years since then have blown by me without much purpose. I still come to Chicago every once in a while, to see family and friends, but I do it without warning, and don't stay too long. Mostly I'm a nomad. I've already roamed across the country and stayed in what seems like a million different places. When I make new friends, I have to be careful about what I say. After a few years, I feel the need to move again.

Mostly what I have left is the investigation. I know if my father is looking down, he has to laugh. Operation Gambat was really my life's work—part of the Master Plan that he would say God had mapped out for me. In a bizarre way, everything I did leading up to it prepared me to help the government get all those convictions.

So what did Operation Gambat really accomplish?

For one thing, there wasn't another Mob hit in Chicago for ten years after I left town, and it's been a rare event ever since. This is not a small thing in a city where, for most of a century, mobsters were whacking each other on a regular basis. Finally, even the Outfit's lowest-level street thug realizes that cases can't be fixed; that you can't get away with murder.

In 1993, after the first eleven convictions in Gambat, a report about my investigation was written for the Illinois Supreme Court's Special Commission on the Administration of Justice. Reforms were recommended, and eventually made, in the Cook County Circuit Court that affected the way judges are appointed and cases are assigned, so it would be impossible for another Pat Marcy to manipulate trials. In addition, the court now has an independent watchdog as a kind of check on the judges.

These days, the old Outfit is a shadow of itself. To put the big bosses away, the Feds used several successful investigations. But I believe that Operation Gambat took out the hit men and the protection of the courts, which had been the foundation for the Mob's power in Chicago. No Young Turks will ever organize street crime the way they did for Tony Accardo. I even played a part in reducing the influence of the Mob on some unions. I know a garbage strike can be a pain in the ass for most people; but for me, it's a sign that the union leaders are finally looking out for the interests of their members, and no longer taking payoffs from the companies that employ them.

Getting Maloney off the bench was another great accomplishment. There's no telling how much more damage he could have done. Of the nine men Maloney put on Death Row, six have now been granted new trials. Two were sentenced to life, but two were aquitted, and the remaining two stand a good chance of release as well. In the words of Judge Ilana Rovner, now an appellate judge: "We may no more treat Maloney as an impartial arbiter for constitutional purposes than a delusional megalomaniac who locks a judge in the closet, dons a black robe and hoodwinks everyone with a credible impersonation of Oliver Wendell Holmes." The lawyers called me to testify in one of these lawsuits, but decided they couldn't use my testimony because I was already so outspoken in my hatred for the man.

Probably the single greatest symbol of my investigation's success is what became of the First Ward itself. After I took down the political organization, Mayor Richie Daley literally took apart the aldermanic district. He split off important parts of the ward until just a little fishhook was left. City Hall claimed that reputable downtown businesses no longer wanted to be associated with the First Ward. Meanwhile, I'm sure the mayor didn't want to see all that power and influence concentrated in one ward any more. So if someone says Bob Cooley changed Chicago's political landscape, it would be true in more ways than one.

All in all, I can take satisfaction from this. A lot of good did come from the investigation, despite the trouble I made for myself, and despite the fact that some decent people were caught up in it, like Judge Shields and Judge Wilson.

But in the last few years, when I've read the newspapers from Chicago, I've seen the accomplishments of Operation Gambat slowly chipped away. One recent *Chicago Tribune* article reported that Operation Gambat ended up with *four* convictions, when the actual number is twenty-four and this doesn't count my contribution to the Rocky Infelice case that resulted in the conviction of nineteen more mobsters. Now, when I read stories about Maloney, they say he was convicted as part of Operation Greylord.

Maybe these are your typical reporter errors or oversights. But I think there's something else at work, too. There are still powerful people in Chicago and Washington who want to pretend that Operation Gambat never happened. Some are embarrassed by the real connections we showed between the courts, our government, and organized crime. Some would like us to forget about all the corruption and cover-ups that remain. Since my investigation never went as far as I wanted it to go, I still hope that there are areas where the Feds and local reporters will pick up the pieces and attend to unfinished business.

For example, in 2002, Bill Hanhardt, former chief of detectives, and once the third-most powerful man in the Chicago Police Department, was convicted of running a jewelry theft ring that stole more than $5 million. This trial came more than sixteen years after my first report to the FBI. Testimony showed that he started the jewel thefts while he was still in the department. No way was Bill Hanhardt just one bad apple. To this date, no one has ever taken a second look at all the officers he promoted and supervised in his last years as chief of detectives. Most Chicago cops are honest and hardworking, but there is also a culture of corruption in the force that makes it harder for the good policemen to do their jobs. It's no surprise to me that the mayor, Richie Daley, continues to promote commissioners from inside the department. Any qualified outsider would start lifting up some rocks, and you can bet that person would find a whole bunch of maggots underneath.

In 2003, Anne Burke, wife of Alderman Ed Burke and now an Illinois appellate judge, was appointed to head the National Review Board monitoring priest abuse for the United States Conference of Catholic Bishops. Did the bishops know that she had once represented a child molester during her years as a defense attorney? Especially a child molester as notorious as James Moffat, the high school principal who was convicted of abusing five of his students? If you knew anything about the Moffat case or the Cammon murder case, even from what you read in the newspapers, why would you ever trust Anne Burke to get to the bottom of a child abuse case? Or even serve on the Appellate Court?

In 2004, the *Chicago Sun-Times* discovered that Chicago was giving $40 million to people with trucks that could be used for city business. The reporters found that most of these trucks just sat in a driveway somewhere and that ten percent of these contractors were Mob associates. Others were politically connected with the Daley administration. Supervising this program for the city was Nick "The Stick" LoCoco. Once, I had represented Nick when he was arrested for bookmaking. I thought I was working without a fee, because he was a "Ward case." When I found out that Patty DeLeo still charged him a thousand dollars, I had an excuse to break from the firm.

You see? Even after all these years, my Mob friends keep popping up with city jobs or contracts. I can guarantee that this trucking program is just the tip of the iceberg. The First Ward spent half a century "embedding" mobsters into city and county government. It's going to take more than a few years to weed them all out—if the mayor and the public really have the stomach to do the job.

Maybe corruption in Chicago is no longer king, but it's still somewhere in the deck. If the city isn't careful, it could start rising to the top once again. When U.S. District Court Judge Marvin Aspen sentenced Alderman Fred Roti, he quoted the philosopher who said, "Those who cannot remember the past are condemned to repeat it."

NOTES

Other sources provide further verification and amplification for Cooley's story or add different perspective. I note these below with my own comments.

Hillel Levin

INTRODUCTION

v. *Chicago's Mafia became the single most powerful organzed crime family in American history.* This statement is not disputed by organized crime historians, but may come as a surprise to casual readers of Mafia books. Some of the most seminal non-fiction works have focused on New York crime families, such as *The Valachi Papers* by Peter Maas, *Honor Thy Father* by Gay Talese, and *Wiseguy* by Nicholas Pileggi. The novel, *The Godfather*, and its screen adaptations may have had the greatest impact on popular imagination, especially in regards to which Mafia families controlled illegal activities in Las Vegas. In fact, by the seventies, Chicago's Mob had chased the last remnants of the New York Mafia out of Vegas. Their victory is chronicled in *War of the Godfathers* (New York: Ballentine, 1991) by former FBI agent William F. Roemer. In his non-fiction book, *Casino* (New York: Simon & Schuster, 1995), Pileggi further details how Chicago mobsters controlled the Vegas gambling industry. In *Accardo: The Genuine Godfather* (New York: Ballentine, 1996), Roemer quotes Pileggi as telling him that during his research on Casino, he "discovered that it was Tony Accardo and the Chicago Mob who really made Las Vegas what it became." (*Accardo*, 220.)

v. *While Mob bosses knocked each other off on the East Coast . . . never came close to achieving.* See notes below for page 83, and "Highlife with the Lowlifes."

vi. *In his 1969 book,* Captive City *. . . in the billions.* (Ovid Demaris, *The Captive City* [New York: Lyle Stuart, 1969], 5.)

vi. *By the seventies, the FBI . . . the Tropicana and the Stardust.* (*War of the Godfathers,* 177; *Casino,* 179 and 267.)

vi. *Bundles of cash . . . to the Outfit's bosses.* (Michael Corbitt, Sam Giancana, *Double Deal* [New York: William Morrow, 2003], 280.)

vi. *Although other urban areas . . . political organization.* In *The Captive City,* Demaris explains how several Capone cronies transformed themselves from street thugs into influential members of Chicago's political establishment. Demaris starts his chapter, "The Clout Machine," with the following 1951 quote from Senator Estes Kefauver, who led the first congressional investigation of organized crime:

"Everywhere we went, the committee found a certain amount of political immorality, but in Chicago the rawness of this sort of thing was particularly shocking . . . There was no doubt in the minds of any of us, after the sort of testimony we heard in Chicago, that organized crime and political corruption go hand in hand, and that in fact there could be no big-time organized crime without a firm and profitable alliance between those who run the rackets and those in political control." *(Captive City,* 93-232.)

vi. *Born Pasqualino Marchone . . . robbery in the Thirties. (Captive City,* 42.)

vii. *Although the* FBI *tried to penetrate the First Ward . . . Marcy was too careful to be caught . . .* Tom Durkin, assistant U.S. Attorney for the Northern District of Illinois, 1980-1993, explains: "It was impossible to infiltrate the First Ward corruption with undercover FBI agents. Pat Marcy only worked with people he had known for years." (Thomas M. Durkin, interview by Hillel Levin, May 2004.) According to Jim Wagner, a former Supervisory Special Agent for Organized Crime Investigations in the FBI's Chicago office, "Literally generations of [FBI] agents had tried to crack the First Ward and got nowhere. We were well aware of their Organized Crime connections." (James W. Wagner, Interview by Hillel Levin, June 2004)

viii. *Harry Aleman, a hit man dubbed the Outfit's killing machine.* (Maurice Possley, "The Mob's Killing Machine," *Chicago Tribune,* May 10, 1998.)

ix. *Before the end of the 1990 . . . Gambat indictments.* (John Gorman and Ray Gibson, *Chicago Tribune,* "5 Indicted In 'Corruption Feast,'" Dec. 20, 1990.)

ix. *When Cooley and the prosecutors . . . a guilty plea.* See notes below for "The Harder They Fall" and chart, "Operation Gambat Cases and Outcomes."

ix. *In the wake of Operation Gambat . . . take action.* See notes below for "Afterlife."

x. *Operation Gambat . . . Organized Crime Strike Force.* See notes below in "Afterlife."

x. *A character clearly based Cooley . . . movie called* The Fixer, *starring Jon Voight.* Turow calls the character, Robbie Feaver, and his book's jacket copy reads: "When the flashy, womanizing, multimillion-dollar personal injury lawyer is caught offering bribes, he's forced to wear a wire." Turow never met Cooley, but had an assistant call him. Voight plays Jack Killoran, who *TV Guide* describes as "a corrupt lawyer in Chicago's political inner circle."

xiii. The Chicago Sun-Times . . . *"organized crime figures."* (Steve Warmbir and Tim Novak, "Mob ties run throughout city truck program," *Chicago Sun-Times,* Jan. 25, 2004.)

xiii. *Meanwhile, Richard Daley . . . Mob influences.* (Gary Washburn and Ray Long, "Daley places his bets on casino for Chicago," *Chicago Tribune,* May 11, 2004.)

CHAPTER 1
A DEAL WITH THE DEVIL

4. *I turned to see John D'Arco Senior . . . for Al Capone.* See notes below for "High-life with the Lowlifes," p. 107.

4. *But whatever D'Arco . . . parcel of the Mob.* In 1969 Demaris wrote, "Of the wards under the aegis of the Syndicate, the First Ward remains one of the most representative in the system." *(Captive City,* 136.) See other notes below in "Crime Pays" and "Highlife with the Lowlifes."

4. *They had bricked up . . . and Jimmy Carter.* Mayor Richard J. Daley often fended off charges of First Ward involvement with Organized Crime. In 1969, when the Crime Commission listed D'Arco's company, Anco Insurance, as "Mob-linked," Daley refused to cut off city business from the firm, explaining, "It's one thing to have facts and another to report hearsay." (John O'Brien, "Daley Questions D'Arco Gang Tie," *Chicago Tribune,* Nov. 7, 1969.)

6. *A couple of weeks later . . . the First Ward table.* In several different trials, Cooley has described his first meeting with Pat Marcy and the subsequent events involving the case he fixed for him. He provided the most detail in *State of Illinois v. Harry Aleman,* No. 93 28787 (Sep. 23, 1987) Transcript of Proceedings at 8-103.

7. *The press dubbed him . . . contract murders.* ("Mob's Killing Machine.") A Chicago Police Department rap sheet from this time shows that Harry Sam Aleman had been arrested on at least 19 occasions from Jan. 1960 (when he was 21) to April 1975, for offenses ranging from malicious mischief to aggravated battery, burglary, grand theft auto, armed robbery, false statements on a mortgage application, gambling and aggravated kidnapping. In most of the cases he was sentenced to probation or the charges were dismissed by the judge. (City of Chicago Department of Police, "Arrest Record of Harry Sam Aleman," IR 12312, Feb. 2, 1975.)

8. *The victim was William P. Logan . . . a shotgun.* (James Griffin and Robert Shanahan, "Homicide Report for William P. Logan," RD#M397025, Chicago Police Department, Sep. 28, 1972.) The initial police report, begun on the night of the murder, included statements from Bobby Lowe, the neighbor witness. These would prove inconsistent with the evidence and other witness accounts—especially his description of the car, murder weapon and number of shots fired. Although he would later depart from these initial comments, and bring his testimony in line with the other witnesses, Lowe's credibility always remained problematic for the prosecution.

8. *Once the coppers . . . spilling out.* One of the first interviews with Almeida was conducted by an FBI agent and police officer. (John J. O'Rourke, *Federal Bureau of Investigation FD-302,* Oct. 18, 1976.)

13. *[Marco D'Amico] was one of the Mob's Young Turks . . . West Side.* During this period, reporters and Mob observers used "Young Turk" to designate the Outfit's top crew leaders like D'Amico, Harry Aleman and William Joe "Butch" Petrocelli (Chicago Crime Commission, "William 'Butch' Petrocelli," Searchlight, Jan. 1979, 7). Although hits committed by Young Turks were first thought to be power grabs, they were in fact enforcement measures sanctioned by the older Outfit bosses. (See "Crime Pays," p. 84.) D'Amico would eventually become the head of all the Mob's sports gambling operations in Chicago and the suburbs. (Daniel J. Lehman, "Gambling Charges Hit 9," *Chicago Tribune*, Nov. 19, 1994.)

14. *Once, I watched him . . . in a pizza parlor.* State prosecutors later considered charging Aleman for the crime, but concentrated on the Logan murder instead. *(United States v. Thomas J. Maloney and Robert McGee,* 91 CR 477 [N.D. Ill. July 19, 1994], Tr. of Proceedings at 235.)

15. *Through Marcy's connections, Maloney was soon to be appointed as a Circuit Court judge to fill a vacancy.* (Jerold S. Solovy, The Illinois Supreme Court Special Commission on the Administration of Justice: Final Report, Dec. 1993, 19.)

19. *The hit, I learned . . . Logan replied, "Fuck that Guinea."* Cooley was given this information by Butch Petrocelli. He first reported it to the FBI (John "Steve" Bowen, FBI 302, on May 13, 1986) and then discussed it again with assistant State's Attorney Patrick J. Quinn when he considered whether to retry Aleman for the murder.

20. *When he announced . . . a bicycle."* (*Illinois v. Harry Aleman,* No. 76 C 6958 [May 24, 1977], Tr. of Proceedings at 674-679.)

CHAPTER 2

COP KILLER

23. *Jim's dad . . . a holdup man.* (Patricia Leeds, "Commandments Daily Guide of This Policeman," *Chicago Tribune*, June 16, 1950.) *The bullet that hit him between the eyes took another twelve weeks to kill him.* ("Policeman Dies From Wound In Holdup Battle," *Chicago Tribune*, April 5, 1927.)

23. *The night of the shooting . . . saw a doctor.* ("Cop Shot in Holdup, Taken on Wild Ride," *Chicago Tribune*, Jan. 24, 1927.)

24. *The dentist was later convicted of Driving Under the Influence . . .* ("Policeman Shot In Bandit Battle Is Near Death," *Chicago Tribune*, Jan. 25, 1927.)

24. *Grandfather raised his head . . . described as "colored . . ."* ("Man Identified As Robber Who Shot Policeman," *Chicago Tribune*, Jan. 27, 1927.)

24. *He later admitted . . . six pistols.* ("Accuse Man In Shooting Of Policeman," *Chicago Tribune*, Jan. 28, 1927).

24. *A few years before . . . a cascade of roses.* A sociologist from the era, John Landesco, writes, "Al's brother was given a spectacular funeral. The coffin was silver-plated and the flowers were said to have cost more than $20,000." (John Landesco, *Organized Crime in Chicago* [Chicago: The University of Chicago Press, 1929], 179-180.)

24. *Grandmother heard the verdict . . . in my career.*" The prosecutor added, "I can't understand a jury returning such a verdict in the face of the evidence." When she recovered, Cooley's grandmother told the reporter: "I am astounded, dumbfounded." ("Jury Frees Pemberton In Policeman's Death," *Chicago Tribune*, Oct. 22, 1927.)

26. *If needed, Mom could . . . about my Dad.* ("Commandments Daily Guide.")

27. *Probably the meanest kid . . . along the way.* We use a fictitious name for this individual who never became a public figure. Although he would eventually make a fortune in the world of finance, he suffered reverses, partly due to alcoholism and resumed the illegal activities of his youth. When he was last in touch with Cooley, he was in a state penitentiary for home invasion.

33. *I was a little midget . . . guy in the world.* Murphy, today a Chicago attorney, remembers that first day of escapades with Cooley and says: "Bob was wild and out of control. Also, for a little guy, he could be very tough in a fight. Part of the problem was that he was away from home for the first time. He came from a deeply religious family and now he was free to sow his wild oats." (William P. Murphy, interview by Hillel Levin, June 2004.)

CHAPTER 3
MARCO & THE COUNT

46. *A few hours later . . . named Richard Speck.* The eight murders were committed during the late night hours of July 13 through the early hours of July 14, 1966. (Steve Johnson and Sharman Stein, "Speck's death fails to end the pain of victims' relatives," *Chicago Tribune*, Dec 6, 1991.)

51. *One day at breakfast . . . no more than that.* According to police records, D'Amico would have been 34. Although well-known to authorities as a rising power in the West Side crew, to this point he did not have a significant record—only one gambling arrest when he was 21. ("The D'Amico Enterprise," *Illinois Police and Sheriff's News*, www.ipsn.org, Nov. 26, 2003.) D'Amico also had several Italian beef stands, often run by members of his crew. (Peter F. Vaira, *In The Matter of Bruno Caruso*, et. al., Docket No. 99-12D, Office of the Independent Hearing Officer, Laborers' International Union of North America, Jan. 10, 2001, p. 25.)

56. *In fact, for several years . . . contorting his hands.* An example of this ad could be found in *The Stalker*. ("Issue #2," DC Comics, 1975.)

56. *He called himself Count Juan Raphael Dante . . . grappling arts masters . . ."* The legend of Count Dante can still be found on the web site, CountDante.com, which is run by his former student, William V. Aguiar.

56. *In fact, Count Dante . . . a wealthy neighborhood.* In one of his last interviews, Count Dante admitted his real name and that his father was a doctor, although he still claimed Spanish heritage. (Massad F. Ayoob, "Count Dante's Inferno: What it's really all about," *Black Belt*, Jan. 1976.)

56. *The Count's "serious problem" . . . the spear still inside him.* (Tony Sowa, "Karate School Feud Flares, 1 Killed, 1 Hurt," *Chicago Tribune*, April 24, 1970.) John Keehan, aka The Count, was no stranger to feuds with competing martial arts schools. He was caught trying to bomb one five years before. ("2 Plead Guilty, Get Probation In Bomb Plot," *Chicago Tribune*, Oct. 29, 1965.)

57. *A supermarket tabloid . . . "The World's Deadliest Fighter Is A . . . Hairdresser!* The front page headline had the subtitle, "Will Cassius Clay Accept Count Dante's Challenge?" (*National Informer*, July 21, 1968.)

58. *During the day . . . along the lakefront.* A lion owned by John Keehan and partner in a karate school was reported to have bitten the mayor of Quincy, Illinois during a photo shoot. ("Chicago Lion Sinks Teeth in Quincy Visit," *Chicago Tribune*, Oct. 8, 1964.)

63. *My biggest trouble . . . macho bullshit . . .* In a story Keehan wrote himself, he says the confrontation was provoked when one of his instructors was "threatened" and he was then challenged by the Green Dragon Society, which operated the Black Cobra Hall. (In court documents and some articles, Green Dragon and Black Cobra are used interchangeably.) He called Koncevic, who ran a nearby school, to help. Keehan writes that he, Koncevic and a student faced twelve armed men. "The police later told me I was crazy to have walked in, but to me the greater the odds the better the fight." Although he concludes, "I blame myself," for Koncevic's death, he adds, "I still look with disgust on the cowardly actions . . . of the complete Green Dragon instruction force . . ." (John Keehan, "Death in Chicago: Count Dante's Own Store of the Killing of Jim Koncevic," *Official Karate*, Oct. 1971.)

CHAPTER 4
CRIME PAYS

67. *It was Jimmy LeFevour . . . on his breath.* In a book about Operation Greylord, the investigation that eventually caught up to the LeFevours, the authors write, "In twenty-eight years as a police officer, [Jimmy LeFevour] never rose above the rank of patrolman in a career that was distinguished only for his drinking." (James Tuohy and Rob Warden, *Greylord: Justice, Chicago Style* [New York: Putnam 1989], 90.)

70. *One of the senior judges . . . his suit jacket.* "During the 1970s and into the 1980s, Sodini franchised gambling court to the highest bidders." (*Greylord,* 16.)

71. *For the first eleven years . . . just to judges.* When Cooley admitted this on the stand during later trials, a defense attorney used his words to label him "the most corrupt attorney in the history of Cook County." In fact, when Cooley started his practice, bribes had become a widespread practice in the court system. In regards to traffic court, the authors of *Greylord* write, "All new judges assigned to major courtrooms were tested immediately by [presiding] Judge LeFevour, and those who did not accept bribes were not reassigned there." (*Greylord,* 27.)

73. *I've never claimed . . . defense attorney.* Cooley's college friend, Bill Murphy, who went on to become a highly-regarded Chicago defense attorney says of Cooley, "He had good trial skills. He was competitive. He wasn't a legal scholar, but he could go to court and be effective." (Murphy, interview.) Another lawyer who watched him in action says, "He could be incredibly skilled at identifying himself with members of the jury. He prevailed in most jury cases that I know about." (Confidential Source, interview.) Ironically, Ed Genson, a renowned criminal defense attorney competing with Cooley during this period would later try to turn his success at jury trials against him when Cooley became a witness (see above, p. 286). But not all lawyers who knew Cooley are unanimous about his ability. One says, "To call him a 'great trial lawyer' is ridiculous. He never prepared for trial like great trial lawyers do. I doubt if he knew how. Instead, he walked into court like he had the verdict in his pocket, and many times, in bench trials, he did." (Confidential Source, interview.)

79. *After the clubs closed . . . in Chinatown.* Cooley testified extensively about the dice games during hearings about Mob influence on the Laborers' International Union (LIUNA). He often saw union leaders in attendance. (Office of the Independent Hearing Officer, Laborers' International Union of North America, *In Re: Trusteeship Proceedings Chicago District Council,* No. 97-30T [July 22, 1997], Tr. of Proceedings at 1058-1066.)

80. *Tony [Spilotro] was a little guy . . . vicious temper.* In *Casino,* Pileggi quotes an FBI agent who spent years listening to Spilotro wiretaps: "[Spilotro] lost his temper faster than anyone I ever knew. There was no slow burn. He went right from being nice to being a screaming, violent maniac in a second." (*Casino,* 150.)

81. *He had a jewelry store . . . his best loot.* The FBI would later charge that the store was a "veritable warehouse of stolen jewelry." (William F. Roemer, Jr., *The Enforcer. Spilotro: The Chicago Mob's Man Over Las Vegas* [New York: Ballentine, 1994], 124.)

81. *Charlie Postl . . . mayors show up.* Demaris writes that FBI agents observed John D'Arco Sr. and Pat Marcy, among other members of the First Ward having "conferences" at Postl's with Mob bosses. (*Captive City,* 152.)

83. *The Outfit, as they called . . . killing each other.* In 1981, *Tribune* crime reporters quoted federal authorities as saying, "All territory west of the Mississippi River belongs to Chicago." (Ronald Koziol and John O'Brien, "Mob's gathering in café gives insight to hierarchy," *Chicago Tribune,* Jan. 25, 1981.) But the power of Chicago's Mob was known long before that. In 1976, FBI agent Jim Wagner arrived in Chicago after six years in the New York City office. (He retired from the FBI in 2000 and spent all but the first of his 31 years at the bureau on Organized Crime.) Comparing the Mafia in the two cities he says, "Chicago was more brutal in its control of their people and interests, and more impatient with people who didn't cooperate." As far as Chicago's control of everything west of the Mississippi, he says, "That information had been received by so many different informants and sources, it became common knowledge early in the seventies." (Wagner, interview.)

83. *They were divided up . . . family name.* Wagner explains the wisdom behind the Outfit's territorial organization. "The New York Mafia's infighting was caused by the fact that it was so fractionalized: first by the family divisions and then by the boroughs they were in. In recent years, New York has moved closer to the sort of cooperative models that Chicago's Mob created." (Wagner, interview.)

Although some law enforcement authorities and mobsters have used different names for the groups listed by Cooley, there is general agreement that there were five that divided the metropolitan area along the four major freeways. In 1983, before the U.S. Senate Permanent Subcommittee on Investigations, then FBI agent Roemer presented a chart listing the prominent members for each of Chicago's five groups. He credited the Chicago Crime Commission for their assistance and used the chart in the preface of his books (e.g. *The Enforcer,* xvi-xvii). The "geographical" organization was also discussed during the LIUNA hearings. (Vaira, 24.)

84. *The five Mafia groups . . . called street tax.* With Cooley's information, the Organized Crime Strike Force would use the street tax system as the basis for a future prosecution that netted crew leader Ernest 'Rocco' Infelice and 17 others, mostly from the Cicero group. (See "The Harder They Fall," p. 305 and further notes for that chapter below.)

90. *I heard that a gang . . . in U.S. history.* A book about the robbery that mentions the missing money was co-written by *Tribune* crime reporter O'Brien: Edward Baumann and John O'Brien, *Chicago Heist,* South Bend: And Books, 1981.

91. *Only the broker . . . were convicted.* The broker, Luigi DiFonzo, was represented

by famous criminal defense lawyer Joe Oteri and gave him a Rolls-Royce as a reward. (Cris Barrish and Jerry Hager, "For the defense, Joe Oteri," *Delaware News Journal*, June 14, 1998.)

93. *For some reason, the Count's name . . . Boston commodities broker . . .* Although the potential involvement of John Keehan (the Count) with the Purolator heist was not widely reported, connections between the robbery and his death were made a few days later by longtime *Chicago Sun-Times* reporter, Art Petaque, in his crime column. Petacque interviewed Christa ("Keehan's wife"), who told him that Keehan was questioned by the police about Purolator and passed a lie detector test, but never left their condo during the three-week trial of the accused robbers. (Art Petacque, "Purolator link? Probe karate whiz's death," *Chicago Sun-Times*, June 1, 1975). Petacque describes the cause of Keehan's death as "shock and internal bleeding," but Christa also talked to the *Black Belt* writer who conducted Keehan's last interview. According to him, "His pale, delicately beautiful young wife found [Keehan] stiff in his bed one morning, his insides full of clotting blood." In this version, Christa attributes his death to an untreated ulcer and "high, hard living." ("Count Dante's Inferno.")

CHAPTER 5

HIGHLIFE WITH THE LOWLIFES

97. *As far as the public was concerned . . . or ignored.* When Cooley first met him, D'Arco had received a pass from the media and the first Daley administration ("Daley Questions D'Arco Gang Tie"), but controversy would later flare around his Mob connections in 1980 when he supposedly influenced Chicago Police appointments by Mayor Jane Byrne (see notes below for page 107).

100. *[The After Hours Club] was a block from . . . The Hungry Hound.* In his report, the LIUNA's Independent Hearing Officer called the Hungry Hound "a convenient meeting place for the main organized crime family in the area." (Vaira, 25.)

101. *Some twenty years later . . . no apparent reason.* "Multimillionaire John E. du Pont was found guilty of murder yesterday, but jurors spared him a possible life sentence, deciding that mental illness played a role in his fatal shooting of an Olympic wrestler:" Maria Panaritis, "Du Pont guilty of killing wrestler but mentally ill," *Associated Press*, Feb. 26, 1997.

102. *Pat never held . . . was secretary.* When FBI agent Roemer testified before the U.S. Senate Permanent Subcommittee, he charged that Marcy was a "made" member of the Chicago Mob and his appointment as Secretary was engineered by one-time Outfit CEO, Sam Giancana. Much of Roemer's information was

based on wiretaps. (William F. Roemer, Jr., *Roemer: Man Against the Mob* [New York: Ballentine 1989], 100.).

106. *But after the death . . . politician in Chicago*. Roti was often portrayed in the press as a puckish Damon Runyan character. "Patronage is a fine art for [Roti]," one article muses. "Nine Rotis are on the city payroll, and as many as 17 relatives have been there at one time. Nephew Fred Barbara received a $10 million hauling contract in 1988 over a minority firm that was low bidder. Another nephew and his son got city grants." (Hanke Gratteau and Ray Gibson, "5 Indicted Men Political Veterans," *Chicago Tribune*, Dec. 20, 1990.) Typically these stories did not mention that Roti's father, Bruno "the Bomber" Roti, had been a mobster or that his nephews—Bruno, Frank and Leo Caruso—were the discredited and brutal leaders of the Chicago local of LIUNA. The Independent Hearing Officer used the Carusos association with Roti as one of the grounds for revoking their membership from LIUNA and barring them from ever holding office in the union. (Vaira, 118.)

106. *He used to say his election slogan was "Vote for Roti and Nobody Gets Hurt."* ("5 Indicted Men.")

107. *Senior was part . . . jury acquitted Senior.* Although there are no records of convictions for D'Arco, his early arrests and association with Capone are documented in several newspaper clips from the time. One has him picked up in a car without a license plate after leaving the funeral for a Capone bodyguard. ("Rio, Al Capone's Guard, Buried In Gangland Style," *Chicago Tribune*, Feb. 28, 1935.) In a far more serious case, at the age of 21, he was one of four arrested in the purse-snatching murder of a 49-year-old woman and "mother of four children." ("4 Youths Held As Police Probe Woman's Murder," *Chicago Tribune*, May 24, 1930.) Although D'Arco was acquitted, one of the others was later convicted. (John W. Tuohy, "Battaglia Brothers," *AmericanMafia,com*, July 2001.) From court files, Demaris cites another instance in 1931 when D'Arco was arrested for armed robbery. Again, a friend, also charged in the crime was convicted, while D'Arco was not. (*Captive City*, 140.) Marcy wasn't so lucky, and even served time for his conviction. In those days, he was known as Pasqualino Marchone. Besides identifying Marcy as an ex-convict, Demaris says his brother, Paul, also did time for robbery, but eventually became an administrative assistant for the Cook County Board of Zoning Appeals. (*Captive City*, 142.)

107. *Pat [Marcy] was a majority . . . the firm.* Demaris shows how an interest in Anco prevented a previous First Ward committeeman from a cabinet appointment by then Governor Adlai Stevenson. (*Captive City*, 141.) Marcy's majority share of the firm was disclosed in his federal indictment. ("Second

Superseding Indictment," *United States v. Marcy & Roti*, No. 90 CR 1045 [N.D. Ill. Sep. 1990], at 3.)

108. *Buddy Jacobson may have . . . to Capone's side. (Captive City, 139-140.)*

108. *With the money from bootlegging, Capone realized he . . . Democrat didn't matter.* According to sociologist Landesco, gang leaders in Chicago had once aspired to become elected officials or party activists on their home turf. But Capone, he writes, was "totally mercenary." He did not want to be elected to office. Instead, he wanted control of the government wherever he ran his various rackets to protect "the profits of illegitimate or contraband commerce." Political ideology did not matter in the least, so Capone tended to take over the party in power. In the suburb of Cicero, which practically became his headquarters, it was the GOP. Capone's Mob took a similar tack with politics in the city, targeting whatever party was in power in each ward. (Landesco, 178.)

108. *After Capone, Tony Accardo . . . made him sound.* FBI agent Roemer writes, "Nobody in history has ever made the impact in organized crime that Accardo has . . . I feel that Accardo's ability to remain un-incarcerated while serving his organization in the very top positions for so long, with all our powers of law enforcement focused against him, is indicative of his immense performance." (*Accardo*, 384.) Roemer claims that the nickname was bestowed on Accardo by Capone himself. (*Accardo*, 41.)

108. *Like Capone, Accardo saw . . . to the First.* At the turn of the century, the First Ward was a "red-light" district. Rival gangs of politicians literally fought (and killed each other) for control. (Landesco, 36-39.) Although the ward eventually expanded to encompass the business district and wealthy neighborhoods, Mob elements retained their control in the apparatus of the Democratic machine. (*Captive City*, 136.)

108. *Buddy [Jacobson] had started . . . executive secretary.* He ran for Alderman in the 20th Ward in 1927. He lost and was convicted of vote fraud in the process (*Captive City*, 140). He lost another race in a bid to be the GOP Committeeman for that ward three years later (*Chicago Tribune*, April 16, 1930). Jacobson changed party affiliation when his 20th Ward was merged with the overwhelmingly Democratic First Ward in 1947. (*Captive City*, 130.) By 1952, he was Secretary for the First Ward Democratic Committee. ("Civic group asks Dems to purge Hoodlums," *Chicago Tribune*, March 6, 1952.)

109. *Then, in 1950 . . . general election.* (Brian J. Kelly and Pat Wingert, "The Man City Hall Whispers About," *Chicago Sun-Times*, April 20, 1980.)

109. *During one wiretap . . . for reelection. (Man Against the Mob, 194-197.)*

110. *By the mid-seventies, the Outfit . . . were in agreement.* These constant changes in Mob leadership are documented by Roemer in *Accardo*, 405-407.

110. *The Hook would have . . . passenger seat.* Cooley described these scenes for the LIUNA Hearing Officer, since the Caruso brothers were closely allied with the Chinatown group. (*In Re: Chicago District Council* at 1093.)

110. *At one point . . . Italian-American Club . . .* In fact, the LIUNA Independent Hearing Officer (IHO) found that here were non-Mafiosi members: "The Italian-American Club was open to all Italian-American persons, many of whom joined for social purposes and were not connected to organized crime. . . . The IHO notes that while some members of organized crime chose to transact organized crime business at the club, it was not the type of club to which only the [Mafia] could be admitted." (Vaira, 45.)

111. *The On Leong Chinese Merchants Association . . . in street tax.* Although the On Leong societies in Chinatowns across America looked, from the outside, like harmless civic groups, they evolved from tongs or gangs. Besides gambling, they became involved with drug smuggling. (Gwen Kinkead, *Chinatown: A Portrait of a Closed* Society [New York: Harper, 1992], 47-49.) For more on the On Leong's involvement with Roti, see "Chicken With Wing."

111. *I realized how vital Pat Marcy . . . on Chicago.* FBI agent Jim Wagner says, "When I came to Chicago, it was astounding for me to see the influence of Organized Crime in the political arena. I wasn't aware of anything at all similar in New York. I looked at Pat Marcy as the connection between politics statewide and the Outfit. As far as the general public was concerned, he was low profile. But those in the know realized that he was the powerhouse. He had the ability to make decisions or get decisions made." (Wagner, interview.)

111. *Pat became so central . . . in Las Vegas.* In his book, *Double Deal,* former suburban police officer and Outfit associate, Michael Corbitt, describes how money made its way out of Las Vegas. For a time, he provided the last leg of the courier service and made the delivery himself to Marcy and Aiuppa. (*Double Deal,* 280.)

111. *Stein was another . . . his workers.* (*Captive City,* 42-43; Also, "Ben Stein, King of the Janitors," *Illinois Police and Sheriff's News,* www.ipsn.org, June 24, 1997.)

112. *[Dominic Senese] ran the Teamsters Local . . . a strike.* Peter F. Vaira, then Attorney in Charge of the Chicago Strike Force co-wrote an internal report for the U.S. Department of Justice. He voiced alarm about the Mob's stranglehold on unions, especially in the Chicago area, and writes: "The picture that it presents is thoroughly frightening." He describes Senese and his local as follows: "[Local 703] represents the produce haulers. The Secretary Treasurer is Dominic Senese, a Chicago syndicate member and a relative by marriage of Anthony Accardo, Chicago Syndicate head. Senese is a powerful man in the Teamsters Union, and has been rumored for a job

with the international. He is currently under investigation for taking pay-offs for awarding health and welfare insurance contracts for his union to a syndicate company." (Peter F. Vaira, "Organized Crime and the Labor Unions," *Organized Crime Strike Force Internal Document*, 1978.) Senese and Ben Stein were rumored to have dipped into Local 703 pension funds to buy a dilapidated hotel. They then sold the property as the site for the James R. Thompson State of Illinois office building. ("Ben Stein.").

113. *Some of the Mob's worst hit men and good enforcers were on the public payroll.* The press reported that Tony Borsellino had a high-paying union job at the city's convention cente one year after he was paroled for hijacking trucks. ("John Anthony Borsellliono Among Kingpins Working at McCormick" *Chicago Tribune*, Aug. 1, 1974.) Butch Petrocelli received a salary from the engineering division of the park district. (*Chicago Tribune*, Jan. 17, 1969.)

116. *Joe Di[Leonardi] was sent . . . a go-along guy.* DiLeonardi told one reporter that Byrne demoted him because he would not stop the vice squad com-mander from raiding Mob bookies. Brzeczeck, the new chief, responded by casting aspersions on DiLeonardi. (Bob Weidrich, "Ex-chief refused to oust Duffy," *Chicago Tribune*, April 20, 1980.) During this fray, John D'Arco Sr. became a lightning rod again. When the *Chicago Sun-Times* looked into his past, the paper said the new police chief defended him, saying, "none of the allegations against [D'Arco] had ever been proved." ("The man City Hall whispers about.")

116. *Although [Hanhardt] made some . . . crew leaders.* More than just a friend with the Mob, Hanhardt practically became family, explains FBI agent Jim Wagner. "His daughter married the son of one Mob boss." (Wagner, interview). For much of his career, Wagner tried to build a case against Hanhardt, ultimately succeeding. In 2001, Hanhardt pled guilty to operating a jewel theft ring that stole more than $5 million. (Matt O'Connor, "Hanhardt gets nearly 16 years." *Chicago Tribune*, May 3, 2002.) See further notes on Hanhardt in "In the Weeds."

119. *Blackie never ceased . . . Jumbo Cummings . . .* (O'Connor, "Ex-Cop Charged As Probe Focuses On Divorce Court," *Chicago Tribune*, May 16, 1992.)

122. *No one was worse . . . was drunk.* D'Amico's drinking and temper caused an arrest in 1978 for "street fighting" on Rush Street, and aggravated battery in 1980. In 1983, he was stopped for D.U.I. and then resisted arrest in the suburb of Palatine (and bit the arresting officer). All these charges were even-tually dropped. ("D'Amico Enterprise.")

126. *I was with my girl in the corner talking to two leaders from the Chinatown crew, Larry Pusiteri, who managed the After Hours Club, and Richie Catazone, an older bald guy.* During his LIUNSA testimony Cooley identified Pusiteri as the manager of the

Hungry Hound and, with Catazone,, a member of the Chinatown group. He also placed them both at the dice games. (Vaira, 37 and 52.)

129. *[Borsellino] supposedly made his bones as part of an elite ring of truck hijackers, and served a few years for a million dollar silver bullion heist.* ("John Anthony Borselliono Among Kingpins Working at McCormick," *Chicago Tribune*, Aug. 1, 1974.)

129. *The next day [Borsellino] was found . . . Accardo's house.* According to Roemer, the FBI tied seven deaths to the break-in, not just the burglars, but their ex-cop fence and a friend who happened to be with him at the wrong time. Supposedly Borsellino was killed to cover Accardo's tracks. (*Accardo*, 13.) Later, when Frank Cullotta, a former member of Tony Spilotro's gang, became a cooperating witness for the government, he identified Borsellino and Butch Petrocelli among the Outfit's most prolific killers. (Ronald Koziol, "Informer ties 4 dead 'hit men' to 24 murders," *Chicago Tribune*, Sep. 20, 1982.)

130. *When I asked Pat . . . over his business.* According to the *Illinois Police and Sheriff's News*, the last time Koppel was seen, she was with Simon at Flapjaw's Saloon. ("Ben Stein.")

CHAPTER 6
A RUN THROUGH THE GREASE

131. *In a heavily accented voice . . . of your life."* (Jay Branegan, "Separate extortion trial set for missing mobster," *Chicago Tribune*, Jan. 8, 1981.)

134. *The next morning . . . Nick's murder.* (Terry Dvorak and John O'Brien, "Witness in Mob Extortion Trial Shot Dead: Scheduled to testify Dec. 8," *Chicago Tribune*, Nov. 29, 1980.)

135. *A few days later . . . expect the worst.* According to *Tribune* reporters, before Butch disappeared, "he was reportedly under investigation for charges of obstruction of justice in connection with the murder of Velentzas." (Jay Branegan and John O'Brien, "2d mobster missing in trial here," *Chicago Tribune*, Jan. 7, 1981.)

138. *The copper and the FBI agent . . . who whacked Nick.* Cooley also made public the handwritten statement he wrote for Renella to counter the agent's testimony. (Jay Branegan, "Separate extortion trial set for missing mobster," *Chicago Tribune*, Jan. 8, 1981.) Police eventually found Renella in Vancouver after tracking his various girlfriends (although he left all of his clothes back in Chicago, they noticed he took his cologne). He pled guilty and was sentenced to seven years for extorting Velentzeas. ("Hid from authorities for 7 mos.," *Chicago Tribune*, March 1, 1982.)

142. *The remains were partly . . . a blowtorch . . .* Although details about the burns and suffocation appeared in the papers ("Informer ties 4 dead"), the information about the blowtorch was provided to me by a Chicago police detective assigned to Organized Crime who helped identify the body.

143. *At some point, the bosses . . . Defense Fund.* The *Chicago Sun-Times* reported a similar theory and had Aleman himself ordering the execution and torture. ("Decomposed body of reputed top mob boss identified," *Chicago Sun-Times,* March 16, 1981.)

CHAPTER 7

CHICKEN WITH WING

148. *It came in July 1981 . . . in Chicago's Chinatown.* Cooley testified extensively about this case in *U.S. v. Maloney.* (*United States v. Maloney & McGee,* No. 90 CR 444 [N.D. Ill. March 19, 22, 1993], Tr. of Proceedings 1802-2122.)

148. *One group was known . . . across the country.* At first, the national On Leong organization was out to curb the gangs, but eventually decided to use them to control all illegal activity in their communities, much as the Outfit did in its territory. (Kinkead, 92.)

148. *"Go meet this guy . . . gambling parlors.* Growing up in the Chinatown area, and then as First Ward Alderman, Roti was well-known to the Chinese and likely to be spotted if he tried to meet with Moy. (O'Connor, "Sentencing Of 'Chinatown Mayor' Closes On Leong Case," *Chicago Tribune,* May 16, 1995.)

151. *I went to meet Barsy . . . in his firm.* Although Cooley did not hold Barsy in high regard, FBI agent Roemer identified him as a prominent defense lawyer and one of the few he "respected." (*The Enforcer,* 222.)

151. *Like me, [Maloney] came . . . John Marshall Law School.* Maloney provided information about his education as a witness. (*Roger Collins, United States v. Welborn,* No. 93 C 5282 [N.D. Ill. June 16, 1999], Tr. of Proceedings at 11). Other biographical details could be found in such articles as: O'Connor, "Ex-Judge Gets Final Fix," *Chicago Tribune,* July 22, 1994.

151. *He put as many men . . . Law and Order.* Maloney had nine cases where he sentenced the defendants to death. (Also, see p. 317 "Afterlife.")In at least one of these cases, Maloney appointed a discredited attorney to defend against the capital charges and permitted the prosecutors to pack a jury with whites when the defendant was black. This defendant has since charged that Maloney's harsh sentence helped camouflage his decision in the Chinatown case. (Ken Armstrong and Steve Mills, "Death Row Justice Derailed," *Chicago Tribune,* Nov. 14, 1999.)

157. *[Eddie Chan] had been a staff sergeant . . . and gambling business.* Chan also quickly bought favor with local authorities by contributing heavily to local politicians. (Kinkead, 92.)

160. *Ed and I were . . . Chicago's City Council.* ("Alderman Edward M. Burke," CityofChicago.org, as of June 11, 2004.)

163. *Cieslik found them . . . misconduct.* During the trial, the medical examiner testified that the victim died of "massive" injuries. Fifteen bones were broken. Meanwhile, Jesse Jackson was not happy with the judge either—for acquitting the third cop. ("Policemen Convicted of Involuntary Manslaughter in Beating Death," *Associated Press*, Dec. 23, 1981.)

164. *Dad died in February 1983.* Cooley spoke to the paper for the rest of his family. "My father was well-liked as a policeman," he was quoted. "He had been in the seminary and he was ultrahonest." ("J.F. Cooley; policeman added to family legacy," *Chicago Tribune*, February 15, 1983.)

168. *The Feds called this investigation . . . South Side group.* The operation got rolling when the FBI bugged the home of a Chicago patrolman related to a Kansas City Mob leader. They could then monitor a meeting of the Outfit's top bosses that included Aiuppa and LaPietra as they discussed selling their Las Vegas hotels to the Kansas City Mob. The feds listened in as they weighed the purchase prices against the amount they were skimming from the casinos. (*The Enforcer*, 244-247.)

168. *Like Byrne before him . . . police department.* In a series of articles, Tribune reporter David Jackson revealed links between Mob associates and Washington's police superintendent, Matt Rodriguez. The chief was reluctant to take action against a dozen cops identified by the FBI as potential mobsters. (David Jackson, "Forbidden Friendships Between Cops and Criminals," *Chicago Tribune*, Oct. 24, 2000.)

169. *Each day after court . . . to follow him.* Cooley testified on this scene extensively in *U.S. v. Maloney* at 76-102.

170. *[Frank] Cullotta's testimony would . . . of all charges.* Roemer devotes a few pages to M&M in his book on Spilotro and calls it a "weak case" (*The Enforcer*, 219-224). This assessment has pleased Maloney, who quoted from the book when lawyers questioned him about his verdict. (*Roger Collins*, 32.)

170. *In the end [Terry Hake] helped convict . . . and they convicted sixteen of them, including Dick LeFevour . . ."* (Solivey, Appendix II.)

170. *But for me Operation Greylord was a disappointment . . . or murder cases.* Although Greylord did not take down the First Ward, it was still among the most successful federal investigations, just in terms of the sheer number of corrupt officials and lawyers convicted. More important, according to FBI agent

John "Steve" Bowen, "Greylord laid the foundation for future investigations by giving us pro-active investigative techniques, like contrived cases, to go after people who were looking for bribes." (John "Steve" Bowen, interview by Hillel Levin, June 2004.) But those techniques had their limits, according to Assistant U.S. Attorney Tom Durkin, who like Bowen worked on Greylord cases. "With Greylord, we attacked fairly notorious corruption. It was so widespread, you could infiltrate it with undercover agents, who were new on the scene. But when it came to the First Ward, only a true insider could penetrate the higher levels of corruption where you had Marcy and Roti and the most powerful judges. They only trusted a limited number of people, which is why they got away with so much." (Durkin, interview.)

173. *I had been on the Colella case . . . to Counsellors?"* (*United States v. Marcy & Roti*, No. 90 CR 1045 [N.D. Ill. Dec. 14, 1992—Jan 12, 1993], Tr. of Proceedings at 421-442.)

176. *[The policewoman] said, "He came . . . kill you. '"* (Linnet Myers and Philip Wattley, "Judge In Cop Beating Case to Transfer," *Chicago Tribune*, March 6, 1986.)

180. *Just as I expected the papers crucified . . . Judge Passarella.* One headline in the *Tribune* read: "An Incomprehensible Verdict" (*Chicago Tribune*, March 9, 1986.)

180. *Passarella met with . . . of the case."* ("Judge in Cop Beating.")

CHAPTER 8
IN THE WEEDS

185. *"Do you need money?" . . . in this city."* As they talked, Shapiro remembers thinking, "Why me?" Although Cooley remembered him from a previous encounter with a client, Shapiro had no memory of Cooley, but immediately he understood his potential. At the time, he says, "Chicago's Mob was still enormously powerful. It was just smarter than the Mafia groups. It was organized smarter—by crews instead of families, and it was run smarter, with the bosses handing union jobs to mollify everyone. Accardo and Aiuppa were just another level above your typical Mob leader, but the key to their success was Pat Marcy. He was the most significant unknown powerbroker in Chicago and his influence was unbounded." (Gary Shapiro, interview with Hillel Levin, June 2004.)

187. *Then Steve said . . . terminal illness?* Bowen explains that after checking into Cooley's background, they still needed to meet him to complete their evaluation. In fact, Dyson's specialty was psychology. Bowen says, "You always want to know where someone is coming from in those first few meetings.

With Bob, we went for a long time really not knowing what his motivation was." (Bowen, interview.)

188. *I was not happy . . . U.S. Attorney.* In fact, the Chicago Strike Force office had to coordinate closely with the Chicago U.S. Attorney (and would be eventually absorbed into each local office). Although Shapiro's title was "Attorney in Charge, Chicago Strike Force," his bailiwick was really Organized Crime. He explained, "The U.S. Attorney had first dibs on Public Corruption, and that's where we determined Bob could help most. Besides, we had the best Public Corruption program in the country. Finding a corrupt official in Chicago was like shooting fish in a barrel." (Shapiro, interview.)

In fact, Bowen was one of the FBI agents assigned to corruption. For Cooley, this division made no sense—the Mob in Chicago was all about public corruption.

189. *I could no longer . . . a lot of time . . .* In fact, Shapiro says, "There was a lot of concern in Washington about Bob maintaining a law practice. It paralyzed things for a while." (Shapiro, interview.)

189. *McCoy had been . . . I'm telling you."* Looking back, Bowen thinks McCoy's challenge was appropriate. "You always start testing the waters to see if he's serious." (Bowen, interview.)

190. *But there was one . . . do you?"* Cooley's comments about Hanhardt were in fact recorded by McCoy in a separate 302. (Jack S. McCoy, John S. Bowen, Marie L. Dyson, *FBI 302*, March 20, 1986.

Although FBI agent Jim Wagner long had suspicions about Hanhardt, these were not shared by agents who knew him best. "It seemed like [Hanhardt] was a friend of the bureau. You could say he even endeared himself to certain agents and supervisors. For example, he was very helpful working on big easy-turnover cases like cartage theft. Nobody wanted to consider the fact that the guy was dirty. As he went higher in the force, Hanhardt became a more difficult issue, because he could affect your day-to-day working relationship with the CPD." (Wagner, interview.)

191. *Steve and Marie wanted . . . I saw John.* Bowen says, "I'm sure we were watching him. Sometimes we were on him and he didn't know it." (Bowen, interview.)

192. *But still, the Feds . . . the bookies.* Bowen remembers, "All that time we were waiting for guidelines from the [Attorney General]. It was as frustrating for us as Bob. At least we could keep him busy with the bookies, and although that was Organized Crime [as opposed to Public Corruption], that side was glad to let us do it." (Bowen, interview.)

196. *"When we told him . . . think of that?"* Shapiro says, "I don't know how Bob heard that, but I was not trying to negotiate a plea or any other sort of deal with him. That was not my job. That was something he had to work out with

the U.S. Attorney [Valukas]. I really wanted to be the guy at the Justice Department he didn't have to worry about—someone he could always talk to." (Shapiro, interview.)

197. *I said, "Fuck you . . . Bill Murphy."* Shapiro says, "If I thought he was serious about talking to a lawyer, I would have stopped talking to Bob and have talked to his lawyer. No matter what. I always respect a witness's right to representation and would never discourage it." (Shapiro, interview.)

Murphy does remember receiving the call from Cooley at that time and remembers being "overwhelmed" by what he heard. He says, "To this day, I think Bob made a mistake. If you knew him, you knew he had a tendency to act impulsively, and I think the decision to cooperate was an impulsive act. He had a good career and he threw it away. Despite his sacrifice, I don't think too many people in the government care about him in the least. They just wanted to use him and say goodbye." (Murphy, interview.)

199. *Somehow Tom and Gary Shapiro . . . on Marcy.* Unlike a bug or a wiretap, prosecutors did not need consent from a judge. However, they still had a fairly complicated process to follow. David Grossman, an FBI agent who became a public corruption supervisor, explains, "We always needed 'predication.' You have to have a good reason to believe someone is involved with criminal activity. In a typical situation, Steve Bowen would draft a request, and I would review it. My boss, the Assistant Special Agent in Charge of the Chicago division, would have to approve and then it would have to get by an assistant U.S. Attorney." (David Grossman, interview by Hillel Levin, May 2004.)

200. *Then I showed him . . . the case."* Cooley discussed a transcript of this recording in *United States v. Marcy & Roti,* No. 90 CR 1045, (N.D. Ill. Dec. 28, 1992), Tr. of Proceedings at 861-862.

200. *I went back down . . . Council Chambers.* Wire procedures eventually changed for public buildings first. Federal agents would get the recording devices inside the building first and install them once the informant was inside. (Grossman, interview.)

202. *A "surprise" witness . . . Tony [Spilotro's] old pal.* Hanhardt retired shortly after Cooley fingered him in his debriefing with the Feds. Roemer bends over backwards to justify Hanhardt's testimony and seems to find nothing fishy about it. (*The Enforcer,* 259.)

202. *Little did I know . . . an Indiana cornfield.* The medical examiner determined that the brothers died from "blunt force injuries from around the neck and head." (*Casino,* 346.)

202. *In the middle of the summer . . . Cook County Circuit Court.* Bowen remembers Cooley being more resistant. "Bob kept saying these contrived cases were 'Greylord nonsense,' and he hadn't come in to just do that." (Bowen, interview.)

203. *"Unless it's real important . . . I said.* (Charles Nicodemus, "Jury Hears Tapes Of Judge Talking About 'Plant' Fears," *Chicago Sun-Times,* July 17, 1993.)

203. *I told him . . . in them."* (Robert Cooley, Adam Stillo, Sr., *Federal Bureau of Investigation Electronic Surveillance* [Raw Transcription], Oct. 6, 1986.)

203. *"You know my nephew Joey? Talk to him."* (Nicodemus, "Jury.")

204. *"As I say," . . . the call."* (O'Connor, "Stillo Found Guilty Of Corruption," *Chicago Tribune,* July 30, 1993.)

205. *"Something about this . . . FBI agent."* (O'Connor, "Judge's Sixth Sense Recounted At Bribe Trial," *Chicago Tribune,* July 9, 1993.)

CHAPTER 9

THE WORST FUCK

209. *"What's the worst . . . not to be trusted."* (O'Connor, "Returned Bribe Discussed On Tape," *Chicago Tribune,* March 20, 1993.)

211. *"You're talking in . . . like that."* (Rosalind Rossi, "Videotape Shows Lawyers Discussing Payoff To Judge," *Chicago Sun-Times,* March 23, 1993.)

212. *I was told that Gary had to go to Washington . . . crashing down around him.* Shapiro denies that he had to go to Washington to overrule Valukas. "If there was a decision to keep Bob out of the Sodini case, I'm sure it was made by Tony [Valukas]. He didn't need pressure from me or anyone in Washington." (Shapiro, interview.)

Scott Mendeloff, an assistant U.S. Attorney, also defends Valukas and says categorically, "I never saw Valukas do anything to interfere with any investigation." (Scott Mendeloff, interview by Hillel Levin, June 2004.)

Attorneys who prefer not to be identified believe that Valukas was simply focused on the Sodini trial and saw Cooley's value to other cases as still unproven. One says, "Tony is very self-centered. He was relatively new on the job, and I think he was being selfish to get as much evidence as he could to win one of the first big cases on his watch." (Confidential Source, interview.)

Another member of the team says, "A lot of us fought like cats and dogs to keep Bob out of the Sodini trial. It was not pretty. And, for a while, we really thought they would call him as a witness and blow everything." (Confidential Source, interview.)

One investigator from the time does believe that Valukas felt threatened by Cooley, and says most of the U.S. Attorneys before him would have felt the same way. He says, "You just had to look at the way we were organized. There was Organized Crime and there was Public Corruption. In most cities that works. However, in Chicago, the Mob actually used corruption to become more powerful. Some U.S. Attorneys had a mindset that it was too embarrassing for the city to make that connection between public officials and mobsters. Valukas started out with that mindset. He lived here and knew he had to return to private practice here. (Confidential Source, interview.)

214. *Anne Burke screamed . . . change their grades.* Besides his position as principal, Moffat was reported to have political clout and was, at one time, "second in command" for the entire city school system. A teacher told reporters he was "worried that Moffat's power would win him an acquittal." (Linnet Myers, Casey Banas, and Terry Wilson, "Ex-Principal Convicted of Sex Abuse," *Chicago Tribune,* March 24, 1987.)

214. *The defendant, Herbert Cammon . . . the wife's murder.* (John Gorman, "Insurer Sues to Bar Death Claim," *Chicago Tribune,* June 29, 1988.)

215. *. . . Tuite brought in Anne Burke . . . to withdraw.* (Steve Neal, "GOP Rival's Ally Tries to Smear Anne Burke," *Chicago Sun-Times,* Aug. 30, 1993.)

215. *An article appeared . . . jury trials.* (Joseph R. Tybor and Mark Eissman, "Judges Penalize the Guilty for Exercising Right to Jury Trial," *Chicago Tribune,* Oct. 13, 1985.)

215. *Later, he was reprimanded . . . female attorneys.* (Charles Mount, "Judge Reprimanded for Sexist Remarks," Aug. 1, 1987.)

215. *Finally, Cieslik had . . . the help of the* Tribune *editorial page.* ("Voters: Kick Out Three Judges," *Chicago Tribune,* Nov.7, 1988.)

216. *"I would never roll over," . . . I'm gone."* ("Maloney Trial," *Chicago Sun-Times,* March 23, 1993.)

217. *"I wonder who . . . right there."* ("Video.")

218. *Maloney called Cammon . . . murdering his wife.* (Linnet Myers, "Man didn't kill wife for cash, judge rules," *Chicago Tribune,* Jan. 13, 1988.)

218. *After reviewing the . . . the policy.* ("Insurer Sues.")

218. *I hoped that Tuite . . . fees.* In fact, by the time the case went to trial before Maloney, Anne Burke had withdrawn as counsel. This is disclosed in a column by *Sun-Times* political writer Steve Neal that tries to be supportive of the Burkes, but probably calls too much attention to the Cammon case in the process. ("GOP . . . Tries to Smear Anne Burke.") See more on Burke and Neal's column in notes for p. 318 below.

CHAPTER 10

CANDID CAMERA

219. *A few years before . . . a bench trial.* (Bowen, FBI *302,* Jan. 4, 1988.) Oberman was the developer who tried to curry favor with Cooley and the First Ward by buying drinks at Faces. (See "Highlife with the Lowlifes," p. 125.)

219. *But Valukas wouldn't . . . a Mob boss?* Steve Bowen explains, "Someone may have told him it was a danger issue, but it was probably just an administrative issue. Because of his position as a state senator, D'Arco was at a new level and that delayed us because we had to do the predication paperwork all over again. These things are a pain, but you can understand why the government wanted to keep us focused in our investigations." (Bowen, interview.)

220. *After Daley and Valukas . . . "conflict" for me.* Gary Shapiro says, "The conflict of interest issues are not something Bob can blame on Tony [Valukas]. I don't think he ever knew about the battle that Tony fought behind-the-scenes to try to work out the problems inherent in an attorney working for the government and simultaneously representing clients being charged by the government. There were people in Washington who wanted him to shut down his practice from Day One. The kinds of conflicts of interest that an undercover attorney wearing a tape recorder all day would have with his clients made his keeping his law practice impossible." (Shapiro interview.)

221. *In January 1988, [Senese] got out . . . drive home.* (Ronald Koziol and Robert Blau, "Gangland-Style Attack Breaks the Immunity of Oak Brook," Chicago Tribune, Jan. 24, 1988.)

221. *Dom didn't talk—in fact . . . down from office.* (Ronald Koziol and James Strong, "Union Chief Reportedly Cuts Mob Deal," *Chicago Tribune,* Feb. 18, 1988.)

222. *Chancery Division of Cook County Court . . . a sting.* "Everyone tends to focus on the criminal courts," says Tom Durkin, who was an assistant U.S. Attorney. "But we were limited with contrived cases. We couldn't create a case with serious criminal charges. Meanwhile, Greylord never cracked the civil courts. Because of the sums involved, Chancery was very prestigious and all those judges seemed very insulated." (Durkin, interview.)

222. *[Marcy and I] went into the lobby . . . shelter racket.* Cooley concocted this tale from the real-life adventures of his childhood friend (whom we call Tommy Dugan). Cooley used to regale Marcy with Dugan's wild and wooly business antics. "Tom and I would have skull sessions with Bob to come up with the contrived cases," Bowen says. "We'd ask ourselves, 'Would this work or would that sound better?'" (Bowen, interview.)

222. *"These guys are scared . . . a year ago."* (U.S. v. Marcy at 488.)

223. *[Marcy] asked who we got . . . a ten-foot pole,"* Marcy said—just as I thought. (U.S. v. Marcy at 491.)

223. *"No,"* Patty said, *. . . about is this."* (United States v. Shields & DeLeo, No. 90 CR 1044 [N.D. Ill. Aug. 19—Sep. 24, 1991] at 363.)

224. *Into Patty's hands . . . "One, two, three . . ."* (U.S. v. Shields at 383.)

224. *Shields would take a bribe, . . . honorable about it.* (U.S. v. Shields 391.)

224. *After the second payoff . . . somersaults."* (U.S. v. Shields at 460.)

225. *I had taken undercover . . . bookies there.* Shapiro explains, "Bob was like our Encyclopedia Britannica of the Outfit. We may have known most of the faces, but he knew connections between groups and individuals that we hadn't dug up before." (Shapiro, interview.)

225. *"Maybe you are a beefer," . . . about someone."* (*U.S. v. Shields* Tr. of Electronic Surveillance CG 183B-2181.)

225. *I gave him $6,000—$5,000 . . . future services.* (*U.S. v. Shields*, ElSur.)

225. *In fact, unknown . . . that much more.* The bug in Shields's chambers was only the second ever authorized for a judge (the first was for Operation Greylord). Steve Bowen says it was installed only days after DeLeo "nonchalantly" claimed he could pay off Shields. Bowen brought in an affidavit for the federal judge to authorize the surveillance. "You could just see the shock on his face. Shields had so much respect in the legal community. Nobody would have expected him to be involved in this kind of fix." (Bowen, interview.)

225. *This one case vindicated . . . run its course.* Durkin says, "I remember taking Valukas the first tape with DeLeo saying he could make Shields 'do whatever we want.' He was as enthusiastic as everyone else and wanted us to take the investigation as far as it would go." (Durkin, interview.)

226. *When Johnny approached . . . fix a case.* A chiropractor friend of the state senator's had been charged with fraudulent billing. (Marie L. Dyson, FBI 302, Jan. 19, 1988.)

227. *On Monday morning, October 31 . . . insurance law.* (Bowen, FBI 302, Oct., 31, 1988.)

227. *He gave me . . . Arthur "Ron" Swanson.* (O'Connor and Ray Long, "Ryan pal lied to grand jury, U.S. alleges: Ex-senator, lobbyist Swanson indicted," *Chicago Tribune*, Aug. 28, 2003.)

227. *Fortunately, Johnny was . . . "Merry Christmas."* (O'Connor, "U.S. Says D'Arco Took $5,000 Bribe On Tape," *Chicago Tribune*, Oct. 10, 1991.)

227. *Now, the Feds told me . . . bullshit like that.* But agents remember there was a legitimate concern about Cooley's safety. Ironically, he had been so successful making cases against high-level officials, some assistant U.S. Attorneys now did not want him to take risks against low-level mobsters. FBI agent Jim Wagner, who specialized in organized crime wasn't informed about Cooley until 1989 and wanted his help with Marco D'Amico. But he remembers, "There was reluctance on the part of those in public corruption to allow him to work on organized crime. There was a concern for the danger involved and the possibility that Bob could be suddenly terminated." (Wagner, interview.)

228. *I thought, "What could say . . . pass a law."* As they did with every payoff, the FBI made note of the serial numbers for each of the bills Cooley used for each

street tax payoff. A report also notes his discussion with Marco about the juice loan for the D'Arco bribe, and mentions that Bob gave a $200 loan to a crew member in a card game, but did not believe the player "will ever pay it back." (Bowen, FBI 302, March 7, 1989.)

229. *In fact, this idea . . . armed robbery.* It was almost too good to be true for Jim Wagner, too. D'Amico had been a tough nut to crack. He explains, "Marco trusted very few, conversed with few, passed money with very few. He was long acquainted with Bob and that was the only reason Bob could get so close." (Wagner, interview.)

230. *[Roti] then wrote the numbers "75" . . . even louder.* (U.S. v. Marcy at 518.)

231. *[Marcy] marched over . . . fucking owners are."* (U.S. v. Marcy at 509.)

231. *[Marcy] said, "The figures . . . to make sure.* (U.S. v. Marcy at 527.)

231. *A week later, . . . the whole thing then."* (U.S. v. Marcy at 667-668.)

232. *As far as I was concerned . . . the Circuit Court.* (U.S. v. Marcy at 481.)

232. *This time, my "client," . . . from their business.* (U.S. v. Marcy at 19-22.)

233. *[After Marcy accidentally puts his hand on Cooley's back where the recording device is strapped.] Once again . . . town.* Steve Bowen, the FBI agent who worked most with Cooley, remembers the incident. He says, "That did scare me. I'm not doing my job if I'm not scared. At times like that we seriously considered shipping Bob out of town and putting an end to the investigation." (Bowen, interview.)

233. *[I] went back to see Marcy . . . for him.* (U.S. v. Marcy at 560-565.)

234. *They meant Pasquale "Buck" Sorrentino . . . Law Division.* Sorrentino had also once been President of the First Ward Democratic Organization and considered D'Arco Sr. his political mentor. (Solivey, 35.)

234. *Rocky Infelice, probably . . . baseball bat execution . . .* Roemer adds that Infelice was a decorated paratrooper in World War II who was dropped behind enemy lines during the Normandy invasion. (*The Enforcer,* 265.)

235. *He was later convicted . . . Hal Smith.* (John O'Brien, "Infelice latest mob boss headed for prison," *Chicago Tribune,* March 11, 1992.)

235. *[Roti] pulled the Chief Judge . . . a piece of paper."* (U.S. v. Marcy at 571.)

235. *FBI agents shadowed . . . the judge.* (Solivey, 35.)

235. *Pat walked through . . . Marcy shot back.* (U.S. v. Marcy at 575-576.)

236. *[Roti] grabbed a napkin . . . my pocket.* (U.S. v. Marcy at 580.)

236. *I made the next payment . . . at one time."* (U.S. v. Marcy at 667-668.)

237. *I couldn't believe it . . . he followed me.*

Although Steve Bowen hid his surprise, he says that this was also the first time that he learned the bug had been discovered. (Bowen, interview.)

237. *"I know you're careful," [Roti] said. "You gotta be," I said . . . Roti walked over*

to each of his two windows and lowered the blinds. Then he turned and said, "What have you got? Four . . ." "Yeah," I said. "Four. That's the end of it." (U.S. v. Marcy at 623-624.)

238. *Later, I heard how a busboy . . . on Monday morning.* The discovery created a splash in local and national news. A few days later, a front page story in the *Tribune* quoted an inside source as saying the camera was part of an investigation that would be "the next step of Greylord." But reflecting the divisions in the U.S. Attorney's office, another source suggested that the discovery of the bug "caught the government off guard and may call into question the ultimate success of the case." (Dean Baquet and Joel Kaplan, "Spy camera tied to Greylord Organized crime, court links sought," *Chicago Tribune,* July 16, 1989.)

238. *For me, the camera was total overkill . . . never talked dirty at the First Ward table.*
To this day, it has been assumed that the Counsellors Row bug was an integral part of Operation Gambat. In fact, it was fought by prosecutors and FBI agents most closely involved with the investigation. One says, "You will find that the Counsellors Row bug is a very touchy topic for us. It was pushed through by an FBI supervisor who had not been in his position very long. He believed that we had to pick up something useful, but it was a very high-risk install and was not worth blowing the access we already had with Cooley." (Confidential Source, interview.) Although little useful evidence was gained with the camera, the tap on Marcy's phone did lead to the charge that he solicited a bribe in return for a judicial appointment to circuit court.

238. *For the next few days . . . various microphones.* Much of the coverage quickly made light of a development that would have been cause for more concern in other cities. (Wes Smith, "Jeepers Peepers: Smile, Covert Cameras May Be Catching Your Act, *Chicago Tribune,* July 17, 1989.)

238. *[Roti] shook his head . . . "It never changes hands here." (U.S. v. Marcy* at 624.)

239. *[Judge Scotillo] confirmed that . . . just an act." (U.S. v. Marcy* at 645.)

239. *We had to come up . . . to block it.* (Solivey, 37.)

240. *[D'Arco] laughed that . . . a lot cheaper." (United States v. D'Arco,* No. 90 CR 1043 [N.D. Ill.], Tr. of ElSur CG 194A-828 for Sep. 14, 1989.)

240. *[D'Arco] laughed, "Roti would stiff . . . the judge's apartment . . . (U.S. v. D'Arco* Tr. of ElSur Sep. 27, 1989.)

240. *In October, I handed him $2,500 . . . the rest for himself. (U.S. v. D'Arco* Tr. of ElSur, Oct. 5, 1989.)

240. *I went to the restaurant where I knew [Scotillo] had lunch . . . [I asked,] "Now Johnny took care of you this time, right?" He replied, "Yeah. He did."* FBI agents also followed Scotillo as he walked from the court to lunch. (Bowen, *FBI 302,* Oct. 19, 1982.)

Chapter 11

Parting Shots for Harry and Marco

244. *"No," [Judge Wilson] said . . . nine years."* (U.S. v. Marcy, Tr. of ElSur [CG 183B-2442] May 16, 1989.)

244. *I said, "I'm gonna . . . about anything."* (U.S. v. Marcy, Tr. of ElSur May 16, 1989.)

245. *[Wilson] said to her, "Stay . . . bad man."* (Illinois v. Harry Aleman, No.93-28286-87, Tr. of Proceedings Feb. 9, 1995 at 253.)

245. *I wanted to approach . . . certifiably dangerous.* Agent Jim Wagner says he was among those who cautioned Cooley about Aleman. "Bob took risks that I believed he should not take, but he was very convinced of his invincibility; that his wit and mouth could always get him out of a tough situation. You need a huge ego to pull that off, and Bob was that sort of unique individual." (Wagner, interview.)

245. *That morning Steve met . . . to stay away.* Wagner did try to follow Cooley at a distance and crossed paths with Aleman. Wagner remembers, "We locked eyes for a moment, and I must say he did have the killer's look." (Wagner, interview.)

248. *I zipped over to the club . . . double payback."* Later court records show Cooley bet a total of $140,000 with Borelli and $775,500 with Abbinanti between Oct. 29 and Nov. 26, 1989. (Vaira, 15-16.)

249. *[D'Amico] wanted to make sure . . . "They're professionals."* (O'Connor, "Reputed Mob Boss Enters Plea," Chicago Tribune, May 2, 1992.)

249. *During the press conference . . . the occasion.* In fact, others involved with the investigation question whether Valukas would or could have a press conference. See notes below for p. 254.

250. *He got into my car . . . around the corner.* Inside the bag were "rubber banded" bundles of fifty-dollar and hundred-dollar bills, all adding up to the $50,000. (Wagner, FBI 302, Nov. 21, 1989.)

251. *[Abbinanti] was ambitious, too . . . City of Chicago.* Abbinanti was on the city's payroll as a truck driver for the Department of Streets and Sanitation. (O'Connor and Ray Gibson, "Reputed Mobster Indicted As Statute Of Limitations Nears," Chicago Tribune, Nov. 19, 1994.) He managed some of D'Amico's beef stands and was also a precinct captain for a ward near O'Hare Airport. (IPSN, "D'Amico Enterprise.")

252. *Wagner had picked . . . the raid.* Wagner remembers, "I spent weeks looking for that house. It had to meet a lot of conditions to keep this project as safe as possible." (Wagner, interview.)

254. *But Jimmy told me . . . everything arranged."* Wagner remembers, "This was as frustrating for me as it was for Bob. I put a lot of work into it, and we knew we

could catch some bad people in the act, but there was absolutely no way we could get a second opportunity. The decision had been made by the U.S. Attorney [Anton Valukas] that Bob had to leave town." (Wagner, interview.)

254. *For some reason, Valukas . . . Attorney General.* None of the prosecutors or agents I talked to say that a Valukas press conference was in the works. Gary Shapiro told me, "Valukas would have never held one at that point. Getting the media involved could have jeopardized everything we did." (Shapiro, interview.) Dave Grossman, then the Supervising Special Agent for Public Corruption agrees. "There is no way we would have stopped an investigation for political reasons." (Grossman, interview.) Then assistant U.S. Attorney Tom Durkin adds, "It would be very unfair to say that Tony Valukas ended Gambat early for his own purposes. He was a very legitimate and determined prosecutor." (Durkin, interview.)

But others involved with the investigation say that Cooley could have been led to believe that an event was coming that would force Gambat to a conclusion. One says, "For Bob's own good we had to get him to stop. He had played out his string and was taking some pretty big risks for low-level mobsters. To be honest, we were all burned out." (Confidential Source, interview.) Another says, "It's no coincidence that Gambat stopped the same week as Valukas's term. You can't tell me he didn't want credit for the investigation. But he deserved it, too. Once things got rolling, he was very supportive of what Bob was doing—in many ways that Bob would not have known about." (Confidential Source, interview.)

254. *One of the agents . . . "Oh, my God."* (*U.S. v. D'Arco* at 4958.)

CHAPTER 12

WITNESS DEJECTION PROGRAM

261. *[Valukas] said, " . . . if you want . . . believe you me."* Tom Durkin says, "I would have told Bob the same thing. Making extraneous statements gives the defense quotes that they can later use against you. Bob was a smart guy and once we explained that, he understood why he shouldn't talk to reporters. As far as I know, he didn't." (Durkin, interview.)

261. *The next morning . . . gambling debts . . ."* (John O'Brien and Ray Gibson, "FBI Sting Targeting Corrupt Judges, Zoning," Chicago Tribune, Dec. 2, 1989.) At some later time, the *Tribune* tried to amend this account of Cooley's motivations. Today, the digital copy of this article contains the following preface: "Corrections and clarifications: Stories published in some editions of the *Chicago Tribune* on Dec. 2, Dec. 3, and Dec. 5, 1989, stated that Robert Cooley turned government informant because of gambling debts and threats against

him because of the debts. Testimony in a subsequent trial showed that this statement about his motivations was not correct."

261. *To make matters worse . . . and my motives.* In fact, FBI agent Steve Bowen came up with the name. He says, "As I got to know Bob and his motivation for helping us, I had tremendous respect for him. He truly did have a conscience and made a pretty gutsy move when he came to us. I never intended for the name 'Gambat' to reflect badly on him. But you have to come up with these names quickly and don't have time to think about it. I had always heard that 'Greylord' really came from the name of a racehorse that one of the FBI supervisors owned. I can see how that could happen." (Bowen, interview.)

261. *Meanwhile, they had different . . . newspapers' clip files.* Despite what Ovid Demaris had written about Marcy in 1969, and despite what Roemer had testified about him to the U.S. Senate in 1983, only after Marcy's indictment did reporters indicate that Marcy had past Mob associations; and even then in a most elliptical way, such as the following: "For most of his years as secretary of the 1st Ward Regular Democratic Organization, Pat Marcy Sr. was a man about whom little was known and much was rumored. Even his name was a fiction, changed after his entry into politics from Pasquale Marchone. But his indictment Wednesday sharpened the focus on one of the 1st Ward's most elusive figures. Over the years, Marcy's name has surfaced repeatedly in discussions of mob activities." (Hanke Gratteau and Ray Gibson, "5 Indicted Men Political Veterans," *Chicago Tribune*, Dec. 20, 1990.)

262. *From the start, almost . . . the truth.* Although FBI agents directly involved with Operation Gambat know that Cooley was not in the Witness Protection Program, many others did not. It's possible that some members of the prosecution team were confused as well. Steve Bowen explains, "I wouldn't even tell the prosecutors where Bob was. Many times when they met with Bob, it was in a 'neutral' location—somewhere outside of Chicago but pretty far from where Bob was actually living." (Bowen, interview.)

262. *Most people think . . . U.S. Marshals Service.* "The Marshals Service provides for the security, health and safety of government witnesses—and their immediate dependents whose lives are in danger as a result of their testimony against drug traffickers, terrorists, organized crime members and other major criminals. The Witness Security Program was authorized by the Organized Crime Control Act of 1970 and amended by the Comprehensive Crime Control Act of 1984." ("Witness Security Program.," *United States Department of Justice Web Site* [usdoj.gov], as of Jan. 25, 2004.)

262. *One wire caught . . . the First Ward."* (Wagner, interview.)

263. *My total income came to $3,200 . . . to $3,400 a month.* (*U.S. v. Shields* at 1016.)

264. *I knew that agents had already gone out to Mob leaders and warned them . . .* The FBI did warn Mob bosses not to harass Cooley's friends or family. Jim Wagner says, "I arranged a meeting with Marco at his attorney's office to specifically tell him that Bob was working with us. I let him know that this was official notification and I didn't want to see any repercussions for Bob, his friends or his family." (Wagner, interview.)

265. *[The FBI agent] told Wilson, "Bob Cooley . . . a witness."* (O'Connor, "US Fights Key Tapes By Cooley," *Chicago Tribune*, July 26, 1991.)

265. *But then, in February, . . . and blew his brains out.* An FBI report also indicates that "Wilson had just been served a subpoena in connection with Chicago case entitled 'United States v. Rocco Infelice; et. al.'" Harry Aleman was among the additional defendants in that case. (Peter J. Wacks, FBI 302, April 13, 1990.)

269. *I had dealt . . . along just fine.* Some of the assistant U.S. Attorneys working on Gambat cases did not share Cooley's view that Foreman was better than his predecessor, Anton Valukas. One says, "Fred was exactly the sort of politically connected lawyer who should have never had that job. He was not nearly the U.S. Attorney that [Valukas] was." (Confidential Source, interview.)

269. *The next day, the* Chicago Tribune *. . . Attorney General Thornburgh replied,* "Stay tuned." (Gorman and Gibson, "Five Indicted in 'Corruption Feast.'")

270. *I knew [Foreman's] real problem . . . the assignment.* Then assistant U.S. Attorney Scott Mendeloff had previously prosecuted judicial corruption, and contrary to Cooley, he did feel that Maloney would be a tough case. "Maloney had a reputation for being a tough no-nonsense guy who was not supposed to be in the pocket of anyone, because he favored the state so much. He knew what trying a case meant and his decisions, even with the fixed cases, had some rationale." (Mendeloff, interview.)

272. *It turned out that . . . could bring charges.* To meet the statute of limitations and not affect another Gambat case already underway, the government kept the indictment under seal for nearly four months. (O'Connor, "Ex-Judge Maloney Charged With Taking Bribes In 3 Murder Cases," *Chicago Tribune*, Sep. 28, 1991.)

CHAPTER 13
"SLANDER MY NAME"

273. *[Genson] was quick to dismiss . . . with corruption."* (Ray Gibson, "Cop, Lawyer, Informant: Odyssey In 1st Ward," *Chicago Tribune*, Dec. 24, 1990.)

273. *Originally, [the case] had more than . . . in Chinatown.* (O'Connor, "On Leong Case Gets Split Verdict," *Chicago Tribune*, Aug. 28, 1991.)

274. *After I came in, the Strike Force . . . Moy in Taiwan.* Cooley also reported to the FBI that former retired Chief of Detectives Bill Hanhardt was paid off by the On Leong while he was Chief of Detectives. (Edwin C. Barnett, Thomas M. Bourgeois, *FBI 302,* May 6, 1987.)

275. *When I made my first appearance . . . by the defense attorneys.* (O'Connor, *Chicago Tribune,* July 1, 1991.)

275. *An article on that leak . . . 20 Judges . . . "* (Ray Gibson and O'Connor, *Chicago Tribune,* June 27, 1991.)

275. *The other leak was . . . to Marquette.* ("Cooley's Credibility on Trial.")

276. *In the words of the* Tribune *. . . "Bribes Were My Life . . . "* (O'Connor, *Chicago Tribune,* July 2, 1991.)

276. *From the moment I appeared . . . afraid of somebody."* (*United States v. National On Leong Chinese Merchants Ass'n,* No. 90 CR 760 [N.D. Ill. July 1, 1991] Tr. of Proceedings at 59.)

277. *The night before . . . Federal Building.* Patrick A. Tuite and Edward M. Genson were then two of the best-known defense counsel in Chicago. They represented nearly fifty Greylord defendants and "had reputations for taking many cases to trial" in both federal and state court. (*Greylord,* 152.) "Tuite speaks softly, politely, and if angry at a witness on cross-examination, he is more likely to use sarcasm than volume. Genson is loud, outraged, and can be grating." (*Greylord,* 155.)

277. *[Tuite said,] "I'm disgusted . . . I bet."* (*U.S. v. Ntl. On Leong* at 332.)

277. *At one point . . . and ten dollars?"* (*U.S. v. Ntl. On Leong* at 216.)

278. *[Tuite] shouted, "Are you trying . . . snake to listen."* (*U.S. v. Ntl. On Leong* at 324.)

278. *[Tuite] said, "I doubt that . . . two of us.'"* (*U.S. v. Ntl. On Leong* at 368-369.)

By sheer coincidence, one of the other defense counsel that day was Bill Murphy, Cooley's friend from Marquette. Of the exchanges between Tuite and Cooley, he says, "I've been doing this for 36 years and I've never seen anything like it. That cross-examination was incredibly personal. Even if you didn't know them, you could sense that each had an intense distaste for the other." (Murphy, interview.) See notes on page 302 for a description of Cooley's cross-examination by Genson.

278. *[Tuite] laughed, "Who did you . . . to these people."* (*U.S. v. Ntl. On Leong* at 368.)

278. *The jurors returned a split decision . . . much of him."* ("On Leong Case Gets Split Verdict.")

279. *From what little . . . into one trial.* One writer who followed the trial blamed the government's central witness, who she describes as "bizarre." She also comments, "The defense leapt on Cooley as an object beneath contempt." (Kinkead, 122.) Gary Shapiro adds, "It was a tough case, and while I thought

Bob did well, our other witnesses were awful. On top of everything else, we had to do simultaneous translation in Chinese, probably the worst language for trial testimony." (Shapiro, interview.)

FBI agent Steve Bowen remembers that On Leong was a depressing start to Cooley's career as a witness. "The day after Bob testified, the press really beat him up, and I remember he was pretty down about that."

279. *[Dan Webb] was considered . . . could buy.* The Web site for Webb's firm, Winston & Strawn, adds that he is "listed in The Best Lawyers in America for both business litigation and criminal law . . ." (Dan K. Webb, Attorney Profile, whywinston.com.)

280. *Like a good trial lawyer . . . I dealt with him. (U.S. v. Shields* at 574-577.)

280. *Banks started off . . . either paid or lost." (U.S. v. Shields* at 760-783.)

281. *"Now you had no . . . pay personally." (U.S. v. Shields* at 810.)

281. *When [Banks] asked about . . . my own choice. (U.S. v. Shields* at 1034.)

281. *Then, before the jury returned . . . any further.* (O'Connor, "Cooley calls DeLeo his cohort in bribery," *Chicago Tribune,* Aug. 23, 1991.)

282. *[Shields] showed the arresting officer . . . a personal interest."* (O'Connor, "Shields Grilled On Drunk Driving Arrest, Tape," *Chicago Tribune,* Sep. 5, 1991.) Durkin remembers, "We found that article in an old issue of *Litigation.* He is a smart, articulate guy, and he presented well on the stand, so I think it helped counter that." (Durkin, interview.)

282. *First [the jury] listened . . . "but it's there."* (O'Connor, "Jury Plays Tape Until All Agree Shields Is Guilty," *Chicago Tribune,* Sep. 25, 1991.)

282. *[Judge Rovner] sentenced the judge . . . denial at trial." (U.S. v. Shields,* Tr. of Proceedings, March 2, 1992 at 35-40.)

283. *Surprisingly, she sentenced Patty DeLeo . . . all tired of it." (U.S. v. Shields,* Tr. of Proceedings, March 2, 1992 at 29.)

283. *[DeLeo] told the judge . . . learned them."* (O'Connor, "Ex-Judge Shields Gets 3-Year Term," *Chicago Tribune,* March 3, 1992.)

283. *Harry Comerford, chief judge need any more.* ("Jury Plays Tape . . .")

283. *As far as the press . . . of evidence . . .* But inside the U.S. Attorney's office, Cooley's credibility and value to the investigation were riding high. Then assistant U.S. Attorney Scott Mendeloff remembers, "Shields looked like a very tough case for the government to win. When we did, it was a real boost to the entire office, and we really needed that after what happened with On Leong." (Mendeloff, interview.)

284. *Genson dismissed the tapes . . . explain the tapes?" (U.S. v. D'Arco* at 297-298.)

284. *From that moment on . . . at Cooley."* (O'Connor, "U.S. Says D'Arco Took $5,000 Bribe On Tape," *Chicago Tribune,* Oct. 10, 1991.)

285. *Again, I explained why . . . here in Chicago."* ("U.S. Says D'Arco . . .")

285. *Suddenly, Johnny's voice . . . to shut up.* (O'Connor, "D'Arco Has A Few Words For Cooley," *Chicago Tribune*, Oct. 11, 1991.)

285. *The* Chicago Tribune *headline said it all . . . on the stand.* (O'Connor, Oct. 18, 1991.)

285. *[Genson] added, "With your father . . . there," I said.* (*U.S. v. D'Arco* at 637.)

286. *[Genson] said, "You tried jury cases . . . lost some."* (*U.S. v. D'Arco* at 1534.)

286. *"I was told he wasn't . . . yours," I answered.* (*U.S. v. D'Arco* at 701.)

286. *Later, I explained to . . . wouldn't name me."* (*U.S. v. D'Arco* at 2027.)

286. *Later in the trial, [Charles] Sklarsky . . . the Strike Force.* (Mary Wisniewski, "Cooley came in on his own, ex-prosecutor says," *Chicago Daily Law Bulletin*, Nov, 5, 1991.)

287. *The reporter for the . . . to the gym."* ("Cooley came in . . .")

287. *According to Genson, Johnny only humored me out of pity, because I was "shabbily dressed" and "driving an old car."* (*U.S. v. D'Arco* at 1527.)

287. *Tape transcripts . . . my sport jacket . . .* (*U.S. v. D'Arco*, Tr. of ElSur Oct. 5, 1989.)

287. *In another . . . like a limo.* (*U.S. v. D'Arco*, Tr. of ElSur Dec. 23, 1988.)

287. *"I was passing . . . a bust-out."* (*U.S. v. D'Arco* at 1529.)

287. *I replied, "I know . . . work this deal."* (*U.S. v. D'Arco* at 1480.)

288. *He demanded to know . . . He's absurd."* (*U.S. v. D'Arco* at 1486-1487.)

288. *[D'Arco] slammed his chair . . . her head off.* (O'Connor, "D'Arco Flies Into Rage At His Trial," *Chicago Tribune*, Oct. 26, 1991.)

288. *As far as the judge . . . human being as there is . . ."* (*U.S. v. D'Arco* at 1145.)

288. *[The judge] admonished Eddy, . . . representing the government . . ."* (*U.S. v. D'Arco* at 1501.)

289. *[The judge] admitted, "I am a very . . . different housing."* (*U.S. v. D'Arco* at 1709-1711.)

289. *"Is there any lie . . . at risk?"* ("15 Days Of Testimony Ends In D'Arco Trial," *Chicago Tribune*, Nov. 6, 1991.)

289. *At the mention of Senior's name . . . to the* Tribune. (O'Connor, "D'Arco Breaks Down During His Trial," *Chicago Tribune*, Nov. 8, 1991.)

289. *"Many times I didn't . . . not pay attention."* (O'Connor, "I Didn't Understand Cooley, D'Arco Says," *Chicago Tribune*, Nov. 15, 1991.)

290. *As proof, [Genson] . . . out each bill.* ("D'Arco Jury Hears Tapes . . .")

290. *"Unfortunately," . . . money."* (O'Connor, "D'Arco Admits Cooley Paid Him," *Chicago Tribune*, Nov. 16, 1991.)

290. *"You lied to Cooley . . . Johnny answered.* (Mary Wisniewski, "D'Arco admits taking money," *Chicago Daily Law Bulletin*, Nov, 18, 1991.)

290. *In a bizarre appeal . . . paying off Scotillo.* (O'Connor, "D'Arco: I Expect 2nd Indictment," *Chicago Tribune*, Nov. 20, 1991.)

290. *Mike Shepard told the jury . . . an eel."* (O'Connor, "Jury Deliberations To Begin On D'Arco," *Chicago Tribune,* Dec. 5, 1991.)

291. *"Because of the strength . . . a credible witness.'"* (O'Connor, "D'Arco Convicted Of Bribe Taking," *Chicago Tribune,* Dec. 7, 1991.)

291. *Judge Lindberg gave Johnny . . . with his wife.* (O'Connor, "D'Arco Gets 3 Years, Is Barred From Returning To Government," *Chicago Tribune,* May 21, 1992.)

291. *Just before he got . . . for that crime.* (O'Connor, "D'Arco Doesn't Fight New Charges," *Chicago Tribune,* Oct. 20, 1994.)

291. *For reasons I don't . . . never indicted.* Prosecutors and FBI agents involved with Gambat are divided about the decision not to indict Judge Scotillo. A prosecutor says, "I've heard the two tapes with Bob [in the street and at the restaurant] and I just don't think there's enough there to indict. If Scotillo had been home the day Johnny and Bob came calling, I have no doubt he would have been indicted and convicted." But an investigator, also familiar with the recordings, argues, "We took Shields with a lot less tape than we had on Scotillo." Another prosecutor adds, "Scotillo is the one case Bob can truly chalk up to politics." (Confidential Sources, interviews.)

291. *U.S. Attorney Fred Foreman . . . "D'Arco Conviction Has Probe On A Roll."* (*Chicago Tribune,* Dec. 8, 1991.)

CHAPTER 14

THE HARDER THEY FALL

293. *Still, even the government . . . four days a week.* (O'Connor, "Marcy Sent To Intensive Care Unit," *Chicago Tribune,* Dec. 19, 1992.)

293. *"It is only the word . . . in this case . . ."* (*U.S. v. Marcy* at 94.)

294. *Both major papers . . . U.S. Senate hearing.* (Rossi, "Curtain To Rise On 1st Ward Bribery Trial," Dec. 10, 1992; O'Connor, "FBI Tapes Will Start In Roti, Marcy Trial," *Chicago Tribune,* Dec. 14, 1992.)

294. *"This case does not . . . old-time politics."* (O'Connor, "Cooley Ties Judge Bribe To Marcy," *Chicago Tribune,* Dec. 16, 1992.)

295. *He went straight . . . live that long.* (O'Connor, "Marcy's Heart Attack May Delay Trial For 6 Months, Lawyers Say," *Chicago Tribune,* Dec. 22, 1992.")

295. *[Marcy] died three months later.* Even with his death, the newspaper headlines still dealt gingerly with their characterization of Marcy. The *Chicago Sun-Times* was boldest: "Pat Marcy Dies, 1st Ward Power Linked To Mob," (Tom Seibel, March 14, 1993.) The *Chicago Tribune* was remarkably circumspect, "Power Broker Marcy, 79, Dies," (Don Babwin and Michael Lev, March 14, 1993) but it did lead with the following line: "Pasquale 'Pat' Marcy, a Chicago political power broker in the notorious 1st Ward and reputed mob link to City Hall, died early Saturday."

295. *Breen admitted that Roti . . . denied everything.* (O'Connor, "Roti Fixed Zoning, His Lawyer Concedes," *Chicago Tribune*, Jan. 13, 1993.)

296. *"You can get away . . . pretty decent thing."* ("Roti Fixed Zoning . . .")

296. *Freddy got a pass . . . the other charges.* (Rossi, "Roti Verdict Split," *Chicago Sun-Times*, Jan. 16, 1993.)

296. *But the judge, Marvin Aspen . . . over $125,000.* (Rossi, "Roti's Sentence: 4 Years, Fine, Imprisonment Costs," *Chicago Sun-Times*, May 14, 1993.)

297. *[Judge Aspen] said, "The power of . . . or corrupt regime."* (*U.S. v. Fred Roti*, No. 90 CR 1045 [N.D. Ill. May 13, 1993], Tr. of Proceedings at 3-7.)

298. *As one reporter wrote, [Maloney] "scowled."* (Rossi, "Ex-Judge Maloney Guilty Of Fixing Murder Cases," *Chicago Sun-Times*, April 17, 1993.)

298. *[Maloney] asked, "Are you . . . take care of yourself."* (*U.S v. Maloney & McGee* at 2765.)

299. *I was the one . . . had no case.* Assistant U.S. Attorney Scott Mendeloff, believes Swano may have flipped no matter what. He says, "I think that underneath it all that Swano was a decent person, and he did not want to be dragged into a trial where he would be tarred with the El Rukns. Whatever his motives, Swano's testimony had to be credible, and Bob [added to that]." (Mendeloff, interview.)

299. *Maloney's lawyer, Terry Gillespie . . . to con you."* (O'Connor, "Maloney's Court Ruled By Greed, Jury Told," *Chicago Tribune*, March 5, 1993.)

300. *[Swano] not only represented . . . with them."* (Rossi, "Trial Opens For Ex-Judge Charged With Fixing Cases," *Chicago Sun-Times*, March 5, 1993.)

300. *McGee called the judge . . . to Maloney.* (O'Connor, "Phone Records Back Testimony Of Trial Fix, Maloney Jury Told," *Chicago Tribune*, March 5, 1993.) 300. *When that company . . . McGee had made.* (Mendeloff, interview.)

300 *The phone records . . . long-lost glove."* (Rossi, "Ex-Judge Trial Winding Up," *Chicago Sun-Times*, April 12, 1993.)

300. *Later, during deliberation, . . . a money order?"* ("Ex-Judge Maloney Guilty . . .")

301. *Scott said, "It is the view . . . People vs. Harry Aleman."* (*U.S. v. Maloney*, July 19, 1994 at 13-14.)

301. *"Thomas J. Maloney went . . . truth is in him".* (Rossi, "Ex-Judge Gets 15 Years, Rips Accusers," *Chicago Sun-Times*, July 22, 1993.)

302. *Judge Leinenweber said, "What you . . . particular cases."* (O'Connor, "Ex-Judge Gets Final Fix: 15 Years," *Chicago Tribune*, July 22, 1993.)

302. *[Genson] called me, "the most . . . a dog's tail.* (Charles Nicodemus, "Mole Sticks To Story In Stillo Bribery Trial," *Chicago Sun-Times*, July 21, 1993.)

The *Sun-Times* reporter also observed, "Genson's angry description of Cooley's history, successfully objected to by assistant U.S. Attorney Scott

Mendeloff, came after two days of cross examination had left Cooley unflustered and his story of corruption unshaken." ("Mole Sticks . . .")

Mendeloff had similar feelings about Genson's performance. "Usually, Ed is most effective when he uses his humor. But with Bob there was a stridency that did not help him or his client. You could see that this had become very personal for him." (Mendeloff, interview.)

303. *Judge Leinenweber told them, "I'm dealing . . . two years . . .* (O'Connor, "Judge Stillo Gets 4 Years For Fixing String Of Cases," *Chicago Tribune*, July 12, 1994.)

303. *Then, after he did his time . . . to the end.* Mendeloff felt sorry for the younger Stillo. "I think he was very marginal to the case, but there was no way the jury could convict the uncle without convicting him. He was always very civil and decent with me. I understood he had a weak heart and that's what killed him." (Mandeloff, interview.)

303. *"A series of circumstances . . . judicial corruption."* (William Grady, "State Agency Appears To Be Punishing Cooley, Lawyer Group Says," *Chicago Tribune*, July 12, 1994.)

304. *Their article began, "Poor, . . . Operation Gambat investigation."* (William Grady, Bill Crawford, John O'Brien, "Informant Wants 'Salvage Of Dignity,'" *Chicago Tribune*, July 13, 1994.)

304. *The agents told me . . . happen to him."* When *Sun-Times* columnist Steve Neal made a tortured defense of her role in Cammon, Anne Burke indicated to him that she had been contacted by the U.S. Attorney's office: "Mrs. Burke, who wasn't the co-counsel in the second trial, said that she cooperated with federal prosecutors who had questions about the 1984 trial. Court records from the case were subpoenaed after a federal undercover witness recorded conversations with Judge Cieslik in which the Cammon case was discussed." But the prosecutors and FBI agents who worked with Cooley and listened to the Cieslik tapes do not believe they were sufficient to get an investigation off the ground. "One says, "We may have had a judge talking about Burke putting pressure on him, but we never had enough to predicate Burke as having fixed other cases." (Confidential Source, interview.)

305. *They convicted Johnny DiFronzo . . . debts in Vegas.* ("Chicago mobsters sentenced for scheme to take over casino," *Chicago Tribune*, May 27, 1993.)

305. *[The Feds] went after . . . the year 2000.* (John O'Brien, "Infelice latest mob boss headed for prison," *Chicago Tribune*, March 11, 1992.)

Strike Force prosecutor Gary Shapiro explains that Cooley was instrumental in tying Aleman to the Infelice indictment. "Until I talked to Bob I didn't know how they were connected. I met him in a neutral location and spent a day with him. That's all it took to charge Aleman and give him another 11-year sentence."

306. *On December 8, 1993 . . . murder case was fixed."* (John O'Brien, "Acquitted Mobster may Not Be Off Hook," *Chicago Tribune,* Dec. 9, 1993.)

Although then assistant State's Attorney Patrick J. Quinn, helped put the retrial in motion, he says, "Jack O'Malley is the one who pulled the trigger and he deserves a lot of credit for that. You can bet that the vast majority of state's attorneys would have let a case like that drop, especially because it was such a long shot." (Quinn, interview.) Another lawyer involved is less charitable. "O'Malley had an election coming up. What better publicity could he ask for?" (Confidential Source, interview.)

306. *[Ackerman] quoted from . . . life or limb."* (Gary Wisby, "Aleman Charged Again In Murder Despite Acquittal," *Chicago Sun-Times,* Dec. 9, 1993.)

306. The Tribune *called . . . case to win."* ("Acquitted Mobster.")

306. *[Judge Toomin] ruled that a fix . . . real."* (John O'Brien, "Exception To Double Jeopardy: Bribery Cited As Reason For New Aleman Trial," *Chicago Tribune,* Oct. 13, 1994.)

307. *Ackerman zeroed in . . .—was dead.* (*Illinois v. Aleman,* Feb. 9, 1995 at 211-213.)

307. *As Allan later joked . . . like a "séance."* (*Illinois v. Aleman,* Feb. 9, 1995 at 259.)

308. *Rizza testified that . . . taken care of."* (*Illinois v. Aleman,* Feb. 9, 1995 at 52-53.)

308. *When he copped a plea . . . like Rizza.* (*Illinois v. Aleman* at 255.)

308. *Pat Quinn brought out . . . fix was in?* (*Illinois v. Aleman* at 197.)

308. *Cassidy argued, the trial . . . reeks."* (*Illinois v. Aleman* at 248.)

308. *One month later, . . . Billy Logan.* (Gary Marx, "Aleman Can Be Retried: Double Jeopardy Doesn't Apply," *Chicago Tribune,* March 10, 1995.)

309. *The judge wrote, "I find . . . of its value."* ("Aleman Can Be Retried . . .")

309. *A panel of the Appellate Court . . . every challenge.* (Possley, "'Fixed' Murder Case To Resurface: Stage Set For Retrial Of Reputed Mob Hit Man," *Chicago Tribune,* Aug. 29, 1997.)

309. *There were the bookie cases . . . Dominic Barbaro.* (O'Connor, "3 More Plead Guilty In Gambling Ring," *Chicago Tribune,* Dec. 17, 1992.)

309. *[Pesoli] copped a plea . . . prison sentence.* (O'Connor and Ray Gibson, "Ex-Cop Says He's Guilty Of Perjury," *Chicago Tribune,* May 5, 1993.)

309. *In November 1994 . . . Ricky Borelli.* (O'Connor and Ray Gibson, "Reputed Mobster Indicted As Statute Of Limitations Nears," *Chicago Tribune,* Nov. 19, 1994.)

310. *Five months after his arrest . . . two years of supervision.* (O'Connor and Ray Gibson, "Mob Leader D'Amico Gets 12 Year Term," *Chicago Tribune,* Oct. 4, 1995.)

310. *I had no trouble linking . . . Chinatown Group.* The Independent Hearing Officer mostly cited Cooley's testimony for the decision to kick the Caruso brothers out of the union. (Vaira, 117-121.)

311. *In the words . . . American jurisprudence.* ("'Fixed' Murder Case . . .")

311. *I had never had . . . this case.* Assistant State's Attorney Scott Cassidy says, "I had never seen that level of security at the criminal courthouse for anyone before, and I haven't seen it since. I'm told there was something similar for the trial of Jeff Fort [El Rukn gang leader], but I think that's the only thing close." (Scott Cassidy, interview by Hillel Levin, June 2004.)

312. *Reporters wrote . . . each day.* (Lorraine Forte, "Aleman's Retrial In 1972 Murder Fills Courtroom With Drama," *Chicago Sun-Times,* Sep. 28, 1997.)

312. *Aleman's lawyer, McNally, . . . an honest judge."* (Possley, "Mob Fixer Tells How He Bought Aleman Judge," *Chicago Tribune,* Sep. 24, 1997.)

312. *Unlike my other Gambat trials, . . . from other sources.* The prosecutors who had worked with Cooley in the past believed he was up to the task. After the Maloney and Stillo convictions, assistant U.S. Attorney Scott Mendeloff went on to other high-profile trials, including the government prosecution against Timothy McVeigh for the bombing at Oklahoma City. He says, "Bob Cooley was the finest witness I ever had. Bar none. And I've had a lot of experience with witnesses in corruption cases. Everyone talks about how good a witness Terry Hake was in the Greylord cases—and I'm a big fan of Terry—but Bob was ten times the witness. You could ask him to describe an incident and then ask for the same thing five months later. The two descriptions would not vary in the least. Jurors loved him and, most important, really believed him." (Mendeloff, interview.)

313. *"I gave him the money," . . . "You destroyed me."* (*Illinois v. Aleman,* Sep. 23, 1997 at 94.)

CHAPTER 15

AFTERLIFE

315. *[Billy Logan's ex-wife] told a story . . . kill Logan.* (Possley, "Aleman Defense: 2nd hit man Did It: Teamster's Ex-Wife Describes Fistfight," *Chicago Tribune,* Sep. 30, 1997.)

315. *According to the* Tribune, *. . . American justice."* (Possley and Judy Press, "Aleman Guilty On 2nd Time Around," *Chicago Tribune,* Oct. 1, 1997.)

315. *When it came time . . . three hundred years.* (Possley, "Mob hit man Aleman Gets 100-300 Years," *Chicago Tribune,* Nov. 26, 1997.)

316. *For one thing . . . rare event ever since.* From 1991 to 1996 (until he was elected to the Appellate Court), Pat Quinn headed the Organized Crime Unit of the Cook County State's Attorney's Office. He says, "During the years I held that position, there were no murders related to organized crime. I directly attribute that to Bob Cooley and his testimony. After him, the hit men

couldn't trust anyone. Even the lowest-level street guys realize that you can't fix a murder case in Chicago. Not any more." (Quinn, interview.)

317. *Of the nine men Maloney . . . release as well . . .* (Ken Armstrong and Steve Mills, "Death Row Justice Derailed," *Chicago Tribune,* Nov. 14, 1999.)

317. *Judge Ilana Rovner [wrote]: "We may . . . Oliver Wendell Holmes."* (Lawrence C. Marshall, "Righting the Wrongs in our Criminal Justice System," *Chicago Tribune,* June 16, 1997.)

318. *After I took down . . . fishhook was left.* (John Kass, "Remap imperils City Council vets," *Chicago Tribune,* Oct. 29, 1991.)

318. *One recent* Chicago Tribune *. . . four convictions . . .* (John Chase and Gary Washburn, "Illinois' Bane: State of shame; Scandal has home in land of Lincoln," *Chicago Tribune,* Dec. 18, 2003.)

Those who were closest to Operation Gambat are the most mystified by this relative lack of recognition for Cooley and his investigation:

Scott Mendeloff is now a partner at the firm of Sidley Austin. He says, "It's hard to overstate the importance of what Bob has done for Chicago, because what he's done has been so far reaching. Getting rid of the First Ward people was essential to cleaning Organized Crime out of City Hall and our court system. This city used to suffer serious miscarriages of justice on a regular basis. Generations of prosecutors and FBI agents know this and realize what Gambat accomplished. Maybe the general public doesn't appreciate it as much because they didn't know how bad it really was here. Ironically, by cooperating the way he did, Bob took a hit to his reputation that cannot be easily removed, but in the process he delivered such a gift to this community. (Mendeloff, interview.)

Tom Durkin is now a partner at Mayer Brown. He says, "What is so unusual about Gambat is how important one man was to the investigation. If he had not walked in the door, it's likely that none of these old cases would have been solved and Bob would have still been practicing law. Without Bob, government prosecutors had no way to get at these people or their transactions. We couldn't even get close. When you look at the Gambat cases, you realize that this was not an inevitable set of prosecutions, waiting for someone else to stumble over them. They each needed someone with his access and initiative for both the indictment and the convictions. Now the city, the legislature and the judiciary are the better for it." (Durkin, interview.)

Gary Shapiro is now First Assistant U.S. Attorney in the Chicago office. He says, "If Bob had done no more than help jail Maloney and Aleman, he would have made a major contribution to the safety of Chicago, but obviously he did much more than that. Even beyond the specific cases he helped us win, he taught us things about the Mob's metabolism and their worldview that led to many more convictions and continue to pay dividends." (Shapiro, interview.)

318. *For example, in 2002, Bill Hanhardt, . . . than $5 million.* (O'Connor, "Hanhardt gets nearly 16 years," *Chicago Tribune*, May 3, 2002.)

For decades, FBI agent Jim Wagner was on Hanhardt's trail. He found success just before he retired. "I finally did it by building a 'Chinese' wall between the investigating agents and the Chicago police assigned to the bureau. Those officers still suffered retribution when we indicted Hanhardt. I think it truly damaged their careers. Their supervisors had expected a warning." (Wagner, interview.)

318. *In 2003, Anne Burke, . . . the United States Conference of Catholic Bishops.* On May 2, 2003, after two years on the board, Anne Burke announced she was stepping down. Two other high profile board members joined her—trial lawyer Robert Bennett, and former White House chief of staff in the Clinton administration, Leon Panetta. It has been assumed that the move was to protest the Bishops' slow progress with the Board's audits into Priest child abuse. (Geneive Abdo, "Anne Burke to leave priest abuse panel," *Chicago Tribune*, May 2, 2004.)

319. *In 2004, the* Chicago Sun-Times *. . . Nick "The Stick" LoCoco.* (Steve Warmbir and Tim Novak, "Mob ties run throughout city truck program," *Chicago Sun-Times*, Jan. 25, 2004.)

319. *When U.S. District Court Judge Marvin Aspen . . . repeat it."* (*U.S. v. Roti* at 2).

Operation Gambat Related Cases and Outcomes*

[1]Conviction (C) or Guilty Plea (P); [2]Supervised Release; [3]Restitution; [4]Probation

Name	Case #	Position Held	Counts/ Charges	C/ P[1]	Date Conv Or Plea	Sentence
John D'Arco, Jr.	90 CR 1043	State Senator	2-Extortion 1-False Tax Return	C	12/6/91	3yrs. prison; supv[2]; $10,000 fine; $7,500 rest[3]; 360 hrs Community service
Pat DeLeo	90 CR 1044	Chicago Corp. Counsel	4-Extortion 1-Racketeering	C	09/24/91	33 months prison; 2 yrs supv; $7,500 fine
Thomas J. Maloney	91 CR 477	Judge	2-Bribery 1-Extortion, Racketeering 1-Obstruction of Justice	C	04/16/92	15 yrs prison; supv; $200,000 fine
Pat Marcy	91 CR 1045	Secretary, First Ward Democratic Committee	1-RICO (conspiracy) 1-RICO 6-Bribery 6-Extortion			Died during trial
Robert McGee	91 CR 477	Attorney	1-RICO (conspiracy) 1-RICO 1-Extortion	C	04/16/92	6yrs prison; 5yrs prob[4]
Samuel "Blackie" Pesoli	92CR 374	Chicago Police officer	2 Counts Perjury	P	05/03/93	11 mos prison; 2yrs supv; $5,000 fine.
Fred Roti	90CR 1045	Alderman First Ward	1-RICO (conspiracy) 1-RICO 5-Bribery 4 Extortion	C	1/14/92	4 yrs prison; 3 yrs supv; $75,000 fine, $17,500 restitution; $550 fine; $1,492/mo prison cost; $1,318/mo supv cost
David Shields	90CR 1044	Presiding Judge Chancery Court	4-Extortion 1-RICO 2-False Statements	C	09/24/91	37 mos prison; supv; $6,000 fine
Joseph T. Stillo	91CR 795	Attorney	1-Extortion	C	07/29/93	2 yrs prison; $10,000 fine
Adam Stillo Sr.	91CR 795	Judge	1-RICO (conspiracy) 1-Extortion	C	07/29/92	4 yrs prison; $100 fine
William A. Swano	91CR 477	Attorney	2-Bribery	P	07/15/91	4 yrs prison; $1,000 fine

Name	Case #	Position Held	Counts/ Charges	C/ P[1]	Date Conv Or Plea	Sentence
Dominic J. Swano	92CR 483		2-Gambling 12-Tax (failure to file)	P	10/8/92	20 mos prison; 1 yr prob
Mark E. Guidi	92CR 483		2-Gambling 10-Tax (failure to file)	P	12/16/92	10 mos prison; 2 yrs prob
Mark D. Hollendonner	92CR 483		2-Gambling 2-Tax (failure to file)	P	12/16/92	4 mos prison; 3 yrs supv; $2,000 fine
Anthony Nolfe	92CR 483		2-Gambling 2-Tax (failure to file)	P	12/16/92	1 month prison; 5 yrs prob
Marco D'Amico	94CR 723		2-Firearms 1-RICO (gambling) 4-RICO (extortion) 2-False Tax	P	05/01/95	12.5 yrs prison; 3 yrs supv; $6000 fine
Anthony R. Dote	94CR 723		1-RICO (gambling) 2-RICO (extortion) 2-False Tax	P	05/03/95	4.25 yrs prison; 3 yrs supv; $10,000 fine
Robert M. Abbinanti	94CR 723	Truck Driver, Chicago Street & Sanitation	1-Firearms 1-RICO (gambling) 2-RICO (extortion) 2-False Tax	P	04/28/95	6.75 yrs prison; 3 yrs supv; $3,000 fine
Roland "Ricky" Borelli	94CR 723	Chicago Police Officer	1-RICO (extortion) 2-False Tax	P	05/09/95	10 mos prison; 2 yrs supv; $100 fine
Frank Catapano	94CR 723		2-RICO (extortion) 1-Contempt	P	05/11/95	15 mos prison; 5 yrs supv; $4,500 fine
Carl R. Dote	94CR 723		1-RICO (extortion)	P	04/13/95	3 yrs prob; $2,000 yrs fine
Frank Maranto	94CR 723		1-RICO (extortion) 1-Contempt	P	05/01/95	15 mos prison; 3 yrs supv
Robert L. Scutkowski	94CR 723		1-RICO (extortion)	P[1]	04/18/95	3 yrs prob;
William L. Tenuta	94CR 723		1-RICO (extortion)	P	05/11/95	15 mos prison; 2 yrs supv
Harry Sam Aleman	93-28786-87		1st Degree Murder	C	09/30/97	100-300 yrs prison

* Sources: U.S. District Court, Northern District of Illinois; except Aleman, Appellate Court of Illinois, First District, Fifth Division

INDEX

ACKNOWLEDGMENTS

We owe the biggest debt of gratitude to the mutual friend who introduced us. He is the supreme investigator and teller of hard truths. Along with many others, we also want to thank Vic Switski and Steve Simon of Acumen Probe, Steve Bowen, Dave Grossman, Jim Wagner, Frank Marrocco, Tom Durkin, Scott Mendeloff, Gary Shapiro, Pat Quinn, Scott Cassidy, Bill Murphy, Mark Coe, Jim Bernard, Marc Brown, and Marc Winkelman.

Finally, our thanks for their patience and insight to our literary agent Nat Sobel, and our editors at Carroll & Graf Publishers: Philip Turner and Keith Wallman.